COLLEGE FOR HUMAN SERVICES
LIBRARY
345 HUDSON STREET
NEW YORK, N.Y. 10014

*Blacks in the
Industrial World*

BLACKS IN THE

THEODORE V. PURCELL
AND
GERALD F. CAVANAGH

INDUSTRIAL WORLD

ISSUES FOR THE MANAGER

THE FREE PRESS · NEW YORK
COLLIER-MACMILLAN LTD.
LONDON

Copyright © 1972 by The Free Press
A Division of The Macmillan Company
Printed in the United States of America
All rights reserved. No part of this book may be
reproduced or transmitted in any form or by any means,
electronic or mechanical, including photocopying, recording,
or by any information storage and retrieval system,
without permission in writing from the Publisher.

The Free Press
A Division of The Macmillan Company
866 Third Avenue, New York, New York 10022

Collier-Macmillan Canada Ltd., Toronto, Ontario

Library of Congress Catalog Card Number: 74-184530

Printing number 1 2 3 4 5 6 7 8 9 10

To the hundreds of black and white men and women whose hopes for the future are evidenced in these pages

". . . Responsible management must have the vision and exert the leadership to develop a broader social role for the corporation if business is to continue to receive public confidence and support . . . There are limitations to what business can contribute . . . the kind of society we want can be achieved only with the full participation of government . . . education, medicine, religion, labor, the arts, philanthropy. . . . We believe business will respond constructively to this new challenge."

> A Statement on National Policy Committee for Economic Development June, 1971.

Contents

CHAPTER ONE	Black people and corporate responsibility	1

PART ONE *The National Experience*

CHAPTER TWO	Ninety years of slow change	13
CHAPTER THREE	The long road to parity	30

PART TWO *The Local Experience*

CHAPTER FOUR	Chicago: Bohemians to young blacks	49
CHAPTER FIVE	Yankee management in Virginia	101
CHAPTER SIX	Middle America and the blacks	141
CHAPTER SEVEN	Racial change in a deep-South plant	174

PART THREE *The Issues*

CHAPTER EIGHT	Making minority policies effective	223
CHAPTER NINE	New opportunities for the disadvantaged	233
CHAPTER TEN	Equal versus preferential practice	275
CHAPTER ELEVEN	The beginnings of some answers	294
APPENDIX	A. *Research methods: did they tell us what they really think?*	305
	B. *Comparative statistical tables*	321
	C. *Structure and manpower of the electrical industry*	324
SUBJECT INDEX		339
INDEX OF INTERVIEWEES		**356**

List of Tables

Table No.	Description	Page No.
2–1	**Employment by Race and Sex, 1930–1960** Electrical Manufacturing Industry	14
2–2	**Employment by Race, 1957–1959** Selected Electrical Manufacturing Plants	27
3–1	**Black Employment, 1960–1969** Electrical Manufacturing Industry	30
3–2	**Employment by Race, Sex, and Occupation, 1969** Electrical Manufacturing Industry, 3,533 Establishments	38
3–3	**Black Employment: Electrical Manufacturing and Six Basic Industries, 1966 and 1968,** By Occupational Group	40
3–4	**An Index of Black Participation in the Electrical Manufacturing Industry, 1966 and 1969**	42
3–5	**Predicting Black Employment,** Electrical Manufacturing Industry, Base: 1966–1969	43
4–1	**Profile of the Hourly Workers,** National Acme–Chicago, 1969	56
4–2	**Job Performance of Hourly Blacks,** Percentage of foremen who judged that blacks do at least as well as the average worker, Acme–Chicago	62
4–3	**Attitude Toward My Job,** Hourly employees by race, age, and work, Acme–Chicago	72
4–4	**Perception of Personal Chances for Promotion** Hourly employees by race and age, Acme–Chicago	76
4–5	**Perception of Blacks' Chances for Promotion** Hourly employees by race and age, Acme–Chicago	77
4–6	**Attitude Toward my Foreman,** Hourly employees by race and age, Acme–Chicago	79

4–7	**Attitude Toward Having a Union,** Hourly employees by race, Acme–Chicago	87
5–1	**Profile of the Hourly Workers,** GE–Lynchburg, 1969	104
5–2	**Annual Turnover, 1966 to 1969,** GE–Lynchburg	105
5–3	**Black Employment by Sex and Occupation** GE–Lynchburg, 1966 and 1969	112
5–4	**Perception of Personal Chances for Promotion,** White hourly, black hourly, and black salaried employees, GE–Lynchburg	116
5–5	**Perception of Blacks' Chances for Promotion,** White hourly, black hourly, and black salaried employees, GE–Lynchburg	116
5–6	**Foreman's Appraisal by Race,** GE–Lynchburg	118
5–7	**Perception of Black-White Relations on the Job** White hourly, black hourly, black salaried, and foremen, GE–Lynchburg	126
6–1	**Profile of the Hourly Workers,** Westinghouse–Buffalo, 1969	146
6–2	**Annual Turnover, 1969,** Electrical industry, Westinghouse, and Buffalo divisions	147
6–3	**Black Employment by Occupation** Westinghouse–Buffalo, 1961	151
6–4	**Black Employment by Sex and Occupation,** Westinghouse–Buffalo, 1966 and 1969	153
6–5	**Perception of Fair Hiring for Blacks,** Hourly employees by race, Westinghouse–Buffalo	154
6–6	**Job Performance of Hourly Blacks,** Percentage of foremen who judge that blacks do as well as the average worker, Westinghouse–Buffalo	155
6–7	**Perception of Black-White Relations on the Job** Hourly employees by race, Westinghouse–Buffalo	160
6–8	**Attitude Toward Working with Blacks,** Hourly employees by race, Westinghouse–Buffalo	160
6–9	**Perception of Preference for Blacks in Hiring** Hourly employees by race, Westinghouse–Buffalo	163
6–10	**Attitude Toward My Foreman,** Hourly employees by race, Westinghouse–Buffalo	167

7–1	**Profile of the Hourly Workers,** Fairbanks International–Memphis	186
7–2	**Attitude Toward My Job,** Hourly employees by race, Fairbanks–Memphis	193
7–3	**Attitude Toward My Foreman,** Hourly employees by race, Fairbanks–Memphis	193
7–4	**Job Performance of Hourly Blacks,** Percentage of foremen who judge that blacks do as well as the average worker, Fairbank–Memphis	193
7–5	**Perception of Black-White Relations on the Job** Hourly employees by race, Fairbanks–Memphis	195
7–6	**Perception of a Black Foreman's Chance for Success,** Hourly employees by race, Fairbanks–Memphis	211
7–7	**Attitude Toward Local Union Leadership,** Hourly employees by race, EWA Local 40, Fairbanks–Memphis	215
9–1	**Profile of Disadvantaged Workers,** Five plants	235
9–2	**Disadvantaged Employees' Reasons or Circumstances for Leaving,** Acme–Chicago, 1969	244
9–3	**Profile of Disadvantaged Employees Who Left vs. Those Remaining,** Acme–Chicago, 1969	245
9–4	**Foremen Ratings of Individual Disadvantaged Workers,** Westinghouse–Buffalo	248
9–5	**Attitude Toward My Foreman,** Hourly employees, disadvantaged, blacks, and whites, Westinghouse–Buffalo	249
9–6	**Attitude Toward taking a Problem to my Foreman,** Hourly employees, disadvantaged, blacks, and whites, Westinghouse–Buffalo	250
9–7	**Reasons for Leaving Raytheon Job Training Center During Training,** February 1968–April 30, 1969	254
10–1	**Perception of Preference for Blacks in Hiring** Hourly white employees, four plants	287
10–2	**Perception of Preference for Blacks in Promotion** Hourly white employees, four plants	290
10–3	**Perception of Preferential Practice by Their Own Foreman,** Hourly white employees, four plants	291

B–1	**Job Performance of Hourly Blacks,** Percentage of foremen who judged that blacks do at least as well as the average worker, four plants	321
B–2	**Company, Boss, Work Satisfaction Index,** Four plants by race and age	322
B–3	**Tolerance of Blacks in the Work Setting Index** Four plants by race and age	322
B–4	**Pro-Union Index,** Four plants by race and age	322
B–5	**Black Employment by Sex and Occupation, 1964, 1966, and 1967,** Electrical Manufacturing Industry	323
C–1	**Number of Employees, Value Added, and Value of Shipments, 1967,** Electrical manufacturing and all manufacturers	325
C–2	**Number of Employees and Value Added, 1967,** Electrical manufacturing and selected industries	325
C–3	**The Fifteen Largest Electrical Manufacturing Companies, 1969**	327
C–4	**Average Monthly Turnover, 1958–1969,** Electrical manufacturing and all manufacturers per 100 employees	333
C–5	**Electrical Machinery and Other Industries Average Hourly and Average Weekly Earnings, 1969**	335
C–6	**Employment by Region, 1967,** Electrical manufacturing industry	337

List of Figures

Figure No.	Description	Page No.
4–1	**Growth of Black Employment,** National Acme–Chicago	55
5–1	**Growth of Black Employment,** GE–Lynchburg	111
6–1	**Growth of Black Employment,** Westinghouse–Buffalo	152
7–1	**Growth of Black Employment,** Fairbanks–Memphis	187
C–1	**Growth of Total and Blue Collar Manpower** Electrical Manufacturing Industry	331
C–2	**Electrical Manufacturing's Share of Total Manufacturing and Durable Goods Employment**	332

List of Exhibits

1.	**"Buffalo Divisions News"**	312
2.	**IUE Buffalo "Union Member"**	313
3.	**Interview Letter**	314
4.	**Research Coding Form**	315
5.	**Contingency Table No. 50**	318
6.	**Analysis of Variance**	319
7.	**Rotated Factor Loadings**	320

Acknowledgments

We wish to thank the Ford Foundation and, in particular, Basil T. Whiting, Project Officer. Theodore Purcell received clarifying criticisms from his colleagues and students at the Sloan School of Management of the Massachusetts Institute of Technology where, as Visiting Professor, he did the final work on the manuscript. Herbert R. Northrup of the University of Pennsylvania, Peter M. Doeringer of Harvard, Dalton E. McFarland and Stanley Stark of Michigan State University, and Timothy B. Blodgett of the *Harvard Business Review* gave valuable suggestions.

The personal interest and confidence of the Officers of the U.S. Equal Employment Commission and the Office of Federal Contract Compliance helped make our data solid. Leaders of the National Urban League and of the National Association for the Advancement of Colored People, by their consultation, helped sharpen the analysis of several key chapters.

The trust of scores of both corporate and local executives, such as Frank J. Toner of the General Electric Company and managers of Westinghouse, the Radio Corporation of America, Western Electric, and Raytheon, was essential. Permitting outsiders access to personal and sensitive issues involving racial relations in a company or plant demonstrates a belief in the value of objective research, and a desire to help solve our social problems.

We are grateful for the trust of the officers of the International Union of Electrical, Radio, and Machine Workers and the Sheet Metal Workers International Union, AFL-CIO, and of the United Electrical Workers.

We are grateful also to our colleagues and research assistants at the Cambridge Center for Social Studies and the Jesuit Center for Social Studies at Georgetown University, especially to William J. Mehok, S. J. Jacqueline Kerr, and Daniel P. Mulvey, S. J., and to our typists Donna and Ellen Woodcock and Judith Alexander, who labored through hundreds of interview transcripts; to Wilbur Mangas and Robert N. Harrington of the Free Press, who saw the book through a long production. Our chief research assistant, Irene E. Wylie, contributed her creative intelligence, patience, encouragement, and self-demanding work to the overall gathering, analysis, and literary presentation of a mass of data.

Finally, we would like to think that the hundreds of black and white workers, foremen, and local union people to whom we listened are the real authors of this "listening" book. Without their thoughts and emotions, confidence and trust, *Blacks in the Industrial World* could never have been written.

Theodore V. Purcell, S.J.	Gerald F. Cavanagh, S.J.
Jesuit Center for Social Studies	School of Business Administration
Georgetown University	Wayne State University
Washington, D.C.	Detroit, Michigan

*Blacks in the
Industrial World*

CHAPTER ONE

Black people and corporate responsibility

The Riot Report states: "The relation of whites and Negroes is our most grave and perplexing problem. . . . We recommend that employers . . . permit Negroes an equal chance with whites to enter all positions for which they are qualified by efficiency and merit. . . . Special attention is called to the fact that opportunity is generally denied to Negroes for gaining experience in business methods through service in responsible positions in business houses."

This is not the 1968 Report of the National Advisory Commission on Civil Disorders; it is the well-documented and readable report of the Chicago Riot Commission of 1919. What has been done to improve the situation in the intervening fifty years? "A lot," one manager says. "Damn little," comments another. Whatever one's criterion for progress, our inner cities have changed little since the riots. The employment gap between black and white young men (except for college people) remains the same.

In the riot cities surveyed by the National Advisory Commission in 1968, Negroes were three times as likely as whites to hold unskilled jobs and those jobs were often part time, seasonal, low paying, and dead-end. Underemployment was as important a problem for Negroes as unemployment. The Advisory Commission stated: "Unemployment and underemployment are among the persistent and serious grievances of disadvantaged minorities. The pervasive effect of these conditions on the racial ghetto is inextricably linked to the problem of civil disorder."[1] The Commission recommended a national

---

[1] *Report of the National Advisory Commission on Civil Disorders* (New York: E. P. Dutton, 1968), p. 413.

minority manpower policy, stressing national economic growth, better job recruiting, vestibule help for disadvantaged workers, more on-the-job training, better chances for advancement and upward mobility, and greater development of new jobs, especially for the disadvantaged.

What progress was made during the year after this widely publicized report? On February 27, 1969, under the auspices of the Urban Coalition and Urban America, Inc., two former members of the National Advisory Commission and the staff director made a second report, "One Year Later." Their findings were grim, even bitter: the United States was "a year closer to two societies increasingly separate and scarcely less unequal."

One way to look at the employment status of black people in America is to estimate how many years it will be before Negroes hold a fair proportion of jobs in each type of work. Let us make some projections based on changes in black participation in the electrical manufacturing industry, for example, between 1966 and 1969.[2] These projections show very modest improvement. Take the figure of 10 percent as a desirable proportion of blacks in the American work force, a conservative norm since Negroes are about 12 percent of our population. Then let us estimate the number of years it will take blacks to hold 10 percent of the positions in each job classification of the electrical industry. Blacks are already more than 10 percent of unskilled and semi-skilled workers, but their progress in the craft jobs, and especially the white collar jobs, will be much slower. If the rate of change seen from 1966 to 1969 continues, it would take nine years to reach 10 percent black in clerical positions; fourteen years for craft jobs; fifty-five years for officials and managerial positions, and eighty-six years for professionals. Moreover, the occupational ladder is constantly changing with more skilled positions supplanting the less skilled. We shall develop the details of these projections in Chapter 3.

A self-made vice president of a major agricultural chemical firm in Houston on reading this said: "My father was born an immigrant from central Europe in 1890. He was on relief. I was born in 1932, one of seven children. In 1956 I graduated from the University of Texas. It took sixty-six years (from 1890 to 1956) for my *white* family to become 'professional.' " However, the forefathers of the blacks now working for this man's company were unwilling immigrants to this country two or three hundred years ago and not one black employee is near to becoming vice president of the company today.

Obviously our statistical projections have limited validity. Growth rates are not constant; no base period is a perfect choice; and hiring policies change. But our figures do show that it will take many, many years for blacks

[2] For earlier projections see Norval D. Glenn, "Some Changes in the Relative Status of American Nonwhites, 1940–1960," *Phylon*, Vol. XXIV, No. 2, pp. 109–222; Leonard Broom and Norval D. Glenn, "When Will America's Negroes Catch Up?" *New Society*, March 25, 1965; Leonard Broom and Norval D. Glenn, *Transformation of the Negro American* (New York: Harper and Row, 1967), Chap. Six.

to reach their full participation in the industrial and business life of this country. It will require not only action by black people themselves, but conscious and systematic manpower planning by the white majority to make the vast changes in employment patterns that are necessary.

WHAT THIS BOOK INTENDS TO DO

We need not belabor the point that the integration and advancement of minority people, especially black people, remains one of America's primary domestic problems. This book presents the attitudes and feelings of management and workers in one representative industry (electrical manufacturing) to one aspect of this problem—employment. We are concerned with the access of black people to jobs in the electrical industry at *every* level, from unskilled to top management. What has management done? What is it doing? What could it do?

Inadequate employment opportunities are only one part of a pattern of deprivation that includes education, housing, and political power; but we will treat these issues only as they directly affect employment efforts. We are also interested in other power centers, such as the federal government, unions, schools, churches, and civil rights groups, mainly as they influence management decisions.

Most of the people and the facts in this book come from the electrical industry. Because of its large size and extraordinary diversity, we think that the insights and conclusions coming from our data will have application to most aspects of American business and industrial life.

This book takes both a national and a grass roots approach to the electrical industry and its minority employment practices. First, we turn our eyes back to the last century to see how racial employment has changed in America. We want to unearth the factors and causes of change. We are concerned with current equal employment statistics and the trends they show. At the four largest companies in the electrical industry—General Electric, Westinghouse, Radio Corporation of America, and Western Electric—we look at corporate policy regarding equal employment opportunity and its implementation. It is especially important also to see what is happening in the plant. How do black workers, white workers, and foremen view one another and the company? Is company policy reaching the factory floor?

To begin to answer these questions we made four major field studies: on Chicago's West Side; in the Middle South at Lynchburg, Virginia; in Buffalo; and in the Deep South in Memphis, Tennessee. In addition, we made two shorter studies of programs for disadvantaged employees: one in East Pittsburgh and the other in the Boston suburbs.

In these field studies we listened to many hundreds of people, blacks and whites, at all levels—managers, foremen, and union leaders, but primarily blue collar men and women—making this very much a "listening" book. One might say: "We've heard it all before." But really hearing the emotions and attitudes of another person is deceptively difficult. Only by listening can we come to understand the racial feelings of individual workers and supervisors, get a feel for the local plant situations, and become sensitive to the human dimensions of fair employment so necessary to future development.

The title of our book, *Blacks in the Industrial World: Issues for the Manager*, stresses our interest in blacks and managers. But we are also concerned about the white worker. Race relations is a two-way street. The black worker will need to listen to the white worker and the white worker will need to listen to the black worker. The manager will need to listen to both. We are concerned about the manager because he is a potentially powerful agent of change. And this is true at all levels of management, from the managers at the top to the foreman who is crucial to any advance in race relations.

SEVEN QUESTIONS

Seven questions are central, and we hope this book provides the beginnings of some answers:

- Do white and black workers differ in the way that they look at their jobs and supervisors? Is there any difference in the work performance of whites and blacks?
- Now that more blacks are getting into factory and office jobs, how do whites and blacks get along at work?
- What kind of management action is needed to hire and advance black people more rapidly, especially craftsmen, foremen, middle managers, and professionals? Is preferential treatment necessary? Will this cause critical white reactions?
- How does management hire, train, motivate, and retain young blacks who are disadvantaged?
- How can the all-important first-line supervisor become racially sensitive and concerned?
- From the black community: Does white big business really intend to hire and upgrade blacks in a hurry?
- What have been the most important causes of change toward improving equal employment opportunities?

In our opinion, these will remain vital questions for the 1970s, if not for the rest of this century. We hope the manager or the general reader can derive some answers from the successes and problems we present. This is partially a how-to-do-it book; but it also is a how-to-think-it book. For we are raising intellectual issues. The balancing of values between concern for both whites and blacks, the issue of preferential treatment, and the social role of the manager are thorny questions. Questions about these issues may yield no perfect answers, but asking the right questions is an important step toward finding answers.

THE CORPORATE IDENTITY CRISIS

Business managers are being asked to hire black workers, not for the sake of more efficient business operations (although this may be the ultimate outcome), but as a deliberate effort to change the forces that are splitting the country along racial lines. The federal government, aware that business has management know-how and cost consciousness, has enlisted the support and even the partnership of business toward improving the employment status of Negroes. Some, including black psychologist Dr. Kenneth B. Clark, say, "Business and industry are our last hope. They are the most realistic elements in our society."

This is part of a new unwritten charter of expectations which asks management to develop programs to confront such complex urban problems as education, politics, race relations, community development, pollution, transportation, and so forth. A new rhetoric of "corporate social responsibility" is being developed.

These concerns have led to what might be called the "identity crisis" of the modern corporation. Management is increasingly asking itself these questions: How directly should the corporation, legally chartered to make motors or mousetraps, become involved not only in supporting traditional community causes but in active efforts to change social and urban conditions and to deal with national power structures? What are the legal, ethical, social, and political boundaries of such efforts? How do these evolving opportunities relate to management's inescapable obligation to provide a product or a service at a reasonable cost and with a profit that will encourage continuity and growth? How shall management keep track of its rapidly changing environment and what is its corporate role in such a society?

It will take time to answer these questions. Much of the theory will develop as executives wrestle with concrete decisions in their own firms. But specific decisions call for policy, for a rationale. This book attempts to advance such a rationale for corporate social responsibility, not so much by theorizing, as by examining the practical applications of theory in specific case situations involving one social problem: minority manpower policies and practices. More specifically, what are the opportunities and the limitations for managers of the major electrical corporations in their responsibility toward jobs for black people, toward white people as related to blacks, and toward the racial relations of our American society as a whole? Clarification of the manager's role in advancing full racial equality at work is the background theme of this book.

EQUAL EMPLOYMENT BEHAVIOR AND RESPONSIBILITY THEORY

Some of the general public, including more than a few college students, see the modern American corporation as materialistic, crass, and unconcerned with the people and environment outside its plant gates. At the same time, there is more and more talk about the social involvement and responsibility of the corporate manager. Talk may remain mere talk, or it may lead to action. In any case, it is important to listen to this talk if we want to understand the changing relationships between black people and the corporate manager.

The conservatives or classicists boldly reject the idea that a manager, or the corporation as a whole, has any responsibility to society beyond his task of making the greatest profits possible. This may seem crass, but first listen carefully to the most articulate of the conservatives, Chicago economist, Milton Friedman:

> . . . Businessmen believe that they are defending free enterprise when they declaim that business is not concerned "merely" with profit but also with promoting desirable "social" ends; that business has a "social conscience" and takes seriously its responsibilities for providing employment, eliminating discrimination, avoiding pollution and whatever else may be the catchwords of the contemporary crop of reformers. In fact they are . . . preaching pure and unadulterated socialism. . . . Businessmen who talk this way are unwitting puppets of the intellectual forces that have been undermining the basis of a free society.[3]

Friedman speaks so strongly because he believes that the greatest social good is to be found in maximum individual freedom. Freedom is best served by dispersing power, and economic power is best dispersed in the market place where the consumer "votes" as he buys. When a manager is diverted from his primary role of profit maximization by some social goal, he not only puts himself at a competitive disadvantage, but undermines the process that creates the conditions for a sound society. Even were the economic system to permit it, Friedman believes that it is inappropriate for a manager, responsible to a *private* group, to make decisions about the *public* welfare. He doubts that the businessman will know how to define the real social questions. He denies that the manager has the right to place public burdens on private stockholders, employees, or consumers. He asks: "Is it tolerable that these public functions of taxation, expenditure, and control be exercised by the people who happen at the moment to be in charge of particular enterprises, chosen for these posts by strictly private groups?"[4]

---

[3] Milton Friedman, *Capitalism and Freedom* (Chicago: University of Chicago Press, 1963), p. 120. See also "The Social Responsibility of Business Is to Increase Its Profits," *New York Times Magazine*, September 13, 1970, p. 33.

[4] Milton Friedman, *op. cit.*, pp. 133–134.

From a very different vantage point—the left—Michael Harrington makes a similar criticism.[5] He is seriously concerned that the business establishment, under the guise of social responsibility, will make decisions about the future of American society which can be decided legitimately only by the American people. Harrington is suspicious of the motives of business, finds the businessman's approach unsatisfactory for understanding social issues, and fears that social decisions made by business will be too far removed from effective public scrutiny.

Chicago businessman Arnold Maremont, from the conservative camp, brings up a major classicist argument against business involvement—the "company store" objection:

> This is, of course, a lot of baloney. Corporations as such have no social responsibilities. . . . Let business stick to making money, government to regulating business, and management as private citizens to contributing their time, talents, and abilities in areas of social action. Any business attempt at social responsibility is in my opinion a phony—as easy to see through as the business benevolence of a few generations ago that built mill towns, factory stores, and kept employees forever in hock.[6]

To sum up, champions of the conservative tradition see the enterprise as an institution primarily to maximize profits for its stockholders. All other claimants are important to management only insofar as they help to maximize profits. If there is real market freedom, they say, let the people decide what kind of a pie they want and in the end this will make for a bigger pie for all.

The modernists challenge the classicists with the assertion that self-interest has not operated successfully to promote the common good. The manager must, therefore, be concerned with certain social issues that do not seem immediately urgent for the self-interest of the corporation or of its managers. The modernists see a growing community of interest between the private and the public sectors, between business institutions and government, with each called upon to make its best and unique contribution to the common good. Government is not an enemy, but an ally and an encourager of private initiative, even in such social matters as training the disadvantaged. Corporate executives must represent not only their stockholders, but also the interests of all other claimants on the corporation: employees, customers, competitors, and the general public. Management takes on something of the role of an umpire, even though it is a player in the ball game. Modernists do not decry profits, for without profits business cannot survive. But profit maximization is not the only concern; the social environment of the firm is of equal concern.

Since the riots at the end of the 1960s some business executives have been using a social responsibility rhetoric which says that business is all but compelled to become actively involved in social problems because the long-run

---

[5] Michael Harrington, "The Social-Industrial Complex," *Harper's*, November 1967, p. 60.

[6] Quoted in the *New York Times*, Business and Financial Section, April 20, 1965.

profits and even the very existence of the corporation depend on a stable society. The corporation is so closely intertwined with its social environment that the health of one is urgent for the health of the other. For example, Gerry E. Morse, Vice President of Employee Relations at Honeywell, states:

> As business leaders we cannot turn away from our direct involvement in this problem [black employment]. It is our responsibility to help find a solution because at the present it has and in the future *it will continue to have a very real and direct impact* upon our economy and *upon the fortunes of our individual enterprises.* This problem will not go away if we disregard it: in fact if neglected, it will undoubtedly grow worse.[7] (Italics ours)

Henry Ford II made this observation soon after the burnings in Detroit at the end of the 1960s:

> Your company and members of its management are engaged in such activities because we believe that business and industry have an obligation to serve the nation in times of crisis, whether the danger is internal or external. It is clear, moreover, that *whatever seriously threatens the stability and progress of the country and its cities also threatens the growth of the economy and your company.* Prudence in constructive company efforts to help overcome the urban crisis are demanded not only by our company's obligations as a corporate citizen but by *your management's duty to safeguard your investment.*[8] (Italics ours)

Another major reason for the developing sense of social responsibility is a change in public expectations. Thomas A. Petit in his study, *The Moral Crisis of Management*,[9] points out that people accepted management's economic power when this country was rapidly industrializing, and large profits to reinvest were necessary to increase the flow of goods and services that the public wanted. Private and social goals were then in harmony. But as America increased in wealth, those who shared in the growing affluence, freed from concern for life's essentials, began to question the right of corporate managers to exercise so much power. If corporate management is to be considered legitimate by the modern public, it will need to show a sincere interest in social problems. Social responsibility today belongs in the corporate survival kit.

Finally, businessmen, frustrated with government bureaucracy, hope that they can handle social problems more efficiently and more effectively than the government. Social responsibility can be seen as a way to put the brakes on Big Government.

---

[7] Quoted in Herbert R. Northrup and Richard L. Rowan (eds.), *The Negro and Employment Opportunity* (Ann Arbor: Bureau of Industrial Relations, Graduate School of Business Administration, The University of Michigan, 1965), p. 123.

[8] Quoted in Robert C. Albrook, "Business Wrestles with Its Social Conscience," *Fortune*, August 1968.

[9] Thomas A. Petit, *The Moral Crisis in Management* (New York: McGraw-Hill, 1967), p. 7.

Amid the rising swell of rhetoric supporting corporate social responsibilities, some writers are calling for caution. Allen T. Demaree, writing in *Fortune* magazine,[10] states clearly that business must continue its new involvement in current social problems, but asks that its managers be "scrupulously realistic in defining the scope of its contribution, and in evaluating the progress it is making." When business promises too much or claims success too soon, he warns, people become cynical. It is then even more difficult to deal with the problem.

A DuPont company publication says that management should not, and indeed, cannot, do the complex job alone.

> No single organization in America, nor any one type of institution has the resources or the experience, or the charter to attack the nation's social and cultural problems in bulk. Such progress as has been made has come through cooperation, through action taken step by step, problem by problem, community by community, drawing upon the multiple talents of organizations that are educational, governmental, cultural, spiritual and commercial in purpose.[11]

A third warning is that setting policy is not enough. Management will not be able to act responsibly until it develops internal structures and communications which will insure the consideration of social values at all levels of decision-making—a kind of social auditing system as a parallel to its financial auditing system.

TOWARD A WORKING DEFINITION OF CORPORATE SOCIAL RESPONSIBILITY

Now it is time to give our own operational definition. Corporate responsibility means a willingness on the part of the corporate manager (acting not only as an individual but as a decision-maker involving his firm) actively and with moral concern to confront certain social problems he deems urgent and to bend the influence of his company toward the solution of those problems insofar as the firm is able to do so. Such responsibility requires that the manager balance intelligently the needs of the many groups affected by the firm so as best to achieve both profitable production and the common good, especially in situations in which he is not required to do so by law or by external pressures which the company cannot easily resist.

There are several elements in this definition. First, the manager is acting not only as an individual but as a corporate agent. Second, he will undertake certain socially motivated actions not required by law or external pressure.

---

[10] Allen T. Demaree, "Business Picks Up the Urban Challenge," *Fortune*, April 1969, p. 103.

[11] *Company and Community*, E. I. DuPont Nemours and Company, Wilmington, Del.

Third, his sense of responsibility will not be based on traditional philanthropy but on his understanding of the complex interrelationships between his firm and society. Fourth, he is concerned with the welfare of people within the firm as well as outside the firm. Fifth, he will be concerned to advance his productivity at a reasonable profit and thereby increase the gross national product. This in itself is an important contribution to the common good. Sixth, there will be a moral component in his thinking. The manager will have to set priorities and make value decisions about the various claims on the corporation.

It is important to distinguish a corporate social responsibility approach from a mere public relations approach. Public relations releases praising the corporation's social contributions are not the same as realistically weaving social values into company self-evaluation and decision-making. And some socially responsible decisions may actually expose a company to increased criticism.

In the responsibility debate between the conservatives and the moderates, the Friedmans and the Fords, this book takes a position. We present our stand in the last chapter only after examining the practical involvement of the firms we observed in the social problem of minority employment. As you go through the book, you might ask whether or not the managers we portray are acting with a sense of corporate social responsibility toward black people. What effect will findings like these have on the evolving identity of the corporation of the late 1970s?

PART ONE
The national experience

CHAPTER TWO

Ninety years of slow change

> *Most Americans know little of the origins of the racial schism separating our white and Negro citizens. . . . Fewer still understand that today's problems can be solved only if white Americans comprehend the . . . barriers that have prevented Negroes from participating in the mainstream of American life.*
>
> National Advisory Commission on Civil Disorders

To understand present and future race relations in American industry, we need to look to the past, particularly to the main factors that influence change. Negro employment in the electrical manufacturing industry dates largely from World War II. Prior to then, less than 1 percent of the industry's employment was black. Why was this so, and what caused the slow improvements?

BEFORE WORLD WAR II

The electrical manufacturing industry began in the 1870s when electric arc lights and power generators first went into very limited commercial production. The following decades saw rapid technological advance and notable expansion. By 1890 Western Electric was over twenty years old, and Westinghouse had been founded. In 1891 General Electric was formed by consolidation of predecessor companies.

Employment in the industry increased rapidly. By the end of the nineteenth century, the industry had almost 50,000 workers. By 1910 the figure was over 100,000, and by the end of World War I, over 300,000. Four hundred and twenty thousand were employed in 1929 just before the Depression, or 4.4 percent of total American manufacturing employment.[1] But very few Negroes

---

[1] All data from Jules Backman, *The Economics of the Electrical Machinery Industry* (New York: New York University Press, 1962), p. 328.

were included among the growing number of electrical employees: in 1930 less than 1 percent were black. (See Table 2-1.)

Table 2-1. Employment by Race and Sex, 1930—1960
Electrical Manufacturing Industry

Year	ALL EMPLOYEES Total	Negro	Percent Negro	MALE Total	Negro	Percent Negro	FEMALE Total	Negro	Percent Negro
1930[a]	383,570	3,095	0.8	298,383	2,919	1.0	85,187	176	0.2
1940[b]	374,684	1,782	0.5	273,483	1,683	0.6	101,201	99	0.1
1950[b]	788,184	19,433	2.5	512,760	11,651	2.3	275,424	7,782	2.8
1960[b]	1,487,412	48,903	3.3	978,259	30,730	3.1	509,153	18,173	3.6

Source: U.S. Census of Population:
1930: Vol. V, Occupations—General Report, Chapter VII, Table 2.
1940: Vol. III, The Labor Force, Part 1, Table 76.
1950: Vol. II, Characteristics of Population, Part 1, Table 133.
1960: PC(1)ID, U.S. Summary, Detailed Characteristics, Table 213.

[a] Gainful workers (10 years and older).
[b] Employed persons (14 years and older).

One major reason for the absence of Negroes was the location of the industry. Electrical manufacturing was a northern industry, concentrated in the Northeast. Moreover, manufacturing locations were mostly in the smaller manufacturing cities. In 1910 less than 2 percent of the population of the northeastern and north central states was Negro, and a good part of this number was concentrated in the largest cities in the Northeast. Negroes were barely present in the labor pool from which the electrical industry drew its work force. Even as late as 1940, only 3.8 percent of the population in the northeastern and north central states was black.[2]

During World War I, the electrical industry was not subject to some of the pressure that led industries such as automobiles or steel to recruit large numbers of southern Negroes, or even to do the limited amount of recruiting done in this period by the rubber tire industry.[3] The electrical industry's labor requirements at that time were more heavily skill oriented than many other industries, and for this work the first and second generation immigrants and older American recruits from rural areas proved adequate. Where unskilled labor was needed, such as in lamp (bulb) manufacturing, white women whose husbands were often working in steel or metals plants proved sufficient.

With the industry emphasizing good benefits and stable or expanding employment, it did not become involved in labor struggles wherein black strikebreakers were imported, as did steel or meatpacking.[4] And unlike

[2] *The Negroes in the United States. Their Economic and Social Situation.* Bulletin No. 1511, U.S. Bureau of Labor Statistics (Washington: Government Printing Office, 1966), p. 66.

[3] See Herbert R. Northrup, Richard L. Rowan, et al., "Negro Employment in Basic Industry," *Studies of Negro Employment*, Vol. I (Philadelphia: Industrial Research Unit, Wharton School of Finance and Commerce, University of Pennsylvania, 1970), Part Two, pp. 51-53; Part Four, pp. 401-402; and Herbert R. Northrup, *Organized Labor and the Negro* (New York: Harper and Brothers, 1944), pp. 172-174.

[4] See Theodore V. Purcell, *The Worker Speaks His Mind* (Cambridge: Harvard University Press, 1952), pp. 46, 51, 318.

heavy industries, such as smelting or steel, or industries with less desirable work, such as meatpacking, electrical manufacturing did not have the concentration of arduous or hazardous jobs that so often became known as "Negro jobs."

During this early period business was under no pressure, of course, from either government or the public to consider Negro employment. The federal government passed no civil rights legislation during the first quarter of the twentieth century, and the more militant civil rights groups focused on political and legal justice. The Urban League, founded in 1911 with an explicitly economic focus, did appeal to businessmen to hire Negroes. But its impact was slight.

EARLY MANAGEMENT POLICY

Despite the small number of Negroes in the industry, management of some large firms became aware of the problem. The following incident throws light on the racial thinking of American managers and unionists of those early days.

It was summer 1917 and World War I was raging. Among the twenty-five to thirty students hired that summer by General Electric's huge and vital Schenectady works was Wendell King—a Negro. On hearing about King's employment, the machinists, represented by the International Association of Machinists, called a strike. Their single demand was that King be fired. General Electric flatly refused. The strike, limited solely to the machinists, lasted eight days.

The following statement, issued by the company, describes management's stand in the case, as well as the fears of the union machinists:

> ... It is not the intention of the company to introduce colored labor into the shops or displace any white labor with colored labor, nor is it the intention of the management to bring numbers of colored people to Schenectady to work in the shops, and we recommend that any objection to the young colored man, Wendell King, remaining at work in the department where he is now employed be withdrawn, and that the Machinists now on strike return to their places and resume work considering the matter at issue as a closed incident.[5]

The strike ended on company terms. There is no record of further racial strife or of company action to increase Negro employment.

We must consider this incident within the framework of its own time. It is significant that GE management was willing to hire Mr. King and take an eight-day, wartime strike rather than discharge him; yet management was not about to introduce Negroes into its shops nor encourage Negro labor to come

---

[5] From newspaper accounts of the incident on file at General Electric Company. *Schenectady Gazette*, June 22, 1917. See also *Schenectady Union Star*, June 21, 22, 25 and 26, 1917.

up from the South to meet the labor shortages occasioned by World War I. As for the IAM unionists, both their fears and their racial intolerance were quite clear.

We can make a more general assessment of early management policy. Many corporations today refer to "long-standing" policies of nondiscrimination. Radio Corporation of America[6] (RCA) cites one of the earliest written merit employment policies, dating from 1919; in 1923 Western Electric[7] included a similar policy in a document defining employment policies. General Electric in 1935 issued a booklet entitled "GE Policies Concerning Wages, Hours, and Working Conditions of Shop Employees." Included was this statement: "There shall be no discrimination by foremen, superintendents, or any executives of the Company against any employee because of race, or creed, or because of an employee's membership in any fraternity, society, labor organization or other lawful organization." The booklet was signed by President Gerard T. Swope, who took an unconventional stance (for the period) in regard to unions. Why the statement was issued is not clear, but Swope's deep concern about social problems may have been the reason. In any case, it does appear to have been the first written policy mentioning race or creed to be announced by a large company.[8]

These statements indicated genuine commitment to an ideal; but practice at the time fell far short. RCA, like most electrical manufacturers, did not employ Negroes in production or clerical jobs before 1941,[9] and integration at Western Electric's Kearny, New Jersey plant in the same year was considered a breakthrough. General Electric followed up its policy statement of 1935 by including a nondiscrimination clause in its contract with the United Electrical, Radio and Machine Workers, yet significant progress in integration would await the war years. As late as 1941, the U.S. Bureau of Employment Security reported its finding that managers surveyed in the electrical manufacturing industry would *not* consider a Negro, if available, for 10,346 of the 20,792 job openings that they anticipated would become available within the next several months.[10]

---

[6] "Equal Opportunity in Employment," statement by Frank M. Folsom, President, Radio Corporation of America, before the United States Senate Committee on Labor and Public Welfare, Subcommittee on Civil Rights, February 23, 1954, reprinted by RCA.

[7] R. G. Lawrence, "Western Electric's Commitment to Fair Employment," in Herbert R. Northrup and Richard L. Rowan (eds.), *The Negro and Employment Opportunity* (Ann Arbor: Bureau of Industrial Relations, Graduate School of Business Administration, The University of Michigan, 1965), p. 137.

[8] See *Community and Government Relations* Bulletin No. 64-3, General Electric Company, April 17, 1964; and Virgil B. Day, "Progress in Equal Employment Opportunity at General Electric," in Northrup and Rowan (eds.), *The Negro and Employment Opportunity, op. cit.*, p. 155. For an account of Swope's remarkable career, including his interest in social work and social problems, see David Loth, *Swope of GE* (New York: Simon and Shuster, 1950).

[9] See Folsom, *op. cit.*

[10] "The Negro's War," *Fortune*, June 1942, p. 9.

Ninety years of slow change

Certain skilled jobs in some plants were undoubtedly closed to Negroes because of contracts with the International Association of Machinists (IAM), the International Brotherhood of Electric Workers (IBEW), or other craft unions; but these unions represented only a small proportion of electrical workers at a few locations. Most likely management was reluctant to face the anticipated reaction of their white workers.

In fact, management rarely had to consider the issue. Gunnar Myrdal in his classic *An American Dilemma* points out that employees and employers alike came to accept the absence of Negroes as "natural."

> ... If an establishment is a "white shop," Negroes generally know this. Few of them ever try to get in—and those few who make the attempt can tell the rest of the Negro jobseekers about how futile it has been. In such cases Negroes are excluded with a minimum of effort on the part of both employers and white workers. Most white people never think of the fact that there is a definite policy to keep the Negro out. The "white shop" is part of the tradition and just seems natural. The issue is not faced. The color bar, although as real as can be, is almost invisible.[11]

Thus, even where locational factors or inadequate educational background did not rule out potential Negro job applicants, it is likely that few Negroes applied because they believed that it would not be a fruitful exercise. Moreover, during the Depression the tiny Negro work force was further depleted, declining at a more rapid rate than did the total work force during these difficult years. Table 2-1 shows that in 1940 only 0.5 percent of electrical employment was black. The very few Negroes employed were generally excluded from production jobs. Despite more progressive policy statements, managements seem to have accepted the mores of the time which limited Negro employment opportunity.

WORLD WAR II AND ITS AFTERMATH

World War II caused a rapid and massive increase in the demand for labor, thereby bringing substantial numbers of Negroes into the electrical industry for the first time. In 1940 the effects of the Depression were still evident. The unemployment rate was close to 15 percent, with 8 million unemployed. In the four subsequent war years, the armed forces increased from a half million to over 11 million. At the same time, American manufacturing expanded to meet war production, and 7.3 million additional people were employed. Unemployment dropped to a historic low of 1.2 percent in 1944; and inevitably the composition of the American labor force changed substantially.

---

[11] Gunnar Myrdal, *An American Dilemma* (New York: McGraw-Hill, 1964), p. 389.

The electrical manufacturing industry was particularly affected by the demand for labor since employment expanded to over 1 million in 1943,[12] more than double the 1940 employment level.

The manpower pressures of massive war production also produced changes in job content and description that favored low-skilled, poorly educated workers. Production systems were redesigned; many low-skilled, repetitive jobs were created; and new electronic products and systems developed in this period required large numbers of low-skilled assembly operations. Lower productivity was tolerated, and government subsidies were available for recruiting and training inexperienced workers.[13]

In addition to changes in the labor market, there was a militant Negro drive, under the leadership of A. Phillip Randolph, for an end to job discrimination. A demonstration march on Washington was threatened, and on June 25, 1941, President Franklin D. Roosevelt issued Executive Order 8802 announcing that discriminatory practices by government and defense contractors were contrary to the public interest. This executive order also established a President's Committee on Fair Employment Practice. David Sarnoff, president of RCA, was an original member of this committee, but he resigned, alleging that the Committee was ineffectual.

A second executive order, No. 9346, was issued on May 27, 1943, with a more vigorous approach that dramatized the need for nondiscrimination. Despite a lack of enforcement machinery it contributed to fair employment in a number of industries by supporting employers desirous of adding Negroes to the labor force against recalcitrant management colleagues and fearful or disgruntled employees. Nevertheless, the labor shortage was the primary impetus for employing Negroes.

The early 1940s saw significant breakthroughs in the number of Negroes hired and some improvement in the kinds of jobs they could get. Among the first to inaugurate change in the electrical manufacturing industry was Western Electric in its Kearny, New Jersey, plant. *Fortune* gives this euphoric account:

> A year ago [in 1941] Western Electric hired Negroes for the first time in its Kearny, N.J. plant and put them to work side by side with skilled white people. The experiment was a full success. No separate cafeterias, no separate washrooms, and no move to get them. The plant is producing highly complicated instruments; neither the work nor its quality was even slightly disturbed.[14]

Furthermore, by the end of the war about 2,000 Negroes were employed by this plant, according to Julius Thomas of the National Urban League.

[12] Statistics from U.S. Bureau of Labor Statistics, *Employment and Earnings Statistics for the United States, 1909–1968* (Washington: Government Printing Office, 1968), pp. 302–303; and *Employment and Earnings*, March 1969 and 1970, Tables B-2 and B-3.

[13] Charles C. Killingsworth, *Jobs and Income for Negroes* (Ann Arbor: University of Michigan Press, 1968), p. 36.

[14] "The Negro's War," *Fortune*, June 1942, p. 9.

Radio Corporation of America recruited Negroes for production jobs for the first time in Indianapolis in 1941 and in Camden and Harrison, New Jersey, in 1942. Despite the fact that very few had any industrial experience, the new workers did well; RCA found it necessary to dismiss "only a very few" whites who refused to work with blacks, and later testified that "there is little ground for the fairly common management fear that the employment of minority groups on an equal basis will arouse resentment among the majority of workers or in the community."[15]

Westinghouse had more trouble at their home plant in East Pittsburgh when they hired black men for the production lines; and rest room facilities were vandalized when black women, originally hired on third shift, gained enough seniority to move up to the same shift with white women. The local union, the United Electrical Workers, supported management in both cases, and blacks and whites were soon working side by side.[16] Similarly, General Electric's major Schenectady plant, scene of the strike incident reported above, has been cited for its progressive policies during the war.[17]

It is difficult to estimate the number and proportion of Negroes employed during the war, since no data are available. It is unlikely, however, that the proportion exceeded 3 percent, and it probably was closer to 2.5 percent— the proportion found by the 1950 census. This would mean that about 30,000 Negroes had jobs in the industry in 1944.[18]

At the end of the war barriers remained in the industry. Negroes were rarely assigned to white collar or supervisory jobs. The significant fact, however, is that Negroes were employed in large numbers for the first time in the industry and were working along with whites. Moreover, the great migrations during the war brought Negroes within the potential work force of many companies for the first time, and offered the opportunity for future black additions to the industry's employment roles.

POSTWAR READJUSTMENT

Although the electrical manufacturing industry declined by approximately 150,000 from its wartime peak in the first postwar year, it recovered rapidly. The orders and demand for its products by both industry and the consumer created enormous backlogs. In addition, the late 1940s saw the first stages of the burgeoning electronic revolution. By 1947 electrical employment was approximately equal to its wartime high. Even in 1949, a low point in postwar industry employment, the electrical work force at 862,000 was about 80

---

[15] Folsom, *op. cit.*, pp. 5–6.

[16] Field notes and interviews.

[17] John A. Davis, "Negro Employment: A Progress Report," *Fortune*, July 1952, p. 103.

[18] This estimate is based on the U.S. Bureau of Labor Statistics data. Census data in Table 2–1 appear to underestimate employment.

percent of its maximum wartime employment and twice its 1940 level, and by 1951 it had passed the wartime peak.

Whether Negroes were affected disproportionately by the postwar layoffs cannot be determined. In any case, in 1950, when employment in the industry was still below the wartime peak, Negro employment as reported by the U.S. Census was 2.5 percent that of total employment, reflecting an absolute increase of about 18,000 jobs for Negroes. Thus in the decade of the 1940s, although Negro employment increased faster than total employment, it started from such a low base that Negroes in 1950 still represented only 2.5 percent of the industry's labor force. (See Table 2-1.)

INTEGRATION ACTIVITIES

The postwar period saw the development of the first programs to employ Negroes, motivated primarily by a concern for integration, rather than manpower needs. Moreover, these programs were designed to obtain positions for white collar as well as blue collar personnel.

In the early part of 1947 the National Urban League established a Management Advisory Committee to place competent blacks in professional and technical positions. A. B. Goetze, then Personnel Director of Western Electric, was most active in initiating the formation of this Committee. In succeeding years representatives of a number of electrical manufacturers, including GE, Westinghouse, and RCA, were active on the Committee and began consulting regularly with the National Urban League at the corporate level.

Also in 1947, Western Electric, with the assistance of Dr. Julius Thomas, Industrial Relations Secretary of the National Urban League, began an executive training program dealing with equal employment opportunities. Some firms commenced informal audits of their own Negro employment, with tentative steps to increase it. Often the commitment of top managers was not effectively implemented. Yet jobs did result, token at first, but they gradually increased for Negroes with key skills.

In 1948 Howard University became the first predominantly Negro university to have its engineering school accredited by the Engineer's Council on Professional Development. The following year, at the instigation of Dr. Thomas, General Electric became the first nationwide company to include the Howard engineering school as part of its regular college recruiting function. Other companies soon followed suit, *actively* recruiting black technical personnel for the first time.

Consultation with the Urban League had little effect on the overall racial composition of the industry. Efforts were directed primarily toward a few individual pioneering breakthroughs at professional and technical levels, rather than toward large numbers of Negro recruits. And fair employment programs were not a high priority. These efforts were, however, the first steps toward voluntary elimination of the strong, although unwritten, barriers that excluded Negroes from many jobs in the industry.

Other developments in the late 1940s also showed concern for fair employment. In 1946 and 1947, Charles E. Wilson, Swope's successor as president of General Electric, served as chairman of the President's Committee on Civil Rights, appointed by President Harry S. Truman. The Committee called for an end to all segregation and discrimination and the passage of effective civil rights and equal employment opportunity legislation. Wilson, who had reissued the Swope nondiscrimination policy in 1941, signed the cover letter transmitting the report to President Truman, stating in part that "... the protection of Civil Rights is a national problem which affects everyone. We need to guarantee the same rights to every person regardless of who he is, where he lives, or what his racial, religious or national origins are."[19] This was perhaps the first call by a major industrialist for such legislation.

In the late 1940s, seven states—New Jersey, Massachusetts, Connecticut, New Mexico, Oregon, Rhode Island, and Washington—followed New York in passing state fair employment practice legislation with enforcement provisions. Thus in the northeastern states where the electrical manufacturing industry was traditionally concentrated, equal employment opportunity had become a matter of law by 1950. In many parts of the South, however, where the industry was beginning to expand, racial segregation was still legal and sometimes required by law.

These first legal steps on Negroes' rights took place during a time when American attitudes toward Negroes were changing. Liberal ideas were more widely articulated during the Depression. The New Deal was characterized by the exaltation of the Common Man. In World War II the United States saw itself as a nation of people opposed to tyranny and oppression. This vision had at least an indirect impact on the American dilemma of racism. If we were freeing people oppressed by Fascism and Communism, we must give some thought to the freedom of American blacks at home.

THE DECADE OF THE 1950s

The Korean War (1950–1953) again drew civilian workers into the armed forces, as well as increasing production and total manufacturing employment. Employment in the electrical manufacturing industry reached 1.3 million in 1953, an increase of approximately 400,000 employees since 1950, a three-year period when the national unemployment rate dropped from 5.3 to 2.9 percent. Increased demand for labor in a tight labor market again meant greater opportunities for blacks.

Since it was a growth industry, electrical manufacturing was not so severely affected as other industries by post-Korean War recession. Although the electrical industry lost 160,000 jobs in 1954, it recovered rather well and

[19] Copy in authors' possession.

employed 10,000 more persons in 1957 than in the Korean War peak year of 1953. The recession year of 1958 cost the industry 100,000 jobs, but by 1960 industry employment stood at 1,467,000, a gain of 134,000 over 1953 and 476,000 more than in 1950.

Within the industry, however, a number of companies felt the 1958 recession more sharply and for a longer period. General Electric employment, for example, fell by more than 50,000 from 285,000 in 1957 to 231,000 in 1959, and did not regain the 1957 figure until 1966.[20] Other companies suffered similar cutbacks, but the electrical industry as a whole increased employment in the 1950s at about four times the rate for manufacturing industry generally.

The kinds of work available also changed markedly during the 1950s. Employment of salaried personnel increased at a faster rate than did that of blue collar workers. Killingsworth describes the shift in government spending:

> The emphasis shifted from aircraft, ships and wheeled vehicles to missiles, atomic weapons, electronic equipment and similar sophisticated gear; and these trends were reinforced by the new undertakings in space flight. The employment growing out of these new emphases and interests was heavily weighted toward the engineer, the technician and the skilled craftsman rather than the low-skilled assembly-line workers. Manufacturing industry generally exhibited some of the same trends, although to a lesser degree.[21]

The electrical industry itself was going through what we might call a technological revolution. An ever higher proportion of engineers and technicians was needed. Nevertheless production jobs continued to expand, so that 338,420 more such workers were employed in 1960 than in 1950. In part, growth offset the impact of automation but delicate electronic assembly also continued to require many semiskilled employees.

Thus while the combination of automation and recession in the 1950s had an adverse affect on Negro employment in the economy as a whole, the percentage of blacks in the electrical industry rose from its admittedly low level of 2.5 in 1950 to 3.3 in 1960. (See Table 2-1.)

THE UNIONS AND BLACKS

During these years, the major unions of the electrical industry had little direct effect on Negro employment and upgrading. Unlike the situations in the building trades and longshoring, hiring and upgrading in the electrical industry were handled by management rather than by unions. (For the structure of unionism in the electrical industry, see Appendix C.)[22]

[20] Data from company annual reports.
[21] Killingsworth, *op. cit.*, pp. 37–38.
[22] For the history of the relationships between Negroes and American unionism, see Sterling D. Spero and Abram L. Harris, *The Black Worker* (New York: Columbia University Press, 1931); Horace R. Cayton and George Mitchell, *Black Workers and the New Unions* (Chapel Hill, N.C.: University of North Carolina Press, 1939); Northrup, *Organized Labor and the Negro*, *op. cit.*; F. Ray Marshall, *The Negro and Organized Labor* (New York: John Wiley & Sons, 1965).

At national or international levels, the civil rights policies of the major unions in the industry varied across a wide spectrum. The International Association of Machinists (IAM) and the International Brotherhood of Electrical Workers (IBEW), loyal to their craft traditions and prejudices, were conservative and exclusive. Like other unions such as the railroad brotherhoods, the IAM formally excluded Negroes from membership prior to 1949 by an explicit provision of its ritual. (Recall the GE Schenectady strike of 1917.) The IBEW never barred Negroes by formal provision, but did so by common consent. After it organized more factory workers in the 1950s, the IBEW accepted Negro members, but many of its craft locals, particularly in the construction industry, vigorously opposed even token integration.

The largest electrical unions were the United Electrical, Radio and Machine Workers of America (UE) and especially the International Union of Electrical, Radio and Machine Workers (IUE). Both the UE, with its left-wing ideology, and the IUE, with its roots in the liberal philosophy of the Congress of Industrial Organizations, took strong stands, at least on the national level, regarding the job rights of Negroes. James B. Carey, former president of the IUE and Secretary-Treasurer of the CIO, became Chairman of the CIO Civil Rights Committee and actively supported Negro employment, although the Committee was quite limited in its power over the autonomous CIO unions.

The formal stance of the electrical unions at both the international and local levels was expressed by typical nondiscrimination clauses in their collective bargaining agreements that "the provisions of this agreement and of the local supplements will continue to be applied without discrimination because of race, creed, color, sex or national origin." Implementation of such policies, of course, depended on *local* union members. Since control over the locals by the internationals in the industry was generally not vigorous, actual plant attitudes and practices depended primarily on the members and leaders of the locals themselves, and grass roots attitudes varied.

We should say a word about union-management seniority requirements as they affected blacks. Since blacks were new employees, by seniority they were last upgraded and first laid off. Yet movement up the job hierarchy in the electrical industry was relatively fluid. There were few long, narrow seniority lines, except in some plants making heavy utility apparatus. The large proportion of semiskilled operative jobs provided opportunities for the unskilled and inexperienced to work at entry jobs and later to advance as they gained knowledge and experience. Seniority systems allowed broad movement within large work areas. Few "black departments" or segregated work areas existed, and we found no record of seniority agreements designed to confine Negroes to specific jobs, as was common in industries such as steel, tobacco, or paper. In the electrical industry seniority was neither a significant bar, nor a spur, to Negro employment.

PLANT LOCATION AND SOUTHERN EXPANSION

We have said that locational factors before World War II reduced Negro participation in the electrical industry since few Negroes lived near the plant concentrations. By the end of the war the great migrations from southern rural areas to the North had altered population patterns, but as the electrical industry began building new plants, Negroes again found themselves at a disadvantage. Many of these new plants were constructed in the more rural areas of the North and West where the labor force was still overwhelmingly white.

In addition, new plants in urban areas were located outside city limits so that companies would be able to construct single-story structures with ample room for expansion, thus avoiding the higher taxes, increased material handling costs, and lack of expansion potential that city location usually involves. Such plants meant great dependence on automobile transportation for employees, since public urban transportation steadily declined throughout the 1950s. Because proportionately fewer central city Negroes owned automobiles than did whites, Negroes had the additional burden of difficult transportation.

The late 1940s and most of the 1950s saw a major expansion of the electrical machinery industry into the South. Most of the plants built there were located in small towns or on the outskirts of cities. In nearly all cases they could be reached only by automobile, again a problem for blacks. In addition, jobs in these plants were much in demand so that electrical machinery employers, like those in other industries, set high hiring standards. Discriminatory education saw to it that proportionately fewer Negroes could meet those standards.

Negro employment was also hindered by the discriminatory policies of southern state employment services. Many companies had their prospective employees screened by state employment offices, which often did not refer Negroes to good jobs. In some states, laws requiring separate wash rooms and eating facilities for black employees made hiring Negroes expensive.

Managements generally accepted southern racial mores, except where individual managers were interested in a more equitable approach. President Price of Westinghouse put his company's position like this:

> It is our opinion that industrial integration does not take place in a vacuum. The degree to which industrial integration can be achieved is influenced greatly by the situations which exist in the communities in which our plants are located. Certainly we can and we do follow policies in our southern plants which are somewhat more progressive than existing community practices. However, we do not feel that in the relatively small communities in which our plants are located that we should be completely out of phase with the community.[23]

---

[23] Remarks by Gwilym A. Price, President and Chairman, Westinghouse Electric Corporation, the President's Committee on Government Contracts, Conference of October 25, 1955, reprint from Westinghouse.

Westinghouse made minor modifications by providing nonsegregated eating and wash room facilities in some states. Yet the Baltimore plants of Westinghouse, opened in the early 1950s, employed Negroes in all capacities, contrary to local custom, and even held company parties in a federal armory because racially mixed parties were not allowed in local hotels.

General Electric, in accordance with its newly developed decentralized organization, left racial policies to individual managers. As a result, at least three of its early post-World War II plants employed a lily-white work force; a few others hired Negroes only in unskilled jobs; while at least four others made significant attempts to employ Negroes on an integrated basis.[24] Thus in the middle 1950s when white workers walked off the job at GE's Louisville, Kentucky, "Appliance Park" complex because Negroes were employed on the assembly line, the strikers were discharged or otherwise disciplined and the integration efforts continued.

One General Electric executive, Dr. Louis Rader, not only pushed integration at the plant under his jurisdiction (Waynesboro, Virginia), but also publicly helped to lead the fight in Virginia which reopened the schools and ended the state's ill-fated "massive resistance" to school integration. Dr. Rader's position, like that of other industrialists so committed, was simple: without good public schools, industry, especially highly technical industry, could not attract engineers and other professionals to live and work in the South. The choice was between following the mores of the Old South, or moving with industry.[25]

The genuine concern of industry managers with the threat posed to effective operations and personnel recruitment by the southern school crisis of the 1950s led many to take a more searching look at their plant personnel racial policies. At the very least, a greater receptivity resulted for governmental integration efforts. Moreover, the problem resulting from the furor over schools made top management more conscious of southern race problems and less willing to believe that adherence to old southern employment mores could ensure tranquillity or acceptance.

Even in the border or northern states, decentralized management unconcerned with corporate equal employment programs produced results inconsistent with corporate policy. The headquarters office personnel recruiter of one large company used several New York City parochial schools as the principal source for secretarial applicants. Since no Negroes were then enrolled in these schools, none were hired.[26]

---

[24] Interview with a former General Electric employee relations executive, February 2, 1970.

[25] For an account of Dr. Rader's efforts and those of executives of other companies, see Herbert R. Northrup, "Industry's Racial Employment Policies," in Arthur M. Ross and Herbert Hill (eds.), *Employment, Race and Poverty* (New York: Harcourt, Brace & World, Inc., 1967), pp. 294–295; and William H. Nicholls, *Southern Tradition and Regional Progress* (Chapel Hill, N.C.: University of North Carolina Press, 1960), pp. 114–123.

[26] Interview with former employee relations manager, September 1970.

In Indianapolis, another major concern was recruiting heavily in 1951. A former member of the employment staff described the situation:

> In 1951 this company was hiring males at a fairly high rate of approximately 100 per week. During initial screening interviews personnel interviewers would indicate on applications "NW" for nonwhites and "W" for whites. There was little or no interest in putting Negroes on the roll so they were rarely hired.
>
> During this period it was noted that one or more of the same well-dressed Negroes were always in the lobby observing who was sent to the shop for interviews and taking obvious notes. This continued for approximately 30 days, during which time we later learned, several Negro organizations contacted our New York headquarters.
>
> In approximately another 60–90 days we were advised to hire a specific number of Negroes. I cannot remember the exact number but it was something like 25. These people were immediately hired.
>
> It would appear that this direct pressure was responsible for these people being put on the roll, and without it they most likely would not have been employed.[27]

FEDERAL AND STATE COMMISSION ACTIVITIES

Although the Eisenhower Administration did not support federal fair employment legislation, a President's Committee on Government Contracts was established on August 13, 1953, by Executive Order No. 10479[28] to encourage nondiscrimination in employment by government contractors. Known as the "Nixon Committee," because it was chaired by the then Vice President, the Committee developed the investigatory and fact-finding techniques, later expanded by the Kennedy and Johnson Administrations as a means of increasing Negro employees among government contractors. A small sample of electrical machinery concerns, including selected plants of major companies, were among those that were investigated and prodded by the Nixon Committee and from which racial employment data were gathered.

Table 2-2 shows data developed by the Nixon Committee inspectors for the last three years of the decade of the 1950s. In general, these corroborate the already noted census data that show both the paucity of Negroes in the industry and the extreme shortage of Negro salaried employees. The variations from year to year are not significant except in the white collar group, but even there the increases may be partially attributable to different plants or companies sampled. The bulk of Negro white collar employment in these years was clerical and was found in large city areas of the North. The 1950s saw increased efforts to expand employment on these jobs, but results continued to be insignificant.

[27] Interview, September 1970.
[28] Previous executive orders had been issued by the Roosevelt and Truman Administrations, as already noted.

Table 2-2. Employment by Race, 1957—1959
Selected Electrical Manufacturing Plants

	ALL EMPLOYEES			WHITE COLLAR EMPLOYEES			BLUE COLLAR EMPLOYEES		
Year	Total	Negro	Percent Negro	Total	Negro	Percent Negro	Total	Negro	Percent Negro
1957	64,489	1,453	2.3	19,989	43	0.2	38,118	1,410	3.7
1958	77,912	1,533	2.0	30,028	224	0.7	40,755	1,324	3.2
1959	76,637	2,083	2.7	30,615	305	1.0	42,222	1,778	4.2

Source: Unpublished files of the President's Committee on Government Contracts (Nixon Committee).
1957—4 companies, 20 plants.
1958—5 companies, 19 plants.
1959—5 companies, 17 plants.

Actions of state fair employment practice commissions (FEPC) also contributed to improved Negro employment in the late 1950s. In New Jersey, what was then known as the Division Against Discrimination began receiving reports of discrimination in the late 1940s and began a campaign that opened up not only an increasing number of blue collar jobs, but also white collar jobs as well. The files of the New Jersey agency reveal steady improvement in this regard in successive inspections of plants of General Electric, Western Electric, McGraw-Edison, RCA, International Telephone and Telegraph, and others. Similar action occurred in Pennsylvania with Westinghouse, in New York with General Electric, in Massachusetts with Raytheon, and in Ohio with RCA and Whirlpool. In all of these states, other electrical manufacturers, including smaller ones, were also inspected and prodded toward increased hiring of Negroes.[29]

The state commissions, unlike the Nixon Committee, made few systematic company or plant analyses and none were made in electrical manufacturing. Nevertheless, as their number grew to include nearly all nonsouthern states, they helped to prepare industry for the civil rights pressures of the 1960s by opening gates for Negroes and gaining acceptance of the principles of fair employment. But it was not yet clear that systematic minority manpower efforts and unconventional techniques would be necessary and considered appropriate by the public.

MANAGEMENT RESPONSE

There is a perennial debate about whether change should be merely encouraged or actively legislated. Businessmen naturally want to avoid government regulation because it can be time consuming and does not always take into account intricate business considerations. Yet how much change occurred without legal pressure?

In the 1950s many firms began a quiet but serious evaluation of their racial hiring practices. Yet most opposed further regulation. Westinghouse

[29] Based upon an examination of the unpublished files of these agencies.

President Gwilym Price probably spoke for many when he addressed the President's Committee on Government Contracts in 1955: "We believe in integration. We believe in integration not only because there are sound, valid and compelling sociological reasons for it, but also because our experience shows there are sound, valid, compelling and hard-headed business and economic reasons for it." But he maintained that FEPC was neither necessary nor wise. When asked whether his participation in the meeting meant that he subscribed to compulsory FEPC, Price replied:

> The government has seen fit to include in its contracts a no-discrimination clause. In accepting government business we obligate ourselves to carry out the letter and intent of that clause. As American businessmen we take pride in the degree to which we honor our business contracts. *However, we do not believe that such clauses are the answer to this problem as much as education and intelligent action are.* Our program of integration was not inaugurated because of FEPC requirements, nor would it end if the FEPC clause were removed from government contracts.[30]

While such a commitment to integration was probably genuine, it is also probable that Westinghouse would not have initiated new programs if there had been no pressure to do so. A memorandum at about the same time from one of the major companies studied showed that pressure from the state FEPC laws and new compliance efforts by the federal government were very important in spurring integration programs. The memorandum stated:

> While it is true that we have had little or no difficulty under our present practice, it is unlikely that we can continue that practice indefinitely in view of these increasing pressures. In addition there are certain advantages in taking a positive position at this time on integration.
>
> If we modify our position voluntarily, and not under compulsion of law or Government fiat, we can develop our own plans of integration. This will enable us to bring qualified Negroes into selected positions. It will reduce the possibility of being compelled to bring Negroes we do not want into positions or activities in which we do not want them.[31]

President Folsom of RCA, on the other hand, testified in favor of federal fair employment legislation when it was being considered by the Senate Labor and Public Welfare Committee on Civil Rights in 1954. The bill was not passed but RCA's support is worth noting. In addition, a former vice president of Inland Steel, William Caples, told the authors that his unsuccessful experience working for voluntary increases in Negro hiring in Illinois made him realize that state legislation was necessary. He supported the Illinois Fair Employment Practices Law, and Inland Steel helped it to pass.

We will see later that the employment provisions in the Civil Rights Act of 1964 did in fact have great impact on racial employment practices.

[30] Remarks by Gwilym A. Price, *op. cit.* (Italics ours)
[31] Confidential material in the possession of the authors.

THE PAST IN RETROSPECT

By the end of the 1950s the electrical industry had made some significant progress in black employment. There were 47,000 more blacks employed than in 1940. Geographic expansion and northward migration of Negroes had eased the restrictive effects of location. Most important, labor shortages during World War II and the Korean War had made it economically necessary to hire large numbers of blacks. Urban League and other civil rights efforts, state FEPC laws especially, and federal investigations had widened the range of jobs open to blacks. Although Negroes were concentrated in low skill jobs, there were some employed in almost every job category. Management was generally committed, albeit passively, to fair employment.

Yet only 3.3 percent of electrical industry employees were black, and obstacles to equal opportunity remained great. Many of the newer plants and some of the older plants were located in areas where Negro population was sparse, where transportation from center city concentrations of Negroes was difficult, where employment agencies discriminated in placements, or where competition for jobs favored the better educated whites. Advancing technology meant many of the new jobs would be available only to applicants with strong educational backgrounds. Industry was not sufficiently aware of the credibility gap between its employment practices and the black community, of subtle practices that excluded blacks, or of the fact that many blacks could have performed adequately had hiring requirements been changed. By 1960 it was apparent that something more than nondiscrimination would be required to increase the representation of Negroes in industrial jobs.

CHAPTER THREE

The long road to parity

Now here, you see, it takes all the running you can do, to keep in the same place. If you want to get somewhere else, you must run twice as fast as that!
　　　　　　　　　　　　　　　The Red Queen in *Alice Through the Looking Glass*

The 1960s brought a marked growth of black participation in the electrical industry. Table 3-1 shows that the percentage of blacks employed rose from 3.3 in 1960 to 7.3 in 1969.[1] At least 78,000 Negroes joined the industry with the greatest growth during 1966.

Table 3–1. Black Employment, 1960—1969
Electrical Manufacturing Industry

Year	Total Employment Percentage Black	White Collar Employment Percentage Black	Blue Collar Employment Percentage Black
1960	3.3	—	—
1964	3.8	1.1	5.6
1966	5.4	1.3	7.8
1967	6.4	1.6	9.3
1969	7.3	2.3	10.5

For more detailed statistics on 1964, 1966, and 1967 see Appendix B, Table B-5. For 1969 see Table 3-2.

[1] We caution that the data utilized in this chapter are not strictly comparable to 1960 census data. Census data are collected by enumerators from individuals; the data utilized in this chapter are based on reports filed by companies with the Equal Employment Opportunity Commission or with other governmental agencies. Moreover, these data for 1964 include only companies that had governmental contracts and, for 1966, 1967, and 1969, those with 100 or more employees. Nevertheless, the size of the samples for all years of the 1960s would indicate that they are quite accurate, and the upward trend of Negro employment is consistent with both our field observations and with trends in industry generally. We feel, therefore, that it is reasonable to assume that the proportion of Negro employment in electrical manufacturing did, indeed, more than double between 1960 and 1969.

Several important influences contributed to this improvement. Pressure from Negro groups intensified; the government became more active; and employment became a more important target for integration. Riots and demonstrations lent a new urgency. An expanding economy created a greater need for labor. Geographical diversification of the industry and migration of blacks into the labor markets of many plants continued. And management began to look more actively for black employees at all levels.

BLACK POWER

We can touch only briefly on some of the major events in the recent rise of active black protest. The successful Montgomery bus boycott of 1955-1956 had already brought Martin Luther King, Jr., to national attention and was the beginning of direct action in the South. Negroes were becoming disillusioned with the judicial and legislative approaches that were based essentially on an appeal to the white man's sense of justice. The southern response to the Supreme Court order to desegregate schools had been massive resistance, and the voting rights bill had goaded the Ku Klux Klan and the White Citizens Council to organized intimidation. Yet the bus boycott showed that Negroes could use their own collective power. In 1960 college students held sit-ins at lunch counters and desegregated hundreds. Older Negro organizations adopted direct action tactics and joined the students and Dr. King in their concern for economic rights and mass action. Business became one of their targets.

In the North Negroes had organized, marched, and boycotted before—for example, during World War II. In 1963 direct action again became an important technique with massive protests against housing, educational, and economic inequities.

Violent and well-publicized anti-Negro reaction in the Deep South and the 1963 March on Washington set the stage for the Civil Rights Bill of 1964. The years 1964 and 1965 also brought the first rumblings of violence in northern ghettos. In 1965 Watts erupted, and in 1967 a wave of civil disorders hit the country. Businessmen in urban areas could no longer ignore the problems of the cities and of the blacks who lived in them.

FEDERAL LEADERSHIP

The federal government was a direct and very important catalyst for change in minority manpower policies in the 1960s. President Kennedy's Executive Order No. 10925 in 1961 differed significantly from earlier presidential orders creating fair employment practices commissions by requiring all companies contracting with the federal government to submit periodic compliance reports giving the number of Negroes employed and the types of jobs they filled.

Most electrical companies had at least some plants covered by this order and thus were sensitive to government pressure.

Prior to 1961 few companies maintained organized quantitative data on racial employment. (Western Electric was an exception.) In some states, racial categorization of employees had been forbidden. Whatever the reason, lack of such quantitative data permitted what Myrdal called the "convenience of ignorance." The compliance reports provided one very concrete tool by which the government and the company alike could judge a plant's racial employment practices.

Also in 1961, the federal government asked the cooperation of business in Plans for Progress—a program for improving the employment situation of Negroes through voluntary company initiative. RCA, Western Electric, General Electric, and Westinghouse all signed soon after the program was announced, pledging to take "affirmative action" to ensure that their non-discrimination policies were implemented. Some plans also included a promise to make a deliberate effort to recruit more Negro applicants. Although Plans for Progress became subject to criticism because performance often did not match public promise, the Plans were at least a symbol that equal employment opportunity had become a more important business goal.

Title VII of the 1964 Civil Rights Act made equal access to employment a legally enforceable right and extended coverage from companies executing government contracts (already covered by executive order) to all firms in interstate commerce beyond a certain minimal size. As the 1960s progressed, the Equal Employment Opportunity Commission, created by the 1964 Civil Rights Act, put increasing emphasis on outreach recruiting of blacks and on a more balanced racial composition as practical indicators of employment policy.

More important are the rules and regulations adopted under Executive Order No. 11246, which set stringent standards for government contractors. For example, General Order No. 4, issued in January 1970 by the Office of Federal Contract Compliance, spells out in great detail for the first time what "affirmative action" requires. This includes: (1) an analysis of all major job classifications and an explanation of why minorities may be underutilized; (2) the establishment of goals, targets, and affirmative action commitments designed to relieve any shortcomings; and (3) the development and supply of data to government organizations, including not only racial occupational figures but also progression charts, seniority rosters, and an analysis of applicants by race for the various jobs.

In fact, General Order No. 4 seems to require the establishment of quotas although it denies that goals and quotas are synonymous. To date the government has not imposed the penalty for violation—debarment from government contracts—because this action would force a court challenge of executive powers, and, more immediately, it might throw many persons out of work, for it would probably close a plant heavily dependent on government contracts.

Yet debarment remains such a threat that no company cares to risk a conclusive showdown, especially over an issue that appears to place the company on the wrong side of social justice.

NEW ECONOMIC GROWTH

The increased pressures toward integration were coming at a time when the economy allowed more rapid hiring since the tightening labor market encouraged an ever widening search for employees.

The economic atmosphere in the 1960s was quite different from that of the 1950s. From 1953 to 1960 the annual increase in Gross National Product was approximately $9 billion or 2.25 percent. From 1960 to 1965 the average annual increase was $21 billion or 4.5 percent. The unemployment rate, which had increased from 2.9 percent in 1953 to 6.7 percent in 1961, declined to 3.8 percent in 1966. From 1960 to 1965 there was a total increase of 5.3 million new jobs. Employment in manufacturing increased by 7.7 percent and in durable goods by about 10 percent. This change was partly due to the economic policy of the new administration which was committed to full employment and therefore was willing to trade off inflationary costs for a decline in unemployment. More jobs meant increased hiring of blacks as well as whites.

Again, employment growth in the electrical industry was greater than in manufacturing generally. The electrical machinery industry added about 600,000 new jobs between 1960 and 1969. By 1966 electrical had become the second largest employer in American manufacturing. This growth was comparable to the enormous buildups during World War II and the Korean War which also brought blacks into the industry in large numbers.

MANAGEMENT POLICY

The fundamental policy difference setting off the 1960s from earlier years is that a significant part of industry became publicly and actively engaged in efforts to change employment practices, with the acknowledgment that new and unconventional methods were to be developed and were necessary to achieve integration within any reasonable span of time.

Growing company involvement and new federal directives led gradually to a systematic evaluation of the total hiring process. Attention turned from preventing overt discrimination to eliminating the more subtle practices that might disqualify Negro applicants. Preemployment tests were analyzed for their validity as predictors of job performance and many that measured qualities not directly necessary for the job were discarded or replaced. Personnel practices workshops stressed the importance of eliminating unconscious discrimination in employment interviews, and some plants employed black interviewers. Companies began to question whether their traditional sources of recruitment reached potential Negro applicants, and some began to experiment with increased employment advertising in the Negro press, with conscious efforts to overcome the widespread assumption that electrical was still a "white" industry.

The same approach was applied to promotions and selection for training programs. One of the first companies to take action in this area was Western Electric when it reviewed its personnel files in 1961 to identify qualified Negroes who might have been overlooked in earlier promotions. Several other concerns inventoried their employees, making a conscious effort to upgrade the existing black labor force. Early efforts were inconsistent in quality, scope, and success; yet it was recognized that traditional methods were perpetuating, or at least not altering rapidly enough, the racial composition of the industry.

Perhaps most important, the compliance reports themselves served as a form of internal audit by which firms were forced to assess their own experience in the matter of racial employment. They were a tool for making judgments of efficiency or inefficiency in the minority employment area, as management had done for years in other areas such as production costs and sales. Although quantified data alone do not provide sufficient information for judging the quality of a fair employment effort, they are essential for giving employment practice concreteness and rationality.

As federal standards were raised, and as executive recognition of the urgency of the problem increased, overseeing equal employment opportunity issues came to be a more important function at corporate levels of the biggest companies. For example, as early as 1963 Western Electric created its first full-time Equal Employment Opportunity (EEO) position at a high managerial level. Parallel developments took place in other companies and also in plant and field locations, with the appointment of full-time EEO managers at most divisional levels and in some of the larger plants.

The establishment of new EEO structures in the firm does not in itself guarantee dramatic progress. The effectiveness and the style of such a department is determined by the priorities set by top executives and by the relative weight given to EEO considerations in the balancing of many competing values. The presidents of all the Big Four made strong statements on fair employment to their management and personnel staffs—a fact increasing the likelihood that affirmative action would be implemented. At least the presence of corporate departments meant that companies were willing to commit executive talent and budget to equal employment opportunity. In some cases they seem to have anticipated OFCC Order No. 4.

The following story of the Westinghouse plant in Vicksburg, Mississippi, is an example of the importance of a strong management stance. The plant employed 660 people making light fixtures. In the late spring of 1965, the plant began a campaign to employ "qualified Negro women for jobs as clerks, stenographers and secretaries."[2] About 4:15 A.M. on Saturday, June

[2] *New York Times*, June 24, 1965.

19, 1965, someone tossed three ignited fire bombs into the garage of the industrial relations manager, damaging his two cars and the garage. Because he managed to put out the fires with a garden hose, the damage was contained.

The Westinghouse security director reacted at once, stating publicly that the company "would not move its plant as the result of one incident." Then added: "But we want to make it clear that we are going to comply fully with government laws requiring equal employment opportunity from firms dealing with defense contracts. We can't throw away 20 percent of our business—it amounts to about half a billion a year in defense contracts alone—because of one plant."[3]

The Westinghouse-Vicksburg plant manager, in a letter to employees, written the Monday after the incident, stated:

> ... I want to make it crystal clear to everyone at this plant that Westinghouse and local management will not tolerate any actions that jeopardize the personal safety of employees. . . .
> Justice and the rights of others must be respected, and we mean to do everything we can to see that they are.[4]

There was no repetition of the incident. The vigorous reaction of Westinghouse and its clear threat to move a $30 million payroll out of Vicksburg forced the leadership of the community to choose between modern industry with integration, or lawlessness and no industry. The bombing was the fourth within a year. Three earlier ones damaged a civil rights meeting hall and two racially integrated restaurants. But it took the strong management reaction to induce community and state action. The local Negro newspaper reported that "the great wall of silence was finally broken"[5] when Westinghouse refused to be intimidated or to tolerate lawlessness.

Before leaving the topic of management policy, we should note that some union leaders were also taking stronger stands. In the late 1960s the IUE conducted a series of vigorous social action conferences for its members, and in 1967 IUE President Paul Jennings was cited by the National Urban League for "outstanding contributions to equal opportunity."

REGIONAL AND LOCATIONAL INFLUENCES

The 1960s continued the regional and locational trends apparent in the 1950s. By 1967, 16 percent of all electrical employees were in the southern states with their larger black populations. Although many managers continued to be cautious about the reaction of white employees and communities in the south,

[3] *Ibid.*
[4] Copy of letter in Industrial Unit Research files, Wharton School of Finance and Commerce, University of Pennsylvania, Philadelphia.
[5] *Vicksburg Citizens' Appeal*, July 5, 1965.

affirmative action programs had been launched by 1966, and black employment had risen to 8.2 percent in 1967. Blacks held fewer salaried positions in the South than nationally, and promoting the first Negro into supervision was a hurdle many plants had not overcome as late as 1970, yet electrical was well ahead of traditionally southern industries such as tobacco, lumber, textiles, and paper.[6]

In the Midwest and Northeast, where the major part of the industry continued,[7] migration of Negroes north had changed the racial composition of neighborhoods surrounding a number of older plants making them "ghetto plants" without trying. But new plants were usually built in suburbs like those on Routes 128 and 495 around Boston, maintaining, if not intensifying, the transportation problems of inner city blacks.

WHAT NUMBERS TELL

Thanks to the reporting requirements of the Civil Rights Act and to the computer, we know not only where white people are working, but where blacks, Indians, Spanish-speaking, and orientals are as well. Dry-appearing tables and columns of numbers actually sketch out a revealing picture of the human condition of black workers in America today. At what jobs do blacks work? How are they affected by company size? How does the electrical industry compare? If blacks were whites, on what steps of the ladder would they then be working? We present an ideal model that leads us to ask a somber question: How long will it take black people to attain their just share of all kinds of jobs and positions in American business?

BLACKS ON THE STEPS OF THE LADDER

During the first half of the 1960s minority manpower stress was on getting blacks into entry-level jobs. Of course, the need to get disadvantaged, underemployed blacks into steady jobs will remain for a long time. But black people are not satisfied with entry-level jobs. Stress in the late 1960s, and certainly for the 1970s, will be on the promotion of black workers into all levels of the corporate enterprise. What do the numbers tell us about blacks' current status on the occupational ladder? We are especially concerned about jobs for black men, since men are so important to the stability of the threatened Negro family.

Most of the increase in the number of Negroes in the industry up to 1969 came in the blue collar area. By that year only 2.3 percent of the white collar

---

[6] See Herbert R. Northrup, Richard L. Rowan, *et al.*, *Negro Employment in Basic Industry*, Studies of Negro Employment, Vol. III (Philadelphia: Industrial Research Unit, Wharton School of Finance and Commerce, University of Pennsylvania, 1970), Part Six.

[7] See Appendix C, pp. 329 ff.

workers were black, in contrast to the blue collar situation where 10.5 percent were Negro. Table 3-2 shows the representation of Negroes by occupational group in the electrical industry in 1969, pointing up the concentration of Negroes in blue collar jobs and particularly in lower rated jobs.

The electrical industry faces a challenge since 38.6 percent of its jobs are white collar; 17 percent of its employees are professionals, mostly engineers, or technicians; and many managers and sales personnel must have engineering or scientific backgrounds. Although the industry is actively recruiting blacks, improvement will be slow. In the past most of these jobs were generally closed to blacks and there is now an educational and credibility gap to be overcome. In addition, 12 percent of electrical employees are craftsmen—another field from which blacks have been traditionally excluded.

Virgil Day, Vice President of GE, put the problem of the credibility gap clearly:

> One of the problems which has come up again and again in discussions with educators whose student bodies include large numbers of Negroes is the lack of recognition of the real opportunities which are open in industry—not just General Electric, but industry as a whole—for qualified Negro applicants.
>
> In the lower grades, this lack of recognition seems to be one of the factors which can breed apathy toward academic achievement. In college, it can predispose many competent young people to shy away from courses which would lead to careers in industry.
>
> "It isn't enough for us to *tell* them about good job opportunities," one of our recruiters was told last summer, "You have to *show* them."[8]

What may be more important is the sad state of primary and secondary education in the inner city and in southern small town or rural schools. It is here that learning is discouraged and future careers so often blighted. For many Negroes to achieve a professional career, family patterns of non-achievement must be overcome, basic skills acquired without assistance at home, and a school which defies learning must be conquered. Companies in the electrical industry have spent thousands of dollars aiding school dropouts, helping programs such as the Opportunities Industrialization Centers, and providing basic education programs to functionally illiterate prospective employees. Inevitably, however, the schools and the basic learning institutions must do a more effective job if discrimination and unequal opportunity are not to be perpetuated.

Increased recruitment and financial support for blacks at first-rate colleges, schools of business and engineering, and at vocational high schools,

---

[8] Virgil B. Day, "Progress in Equal Employment Opportunity at General Electric," p. 161, a chapter in Herbert R. Northrup and Richard L. Rowan (eds.), *The Negro and Employment Opportunity* (Ann Arbor: Bureau of Industrial Relations, Graduate School of Business Administration, The University of Michigan, 1965).

Table 3-2. *Employment by Race, Sex and Occupation, 1969 Electrical Manufacturing Industry 3,533 Establishments*

Occupational Group	ALL EMPLOYEES Total	Negro	Percent Negro	MALE Total	Negro	Percent Negro	FEMALE Total	Negro	Percent Negro
Officials and Managers	137,731	1,265	0.9	134,087	1,136	0.8	3,644	129	3.5
Professionals	176,851	1,844	1.0	171,489	1,745	1.0	5,362	99	1.8
Technicians	124,664	3,921	3.1	113,766	3,471	3.1	10,898	450	4.1
Sales Workers	24,438	158	0.6	21,724	114	0.5	2,714	44	1.6
Office and Clerical	211,348	8,243	3.9	63,058	2,750	4.4	148,290	5,493	3.7
Total White Collar	675,032	15,431	2.3	504,124	9,216	1.8	170,908	6,215	3.6
Craftsmen	210,937	8,861	4.2	194,336	7,166	3.7	16,601	1,695	10.2
Operatives	664,749	76,593	11.5	289,418	31,742	11.0	375,331	44,851	11.9
Laborers	169,545	21,616	12.7	77,027	10,646	13.8	92,518	10,970	11.9
Service Workers	27,411	5,253	19.2	23,316	4,525	19.4	4,095	728	17.8
Total Blue Collar	1,072,642	112,323	10.5	584,097	54,079	9.3	488,545	58,244	11.9
Total All Workers	1,747,674	127,754	7.3	1,088,221	63,295	5.8	659,453	64,459	9.8

Source: Preliminary Equal Employment Opportunity Commission data.

plus cooperative programs between business and Negro colleges and universities are beginning to make some encouraging changes. But it is only a beginning.

For the 1970s, business will also have to concentrate on developing and upgrading the blacks it already employs. It is a common practice in many companies to use company training programs and to support off-plant study programs for employees in order to prepare operatives for craft jobs, competent hourly workers for first-line supervision, hourly testers for higher rated technical jobs, and so forth. These internal channels for education and upgrading are beginning to increase the number of blacks on the middle and upper rungs of the ladder. They could be more fully and imaginatively used.

What About the Issue of Jobs for Negro Men? In the 1960s women's jobs were integrated more quickly than men's. Table 3-2 shows that 5.8 percent of all men and 9.8 percent of all women in the industry were black in 1969. This is true partly because a much larger proportion of men's jobs are white collar (46.3 percent) and integration has been slowest for both black men and black women in white collar positions. In blue collar jobs in 1969, only 9.3 percent of the men were black, as opposed to 11.9 percent of the women, with the greatest discrepancy in the craft category where blacks have had difficulty obtaining training. (See also Appendix Table B-5.)

DOES COMPANY SIZE MAKE A DIFFERENCE?

It has been suggested that large firms will be more active and successful in employing and upgrading blacks than will small firms. We found, however, that in 1968 the twenty largest electrical manufacturing firms had work forces of 6 percent black while the electrical industry as a whole had 7 percent black. Of the twenty, the four largest companies ranked 2nd, 3rd, 7th, and 12th, in their percentages of blacks, ranging from 4.9 to 8.6. The next four ranked 1st, 14th, 18th, and 19th, with percentages of blacks ranging from 2.2 to 18.6. One of the twenty largest employed only 0.7 percent black. The location of a company's plants and the proportion of its jobs calling for high technical requirements seem more important than size.

HOW DOES THE ELECTRICAL INDUSTRY COMPARE?

A look at other industries will help us to evaluate racial integration in the electrical industry. In 1967 6.4 percent of electrical employees were black compared to the 8.4 percent average of all manufacturing industries reporting to the Equal Employment Opportunity Commission. The electrical industry, however, was slightly ahead of the all-manufacturing standard in white collar employment.

Table 3-3. Black Employment: Electrical Manufacturing and Six Basic Industries, 1966 and 1968 By Occupational Group

Occupation	AUTOMOBILES 1966	AUTOMOBILES 1968	AEROSPACE 1966	AEROSPACE 1968	STEEL 1966	STEEL 1968	RUBBER TIRES 1966	RUBBER TIRES 1968	PETROLEUM 1966	PETROLEUM 1968	CHEMICALS[a] 1966	CHEMICALS[a] 1968	ELECTRICAL[b] 1966	ELECTRICAL[b] 1968
Officials and Managers	1.2	1.4	0.4	0.6	1.0	1.3	0.6	0.9	0.2	0.3	0.2	0.4	0.4	0.8
Professionals	0.6	0.7	0.8	0.9	0.2	0.5	0.3	0.8	0.6	0.7	0.5	0.8	0.7	1.0
Technicians	1.2	1.5	1.9	2.1	1.4	2.2	1.3	2.1	1.3	1.7	1.5	2.5	2.2	2.9
Sales Workers	(c)	(c)	0.3	0.6	0.3	0.3	7.5[d]	5.0[d]	2.4	2.7	0.3	0.7	0.2	0.6
Office and Clerical	3.8	4.4	2.8	3.4	2.3	2.9	1.4	1.9	3.9	4.8	1.8	3.2	2.0	3.2
Total White Collar	2.1	2.4	1.5	1.7	1.4	1.9	1.4	1.6	2.0	2.4	0.9	1.6	1.3	2.0
Craftsmen	3.0	3.3	4.6	5.4	5.9	6.3	2.3	2.8	1.9	2.2	2.2	2.9	3.0	4.0
Operatives	20.2	21.3	11.9	13.5	17.8	18.7	11.6	12.8	6.8	7.3	7.6	9.9	8.4	10.2
Laborers	27.6	29.1	22.4	20.7	27.7	28.7	17.1	22.8	19.7	18.0	25.8	22.4	9.9	13.0
Service Workers	27.2	27.3	22.2	23.2	19.1	20.0	30.4	29.2	24.2	21.5	22.9	23.0	17.5	18.9
Total Blue Collar	17.6	18.6	9.0	10.0	16.1	16.7	10.8	11.7	6.3	6.2	8.0	9.2	7.8	10.0
TOTAL	13.6	14.5	4.8	5.4	12.8	13.3	8.1	8.3	3.7	3.9	5.0	6.0	5.4	7.0

[a] There is a possible 1-2 point downward bias in this sample.
[b] Interpolated from 1967 and 1969 Equal Employment Opportunity Commission data.
[c] Few sales personnel combined with office and clerical.
[d] Including many nonsales personnel; actually very few Negroes in this classification.

Source: Herbert R. Northrup, Richard L. Rowan, et al., *Negro Employment in Basic Industry*, Studies of Negro Employment, Vol. I (Philadelphia: Industrial Research Unit, Wharton School of Finance and Commerce, University of Pennsylvania, 1970), Part Six, p. 727; and data in authors' possession.

The long road to parity

Table 3-3 showing employment by race in the electrical industry and six other industries in 1966 and 1968 gives a more detailed breakdown. Black percentages in 1968 ranged from 3.9 percent in petroleum to 14.5 in automobiles. Electrical ranked well behind automobiles and steel—industries with many semiskilled jobs. Electrical also ranked behind rubber tires—an industry with an early tradition of "Negro jobs," but fast eliminating such jobs by automation. Electrical was ahead of chemicals, aerospace, and petroleum—industries all more technically oriented than electrical.

The electrical industry has a middle rank for employing blacks in white collar jobs, but the variation among these seven industries in employing blacks in these jobs is slight. None employed more than 2.4 percent. Table 3-3 shows the electrical industry to have the highest percentages for professionals and technicians and to be increasing its black employment at a rate comparable to, perhaps a little faster than, that of the other industries.

ONE MODEL OF BLACK PARTICIPATION

If blacks were whites, what sorts of jobs would they hold in American business? Let us construct an ideal model of what employment patterns would be like if the percentage of blacks in the electrical industry, and then at each of its nine occupational levels, were equal to the percentage of adult blacks in America generally.

Let us say that blacks ought to be represented in American industry and in the electrical industry at 10 percent of the working population at all levels. Actually this is, if anything, a conservative figure since blacks are about 12 percent of our total population and their unemployment rate is generally at least twice that of whites. The 10 percent target for participation should be used only nationally, since in any given local labor market the black proportion could be well above or below the 10 percent.

Using the 10 percent black participation rate as a base, we construct a simple model of black participation in the electrical industry. (See Table 3-4.) First, we take 10 percent of the total number of employees. The resulting figure we call "imputed black employment." For the entire electrical industry for 1966 this figure is 170,623, as shown in Table 3-4. Second, we see how many blacks are actually employed. At a black participation rate of 5.4 percent (instead of the ideal 10 percent), the actual number of blacks employed in the industry in 1966 was 92,115. The actual was short of the ideal by 78,508. We now find out what percentage the actual number is of the imputed or ideal number. The resulting percentage gives us an index number of black participants. For example, blacks have an index number in 1966 of 54.0 for the entire electrical industry. This means that they participate at 54.0 percent of the ideal (which we set at 10 percent). There was some improvement in 1969: In that year blacks participated at 73.1 percent of the 10 percent ideal. But notice that most of this improvement was at the blue collar level.

The national experience

Table 3-4. An Index of Black Participation in the Electrical Manufacturing Industry 1966 and 1969

Occupation	All Employees	Imputed No. of Blacks[a]	Actual No. of Blacks	Black Deficit (−) Excess (+)	Index Number[b]
1966					
Officials and Managers	117,227	11,723	509	−11,214	4.3
Professionals	175,987	17,599	1,282	−16,317	7.3
Technicians	113,008	11,301	2,508	− 8,793	22.2
Sales Workers	21,232	2,123	53	− 2,070	2.5
Office and Clerical	203,179	20,318	3,969	−16,349	19.5
Total White Collar	630,633	63,063	8,321	−54,742	13.2
Craftsmen	203,873	20,387	6,057	−14,330	29.7
Operatives	689,789	68,979	57,672	−11,307	83.6
Laborers	155,546	15,555	15,439	− 116	99.3
Service Workers	26,389	2,639	4,626	+ 1,987	175.3
Total Blue Collar	1,075,597	107,560	83,794	−23,766	77.9
Total All Workers	1,706,230	170,623	92,115	−78,508	54.0
1969					
Officials and Managers	137,731	13,773	1,265	−12,508	9.2
Professionals	176,851	17,685	1,844	−15,841	10.4
Technicians	124,664	12,466	3,921	− 8,545	31.5
Sales Workers	24,438	2,444	158	− 2,286	6.5
Office and Clerical	211,348	21,135	8,243	−12,892	39.0
Total White Collar	675,032	67,503	15,431	−52,072	23.0
Craftsmen	210,937	21,094	8,861	−12,233	42.0
Operatives	664,749	66,475	76,593	+10,118	115.2
Laborers	169,545	16,954	21,616	+ 4,662	127.5
Service Workers	27,411	2,741	5,253	+ 2,512	191.6
Total Blue Collar	1,072,642	107,264	112,323	+ 5,059	104.7
Total All Workers	1,747,674	174,767	127,754	−47,013	73.1

[a] Figured at 10 percent rate.
[b] Percent actual of imputed; 100 percent = parity.

The 10 percent model is also applicable to each of the nine job categories. For example, 117,227 people working in the electrical industry in 1966 were "officials and managers." Therefore we can assert that 10 percent of this number or 11,723 blacks should be officials and managers, but actually there were 509. The deficit gives us an index number of 4.3. This means that as officials and managers blacks participated at only 4.3 percent of the ideal in 1966.

Table 3-4 shows the extent of integration in the electrical industry in 1966 and 1969 in relation to our ideal model. Integration in 1966 was very limited. Blacks held their fair share of employment only as laborers, and were overrepresented as service workers. They were near parity (83.6) as operatives but very poorly represented as craftsmen and in white collar work.

By 1969 blacks were overrepresented in all blue collar categories except craftsmen, where blacks participated at 42 percent of the ideal. The electrical industry has quite rightly continued recruiting disadvantaged blacks despite the overrepresentation in less skilled jobs. Index increases between 1966 and 1969 were smaller for white collar employment. Black managers and officials

The long road to parity

were still less than 10 percent of the ideal and technicians less than one third. Improvement was greatest in the clerical field where blacks reached 39 percent of the ideal.

The changes from 1966 to 1969 show an interesting paradox: in white collar jobs total employment of blacks increased by more than 7,000, yet the deficit of blacks in white collar jobs decreased by only 2,760. One is reminded of the Red Queen in *Alice in Wonderland*: "Here it takes all the running you can do to keep in the same place. If you want to get somewhere else, you have to run twice as fast as that!" Even though blacks might be said to be running very fast with a 7,000 person increase, total industry employment was increasing almost as quickly. To make progress, blacks would really have to be hired twice as fast. Let us look now more explicitly to the future.

HOW LONG WILL IT TAKE?

How long will it be before black people have their just share of all kinds of jobs and positions in American business? We return to the projections cited at the start of this book. We can see now that improvement in black percentages between our base years of 1966 and 1969 was great—equal to the advances in the ten years between 1950 and 1960. We have seen that this improvement was related to economic expansion, government and civil rights pressure, and managerial affirmative action. Table 3-5 shows projections based on 1966 to 1969 increases. While they are optimistic projections, they show that it will take years before blacks are 10 percent of the various white collar jobs.

By 1969 a 10 percent goal had already been achieved in the less skilled

Table 3-5. Predicting Black Employment Electrical Manufacturing Industry Base: 1966–1969

	Participation Index Numbers 1966	1969	Three-year change in index numbers	Deficit (or excess) of 1969 index number from 100%	Years to achieve 100%* integration at 1966–69 change rate
Officials and Managers	4.3	9.2	+ 4.9	−90.8	55.5
Professionals	7.3	10.4	+ 3.1	−89.6	86.7
Technicians	22.2	31.5	+ 9.3	−68.5	22.2
Sales Workers	2.5	6.5	+ 4.0	−93.5	70.2
Office and Clerical	19.5	39.0	+19.5	−61.0	9.3
Craftsmen	29.7	42.0	+12.3	−58.0	14.1
Operatives	83.6	115.2	+31.6	+15.2	achieved
Laborers	99.3	127.5	+28.2	+27.5	achieved
Service Workers	175.3	191.6	+16.3	+91.6	achieved

* 1969 deficit from 100 percent parity divided by the preceding three-year improvement. The quotient is then multiplied by three.
For example, to overcome a 90.8 deficit with improvement of 4.9 every three years, it would take (90.8/4.9 = 18.5 × 3) 55.5 years.

jobs. At the 1966 to 1969 rate our projections show that it will take fourteen years for blacks to hold 10 percent of craft jobs; clerical positions should be integrated in nine years, and technical positions in twenty-two. Sales positions will not be integrated for seventy years; professionals for eighty-six; and managers and officials for fifty-five. The white collar picture is hardly encouraging.

We use these projections only as illustrations of what could very well happen. We do not propose them as holding a high degree of precision. Three factors could either raise or lower the years required for blacks to achieve parity: first, factors regarding the business cycle and its requirements. The period 1966 to 1969 was the culmination of the most prosperous decade in the history of America. Unemployment during that decade steadily declined, and in 1966 was at 3.8 percent or 2.2 percent for the insured unemployed and in 1969, 3.5 and 2.1 percent, respectively. A growth rate based on a three-year period within this decade would be very optimistic. Recessions during the 1970s or 1980s would lower the growth rate, though wars, of course, would raise it. Furthermore, the constant American trend toward a greater proportion of technical jobs as opposed to semiskilled jobs will make it more difficult for many blacks.

Second are factors regarding the status of blacks and their attitudes. During the 1960s, blacks participated more fully in apprenticeship training programs, vocational schools, and business and engineering colleges—the main routes to craft and white collar positions. But it is anybody's guess whether this increased participation in prebusiness education will grow. Whites are also competing for these educational chances, and we are back once again to the Red Queen! Housing, neighborhood, and family conditions also affect the preparation of a young man or woman for a business position. In addition, blacks may prefer some occupations to others and this could raise or lower their participation. If separatism in the black community grows, it will lower black participation, but our guess is that many blacks will want industrial jobs.

Third are factors regarding civil rights laws and white reactions. Further pressure of laws and courts may increase black participation, unless such pressures develop into legalisms that will alienate whites and the white managerial power structure. White backlash and the resulting polarization of the two races remain an ever-present possibility during the 1970s, but our findings do not predict polarization as necessary or likely.

Any one of these three factors, especially the business cycle, could lower or more likely lengthen the time predicted. Full black participation in American business could easily take much longer. Unless drastic improvements are made, black people will not be equitably represented in white collar jobs in the electrical industry, or in any other American industry, for years and years.

Will black people have the patience? Does American industry have the time? Can our society assume the right to wait so long?

PART TWO
The local experience

Turning from historical and national experience, we come to the important level of the plant. The next chapters focus on black employment in four settings. What are management practices at the grass roots level? What are the racial feelings of black and white factory workers and the forces influencing their behavior? These are our "listening chapters," enabling the reader to hear the feelings of workers from backgrounds and with values often quite different from his own.

The four chapters are the fruit of over two years of listening to and analyzing the views of over 450 black and white workers, foremen, managers, and union and community leaders at plants in four different cities. In every case we lived in or near the black communities, getting to know the people there. We hope that the real authors of these chapters are the plant people themselves; we only want to relay their story to you.

Our main interest in each plant was the blue collar workers. We chose sixty blue collar people in each case, by mathematically random numbers, so that these samples might speak with a minimum of error for the populations from which they were chosen. Tables and statistics on employee attitudes are based on these interviews. We use quotations, disguising all names, to give a fuller picture of workers' attitudes, with a note on whether the person represents a majority, minority, or unusual viewpoint. Our comments and statistics on foremen's and union leaders' attitudes are also based on random samples, unless otherwise indicated.

Did these people tell us what they really think? Our evidence indicates that, for the most part, they spoke with remarkable openness and frankness. A few, of course, did not. We think that our being priests as well as social scientists helped to win the workers' confidence. A fuller description of our sampling and interviewing methods is given in Appendix A.

We wanted plants that would give us a wide variety of factory and local characteristics, so as to be fairly typical of industrial America. We wanted to enter both the North and the South, in cities where blacks were rather few, and where they were nearly a majority. We wanted plants where many women worked, and others where most employees were men; some where employees did piecework, and others where workers were stationed along moving assembly lines. We were curious about the influences of different unions (or no union) on racial relations.

We settled finally on the National Acme* plant in Chicago, an older plant making large electrical equipment on traditional assembly lines and having more than one union; the General Electric plant of Lynchburg, Virginia, a relatively new plant of more than 4,500 men and women producing mobile radios and communications, not unionized; the Westinghouse–Buffalo plant, organized by the International Union of Electrical Workers, and building electric motors and industrial controls; and the Fairbanks International* plant in Memphis making small electrical components and organized by the Electrical Workers of America.*

* Fictitious names

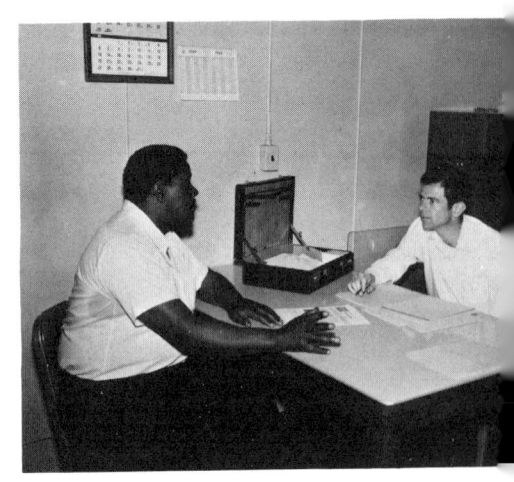

TOP LEFT Twenty-five-year-old Sheldon Cottrell, checker and Sergeant at Arms, IUE Local 1581, shows Theodore Purcell around the Westinghouse plant at Buffalo.
TOP RIGHT Richard Jones tells Gerald Cavanagh about Buffalo's ghetto. Jones, a plater, has worked for Westinghouse more than 20 years.
BOTTOM Gerald Cavanagh asks Mrs. Frances Berger how people get along in her assembly unit at the General Electric plant in Lynchburg, Virginia.

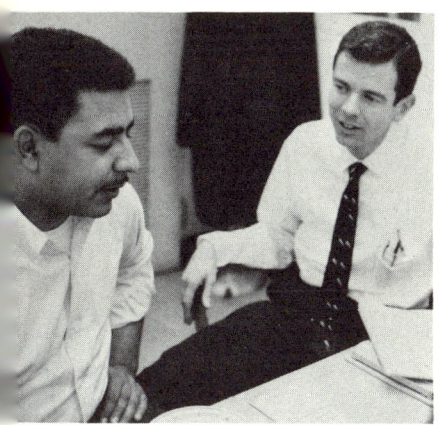

TOP LEFT Leo Skowranski describes tool and die making.
TOP RIGHT Dale Hawkins, Westinghouse motor winding and connecting supervisor, gives a foreman's view.
MIDDLE LEFT St. Claire Anderson, photographic dark room operator, describes GE's Lynchburg plant as he has known it in the past ten years.
MIDDLE RIGHT Theodore Purcell and Levi Morris, technical writer at the same plant, discuss promotion opportunities for blacks.
BOTTOM Foreman Powell discusses the work with one of his employees. Westinghouse, Buffalo.

CHAPTER FOUR

Chicago: Bohemians to young blacks

It's just a job, because there's really nothing to it. Place the motor. Put the housing on, tighten it. A twelve-year-old could do it.
William Fleck, young black production worker

This is the story of what may happen when a large manufacturer in a sprawling northern metropolis like Chicago needs to expand, but finds its traditional ethnic labor supply drying up and newly black neighborhoods beginning to surround its plant. Management must now deal with what has become known as the New Work Force—blacks, Puerto Ricans, white mods, Appalachians. What problems does management face in such a situation and, especially, what are the new workers like? How do they think and feel? Management needs to listen to them. Also, what are the reactions of both the older ethnics and the few younger, mostly southern whites? What are management's corporate responsibilities to these people as employees as well as to them as neighbors in a large city? How will management operate a competitive plant with this New Work Force? Here is the story of one company's experience at the National Acme Electric Plant in Chicago, Illinois.

National Acme Electric's* plant on Chicago's west side started in 1908 but it was not until 1961 that Local 852 of the Electrical Equipment Workers,* AFL-CIO, won bargaining rights for the majority of hourly paid workers. The International Brotherhood of Electrical Workers, the International Association of Machinists, the Teamsters, and the International Union of Operating Engineers also represent some employees.

National Acme makes products such as lift trucks, golf carts, lawnmowers, and other large electrical equipment. As a part of the electrical equipment industry, this business is profitable and growing rapidly with the

*Fictitious name.

population expansion in America. But the business is also somewhat cyclical and highly competitive with some of Acme's rivals who do not have to deal with the so-called New Work Force. Most of the factory work at Acme is assembly where manual dexterity and application are more important than education.

THE NEIGHBORHOODS

The Acme plant is located five miles west of the Chicago Loop, between black Lawndale and all-white Cicero. Close to half of the blacks in our sample of hourly workers at Acme lived in Lawndale and neighboring Garfield Park, while about half of the white employees made their homes in Cicero and Berwyn.

There were few Negroes in Chicago before World War I. By 1920 the city had 110,000 blacks, 4.1 percent of Chicago's population.[1] Chicago's black population continued to grow. By 1950 it reached 492,000. By 1970 it was estimated that there were over 1 million blacks in Chicago, or about a third of the population within city limits. Chicago's ghetto began just south of the Loop along the Penn Central Railroad tracks. It spread to the south, the northwest, the west, and, with a few suburban incursions, to the far south side.

LAWNDALE

The black wave hit the Lawndale west side area in 1950. North Lawndale at that time was 13 percent black. By 1960 it was over 91 percent black. In addition to this rapid turnover, Lawndale has now packed 125,000 people into a smaller residential area than Cicero has for its 69,000 people. At the 1960 census, only 18 percent of the 50,000 housing units in Lawndale were owner occupied, and 14 percent were officially "substandard condition." There has been virtually no new housing in Lawndale since 1930, and most of the housing was more than fifty years old.[2] In 1960 the median family income in Lawndale was $4,980 (Cicero, $7,300); unemployment among males in Lawndale was 10 percent (Cicero, 2.9 percent). A special labor department study in 1966 showed underemployment among blacks in Lawndale to be about 34 percent and unemployment is actually higher than the official figures, because a large number of black men disappear from the census rolls. As for education, the median school year completed is 8.7 percent (Cicero, 9.7).[3]

[1] See *Commentary on Areas of Negro Residence Map: 1950, 1960, and 1964* (Chicago: Urban League, 1965).

[2] The census and statistical information in this report are taken from Evelyn M. Kitagawa and Karl E. Taeuber, *Local Community Fact Book: Chicago Metropolitan Area, 1960* (Chicago: University of Chicago Press, 1963). Lawndale is discussed on pp. 72–73, Cicero on pp. 178–179.

[3] The discrepancy in education is greater than it appears since the quality of education in ghetto and southern black schools is often inferior.

The authors lived during the spring of 1969 at (Catholic) Presentation Parish, one of the few institutions left in Lawndale that had not changed hands or fled in the last ten years. Former Jewish temples with Hebrew inscriptions over their doors and white Protestant churches line wide, tree-shaded Independence and Douglas Boulevards. They are now used by black Baptist congregations. Trash and broken glass strewed many of the streets and yards of Lawndale as did an occasional derelict auto with flat tires or broken axle. At night small pieces of broken glass reflected the bright street lights in strange, silent urban beauty—beauty that disappeared during the day when the glass was seen for what it is. Night brought both fears and joys. Burglaries were common and muggings were a constant threat. But from early afternoon until almost midnight there was the noise of seemingly thousands of children playing in the streets and the lots. Forty-six percent of Lawndale's population was under eighteen years of age. A number of the homes of gray or brown stone or brick had a solid appearance and here and there one saw a homeowner trying valiantly to protect a struggling patch of grass with sticks and strings doing guard duty along the front of his property. Two or three-story stone houses were tightly packed in the congested area with an occasional apartment building to break the monotony.

A generation gap often exists between older blacks and their sons and daughters. The peer group has a greater influence on teenagers than do the parents, both of whom usually work—if indeed there is a father at home. A recent sociological survey in Lawndale showed that 68 percent of the adults sampled there, in spite of the "black is beautiful" movement, were still insecure with their blackness and showed a hesitation toward positive identification with their race.[4]

CICERO

It is only too easy to label Cicero. One thinks of the fact that Al Capone made it the center of his activities years ago. Actually, Cicero is a clean community with neat little frame and brick houses and well-kept lawns and trees. There is little delinquency or poverty. The population has remained stable since 1930 though young ethnics are moving out and Appalachians moving in. The people are proud of their homes, their churches, and their schools. Most residents are foreign born or of foreign parentage. Bohemians lead with approximately 35 percent, followed by Poles, then Slavs, Hungarians, Russians, Lithuanians, Germans, Italians, Greeks, Spaniards, Irish, Scotch, English, Scandinavians, Mexicans, and, recently, some southern whites.

But Cicero strongly resists integration. Although 15,000 Negroes work in Cicero during the day, not a single black family lives there at night. Residents are cold toward anyone who suggests integrated housing. "Letters to the

---

[4] Thomas Honore, "Indications of Racial Identity in Lawndale," unpublished paper dated May 1, 1969.

Editor" in the *Cicero Life* are firm and consistent in their protests against men such as the Reverend Roger Dahlin of Gethsemane Lutheran Church who "doesn't have this community at heart. He has been working toward integrating Cicero and Berwyn for many years." One resident of Berwyn, a town bordering Cicero to the west, writes:

> I am sick and tired of everyone who likes to live out in Berwyn and Cicero constantly being criticized for everything our town stands for. If they don't like it here, they should move to Chicago where they can live, shop and try to educate their children in a Negro district.

Jasper Parker, a forty-eight-year-old Acme employee from Cicero, was unusually outspoken. Although his history was inaccurate according to management, his description of community feelings showed us the stereotypes and fears that nourish hate.

PURCELL: Do you have any Negroes there at all?

PARKER: No. Our town is dead set against them. They were allowed to live in there twice and both times wound up raping the white women. The women were afraid to go out at night.

PURCELL: Where did they live in Cicero?

PARKER: They first time were livin' all over Cicero. That was in the early 1900s, yes, when they run them out. Then they came back in about 1932 and were livin' on the I.C. Railroad. Every night there was fightin' among themselves. They're drunk and chasin' women tryin' to rape 'em. And one they did rape. When that happened they told the railroad either to get rid of 'em or build an area for them and keep 'em in....

PURCELL: Do you think they'll ever get into Cicero?

PARKER: Oh, I imagine they will eventually, 'cause most of the old-timers are movin out.... The old people are dyin' off and gettin' all new people in. Gettin' some Mexicans, Japs, yes. So it ain't long after that, well, when you start. They'll start gettin' in, but they're tryin' them out in Berwyn.... See what they don't like is that if they'd live like you or I— take care of the property you're livin' in, to keep it lookin' nice or try to keep the landlord, if you're rentin', but they don't. 'Cause I worked with one. He was a real nice guy at work. He invited me over to his house. I went over and he had a four room flat, and there's four families livin' in four rooms. He told me, "Well, what the heck," he said, "my landlord's chargin' me so much rent that's the only way I can pay it."

A very different attitude came from a young white worker at Acme: Twenty-eight, Norma Haynes moved to Cicero from the Deep South. She described a violent attack on a young black boy looking for a job:

> And then this young colored boy was ridin' toward Cicero huntin' a job on a bicycle. These three white guys, one of them lived right next door to

my aunt, killed him with a baseball bat. This is the kind of hate I'm speaking of.... It's terrible and to me hate is like a cancer. Once it gets inside of you, it devours.

Hatred is still based partly on fear. Neighborhoods in Chicago have usually gone from all white to all black. Paul Shephard, a manager at Acme, explained how Cicero saw it: "There is no such thing for Cicero as integration. It's inundation. All they do is point to what used to be mostly white—Lawndale."

Cicero, however, was expected to remain virtually all white through 1975. Industrial Area Foundation leader, Saul Alinsky, used to say that the quota system might be a way of avoiding the no black to all black experience. Residents in Austin were experimenting with this approach.

People like those in Cicero are the New Middle America. They feel threatened, and the threat is largely economic. Robert C. Wood, former Secretary of Housing and Urban Development, gave the following description of "the forgotten American":

> He is a white employed male ... earning between $5,000 and $10,000. He works regularly, steadily, dependably, wearing a blue collar or a white collar. Yet the frontiers of his career expectations have been fixed since he reached the age of 35 and he found that he had too many obligations, too much family, and too few skills to match opportunities with aspirations....
>
> [He] lives in the gray area fringes of a central city or in a close-in or very far-out cheaper suburban subdivision of a large metropolitan area. He is likely to own a home and a car, especially as his income begins to rise. Of those earning between $6,000 and $7,500, 70 percent own their own homes and 94 percent drive their own cars.[5]

The Forgotten American believes that both the wealthy upper classes and the poor blacks have political power and economic benefits of which he is deprived. He feels that his taxes are high in relation to the benefits he is receiving. He owns everything on credit. He feels hemmed in in the American society with less and less chance for success. He is resentful: "They think they've heard from Black Power, wait till they hear from White Power—a little slob, G.I. Joe, the guy who breaks his ass and makes this country go. Boy, he's getting sick and tired of all this mess. One day he'll get fed up and when he does, look out!"[6]

It would be a mistake to dismiss all-white Cicero and Berwyn as mere manifestations of white racist communities. There are strong ethnic backgrounds in these communities; the melting pot has not melted; and there is a need for people to have something to identify within a largely impersonal

---

[5] Peter Schrag, "The Forgotten Americans," *Harper's*, August 1969.
[6] "The Troubled American: A Special Report on the White Majority," *Newsweek*, October 6, 1969, based on a Gallup Poll.

society. The third generation remembers what the second generation would like to forget. The problem is not purely racist; it is *also* racist.

EQUAL EMPLOYMENT OPPORTUNITY— BLACKS JOIN THE WORK FORCE

Acme, like many American factories, was originally a "family" plant, drawing its labor supply from the ethnic neighborhoods that surrounded it. Most new employees were recruited and recommended by men and women who already worked in the plant, and whole families often ended up at the plant together.

In the late 1940s and early 1950s Acme began to employ some Spanish-speaking people and some southern whites—both now forming substantial parts of the work force. Very few blacks were hired before 1963. They began moving into neighboring Lawndale in the 1950s, but from 1958 to 1962 Acme did very little hiring. Instead, the hourly work force was reduced by approximately 50 percent while the plant was reorganized to reduce costs, improve quality, and increase productivity. When the work force was later increased, the older service employees had to be returned to their former jobs before new people could be hired or promoted.

In 1963, with an expanding market, Acme increased its work force by 25 to 30 percent. Since Acme's traditional source of labor had almost disappeared and Lawndale and Garfield—the major remaining sources of applicants—had become almost entirely black, Acme began hiring large numbers of Negroes and adding more Spanish-speaking. Figure 4–1 shows the increase in the percentage of blacks during the 1960s. The sharp rise in 1966 and drop in 1967 reflects a short-lived second shift at the plant. Between 1963 and 1970 almost a completely new type of work force came to work at the National Acme–Chicago plant.

By January 1969, shortly before our field study, 31 percent of the hourly workers (1,136) were black and another 21 percent were Spanish-speaking. White factory workers had become a minority in a very short time. As recent hires, however, blacks and to a lesser extent Spanish-speaking workers were concentrated in less skilled assembly jobs. While 37 percent of all operatives were black in 1969, only 5 percent of the craftsmen were black. On the white collar level, 6.5 percent of clerical workers, 1.1 percent of technicians, 2 percent of professionals, and 1.9 percent of the managers (mostly foremen) were black.

PROFILE

The recent arrival of the blacks was apparent when we looked at the backgrounds of the black and white hourly workers whom we interviewed. (We also interviewed Spanish-speaking employees, but the focus of this study is

Chicago: Bohemians to young blacks 55

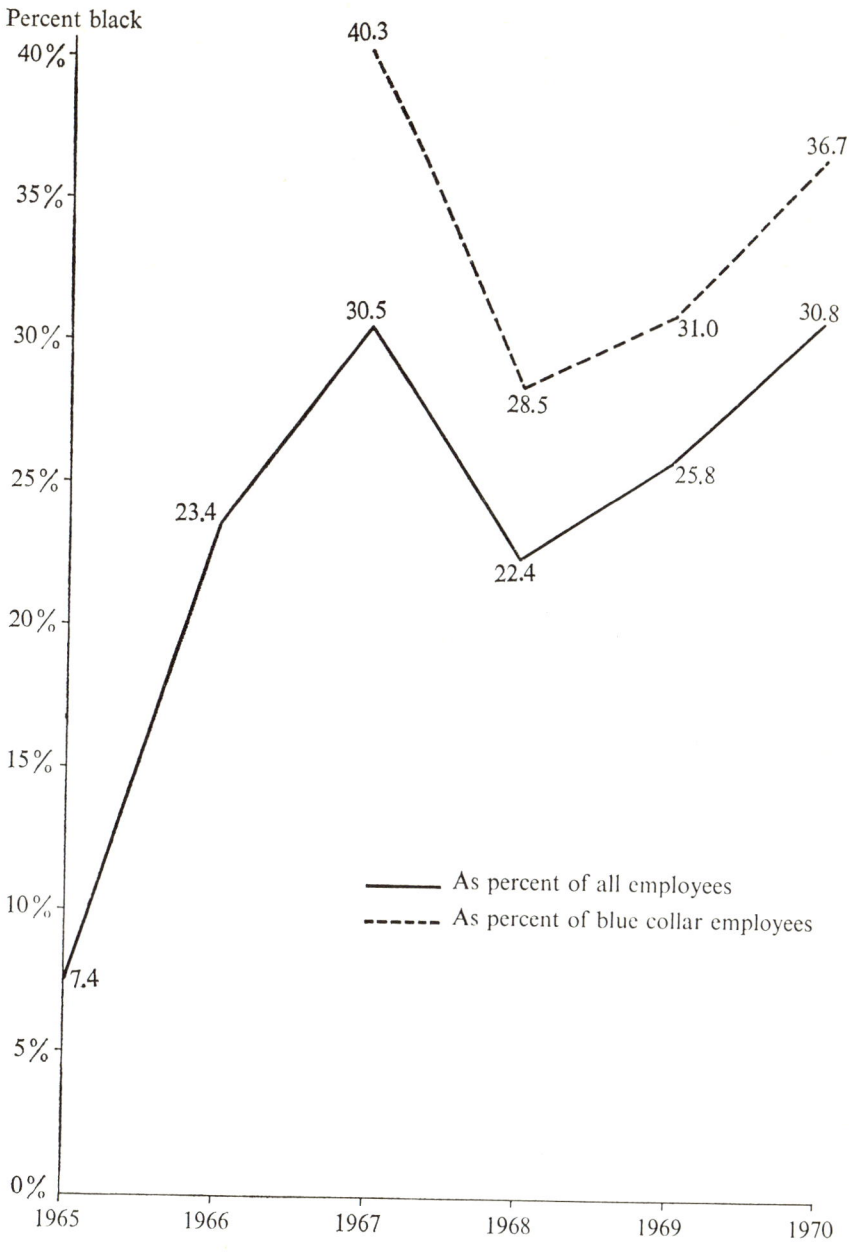

FIGURE 4-1. **Growth of Black Employment
National Acme-Chicago
January 1965 to January 1970**

black and white workers.) Table 4-1 shows that the white employees were considerably older than the blacks; they had been working at the plant much longer; and they held a larger proportion of the skilled jobs and the jobs on the day shift. With more seniority and more highly skilled positions, average pay for whites was naturally higher. Blacks on the average had more education than whites, many of whom finished school twenty or thirty years ago when it was unusual for working class people to finish high school. Most blacks and a third of the whites were born in the South. As expected, most blacks lived in the city while more than half of the whites lived in the suburbs.

Two of these differences seemed especially important in understanding the attitudes of black and white employees toward one another and toward

Table 4–1. Profile of the Hourly Workers National Acme–Chicago, 1969*

	Black	White
Age		
29 and under	65%	13%
30 to 39	20	20
40 to 49	7	30
50 to 59	8	28
60 and over	0	9
Average age	30 years	44 years
Education (highest grade completed)		
Some college	8%	5%
High school graduate	36	21
High school 3 & 4	40	38
High school 1 & 2	16	10
8 grades or less	0	26
Average grades completed	11 grades	10 grades
Birthplace		
Middle South	4%	5%
Deep South	76	28
Northeast	0	5
Northcentral	20	55
West	0	2
Outside of U.S.	0	5
Residence		
City	96%	42%
Suburbs	4	58
Skill level		
Craftsman	4%	24%
Operative	96	76
Shift worked		
Day	55%	79%
Evening	45	21
Date hired		
1930–39	0%	14%
1940–49	4	35
1950–59	4	23
1960–64	0	5
1965–66	43	0
1967	16	7
1968	29	16
1969	4	0
Average years of service	3 years	16 years

* The profile and attitude tables in this chapter are weighted projections from the random sample.

their work. A big age difference was likely to mean some difference in values, regardless of race. At Chicago the race and age differences reinforced each other since 65 percent of the blacks and only 13 percent of the whites were under thirty.

Second, the natural results of a promotion system based largely, although not entirely, on seniority might have seemed to be discriminatory. Almost all blacks were recent hires and were therefore disproportionately represented in entry level jobs.

THE NEW WORK FORCE

Many of the new young blacks are untrained and not now motivated to meet the needs of industry. They are products of a system which gave them little vocational guidance. They are impatient to advance and improve their lives, despite their lack of experience and training for quick advancement. They are products of a ghetto system teaching them that power comes through physical force. They know they want something desperately, but they are not sure exactly how to reach it. Group membership is the most important thing in the lives of these young men; they often lack a father image and find the security, the authority, and identity that they seek in their youthful companions. "Making it" for young people like this is usually determined by group values. For many of them, their first job at Acme will be a frightening experience— the noise, strange sounds, the demands of factory life. And many come from a culture that develops an expectancy of failure.

The new type of work force meant more and different employment office efforts. In the one-year period of 1966 when a second shift was being added, of 40,000 people applying, 5,511 received preplacement examinations, 4,879 were approved, and about 3,000 reported for work. Of the approximately 3,000, 2,100 quit or were discharged, leaving a net of 779 employed.

At about that time height and weight minimums were modified. Available preemployment tests were found to be of small value in predicting job performance and were dropped. A high school education requirement, established in 1958, was lowered in the early 1960s, and educational requirements were dropped altogether in 1966.

The challenge to the employment office was to determine which of the many applicants were likely to stay on the job. An obvious criterion was previous job record. Acme experimented with a "values interview" to correlate the applicant's attitudes and whether or not he stayed with Acme. But the effort was not successful. The employment office also had exit interviews to uncover problems and to learn what sort of person was more likely to stay. The effort had some success, but too many workers quit without notice and locating them was very difficult. At the time of our survey almost the entire burden of selection at Acme was on the employment interviewer. Although those men were skilled and experienced, they had few tools at their disposal to help them in making such difficult judgments.

The New Work Force often brought major health problems to the plant: for example, hypertension (eight times that of a comparable southwestern rural group). Such hypertension may indicate that the black's supposedly unconcerned attitudes and jokes are often a cover for unresolved tensions and frustrations. There were also problems of decaying teeth, defective vision, and lack of body hygiene.

Dr. W. O. Alexander, former Medical Director of the Acme plant, stated that initial rejection for employment (14 percent in 1966) was often eventually greeted by appreciation. The staff were able to direct many to free dental clinics, and several returned the same day for completion of the examination. One-third of the disqualified returned following corrective therapy. On several occasions friends, relatives, and clergymen called to thank the medical staff for encouraging the individual to remedy his physical problems so that he could obtain a job. The lower levels of physical and mental health indicated here also affected those men actually hired. That same tension and sickness also contributed to turnover and absenteeism.

One final point about the New Work Force: How did Acme–Chicago management see its responsibility toward them? One executive suggested four influences on the company's minority policies and practices: the initiative of company executives; the need for more employees; "the realization that other methods have failed and that business probably has the best chance to resolve the country's most significant challenges"; and the desire to improve the company image in the community.

This manager measured the degree of Acme's success in carrying out such affirmative action programs by this main criterion:

- The distribution of minorities through occupational job classifications.

His next two criteria were:

- The improved income level of minorities at Acme;
- "The comparison of results with other companies; and the amount of advice and counsel we at Acme are asked to provide them."

WHITE REACTION TO THE MANY NEW BLACKS

The old-timers at Acme would often recall the "good old days," the "close-knit feelings between management and worker," the company picnics and parties, days when "you could stand around and shoot the bull for a while," when "it was almost a pleasure to come to work." Now those same employees wonder what has caused the less relaxed, less personal atmosphere at the plant over the past twenty years. For many of these whites it was not just a coincidence that there had been a dramatic increase in the number of blacks at Acme.

Leonard Boler, a white, forty-seven-year-old electrical checker from North Carolina, reported that 50 percent of the workers in his department were Negro.

BOLER: It seems to me that's all the companies do hire now.

PURCELL: A lot more comin' in, huh?

BOLER: That's all they *hire*, and if the trend continues, I think the whites'll be in a minority, which I don't think is a good policy either.

PURCELL: I saw one white girl in the employment office the other day; all the rest were blacks.

BOLER: Yeah, yeah. That's the way it is all the time. Maybe the white people that have friends working here wouldn't recommend the place to their friends any more . . . an older man retires, well, any new help is all colored. It seems that way to me. (laughs softly) . . . I think they should hire more white people.

Charles Eliot recalled his acceptance as the first black production worker and observed that racial tensions become more overt when the number of blacks increases:

> Wherever there's one black, he gets along the best of all where there's all white. No matter what happens, everyone takes him in as sort of a personal thing. But when it becomes a mass, then he becomes a problem. Where there's only one or two, the guy may resent it right away but he takes to you a lot faster. I don't know what he think—you're an orphan and he wants to be a big brother to you.

Blacks and whites got along reasonably well on the job, as we shall see. But many older whites, Polish, and Bohemian were quite critical of the new blacks. Fifty-four percent of the white hourly employees felt that blacks did their jobs as well as the average white worker. But 30 percent disagreed. Although the critics were a minority, they represented a point of view to be reckoned with.

Spanish-speaking Cesar daCorta, a salvage man, had a whole list of indictments against black workers:

> They drink coke, eat lunch, and no pay. Go out through the line. They don't want to pay for nothing. . . . Some he no give a damn. He drop his garbage any place . . . they drink, too, on the job. Marijuana, they smoke. . . . Drunk driver drive a truck, too . . . the bosses are scared of them. . . . These people break everything too.

Mr. daCorta berated Negroes more than most of his co-workers, but there were other critical whites:

STANLEY OLSZAK: Oh, shit. They're forever tardy, and absent. Their housekeeping—it's terrible.

MARJORIE SMITH: They're more wasteful. They don't care whether they do a good job or not. They figure, well, "if you don't like it—you do it." They don't have the energy like a white person has . . . maybe some of 'em will, but not all of 'em.

JAMES SIFNAS: You have white guys that're just as lazy as the black guy. But there's more black that are lazy than whites.

RAPHAEL MENDEZ: Sometime worka hard, sometime . . . a lot of colored guy is lazy. Get a scratch, go to the nurse. All the time. I can't.

SUZANNE STRAUSS: John's the exception, he works good. The other ones are, well, there're two stockmen who are slow as molasses. We're always goin' down because we're out of parts. . . . One girl refuses to do work—it's too much for her. And she gets away with it. They take the work away from her and give it to a white girl.

While such negative criticism may have much truth, it is important also to listen to the more moderate whites and young blacks later on in this chapter.

A NEW THREEFOLD PROBLEM: TURNOVER, ABSENTEEISM, TARDINESS

When the authors proposed this research to the foremen at Acme–Chicago, they also asked the foremen what questions they had on their minds. What would they as supervisors like to get out of our listening to their employees? These were their concerns:

- Why do we have so much absenteeism and tardiness? Why have things changed so much in the last few years?
- Why is there so much turnover? These men get good wages.
- Why do men quit? If you ask them, they tell you nothing is wrong. A guy will have good attendance for two-three weeks, then he just doesn't show up.
- I find I can't communicate with these new employees, especially the blacks. What are they looking for?
- Does the paycheck motivate them to get to work? If it does, then why do these guys refuse to work overtime, especially on Friday night and Saturday?
- We've had some fights and even an office that was broken into. Is this because there isn't enough discipline in the plant, or because we are too strict?

THE PROBLEM IN FIGURES

Turnover went from 18 percent in 1963 to 37 percent in 1968, with a high of 57 percent occurring in 1966 at the time of a short-lived second shift. A special in-plant study on 1968 hires showed that of the 1,599 persons who were brought on board in 1968 (excluding summer hires), 830 or 52 percent were no longer with Acme at the end of the year. Sixty percent of those 830 left during the first four weeks, and 92 percent left before the end of the three-month probationary period. About 78 percent left voluntarily; they were not discharged for nonperformance or violation of established rules and practices.[7] The turnover rate among whites hired in 1968 was even higher than that for blacks, and the Spanish-speaking were close behind. Since most of the new hires were black, however, most of the people who quit or were fired were black.

Absenteeism followed the same pattern as turnover. From 2 percent in 1963, it rose in 1968 to about 4.8 percent, with peaks in 1966 as high as 9 percent. This meant that nine out of 100 workers were absent on an average day! A study during January of 1967 found that a mere 15 percent of the work force was the cause of 75 percent of the absenteeism. Who were those men? Where did they work? What was the cause of their high absenteeism?[8]

In attempting to answer these questions, the report came up with several variables: Absenteeism was high in the assembly job classification, among employees under thirty, and among Negroes. The variables overlap considerably, since about two-thirds of the hourly employees under thirty were Negro and most worked in assembly. Young whites were also likely to work in assembly.

Ralph Morgan, an employee relations manager, explained that absenteeism was costly to Acme for a number of reasons:

(1) To account for the absenteeism, the company may be forced to hire more men than it would strictly need;
(2) Some units must work overtime to make up for lost production;
(3) Inexperienced and less efficient people may be put on the job;
(4) Employees sometimes resent being transferred to fill in on other jobs;
(5) Gaps and inexperience slow the production rate.

Two personnel officers who had been close to these problems at Acme over a number of years, Don Keith and Andrew Rouse, both claimed that turnover, absenteeism, and tardiness were as much a problem with young whites as with young blacks; and the facts bore them out. The problems were not simply race problems but were also youth problems. Acme was coping with the New Work Force.

THE FOREMEN EVALUATE THEIR BLACK WORKERS

Most of the foremen sampled reported that the blacks they supervise did as well as the rest of their work force in most work qualities. The major excep-

---

[7] "An Analysis of 1968 Hourly Hiring and Removal Experience," an unpublished in-plant Acme report, p. 8.

[8] "Absentee Survey," January 1967, an Acme in-plant report.

tions were absenteeism and tardiness, where a majority found that blacks were below average. Table 4-2 shows that while some foremen had special difficulties with blacks, others were apparently able to handle them successfully.

Table 4–2. Job Performance of Hourly Blacks
Percentage of foremen who judge that blacks do as well as the average worker
Acme–Chicago

	Better	About the Same	Worse
Quantity of Work	11%	78%	11%
Workmanship	0	78	22
Attendance	0	44	56
Promptness	0	44	56
Accepting Responsibility	0	67	33
Personality at Work	0	100	0
Discipline at Work	0	78	22
Ability to Learn the Job	0	100	0
Promotability	0	100	0

Our random sample included six white foremen, two blacks and one African. In addition we interviewed three other black foremen. When we looked at the total group, we found that black foremen judged their black employees more favorably and tended to make more perceptive distinctions, although they could be very critical. Over half of the foremen in the sample said that black employees tended to be poorer on absenteeism and tardiness. (Two-thirds of the white foremen and half the black foremen were so convinced.)

Let us listen to some foremen describe their problems with the New Work Force. The white foremen first.

George Yanchuk, twenty-six-year veteran with National Acme and a foreman for ten years, said that it was the new people who gave him absenteeism headaches. He complained that they were interested only in their paycheck and had a little regard for quality.

Ed Kolinski, a foreman for twenty-two years, when asked if the blacks are poorer than average on absenteeism and tardiness, said: "I would say so, I would say so. They all seem to have the same problem. Either they gotta be in court, or they have a home problem, or they have a car problem. So I think the majority of the people that I have out there have the same problem."

Some foremen not rating blacks poorer than average in absenteeism and tardiness admitted that there were individual young blacks who had very bad records. But they refused to generalize to all blacks. For example, one black foreman, Harry Ellcock, described the absent and tardy-prone employee:

> They are the young people. I'd say between twenty-three and twenty-six. And they're the ones who really don't want to work no overtime. And they take these days off. They're used to working only three or four days a week, so it's in them. So how long does it take to change

them? You try to change them by talking to them, and by giving them a verbal reprimand and maybe a warning notice. But then they slack from under you again with that same absentee problem or tardiness.

A common complaint of both foremen and personnel men was that those who got wage garnishments—wherein the plant is ordered by the courts to set aside a portion of a man's wages to pay a debt—were also those who were the most absent-prone and the most reluctant to accept overtime, even though they needed the money.

One-half of the white foremen surveyed thought that blacks did not accept responsibility readily, whereas all the black foremen thought they did at least as well. Ed Kolinski, quoted above, told us that the problem really narrowed down to a few:

KOLINSKI: A majority of 'em will do as they're shown. Teach 'em to do what you're told and they'll do that.

CAVANAGH: Do they have initiative, do they see themselves what their responsibilities are?

KOLINSKI: Some have, but the hard core [he does not necessarily mean men classified as hard core], you've gotta everyday come up and prod 'em. . . . It's not the fault of the people they're gettin' in. It's the type of environment these people had. About five or six percent think everythin's gonna be given to 'em.

According to Foreman Jack Grossman, responsibility and motivation were closely linked. He saw a lack of these in the New Work Force.

> I think the caliber of these people we've gotten in the last few years has deteriorated a little. I think it's motivation more than anything. A little laxity on their jobs, a little carelessness. I think the old-timers were expected to do certain things, and I think they took it on their own to even do something over and beyond what their job would normally call for. I think the old-timers never drew the line as close as some of your newer people.

Grossman felt that the potential was there, but that the blacks had to be motivated. Too many of them looked for the easy jobs and were not willing to work to build up their own qualifications for higher paying jobs with more responsibility.

Foreman Fred Dawson, who had a large number of blacks in his second shift work group, blamed some of the problem on assembly line work. He felt that blacks sometimes just did not care: "See, sorta like a resentful attitude they have to be here. To be tied down to a conveyor line and work of that type. But you take the ones like on an individual job, press work or anything like that, and they work a little differently."

Twenty-two percent of the foremen rated the blacks poorer on discipline at work. These men felt that blacks were more difficult to supervise. Dawson was one. When asked how he found it to supervise blacks, Dawson said: "Mmmm. Very hard. Like I said, they *defy* you. As a white man, I've put up a battle. And every time you do tell 'em something—and if you use a voice that's a little rough—they're very resentful. Very."

The New Work Force sometimes makes unrealistic demands. A popular and effective young black foreman, Harry Ellcock, described them:

> They really thought that instead of—and this is what they told me, no kiddin'—instead of tellin' them what to do, that I should *ask* them. I should go to each individual: "Will you please do such and such a thing?" But that wasn't my job to ask. I give you your job, tell you what to do. And you're supposed to do it.

High turnover was also a strain on the foreman. He constantly had new men to train and to get to know. Some of the old-timers found this wearing because so many of the New Work Force came in "with a chip on their shoulder." Turning again to Ed Kolinski:

> When they first come in and you put 'em on jobs, they show a slight belligerence. After they're on for a while, they get to know you and they talk to the other people, they start to get relieved of that chip on their shoulder. And all of a sudden it gets to a point where they already know you, and they know how you're gonna act; and it sort of vanishes away.

Louis Tobias, a production-oriented plant manager, was an older man with years of experience. High in his praise of the old days at Acme, Tobias found the New Work Force and the unrest of urban Negroes hard to understand.

TOBIAS: They really lack any pride in completing any job. They really must lack pride in themselves, because our attendance is not good. Absenteeism is bad. You don't have pride in what you're doing and in the company you work for. They don't give a damn. We have a fine plant here. Acme is a fine company. We have a very clean plant. Our pay is comparable or better than the surrounding industries. Our work has been absolutely steady. Our benefits, such as insurance, pension plans, savings plan are excellent. They all can participate in any of these. I don't know what else they'd ask for.

PURCELL: Yet in the old days the attitude was different?

TOBIAS: Oh, it was entirely different. In the old days the attitude was pro-Acme. Today, it's a place to come, put in eight hours, and get as much money as I can for as little work as I have to put out.

PURCELL: And the question is why?

TOBIAS: I think I know the reason why: this minority business that's stirred up all over the country. They're being allowed to get away with all these acts, and it's drifting off into all the others. And you see them on TV running down the street carrying stolen goods. God, when I was a young man, and I seen an officer of the law, I didn't step out of line. We were deathly afraid of the law enforcement. Today, they could care less!

In spite of his concern about the new young blacks of the cities, Mr. Tobias was open enough to try for better communications, as we shall see.

We have presented the problems. We must remember, however, that some foremen indicated that they did not have much trouble with blacks. Walter Jezak represented this point of view. Jezak was forty years old and had worked his way up through the plant to his current job. He was one of the best-liked foremen in the plant. Four of his men that we talked to said that they got along well with him and rated him as being very approachable, even for a personal problem. Jezak had this to say about the New Work Force:

> I say this honestly, when they are properly instructed and advised as to what is expected of them and shown the importance of this small part—that they may feel that they are contributing to a completed product—I find very little difference in whether the man is black, white, Spanish or whatever.

Special problems with the New Work Force were added to a job that was already difficult. The assembly line foreman at Acme–Chicago had no easy task. Louis Tobias, quoted above, described himself: "I generally reek with self-confidence, and I'm not backing up for anybody. I'm on firm ground, and I'm going to stay there." Tobias admitted that the foreman's job was a tough one:

> It's like being on the front line in Vietnam. They are underpaid for what they have to go through and what they have to do.... Get on that final assembly line, you're in the big leagues then. You've got forty or fifty people looking at you, watching every move and every decision that you make, and how you handle people and what a guy can get away with and what he can't get away with. You're damn right it's a tough job.... It's getting to the point now where you get men that won't want to be a foreman. Management's gonna be suffering.

Old-timer Stanley Olszak, now a section leader, but once a foreman, was not sorry that he no longer had this greater responsibility:

OLSZAK: That foreman is just a punchin' bag for everybody, that's all.... A foreman today isn't like it used to be. I'm talking as far as authority goes.... You had your own way many years ago.

CAVANAGH: Was it that way then? Was the foreman a punching bag when you were foreman?

OLSZAK: Well, naturally, you got all the boys crying on you. Then, from management, you're always pressured.... You're responsible, don't forget. You get a hell of a lot more responsibility.

Almost all the foremen interviewed felt that the company could do more to help them with their job, but only one of twelve said that he did not like his job of supervising.

THE WORKERS TELL US ABOUT THE PROBLEM

We saw two major reasons for turnover, absenteeism, and tardiness among young blacks at Acme. First, their background had not prepared them for the rigidly scheduled life in an industrial plant. Second, the type of work (often assembly work), relations with foremen, and advancement opportunities were often unattractive. The New Work Force might express dissatisfaction with the job and company by missing days, coming in late, or quitting. An index of attitudes toward the total working situation showed that young blacks were dissatisfied as frequently as they were satisfied. On a scale from 1 (very unfavorable) to 5 (very favorable) young blacks scored 3.0 compared to older blacks with 3.9 and whites with 3.8.[9] Naturally these problems overlap. A man or woman might be ill at ease in an industrial situation partly because of personal background, partly because of the job situation, and each of these problems would affect the other.

We shall look first at the backgrounds of the New Work Force and then at their reactions to their job, chances for promotion, and their foremen.

THE NEW WORK FORCE NEEDS MORE ORIENTATION AND COUNSELING

One of the reasons for turnover and absenteeism was that the new employee's value systems, goals, and world views, whether articulated or not, evidently did not mesh with that which was demanded of a person working in an industrial plant. While this was not a new finding, it was still overlooked. Many of these young people, black or white, had little understanding of the need for being at work on time every day, the problems of running an assembly line, the inconvenience to others caused by absence, and so forth. A day lost from work meant only the loss of a day's pay for them. They might not *need* that day's pay. They might be making more money in a day at Acme than in a week in Mississippi or at a local gas station in Chicago.

The will to get to work every day and on time does not come naturally; it is learned. The experience of industry in trying to build up a work force in South America, Asia, and Africa attests to this. American family training and school systems have tended to support the habits necessary for an industrial society, but they have not been so effective in many parts of the black com-

[9] There were so few whites under thirty that a breakdown by age might be misleading.

munity where men and women could not until recently look forward to industrial employment.

Three-fourths of the blacks in the plant were born in the rural deep South. In the South, work hours on the farm were more flexible. A certain amount of work was to be done, but scheduling the work was in the hands of the individual. The industrial environment made very different demands. Lawton Pierce, a black skilled tradesman in the plant, reflected on the importance of an employee's background:

> They bring their traditions, their ways, their modes with them. They were southern in performance. They had a certain amount of work to do, and they got it done in a day's time. But they didn't have to start at eight o'clock. Not only the blacks, but what we call the hillbillys are the same way.

Job hopping and poor attendance, however, were not restricted to rural blacks. Thomas Ramsey, a white utility assembler, told about a good friend of his who had worked with him for five years and quit just a week previously to take another job:

> He told me that he felt he was being pushed around here lately. . . . He isn't going to get more money, and he's got further to go to work. But he say he's got an easier job, and he hopes to work his way up. He thought he was being pushed around by his foreman; but I told him I didn't think he was. He called in sick for a couple of days. He called me up one night and said, "Tell the foreman I've quit."

> So I guess some people like a change once in a while. Some people are restless, and they can't help it. It's just a way of life. But the guy had been here five years, and he was a good guy, a good worker.

World and local conditions, the Vietnam war, and the draft have been unsettling. Benjamin Howard, a fifty-year-old black trucker, saw them as an important factor in absenteeism:

> These fellows figure they got nothing to look forward to but to be drafted. So he better squeeze as much life in a short space of time. . . . They whoopin' it up, havin' a good time, because they don't know when they going to be called to Vietnam. They don't think like an older guy is thinking about security and his home and family, about taking care of his money. But these young guys figure that every day is a day to live.

This restlessness was almost a way of life with many of the young. Personal fulfillment through a diversity of experiences, on and off the job, was of great importance. Some valued their leisure more than money. One foreman quoted a black explaining that he needed his Saturday rest and exercise: "Can't you see how pale I is?" This attitude was in sharp contrast to the older Bohemians and Poles who would and will work *any* overtime that might be offered to them. Yet we also ran into several other men at the Acme plant who found it neccesary to "moonlight," to hold a second job, in order to put food on the family table. And it was precisely the fatigue caused by the second job that often made the man absent and late at Acme.

Many of the young are not yet ready to take on the responsibility that comes with a family. Todd Atkins, who had a poor attendance record himself, explained how hard it would be to just move on if he were married:

ATKINS: Most people still ne'er worked no more than 'bout three days befoh they quit. Some of 'em don't even stay there a day.

CAVANAGH: Is that right? Some guys that come on the line?

ATKINS: That come on the line.... And you know 'bout a man. He's desperate for work, 'cause you catch most these dudes comin' out of school. They not lookin' for no jobs, 'cause they probably work awhile, work two to three weeks, and they quit. They've gotta walk the streets, and do that kind of work.

CAVANAGH: If you have some money. You need some money, though.

ATKINS: Yeah. You know, most kids raised in the North, they just carry on 'til they git somethin' to eat—probably lookin' for book work.

CAVANAGH: How about if a guy had a family, though. That'd be kinda hard, if he didn't have a job, wouldn't it?

ATKINS: If he had a family, it'd be *kinda* hard? It'd be *hard*! They probably find you a job you don't want, but you have to stick with it. If you got a family, you got to feed 'em, and so he have to stick with the job.

Atkins has since left Acme. Of the three men who have left the plant since we talked to them, only one was married. And he was twenty-five years old with no children.

For Richard Masterson, another black assembler, Atkins was right: His family tied him to his job:

MASTERSON: Right now I'm not satisfied, but I know I gotta do it, because I gotta family. I'm not gonna make dem suffer for something that I don't like. So I do the job. And thass why I do it.

CAVANAGH: Is there much of a problem of guys coming in late or missing work in your unit?

MASTERSON: No. They don't have any problem too much because mostly everybody in there is married.... Just about everybody I talk to—they married and they gotta family. They tell me, "Yeah, man, that's the reason why I stick with it. 'Cause I gotta family and dey got to eat." Mostly everybody on that end of the line, they really loves their families.

But there were more Todd Atkins' than Richard Mastersons.

Ambrose Cairns, a new Negro foreman, described the absentee-prone type of employee. He felt that men who were separated from their wives found that a job created more problems than advantages.

> It's a young fellow; you find them between the ages of eighteen and twenty-two. And it's usually a single fellow. Or a fellow that's home been wrecked. You know, broken home and he's back on the street, married and separated. Not divorced because the average man over there has separated. Wife won't get a divorce or he can't afford to get a divorce. Most of them won't get a job at all and the reason why—it's a lead weight. When they leave their wives, most of them don't want a job. Because they feel they have to support their wives, and their kids. And they'd rather just be without a job, without income.

Another very serious problem is false expectations. The young person may have thought that he would make more money, get a quick promotion, or that the work would be easier or more interesting. To show his disappointment and frustration with the company and the job, the young man often simply did not come to work.

A twenty-six-year-old black transferman, Elliot Thompkins, who had been with Acme for less than a year, told about his false impressions:

> Well, I guess, for the work you do, they're not payin' you the money you're supposed to be getting. They tell you one thing over there when you go for employment. Then you get here, it's another thing. They say you'll be makin' this and that. But when you get here, you won't be makin' that. I don't know what they been sayin'. Plus, you have to do a whole lot of work, and they're not holding to their promises.

Incentive pay is difficult to explain. It is even more difficult to explain to the young man with high, unrealistic aspirations and expectations. And yet wages are an extremely important element in the attitudes of the New Work Force toward their job. If pay is not what they expect, chances are they will become dissatisfied with their job.[10] The problem of false expectations will come up again as we look at blacks' reactions to the job, training, foremen, and promotion. A twenty-eight-year-old, well-educated black foreman, John Afesi, believed that helping a man develop realistic expectations was a crucial part of orientation.

> I think that there is a need for personnel or some training program for these people to be clear on expectations. Because their expectations are way too high for what the company or any organization can offer....
> Because if a guy has a high expectation and feels that he is cheated by the organization, then that organization as far as he is concerned is useless.

Two middle-aged blacks who had come up the hard way, Lawton Pierce and Benjamin Howard, had some insights on the attitudes of the New Work Force. Pierce had been thrown out of a number of schools, but he finally got his high school degree from a school for problem teen-agers. In 1969 he held

---

[10] "Absentee Survey," *op. cit.*, p. 1.

a well-paying and responsible craftsman's job. Pierce pictured the young man, much like himself, coming into the plant for the first time:

PIERCE: I think a company has an obligation, not only to give a person a job. I think they have an obligation to orientate the person to the job and the particular people they are working around.

CAVANAGH: What would you do if you were in a position to make changes in orientation?

PIERCE: Well, that'a a tough question. In the sense that we're here to make money. We have a production schedule. Every man has a job to perform. The top of the list goes to giving me a certain amount of pieces for an eight hour day. And it goes down the line.

Pierce was making a key point for a competitive industry such as electrical equipment: they have to meet competition.

PIERCE: What I'm saying is: if my people had some history of a past. . . . But for them there is no past. So it's unfair to bring a person in here—possibly the guy's just out of high school or didn't finish high school. He walks in here. He might be here a month before he actually found out what we're making in this place, because he's stuck in one part of the plant. Well, I think he should be orientated to how his job, how the whole structure is put together.

But, now to ask the company to go out on a limb and to give the hard-core employee a job, and then teach them all the other things, in my opinion, it's a little too much to ask of a company. But, if the company is going to make this investment, then it's only a small investment to go a little further.

Benjamin Howard was a twenty-year black Acme veteran. He drove an electric truck, but began at the bottom, unloading trucks at the receiving dock. He said that he would like to talk to some of the young men coming into the plant:

> When a young fella come in, he should have one of the older fellas like myself that come up the hard way, talk to these guys. I'd tell them, "You're makin' over a hundred dollars a week. You can afford to buy a car. When I come up, I couldn't buy the hubcaps." We had two or three families livin' in one flat to pay the rent. We had it rough. Now, they got all these opportunities. "Now let's knuckle down an' take advantage of it, fellas! An' if you don't want to work, don't tell the man you wanna work. Leave the job open for some guy who does wanna work."

It would seem that some of the straight talk that both Pierce and Howard recommended would help. Both "came up the hard way." Both were direct, honest, and mature. They were not Uncle Toms, yet they had the wisdom that went with experience both in living and working. In Pierce's words, if Acme was going to bring in new young workers, then "it's only a small investment to go a little further." And perhaps this small early investment would save much later on.

Assuming a theoretical conservative hiring cost of at least $200 per man, turnover at current rates could mean an annual cost to Acme of nearly $180,000. There is a loss to some employees of confidence, stability, and the chance for security for their families (almost half of these men are married). It may be just one more job in a cycle of temporary work and poverty. Society loses because of additional welfare or unemployment insurance costs. Yet we must admit that one plant in the cost-competitive, cyclical electrical equipment industry may not easily stand such expense, especially when other competitive plants do not have need for these expenses.

Acme management was aware of those problems and had drawn up many proposals for improving orientation. After the sobering experience of the 57 percent turnover in the mid-sixties the then Director of Employee and Community Relations argued for one full week of "Job Education Training." There was a great deal of discussion of his thoughtful and detailed proposal but it was not implemented at that time. One department did provide a somewhat fuller orientation when they added a second shift in 1968. This, plus attempts to help the new employee find a suitable job for himself, did lower turnover slightly.

Until 1969 the official orientation at Acme was a two-hour slide lecture on the employee's own time. Twenty to thirty people in a group heard a maze of detailed information on: wage systems, incentives, safety, upgrading systems, department organization, pensions, benefits, personal conduct, penalties for absenteeism and tardiness, suggestion system, quality, and much more. So much new information was thrown at the novice employee that Acme's own studies showed only a small fraction was remembered. (In 1969 Acme began a government-financed vestibule training program which provided extensive orientation for disadvantaged workers. We discuss this in Chapter 9.)

A subject of continuing debate at Acme and elsewhere is: Who has the primary responsibility for orienting a new employee and helping him to understand the importance to the company of himself and his job? Is it the foreman or the Employee Relations Department? The peer group is also important as we shall see later.

One of the departments ran a special counseling program for absent and tardy-prone employees in 1967. The counselor was a black man, Ed Taylor, promoted from the plant to Employee Relations. Although Taylor counseled only a small number of men in brief sessions, he felt he was able to get some of the individual reasons behind a man's absenteeism. An in-plant study also indicated that attendance improved in the group Taylor counseled, although layoffs, beginning during the counseling experiment, may also have affected absenteeism by increasing the fear of losing one's job. Taylor, along with most

Acme personnel men and many supervisors, felt that counseling should be continued on a much more extensive basis, but it was dropped at the time and resumed in mid-1969, at least for the men in a new job training program. (See Chapter 9.)

Acme also tried other techniques to increase attendance. An open house for families in the plant seemed to increase pride in the work. Games, contests, and occasional free lunches brought temporary improvement in attendance, but were no permanent solution.

ASSEMBLY WORK AS MONOTONOUS AND UNCREATIVE

Another reason for turnover, absenteeism, and tardiness was the work itself. The old problem of employee reactions to the assembly line had a new angle as more and more of the people who came to work on it were both black and part of the New Work Force. Table 4-3 shows that many young blacks

Table 4-3. Attitude Toward My Job
Hourly employees by race, age, and work, Acme-Chicago

	Black	Young Blacks*	Older blacks	Blacks in Assembly	White
Favorable	55%	31%	100%	25%	62%
Uncertain	25	38	0	25	36
Unfavorable	20	31	0	50	2

* Young—29 or under.

dislike their work, while black workers over 29 are contented with their jobs and whites (most of them being older) are relatively satisfied. Type of work is also an important factor, with blacks in assembly least satisfied.

We recall that an Acme study described the "absent-prone" employee: "Negro male, under thirty, working on an assembly job, in a unit of more than thirty-five employees, with less than two years' seniority." When we look at the attitudes of the black men in assembly, we find that only 25 percent like their job and 50 percent say they do not like it.

Let us look more closely at the attitudes of the New Work Force toward the assembly line. In one major area there were two main sections of assembly work: the beginning of the line where we found most of the heavy work, such as placing chassis on the line; further up was the less strenuous hand work and testing. These latter more-skilled and higher-paid jobs were filled largely by white workers. Because they were new hires with less seniority, Negroes often found themselves on the heavier jobs at the beginning of the line. This accounted for some black resentment. Most assembly workers said that their job required very little skill. Many were ashamed. Listen to several young black assemblers:

JAMES RICKER: The job really doesn't take much training. You can learn it in—oh, gee whiz—a matter of seconds. You're not doin' anything complicated

> that would take maybe a day or two to train you in. Maybe you might have to put on a nut here and tighten it up, which I do. Maybe run a wire through a hole and tighten it up, and put a fitting on it.

WILLIAM FLECK: It's just a job, because there's really nothing to it. Place the motor. Put the housing on, tighten it. A twelve-year-old could do it. It's very easy.... I'm gonna look for a job somewhere else.

HARVEY NORTON: It ain't nothin' to learn. You just grab a chassis and drop it. (He laughs.)

The chuckles and self-devaluation of these comments on the skill required for the job seem to exhibit a sense of inferiority.[11]

Even though the assemblers agreed that little skill was required for their job, many felt that they got too little training for the job. While 80 percent of both assembler and nonassembler whites and nonassembler blacks felt that they received adequate training for their jobs, only 50 percent of the blacks on the assembly line felt that they were adequately trained.

The new young worker often lacked basic information and a sense of the importance of his job, according to a young, articulate black union officer, Art Lewis. When asked what he thought the basic causes of tardiness and absenteeism were, he replied:

> They don't feel a part of this operation. They don't get enough responsibility. In other words, they're just like robots, just like a machine. You come in, and you put a screw in. You do this constantly, day after day. I think there should be more informative meetings between the company and the people. I mean assembly hours. I mean you got to invent how important this product is to an individual, make him feel a part of it.

Foreman Charles Eliot agreed that it was important to explain every job to the new worker in terms of its contribution to the final electrical equipment: "Give him a little responsibility that he can take a part in it, and feel pride in it."

Alfred Porter, another young black with several years' service, described the boredom of a repetitive job:

> I do this job every day. It's all right, but you get bored sometimes on one job. You feel you want to be switched around sometime. But I never gets the chance to get the opportunity to do another job, or a job that's maybe a little easier. I'm forever on the same job, every day.

But some men resented being moved from job to job. Fred Mitchell and James Ricker, black assemblers, felt the same way:

---

[11] For similar findings see Charles R. Walker and Robert H. Guest, *The Man on the Assembly Line* (Cambridge: Harvard University Press, 1952), p. 152. See also Judson Gooding, "Blue Collar Blues on the Assembly Line," *Fortune*, July 1970, pp. 64ff, and "It Pays to Wake Up the Blue Collar Worker," *Fortune*, September 1970, pp. 133ff.

MITCHELL: Some of them's being switched to a higher skill level job without getting higher pay. I don't think this is fair. And sometimes this happens several times a week. I don't want to be switched around. When I come in every day to work, I want to know what I'm doin', you know?

RICKER: I had to change quite a few times when I first came to work here. Oh, man. I didn't want a job like that, having to work here one day and over there the next. I wanted a permanent job to work on.

Once a young disadvantaged person learns his job, he has some confidence in his ability to do it. To move him may be painful.

Listen to Russell Simpson, a young black with three years' experience at the plant, as he described how difficult it was for the individual to take pride in his own work.

SIMPSON: I don't know anybody out there. It's all right sometime but I hate the thought of comin' here all the time. You know, same thing. Like when I was workin' at Sears. If dey had paid me more money I probably would still be working there, because I liked it. I had more responsibility there on the job. I had a much better attendance workin' there. I was there every day. If I didn't come in, then they couldn't do it. Dey couldn't go bring over somebody and say: "Go do Russell's job."

PURCELL: This had to be done by you?

SIMPSON: Ahuh. A good example is this one guy who's a friend of mine. He had a bad record, you know. Every week he was at least late twice. Off all the time. He put in for upgrade, and then they made him an inspector over there. And now, every day he's here, every day.

Blacks in assembly, however, were particularly skeptical about their chances for promotion. Seventy percent felt they did not have a fair chance. The fact that so many blacks thought they were working on dead-end jobs with no chance for upgrading or promotion may be a significant factor leading to job dissatisfaction, absenteeism, and turnover.

In conclusion, we recognize that much of what we say has been said years ago: Walker, Guest, Herzberg, Blauner, Chinoy, Purcell, Kornhauser, and others all point out a high degree of anomie or alienation among workers performing repetitive, conveyor-paced tasks, be they black, white, Spanish-speaking, or whatever. The repetitiveness of the line may bring feelings of domination by the job, futility, isolation, powerlessness. It is not surprising that the highest turnover and absenteeism are found among assembly work groups.

Today this old problem has a new dimension as more of the assemblers are young, black, and from the New Work Force. These people come to work with feelings of insecurity from their families, from failure at previous jobs, burdened by the whole problem of racism in this country. More than the Bohemians of earlier days, these men need a sense of fulfillment in their work, even though they themselves might be unaware of the need.

One might argue, as does one National Acme executive, that "mass assembly is the easiest type of manufacturing situation for blacks to be thrown into en masse, but it may not be the best 'first exposure' for them, due to the nature of the work and the lack of opportunity for genuine individual identity." We know that job redesign would be expensive and difficult. But this goal should not be dismissed too readily.

On the other hand, it is assembly jobs that are available at Acme now. Blacks in Chicago need work; Acme needs employees. It seems likely that for the next ten years, if large electrical equipment is going to be built, black people from Chicago are going to help assemble it.

THEY ARE ANXIOUS TO MOVE AHEAD

Promotions and upgrading are important to any workers but especially to black workers and to the New Work Force. Blacks generally have less seniority, yet many, especially the younger men, are anxious to get a better job. Not getting that job, or seeing little hope for getting it, can result in accusations of discrimination, justified or not, and eventual frustration.

Upgradings within the hourly ranks at Acme-Chicago are covered by a collective bargaining agreement with the Electrical Equipment Workers. Although seniority is an important element, especially at less skilled levels, more weight is given to ability than in many contracts, as can be seen in the following:

> When considering an employee's qualifications for promotion or transfer to a higher rated job, ability will be the chief consideration in all cases. In the case of two employees with approximately equal qualifications seniority shall be taken into consideration as an important factor in promoting or transferring to a higher rated job.

Acme called its upgrading and promotion system the Planned Upgrade Program. An employee could apply in advance for any job or jobs which interested him and for which he felt he had some qualification. Employee requests were filed in the personnel office and the most qualified applicant was chosen when a position opened. No further requests were accepted once the job was open. Both the foreman and the personnel department had to approve the selection.

Paul Shephard, a manager at Acme, was quite convinced that this emphasis on ability has permitted "... minorities with relatively no service to move up quite rapidly in our hourly work force to the mid-skill, and in some cases, higher skilled positions."

The question is, how did employees, especially blacks, feel about their opportunities?

Table 4-4 shows young blacks pessimistic about their chances for promotion while almost half the white workers and almost all the older blacks are confident. Many of these young blacks had little service, of course, but their feelings are an important clue to turnover and absenteeism.

Table 4-4. Perception of Personal Chances for Promotion Hourly employees by race and age, Acme–Chicago

	Black	Young Blacks	Older Blacks	White
Favorable	39%	13%	88%	48%
Uncertain	20	25	11	29
Unfavorable	41	62	0	23

Aaron Hurley, twenty-five, a black assembler with three years' service, thought his chances for promotion were not good. We asked whether he had put in for a promotion:

> About twenty or thirty times. You know those upgrade slips you fill out? About every three months you fill one out, and you hear nothing from it. They send it back and you have to refill it in a period of eight to ten days and send it back in. Well, I did it about four or five times. . . .

Hurley saw several reasons why he had not been promoted:

> There's no colored guys that got the job. You know what it looks like don't you. . . . ?

> I think seniority is still standing in the way. . . . I could start off now and do the job completely but I hadn't been here for four years and he's been here sixteen years. That makes him get the job. . . . I think the job should be based on skill and ability, stuff like that instead of seniority, but it's not in the union contract. There's nothing you can do, but just follow.

Thirteen-year veteran Baldamar Gomez was also skeptical: "Oh you can put in for anything, but when the opening occurs they get somebody else. This is all the management, you know?" James Ricker, a young black assembler, was asked if he would recommend the job to someone else: "I would let them know there's no chance of advancement in the job you're on. As far as pay, you can make it here. If you were looking for advancement, I'd say no, don't come here. Because there's no chance of it."

Other employees, of course were quite favorable. For example, hard-working young black conveyor man, Richard Sims, age thirty-one:

> Promotion? I think the chances are good for promotion. There's only one thing about promotion, you just have to wait your turn. That's all. And this is what, this is what so many people fail to understand, see. They think if they put in for a higher paying job, it should be laid in their lap right then and there. But, see, it's not that way. Because you have to wait until these jobs are available. And they have to, they also have to go by seniority.

Carmen Roland, twenty-eight, secretary, said: "If they take advantage of the opportunity to put in a Planned Upgrade form, there's nothing for 'em to happen *but* an upgrading."

Thirty percent of the blacks interviewed and 47 percent of the young blacks relate promotion problems to racial discrimination, as seen in Table 4-5.

Table 4–5. Perception of Blacks' Chances for Promotion Hourly employees by race and age, Acme–Chicago

	Black	Young Blacks	Older Blacks	White
Favorable	66%	47%	100%	90%
Uncertain	4	6	0	5
Unfavorable	30	47	0	5

Management, however, felt that its Planned Advancement System allowed it to insure equal opportunity for blacks, and reported that, in 1970, 74 percent of the upgrades were minorities.

For Harvey Norton, also a young black assembler, discouragement with promotion was directly related to absenteeism. He put in for upgrading in the first years he was at the plant:

> I've tried upgrading about three times. You get upgraded by seniority and your record as far as showing tardiness and absenteeism and stuff like that, which I think is good. When my record was good that was when I applied, and I didn't get no results from it. I heard nothing from it.... I just got discouraged, and I said: "I won't even bother with it."

Norton knew his attendance record was not good. He felt he had no chance for promotion in any case. Foreman John Afesi agreed that motivation and chances for promotion were closely linked: "Most of them are really hard workers—if they see a future." He reported a case quite similar to that described by Russell Simpson in the preceding section: A man was promoted to inspector and his attendance record vastly improved. Another manager spoke of a young black secretary who was part of a pool; she was not responsible to one person and her attendance record was poor. Once she was made a personal secretary, she was in on time every day. But how many of the people who would be happier with a more responsible job can management realistically promote?

Quite often the young black man has an erroneous notion of what contributes to giving a man promotion. He may be either too discouraged or overly optimistic. Black militants come into the plant very conscious of centuries of prejudice and discrimination. They have read that white society, the Establishment, is making some efforts to correct injustices, and this may lead them to expect rapid promotions with little effort. Here again, straightforward, thorough orientation is necessary.

Foreman Jack Grossman told us this about the black man's motivation and what his solution would be:

> I do think they have to be, I think a lot of 'em have potential. But, boy, I think they have to be motivated, and I think this is where society as a

whole is failing. I think their own race is failing. I think if the same effort as they put into some of these here agitating incidents were put into getting people that're looking for counseling. . . .

Grossman said that much can be done to build up the black man's motivation. He would like to place the responsibility on society as a whole and on black society in particular. How much of that responsibility does Acme share?

Acme had several programs designed to help hourly employees move up. Management felt that the best source of minority craftsmen and foremen would be training from within and that in fact they would have to find much of their talent of any race on the factory floor. The Acme Apprentice Training Program, a four-year course to prepare skilled craftsmen, was begun in the mid-sixties and later expanded. It was clearly needed. A plant study of the skilled craftsmen at Acme in 1967 showed that they were, on the average, fifty-two years old, had twenty-two years' service, and that 60 percent would retire within ten years. Retention was excellent and Manager Paul Shephard said that the program was working well, despite the fact that minority trainees did not have as good an education background as the whites. The program provided an important opportunity for a few.

"Acme High School" was established in 1966 in a joint venture with the Chicago Board of Education. This was the first program of its kind in National Acme. Employees could attend classes in the plant, on their own time and at no cost, toward a high school equivalency degree. The program seemed to have good potential (two graduates became foremen). But relatively few employees participated and even fewer minority group members had attended. (Blacks and the Spanish-speaking were often ashamed to admit they were undereducated.)

In addition, Acme sponsored a Credit Seminar, another National Acme first. The hundred employees who had received wage assignments were encouraged to take the course. The Employees' Credit Union has also counseled individuals with credit problems.

THE NEW FOREMANSHIP

The answer to a New Work Force with tendencies to turnover is a "new foremanship." We think this is a necessary phrase, although it may seem contrived at first. The first-line supervisor in the American factory has been called many things, aside from four-letter words. He has been extolled, praised, and blamed. He has been called "the foreman—key to worker morale"; "the marginal man of industry"; "the master and victim of doubletalk"; "the forgotten man"; "the man in the middle"; "the member of two organizational families." Many of his functions of the early days when the foreman was really a boss have been taken away from him by staff people. He is now supported by utility and repair men, by technical specialists, by counselors, by an industrial relations department, by a vestibule training program, and so forth. Yet we expect him, among other things, to get out production, keep quality high, rearrange his men when someone is absent, and be a father confessor. He has been trained and sensitized. He has been told that he is a crucial person in the success of the American factory, although he has not always been paid enough to encourage men to want to take on such responsibilities. In view of all this lore and literature and language, what new could we say here? What we have to say and to listen to is not new, and yet, in a sense, it is new. But first let us present our findings.

ATTITUDES TOWARD THE FOREMAN

Most of the workers, both black and white, at Acme–Chicago were satisfied with their supervisors, as we see in Table 4-6. This is an important fact.

Table 4-6 shows, however, that young blacks are much less favorable toward their foreman. One-quarter are clearly discontented and more than a third more are ambivalent. This gives us an important clue to the turnover problem. Older blacks and whites are overwhelmingly favorable. Moreover, if we consider the Chicago work force as a *whole*, the foremen seem to be well enough liked.

Table 4–6. Attitude Toward My Foreman
Hourly employees by race and age, Acme–Chicago

	Black	Young Blacks	Older Blacks	White
Favorable	55%	38%	88%	100%
Uncertain	29	37	11	0
Unfavorable	16	25	0	0

Listen, for example, to Norma Haynes who was a bench assembler in the factory. She was young, twenty-eight, came from the South, was married, and lived in Cicero. When asked about her foreman she said: "Well, in my opinion I have a good foreman. He's a good guy. Our supervisor makes me nervous. But my foreman—he's a champion. You can talk to him if you got any problems or something. And he'll listen to you."

PROBLEMS IN THE FOREMAN RELATIONSHIP

We looked more closely at problems, despite the generally good relations, because inadequate relations with the foreman supplies one clue to the turnover problem.

Harvey Norton, one of the young blacks discouraged about promotions, had little respect for his foreman. Norton worked in a department with a high absentee rate and had an attendance problem himself. He expressed himself freely, was happily married, and seemed to be well adjusted. He had heard other guys say that foreman Havlin was "a prejudiced son of a gun," but wanted to make up his own mind. Now he admitted that:

> He is not an understanding man, you know. To get more out of the guys—he is like a baby, you have to pacify him. You have to bend way over to try to find out what he wants. . . . He is not competent in handling people. Now, everyone will agree 100 percent with that. They had five or six grievances filed against him, and everyone in our department signed them.

A bit later he described his former foreman, Walter Jezak, suggesting that the problems in the unit were related to the style of his current foreman:

> Our foreman that was there got another job. He had been giving the guys a lot of breaks. *But the guys had been doing extremely good for him.* He palled around. He worked harder than the employees did . . . getting around, gathered jobs that were supposed to have been done; and he would do it. We had little arguments, but it was never nothing.

Cyril Ford, a forty-three-year-old, highly regarded black in final assembly, also suggested that relationships with the foreman had a very important effect on turnover, absenteeism, and tardiness.

FORD: I believe that is the real trouble here at Acme, as far as the guy being absent and this lackadaisy way of doing. This is the way the guys show they resent a guy, is halfway doing their job. Don't care if they do the job or don't get here on time. That's a lot of resentment. This is the way they can show that "I resent you." You can't come out and tell a guy like you want to tell him. This is a form of expression that you can tell a guy "I don't think you so big," and "You don't know your job so good either."

I've talked to several of the fellows. I say: "Man, why don't you get here on time?" "Aw, Ford, you know I gotta work for this so-and-so. I don't give a damn if I get here or not."

It may not be easy for a foreman to establish good relations. If the new employee is frightened and aloof, he may appear to have a chip on his shoulder, to be uncommunicative and defensive, and not to be trusted. A foreman then feels he cannot relax and trust the new worker. This lack of an ability to communicate and trust easily leads to the employee's dreading to get up in the morning to come to work, leading to absenteeism and eventually to another drop-out.

There seems to be a link between a lack of understanding between a foreman and his work group and high absenteeism, turnover, and tardiness. We feel that an open, concerned, and supportive foreman is more likely to be successful. Is this achieved at the expense of plant discipline and, ultimately, productivity? The same foreman who is supportive must also be straight-

Chicago: Bohemians to young blacks

forward, just, and honest in enforcing discipline—not only for the sake of productivity, but ultimately for the sake of the worker.

We turn now to those aspects of management style that we found to be necessary with the New Work Force to keep absenteeism, turnover, and tardiness within reasonable bounds: (1) a personal interest in the worker; (2) effective communication with the individual worker; (3) honest and fair discipline.

THE FOREMAN'S INTEREST IN HIS PEOPLE

To be supportive, a foreman must be open to his workers and be interested in them. In order to get some information on the importance and the frequency of these qualities in the foremen, we asked: Do you think you could take a personal problem to your foreman? Do you think it helps to have the sort of foreman that you could bring a personal problem to? The positive response the employees gave to these questions provided a graphic and sympathetic picture of the type of foreman they would like to have:

JAMES RICKER, twenty-three, black assembler from Alabama: If a man has a personal problem, he may not be able to perform his job right. If the foreman can help him in any way on his personal problem, you have a better employee. A foreman should show interest in an employee, not only because he's on a certain job, but even in his personal matters. As a matter of fact, I think that this is one of the things that makes a good foreman.

GARY ROGERS, nineteen, white apprentice, when asked about his foreman: Norton is tremendous. If there was any foreman I would want to work under for the rest of my life, it would be Matt Norton; ... if you have a problem at home, you can go to Matt Norton and talk to him. He's a very reasonable, very soft-spoken man. He's the type of foreman who's busy but he'll find time; and he'll go out of his way for you.

DEWITT DRAPER, thirty-three, Negro finisher, described his foreman, Charles Eliot: He never jump on you. That's one good thing. The way he goes about things, it's easy to understand. You know you got a foreman, but you feel like he works right along with you, so you're not scared. He's never sayin' "You're doin' this wrong!" but "This way might be a little easier for you." This is where the foreman comes in. Show him, help him. This makes the job bigger and better. . . .

Eliot, the very well-liked black foreman agreed:

ELIOT: All reprimands should be done in private. It should be done alone, so that he can go back and tell the guys that he give me hell instead of me givin' him hell. Then he feels a lot better, see? . . . I personally take time to walk around, because it pays a lot of dividends.

PURCELL: Yeah, it does pay off, does it?

ELIOT: Yeah, it pays off because the kids, they got to know that you care. If they feel that you're not interested in 'em, they don't take interest in the job.

A younger but quite successful black foreman, Harry Ellcock, made much the same point: "I think that this is the type of relation that you should have with your employees. Not being mean and harsh to them, you know, 'I'm the boss.' You have to get to know the people because the people makes you. The foreman is nothin' without the people."

Personal relationships, even at work, seem to be more important for younger workers than they are for the old-timers. If the younger worker has a good, positive relationship with his foreman, it will influence the worker more positively than "loyalty to the company" or some other abstract concept.

In statistical terms, the answer to our question "Could you take a personal problem to your foreman?" came out as follows: Eighty-six percent of the whites, a large majority, and a majority of the blacks, 51 percent, felt that they could take a personal problem to their foreman. Admittedly, many people will not take such a problem to their foreman; yet feeling that they might do so is important. These data show a rather successful performance on the part of the Acme foremen.

At the same time we again found a distinct racial difference, understandably perhaps, with the whites much more confident than the blacks. If we were to take simply the blacks under thirty, we would find a smaller percentage still, with only 38 percent saying that they could take a personal problem to their foreman. Of blacks on the assembly line, only 30 percent felt they could do this. On the other hand, of the blacks who were not working directly on assembly, two-thirds felt that they could take a problem to the foreman, showing again perhaps the specific problems of the assembly line and the foreman who is a supervisor of an assembly line.

BETTER COMMUNICATIONS SHOULD HELP

Communications is a tired word, yet a perennial challenge in factory life. To communicate, whether orally or in writing, is an old National Acme tradition, but it is sometimes ignored by managers who are under pressures of cost and production. As a more systematic approach to the communications issue, Acme has conducted "round table meetings" in some units on common problems such as quality or safety. A young foreman in a components group, Mario Iannelli, found these small meetings in his office successful:

IANNELLI: This is the key I think to really understanding these people—make 'em a part of the plant—more informative meetings. We are going this route. And this has revealed the attitudes of these people and has given me an insight that, gee whiz, here's a problem that's really plaguing these people.

PURCELL: You get a small group of people regularly in your office?

IANNELLI: Right. Mainly to see that they're given a fair understanding of what we expect, and to see what their problem is. . . .

Louis Tobias, whose criticism of the New Work Force we heard before, saw communications as one answer:

> I'll tell you, Father, I sincerely believe this. The people today need more personal contact. I might have foremen that have sixty or seventy people—that's probably too many. . . .
>
> I heard it from two yesterday. One white and one black. The white one says, "You know, I talked to that general foreman yesterday for the first time in eight months—first time he's bothered to talk to me." And he was hurt about it. And the Negro says, "First time I ever talked to the general foreman, he says you better go on that job or you're going to have to go home." Now you see they felt very hurt about the fact that they hadn't been recognized and they hadn't been talked to. And I'm sure this is the way we're going to have to go. . . .
>
> I'm also starting a program (and I've asked Employee Relations to help me) on foremen holding meetings with five or six different people every day. When you've finished that two hundred people, start over again. But I need help to do that, I need fresh ideas into their heads. Because the foreman is busy. He's busy trying to run that damn line. And his mind is crowded with quality, his scrap, his attendance, getting cost reductions, getting suggestions. There's a thousand things this guy has to do. . . .

Tobias' proposal got support from an intelligent young black assembler in his plant Jeremiah Collins. Collins felt that this sort of small meeting would be successful, providing that it was informal enough to encourage free and open discussion among the workers and their foreman:

> They should split up all the units. You should get these people together and talk to them. Because the union only have maybe a half of the people out here. And they don't go to the union meetings. But split the units up, and have your own little meetings, in your own group. And have *open* discussion like you want to talk to your foreman. And let him be the head of things, and *then* may be you can get up and talk to him the way you wanted—openly.

Collins felt that the other employees *would* bring up their problems at these meetings if they had the opportunity. Collins himself had many problems and suggestions. He was critical—and constructively critical—of his foreman, his job, and the company. He quit his job in September 1969. Perhaps if Tobias had acted more quickly on his proposal, Collins would still be at Acme.

The foreman is the central figure here, and many are aware of the need. With some planning the foreman could be given time, help, and encouragement to communicate better with his workers. Such communication would help to lower turnover, absenteeism, and tardiness. This is a truism, of course, but it is especially important to have a new type of foremanship to deal with the New Work Force.

NECESSARY DISCIPLINE

Fair and honest plant discipline is also very important for the New Work Force. The rising need for personal concern for the individual worker, and better communication with him, does not lessen the need for plant discipline. Perhaps a new style of discipline is called for, but discipline is essential.

When asked about discipline, Paul Shephard, a manager at Acme, admitted:

> It's clear from the record that in certain areas, we are too lax. Because if you look at a given area that has minimal discipline (and this has been done in two of our departments now), you'll see a correlation between that and high absenteeism. Then you look at other areas that have pretty tight discipline, and absenteeism is much better.

In explaining the correlation, Shephard continued: "If an individual or group of them get the feeling that the foreman doesn't care that they don't come in, or that they're tardy three days a week, they'll be tardy."

Harry Ellcock realized the difficult position he and his fellow foremen were in. He was well aware of the atmosphere that could be created when discipline was not administered fairly and consistently. Ellcock described a man who had been coming in late regularly: "So I said: 'The next time that you come in at twelve, without calling me or anything, I'll send you back home.' And I sent him back home. The last two weeks I've been watching, and he hasn't been tardy. And he's been here the full week." He could see what would happen if the foreman had two standards. He told about another tardiness problem:

> I said, "Just takes a second to put a dime in and say, well, look, I'd like to come in a little late; I have this problem." But they don't call! So okay, you let him go. So two or three days later, another man does the same thing. Then what do you do? Can't send them all home. So pretty soon, everybody starts doing the same thing, and this is getting out of control. If you don't stop it, then you're in trouble.

Foremen were unanimous in their insistence that uniform plant discipline was essential. A young black supervisor, John Clay, rejected a double work standard for the disadvantaged after they had learned their job, because he wanted them to succeed. He felt that perhaps too many of the foremen were afraid of the young blacks: "Don't let the black employee do it because he is black and you expect it of him." Clay is convinced that uniform and fair discipline will result in "less termination of these kids, hard kids, poor kids, kids that we have here."

DO THE FOREMEN GIVE PREFERENTIAL TREATMENT TO BLACKS?

We found a decided majority of white workers (70 percent) saying that there was no preferential treatment given by the foremen to blacks. Understandably, all the blacks felt that way. However, some whites were uncertain and some (15 percent) felt that there was preferential treatment. We shall quote only a few of the dissatisfied, since their views were the sensitive ones. Steve Michner, veteran white mechanic, expressed this resentment: "I think they're too easy with 'em. You take a colored guy: if he does anything wrong, he won't be punished for it like a white guy. The white guy, he'll git it right away." Verna Comeau, assembler, said: "They cater to the colored. If I did some of the things they did, the man would say 'There's a door. Get out!' . . . I think the whites should start hollering 'Discrimination' and maybe we'd get away with it." Louis Grovitz, general foreman: "Whites are using the term now 'The first thing they ask you is if you're black. If you're black you've got the best chance.' "

Whites were sensitive to any kind of preferential treatment for blacks. They remembered the days when if a man could not qualify or could not do the work, he was fired: "I worked to get where I am, and that's what I figure everybody else should do."

WHAT HAVE WE LEARNED ABOUT THE NEW FOREMANSHIP?

Is it true that the foreman is a master key for unlocking the turnover, absentee, tardiness problem? The problems of the assembly line foreman are not new. Fifteen years ago an elaborate study of the foremen on the automobile assembly line proclaimed, as its basic assumption, "that the fuller development of the character and personalities of men and women while at work, whether men or management, is called for and is *possible without forfeiting the advances and advantages of modern technology.*"[12] In this whole process, Walker, Guest, and Turner see the foreman as a central figure, for he must direct and arrange the "non-engineered men" on whom the engineering process depends. And he must try to offset for his men the frustrating effects of the assembly line. To do this, if possible, he will build small work group teams. The problems of the auto assembly line of fifteen years ago are the same problems of the electrical equipment assembly line of today. The difference is

---

[12] Charles R. Walker, Robert H. Guest, and Arthur N. Turner, *The Foreman on the Assembly Line* (Cambridge: Harvard University Press, 1956), p. 148.

that we do have a New Work Force and, therefore, we need a new formanship even more urgently. We have stressed the foreman's perception, interest, and communications with his people. None of these are new. The only thing that is new is the urgency that problems be solved by understanding and well-trained foremen. What is interesting about all this is that it will affect not only the black disadvantaged New Work Force people, but white workers as well.

THE BLACK POWER MOVEMENT

Black workers at Acme were naturally influenced by national black thinking in the late 1960s on the subject of Black Power. "Black is Beautiful" and "Black Pride" came to the fore. Here are some of the reactions of National Acme workers to this:

FOREMAN HARRY ELLCOCK, thirty-four, Negro: When I think of black power or black is beautiful, I think that the Negro man as a whole is growing up.

NORMA HAYNES, twenty-eight, white from Mississippi: It was so strange for me when I first came up here to see that some of 'em are really proud to be black. I've never seen anything like this before. But I think that's the way they should be.

OTIS POWERS, twenty-five, Negro: I dig it. Yeah, I dig it. I think it's bringin' us closer together within ourselves . . . all the black over there are from down South, and they just don't talk about it. But you can just mention two or three words to them, you can look at their expression and tell they really believe it.

THOMAS RAMSEY, thirty-three, white: They want to better themselves. That's just fine. But some of them have a very high and strong attitude that should be brought down to earth. This is a minority group, not a majority of them. They have been taught so much to hate white people that some of them actually do have a lot of hate in their hearts.

JOHN DAHLE, forty-seven, white: These guys want the black power. Black power, black power—it seems to me when they get into the plant, they want the whole thing or nothin'. They wanta move up, right when they hire in. They want your job. They don't want the one they got. They want *yours.*

LAWTON PIERCE, forty-three, Negro: Today there's a little static in the air. And I think it's been brought about by the militants. The white man looks at every black man as being a militant.

JOHN AFESI, twenty-eight, Negro supervisor: When this idea of black power came out, I loved it in the economic sense. . . . But it got twisted out of shape. . . . Knocking down walls of boarding houses, you can never stand for because it is destructive. And a destructive man finds it very difficult to change and become a constructive thinker. [Not long ago Mr. Afesi had his head smashed in a ghetto mugging. He died the next day.]

The diversity of views expressed here, as the Negro tries to find his own identity and gain pride, perhaps makes the events that follow more understandable.

THE AFRO-AMERICAN COMMITTEE

A caucus of black employees led by intelligent and angry twenty-seven-year-old Jorel Hadden was formed in 1968 at the Acme plant. It was known as the "Afro-American Employees Committee," or as "The Concerned Acme Employees." The aims of the organization were both to get blacks into more power in the union and to get blacks into better jobs in the plant by increasing promotions, especially in Hadden's department where there was not one black control man or utility and repair man, the principal upgraded positions. Nor were there any black supervisors at the time. Further, some of the supervisors in this department had a reputation for being rather hard-nosed, production-oriented, old-line types.

National Acme has never agreed to a union shop contract. Local 852 of the Electrical Equipment Workers holds around half the workers according to interviews with union people. Nevertheless, we found majority support for the union with slight racial differences of greater black union allegiance, as seen in Table 4-7.

Table 4-7. Attitude Toward Having a Union
Hourly employees by race, Acme–Chicago

	Black	White
Favorable	67%	59%
Uncertain	25	14
Unfavorable	8	27

The Afro-American Committee received support from the larger Chicago Black Labor Federation, a successor of the splintered Chicago Congress on Racial Equality (CORE).[13] They presented their list of grievances to the union, Local 852 of the Electrical Equipment Workers. Local 852 leadership purportedly had not been enthusiastic in pushing for blacks. Hadden's group then began a campaign to encourage blacks to sign up as members of the Committee and subsequently to support the Committee's slate in upcoming union elections. When the elections came in January, Hadden ran for President of Local 852 against the incumbent, Joseph Daniels. A former chief steward, Alfred Porter, also black, ran for member of the Executive Board on the same ticket with Hadden. A part of Hadden's platform was to get the local out from under the conservative policies of the International, perhaps

---

[13] A Chicago newspaper in the possession of the authors, June 15, 1968.

even to make the local independent: "I don't go along with somebody from Washington telling us what we should do out at Acme."

From the outset most Acme employees interpreted early Committee handbills addressed "To Our Black Brothers and Sisters" as an attempt to run on a black separatist ticket. Hadden's supporters publicized meetings that were held next door to the Black Labor Federation offices on Chicago's south side. José Rosario, a Spanish-speaking officer of the union, and others said that these meetings were not well attended. On election day Hadden lost; he received only 137 votes. George Mathews won the local presidency with 338 votes, and Joseph Daniels received 207 votes.[14]

Out of 1,600 in the union, only 682 cast their ballots. Thus, contrary to the assertions of the Students for a Democratic Society (SDS) in the Progressive Labor Party newspaper,[15] Hadden did not even carry the black vote, since there were close to 600 black union members.

Viola Gladden, a black in another department, told why she believed Hadden was defeated:

> I think we kind of brought it on ourselves. I think he could have won if he hadn't just campaigned for one side's support—like soul sisters and brothers. He needs everybody's support, but he only would issue handbills to the Negroes mostly. I guess this is why a lot of white didn't vote for him.

Ora Mullen, a capable young expediter and a member of the Afro-American Committee, defended Hadden, his policies, and his strategy:

> During the summer Jorel said he wanted to try to get more black people in positions within the union itself. It was interpreted that he was trying to form an all-black bloc, which he wasn't. He was trying to form something for the good of all the people within the company, providing these people could get into office in the union. But blacks are so critical of each other, and they were worried about what the management would think if one of them supported Hadden. His idea was to work and build, get within the union, try and communicate straight with the people themselves, and try and correct things between the people and management.

George Mathews, who defeated Jorel Hadden as President of Local 852, also drew support from blacks with his black vice president, Art Lewis. After his defeat for the union presidency, Hadden turned directly to the company with his list of grievances. Tensions mounted over the summer of 1968. In the opinion of the Afro-American Committee, little had been done to redress their

---

[14] A Chicago newspaper in possession of the authors, June 15, 1968.

[15] Their article, which was widely quoted in SDS and Peace and Freedom Party literature and handbills, is grossly inaccurate. The article claimed that Hadden received two-thirds of his vote from whites. If that were so, he then received only forty-five black votes.

grievances. Hadden spoke of the atmosphere in the plant:

> I think the real problem was the atmosphere created by the white people out there: it was sorta like a plantation, and the black people naturally resent this. You go to work, look down the line and see everybody on the line is black, especially everybody on the harder jobs. If you've been to the assembly line, you'll notice that everybody at the beginning of the line are black. And everybody at the other end, where the work is clean and you do nothing but check the equipment—most of these people are white. And when you look down the line, all the cats are black. Everybody standing around looking at you working are whites. And this is the atmosphere that kinda antagonates black people especially.

It was a collision course between a strict old-line management and a young inexperienced Committee of about three dozen who had had little experience in industrial jobs before.

THE 1968 BLACK WALKOUT

The occasion for a confrontation occurred in July 1968 as a result of an assembly line altercation between a Spanish-speaking employee and a black. In accord with plant practices, both were suspended. Following an investigation, including testimony from both black and white witnesses, it was found that the black worker was the aggressor. He was subsequently fired, and the Spanish-speaking employee returned to work. Seizing that opportunity, Afro-American Committee members who were concentrated on one assembly line sat down for about fifty minutes in protest.

A larger confrontation occurred on the following Monday, July 8. Management learned that Jorel Hadden and his Committee had "called a press conference" for noon that day "to announce another sitdown." Confronted with this by his manager, Hadden was advised of the disciplinary implications of such action and urged to use the normal grievance procedure for airing his problems. Hadden rejected the advice and at noon led the second sit-down at the front of the main assembly line. Hadden mounted a platform and shouted to the other blacks; he was the only one talking, and the other blacks were quite silent At that point, with the possibility of confrontation between employees who wished to work and those who did not, management decided to send all of the shift home. A shout went up from the men on the Committee. It seemed to be a victory for them; they had shut down the plant.[16]

According to one management account, on Tuesday morning about twenty blacks picketed outside the plant. Many blacks came to the plant, saw the pickets, did not want to start any trouble, so went back home. DeWitt Draper, forty-year-old assembly man, described his reaction: "You had these guys out in front of the plant with the cars and the police here, so I just

---

[16] The Progressive Labor Party newspaper claimed that 700 blacks joined the walkout. This was again inaccurate. There were only 350 blacks in the departments involved.

turned around and went back home, because I want no part of the thing." A few went into the plant to work. The younger men on the striking committee criticized those blacks, typically women or older men, who did not support the walkout. Jeremiah Collins, also an assembler, said: "They couldn't get together, because half the blacks worked and half didn't. So they weren't together. They're pretty disgusted. They feel's though they didn't get anything. Which they didn't actually." On the other hand a recurring criticism of Hadden was that of Delvin Pace, a young black, active in the union: "He was gonna discriminate for the ghetto. He was talkin' about the soul brothers and that. Well, you can't have just the soul brothers, you've got other brothers out there too."

On Wednesday, July 10, the National Labor Relations Board announced that it would investigate National Acme's charges that the Black Labor Federation and the Afro-American Employees Committee led an unauthorized walkout. By that time thirty-three black employees had been suspended for engaging in the stoppage. Following a thorough review by management to determine the leaders of the stoppage, Hadden and one other employee were fired. Others of the thirty-three received discipline ranging from time off without pay to written warnings for their participation. Local 852 of the Electrical Equipment Workers Union had also issued a handbill pointing out that the strike was illegal and urging all employees to return to work. By Thursday morning production was almost back to normal. Many months later the NLRB charge was dismissed with warnings to the Committee and the Black Labor Federation against recurrence. The episode ended, and the Afro-American Committee died on the vine.

CONCLUSION

It is significant that the Black Power episode ended peacefully, in view of the 1969 and 1970 violence in Detroit auto factories, such as at Chrysler Corporation, under the leadership of DRUM (the Dodge Revolutionary Union Movement), and the trouble at the Ford plant in Mahwah, New Jersey.[17] The bulk of both black and white Acme employees rejected a protest appeal that they apparently perceived to have racist overtones in favor of "working within the system" to achieve their goals.

It is also significant that both National Acme and the Electrical Equipment Workers Union responded constructively to the demands of the Afro-American Committee. By the end of 1968 two black men had become the first Negro supervisors in the Acme plant. Although they had previously been in training, the Committee's action, in the authors' opinion, speeded up their appointments. As for Local 852, it elected its first black vice president in 1968, Art Lewis. In 1970 Lewis was elected president, the first Negro to head Local

[17] See *Newsweek*, June 29, 1970.

852. However, Lewis lost to a conservative white in the summer elections of 1971.

NEGROES AS SUPERVISORS

In 1969 Acme-Chicago had nine black foremen, all recently appointed. Interviews with management, foremen, and employees indicated that the new black foremen were doing well, and that most employees were open to the prospect of more black foremen.

WHITE MAN WORKING FOR A BLACK BOSS

Only 17 percent of the whites sampled from the Acme work force thought that a significant number of people in their work group would have difficulty adjusting to a black supervisor although one-quarter were uncertain. Only one of the twenty said that he personally would not want to work for a black. No whites said that a black would not be able to do the job in the long run.

One of the new black foremen was the well-liked and capable Charles Eliot. He went through the foreman training program, and had had considerable experience dealing with people even before being made foreman. Typical of the reactions of whites toward him was the following from Frank Luzzio, a section leader who had been with Acme for thirty-five years. When asked if he knew of any black foremen in the plant, Luzzio replied:

LUZZIO: Would that be the fellow that works in the back there? Eliot, his name is. Wonderful fellow. Wonderful fellow. Talk to him, he seems to be nice and everything. Polite. No trouble with him.

PURCELL: Be all right if you had a colored foreman, do you think?

LUZZIO: Well, it all depends on the guy. But I notice Eliot—he's pretty easy with his men, really nice, talks to 'em, he's not rough. Like everything else, you've got the good and the bad in white or colored or anything.

John Dahle, a forty-two-year-old white assembler, did indicate resistance to a black foreman accused of giving blacks preference.

DAHLE: We got this colored, black foreman in the department where I used to be, and all the time the whites don't wanna *work* in there because they claim there's partiality if they're all *black*.

PURCELL: The black foreman then favors the blacks against the whites?

DAHLE: Yeah! That's what these people've been tellin' me that works back there. Most of the people that I've been workin' with for years here, a lot of 'em, are over there, workin' now on the line I'm on. Because they no longer wanna work in that department. They claim it's just a *hole*.

Verna Comeau, a white fifty-three-year-old assembler, was probably most typical of the white workers in her attitude toward a black foreman. While the researchers sensed a tinge of hesitancy, Verna said that it would be fine so long as "he's a decent person, knows how to handle people, how to talk to people. They'd have to have an education, a training of being a foreman, because you have to respect somebody."

The Spanish-speaking at Acme, who have traditionally been hard workers and willing to accept company policies, all agreed that they would have no problems in working for a black foreman. Salvage man Cesar daCorta felt there was no discrimination in the plant, and believed he would get equal and fair treatment from a black foreman. When asked what would happen in his work group if a black foreman were appointed, he said:

DACORTA: Have to be my foreman. Nothing nobody can do.

CAVANAGH: Would it work out all right?

DACORTA: Oh yeah! It would work all right. Because when you get to be a foreman, it's supposed to be you got more education than I do. Right?

In short, the researchers found that both the whites and the Spanish-speaking would accept a black foreman readily so long as he had the qualifications for the job.

BLACK MAN WORKING FOR A BLACK BOSS

How do blacks respond to a black foreman? Many whites might think that blacks would be pleased with any foreman of their own race. Some managers might hope that appointing black foremen would satisfy discontented young black workers. As expected, we found that most blacks were favorably inclined toward having a black foreman, and three-quarters were sure he would be accepted by the work group. But the experience of the new black foremen at the Chicago plant showed that they did not automatically receive the support of their black employees. Employees test any new foreman to see how much they can get away with, and the new foreman himself is not always sure how demanding he ought to be and how much power he has. Any man coming up from the work group has to prove himself to black employees as well as to whites. Like the Polish and Bohemian foremen before him, he has to cope with inappropriate demands from men and women who want to be considered special buddies.

Mayer Grushow, a thirty-seven-year-old pipe fitter, said that the blacks gave the new black foreman more headaches than did the whites:

GRUSHOW: I had one area in my department where they have a colored foreman, and the people that gave him the hardest time were the colored. He doesn't seem to be a *bad* person, a *bad* foreman. I think he's young and inexperienced. I think he's probably not sure how to handle people, because he was sort of plucked into being a foreman without really being groomed for it. He struggled with both the white and the colored. But where he figured he would have no trouble with the colored, and they would kind of help him and make his job easier, a lot of them resented it, I guess. He used to have his biggest headaches from them.

CAVANAGH: Is that right? They'd give him a hard time?

GRUSHOW: He has a lot of girls. The white girls would more or less go along with him, and the colored girls would cuss him up and down.

CAVANAGH: Do you think it's just because he's new?

GRUSHOW: I don't think a foreman is born. They have to develop into a certain attitude to where they're accepted and the attitudes sort of fit in with the people. I think it's all touch and go when they make you a foreman. Everybody has to change.

Ora Mullen, a black expediter, raised the common charge of selling out in speaking of Alvin Jennings: "I think he got his job through sellouts. I've met guys over there with seniority that were more qualified for the job.... I don't think he's his own man. I think this [higher supervisor] is pulling strings for him." Alvin Jennings, the most controversial of the black foremen, was chosen under pressure by a supervisor who referred to new disadvantaged workers as "jungle bunnies." Jennings undoubtedly felt great pressure to impress his supervisors and perhaps to keep his black employees in line. It is not surprising that he had difficulties. Several people who worked with Jennings evaluated him:

SYLVESTER TATE: I'm not too interested in a black foreman. . . . I want to see a *qualified foreman.*

CYRIL FORD: They picked him out of the ship room. But if they goin' to use him as a foreman I think they should teach him. I mean, he's a fellow they picked at random, for political reasons or somethin', and set him up there to kind of shish things now. . . . The company might figure, "Now, we'll make an image and we'll give them this guy." But those kind of things create more wrong and distress and frustration than they do good.

LAVERN WOICZAK: He walks around to me with his nose in the air.

NEAL MITCHELL: He was picked by the superintendent, and that's the way he got in to be foreman. . . . He's real nice in a way. I think the majority of black employees go along with him.

ART LEWIS, a union official: I think he promised one of the [union] leaders that he could control the blacks once he got in there . . . and I think he stepped into water a little above his head. However, I'm hoping that he pull through.

Conversations with the other new black foremen showed that they recognized special problems in supervising blacks and most were coping with them quite well. Ambrose Cairns, twenty-nine-year-old black foreman, put the dilemma graphically when asked if he thought it was an advantage to be a Negro supervisor:

> I know it's a big responsibility. Because they expect more out of you. In fact, they [black workers] expect a lot of special attention. They want to converse with you, talk with you. "I want this job. What's the meaning of me not getting an upgrade? Do this for me, and do that for me." It's a lotta problems.

He recalled that his former buddies from the line said, "Now Cairns, don't give me no hard job." When they didn't like their job, they came to him crying and saying, "Cairns, I can't do that job." But he went on, "I know the excuses they use on those jobs, because I used them myself." Cairns occasionally still sees some of his old friends from the Acme plant after work hours on the south side. He quoted them:

> Most of them say, "Cairns, we got you this job. If it wasn't for us you wouldn't have a job. You should look out for us, you know." I say—well this is where I'm bagged up against the wall. So I tell them, "Look here, you got your job, I got mine. We got our regulations, you got your regulations. I'll do the best I can. You do the best you can."

Cairns credited these attitudes to the black movement in the country, and even to the walkout in the plant, which he felt had given the blacks a sense of racial solidarity.

Sidney Pope, a black engineer, focused on the dilemma the black salaried worker was in with management pressures on one side and demands of his fellow blacks on the other:

> Management is expecting one thing out of you, because they're paying a salary. Okay. And then your fellow black man is expecting another thing out of you. You're walking really a thin line. The way I have been able to conquer the situation is that I tell all my soul brothers basically this, "Now, we will laugh and joke and talk. We can talk about the weather and everything else. But we will not discuss company business." And this has worked out tremendously well, because they respect me for this, because they know the position I occupy. But if I try and underline it in any kind of way, I have really lost their respect. *Plus* the fact that management knows, I'm *supposed* to represent them. But by the same token, they're just wondering *whether* or not I'm giving my fellow soul brothers secrets. So, as you can see, it's a pretty precarious position to be in. . . .

Harry Ellcock, one of the first black foremen, also found it difficult initially to establish new personal relationships with blacks:

> I don't think the people were familiar with taking orders from a Negro. They don't have that fear. I'm not saying that they should be afraid of

anyone. But they didn't have that *fear*, and they figure, "I can talk to you." And if I meet them on the street, they can come to talk to me that way and they figure, "I know him; we came up together." And they figure they can do anything because they know you. Whereas with —— or —— [white foremen], they have this certain fear.

Ed Kolinski, a white foreman who used to be Ellcock's supervisor and was still a close friend of his, observed that although Ellcock had problems at first, his people "seemed to be a little loosened up." Kolinski felt Ellcock had licked the problem by gaining his workers' respect by treating all of them equally.

John Clay, another new black supervisor, felt he had no special problems:

> I have no fears of anyone saying I'm more lenient or more stringent on my black employees than my white employees. If a black supervisor has these fears, then the black supervisor has a tendency to be harder on the black people than he is on white people.... He's trying to prove to himself and the people around him that he's not showing favoritism. It's not fair to the black employee, because in order to show that you aren't showing any favoritism, you are showing favoritism against him. But I don't have these fears.

What can we learn from the experience of the black foremen at Acme–Chicago? First, color does not automatically create good social relations. If a black foreman succeeds, it is because he is a capable, open person who earns the respect of his work group. However, his background may make it easier for him to understand his black men. The black foremen we interviewed tended to make more perceptive distinctions between their workers. More black foremen also judged their black workers favorably.

Management needs to choose someone who can relate to young blacks as well as to management. But they cannot expect a foreman to quiet militant blacks just because he himself is black. This would seem to be an excessive burden. The black foreman may often need extra support during the transition period when his former buddies are learning to accept him as a supervisor.

MANAGEMENT AND PROFESSIONAL BLACKS—MADE OR FOUND?

Like most other industrial plants, Acme found it difficult to locate and attract college educated Negroes. One manager, Paul Shephard, presented the problem:

> Howard University, if I recall, will graduate somewhere around seventy-five Negro engineers. And they'll be deluged by over 1,500 companies. Well, Chicago is a perfect example of a very high scarcity of qualified

minorities to come into professional positions. And this is our number-one problem. We're trying as many different ways as we know how to attract them, and so far our batting average is not so good.

Shephard accurately saw training and promotion from within as the only viable answer for Acme. When asked about the five black foremen who were named within a recent year, Shephard said: "But they all came up from the ranks. So this is one of your very, very necessary requirements—that you train from within. This may be what we have to do more and more as we go down the pike, because of this scarcity."

Some black salaried workers, however, suggested that, at least in the past, management was slow to promote blacks who were talented. Sidney Pope, a thirty-six-year-old black engineer, said that for a black to be promoted he had to be twice as good as anyone else. When asked if he thought this was still true, he said:

> Yes. He has to be so outstanding or so dynamic that his qualities, if you try to hide them, it would be noticed by others that you're tryin' to hide 'em—especially when you're trying to move up in higher echelons of management. Inadvertently hidden prejudices will come out when you have people competing for a job, you know.

One young Negro at Acme who worked in the office said that management was not willing to take a chance with blacks to see if they *were* qualified to do the job. Lewis Stickney emphasized that the company must be willing to take chances:

STICKNEY: You have to take a few chances, I think. There's a mania about Negroes being in a position. Either they're gonna be show pieces, or they're gonna be extremely capable and you don't expect that they can fail. All right, get ready for the fact that they're gonna fail, just like a lot of other people gonna fail.

PURCELL: Not everybody makes it.

STICKNEY: Not everybody makes it. And so the company has to take a few chances, go out on a limb. And if a guy falls on his face, don't throw up your hands. Look for somebody else to replace him.

Stickney suggested that a major restraint on appointing blacks to salaried positions was the anticipated rejection of the white work force. As one of the first Negroes in the office in 1964, Stickney recalled how well accepted he was, and he criticized management for lack of faith in their own white employees:

STICKNEY: There were not any [Negroes] upstairs when I moved over here; although, after I was there, somebody else showed up. They started hiring a few more. But I've had no problems.

PURCELL: So that's great, you really broke the ice.

STICKNEY: Well, I don't feel like it's nothing to be proud of, myself, because it just shows that the company was much more ready than it thought it was. It has very little faith in the white people that worked on the jobs. I mean, that's really what they're saying: "We don't know if our white people are ready to accept Negroes."

Whites were considerably more open than management had predicted. Stickney's experience will be repeated often in many American offices during the 1970s.

According to John Clay, a recently appointed black supervisor, one reason Acme has difficulty attracting black professionals is that "room at the top for advancement is very limited, very limited." It is not enough to offer a job to black graduates. Especially today, they must feel that there is an opportunity to move higher in the company.

James Pesch, a likable and popular employee relations manager, said that today the black man at Acme has an excellent chance for promotion if he is interested and capable; it is "the black man's world now." A black with an education may now have an even better chance than his white counterpart. But therein lies a problem for both Acme and blacks: Such men are not easily found.

HOW THE RACES WORK TOGETHER

The social atmosphere on the job can be a very important influence on job satisfaction. We observed that relationships with co-workers seemed to be especially important for the young and disadvantaged. For example, in a department at Acme where many workers made no attempt to welcome new men, turnover was very high. We were particularly interested in how the rapid influx of blacks and Spanish-speaking people into an ethnic plant affected interpersonal relations.

The interracial picture was not simple but the results on the whole were encouraging. We noted at the beginning of this study that many older whites missed the friendly, relaxed atmosphere of the "good old days." Certainly, racial change was not the only influence, but for some it was important. Stanley Olszak, a sixty-two-year-old section leader, felt that there was an underlying hostility between blacks and whites: "You know damn well they don't like white people. They *don't*. I don't hear too much of it, but I get wind of it every once 'a while. They don't like them. Well, I guess the whites don't like the colored, either."

For Nelson Kadey, however, another veteran Acme employee, working together has reduced tension.

I'd say in the last six months, they've been gettin' along swell with the whites. They come along and they'll talk to ya. Let's face it, we're both leery. We don't wanna go an' question them. They don't wanna question us. But when you *work* with 'em, well you've *got* to get together some. You say, "Goddam, you, get over there—move over or somethin'." See? Right there he'll holler right back at you. Before you know it, first thing, you'll help him out. He'll help you out. It works nice. See?

Lawton Pierce, a middle-aged black skilled electrician who had been working for Acme for sixteen years, also told us that race relations were improving.

I know the people here. I've seen their attitudes change. I've seen their eyes opened up. And we have here men that I've talked to fifteen years ago; they think different today. They were prejudiced, but prejudiced out of ignorance. They don't have the shackles any more. What caused it? *The being able to work around a different ethnic group, of being able to watch him function, to find that, given the opportunity, they like the same things.* They cultural minded, and they have the same aspects as anyone else. (Italics ours)

For many of the workers in the plant, perhaps especially the 76 percent of the blacks and 28 percent of the whites who had come up from the deep South, work at Acme was the first sustained contact they have had with the opposite race. Coming from segregated neighborhoods, segregated schools, and segregated recreation areas, many of the old clichés and myths melt away when they get to know the person working next to them in the plant. Thomas Ramsey, a thirty-three-year-old white repair operator from Mississippi, had come to accept the black man, although to him basic differences still seemed to exist:

CAVANAGH: Have you gotten to know colored people better, would you say, since you've been here?

RAMSEY: Oh, yes. Yes, yes. Very much so. In fact, when I was a kid in the South, colored people didn't live very close to the white people. I was raised in the country, and we were never around them much—just what I heard when I was a kid. In the South, even my mother would say, if I was being bad: "Son, you'd better be good or the niggers are going to get you." I guess the people didn't know any better or something. I guess my attitude has changed more about them. It's really hard to say. There seems to be a difference in the colored and the white to me, but it's not a bad difference—it's just the way of life.

Problems do remain. Racial separation at lunch and breaks is common. Black foreman Ambrose Cairns described arguments that polarized along racial lines: "They get along pretty well. But when they get pissed off out there, and I mean pissed off, then they choose sides along racial lines. You hear the conversation getting vulgar and loud, real loud...." And white utility assembler John Dahle pointed out that local and national events can increase racial tension in the plant: "They work together as well as is to be expected. If there's somethin' goes on outside of the plant, it gets in here somehow. Then they're all bunched together like a bunch of geese, and have their little conference. They stick together like a leech."

Black-white relations were also affected, at least subtly, by some whites who felt that many blacks performed poorly on the job and that they owed their jobs to preferential treatment. Similarly some of the few blacks who felt that they were discriminated against resented white workers.

Nevertheless, when asked to summarize how blacks and whites got along on the job, almost all the foremen and employees, both black and white, reported that workers of different races got along well. Acme–Chicago is probably better integrated than most public and private local institutions.

CONCLUSION

Acme's central problem with the New Work Force is turnover, absenteeism, and tardiness affecting both efficiency and cost of production. The problem is partly racial and partly a youth problem. We cannot weigh in precise terms the share of these two influences.

Suppose that as listeners we asked the black and white Acme workers we knew to summarize their feelings and thoughts for this conclusion. Their answers, put in the words of the authors, would be as follows: "We want more orientation as we begin our jobs, real efforts to understand us on the part of our foremen, counselors, and fellow workers. We would like to see what can be done about redesigning assembly line jobs so as to make more cohesive work groups and provide the sense of identity, responsibility, and dignity that we deeply value. Many of us also want a chance to move up."

Acme–Chicago has indeed responded constructively to the challenge of the New Work Force by experimenting seriously with its new, rather extensive federally financed manpower orientation program to prepare 400 men for the work force. If the experiment proves successful, it will doubtless be expanded.

Should management go to the root causes of New Work Force problems? As National Acme gets more deeply involved in rehabilitation through its manpower program, will it be led to try to *prevent* the early underdevelopment of black youth in Chicago? The company is paying taxes in Chicago. Should it see that its tax money leads to better schools, housing, and transportation? The result would be a less expensive and less discouraging job of rehabilitation when the new worker comes to the plant.

Should or could management also try to do something about the Negro (and white) family problems in Chicago, since the fatherless family unit is a serious cause of subsequent worker alienation? There is small cause for optimism about such urban problems, but if they are not solved and polarization grows, the alternatives are worse.

Of course, Acme's main task as a corporation is to produce quality equipment at a profit in a highly competitive market. But time and money spent to get more deeply at the root causes of human degradation would seem to be a good investment both to get potential markets for National Acme equipment and to avoid the expensive costs of worker rehabilitation.

What future will come with the 1970s? We may assume that the electrical equipment industry will continue to grow as the American population grows, and that National Acme will continue to meet its competition. Actually, Acme is currently constructing a large new plant complex near Philadelphia in order to manufacture even more equipment.

From the operating manager's point of view, one of our most encouraging findings was that National Acme was able to bring in large numbers of the New Work Force with no adverse effects on its product quality. In fact, several quality control managers reported that National Acme equipment tests even better today than in the past.

A key unknown is this: If the hourly work force at Acme becomes predominantly black, will whites seek employment there? Will Acme white employees harbor fears, resentments, or hostility? We cannot foresee the answer to this, but our findings of a rather small amount of white backlash are at least encouraging. In addition, the Spanish-speaking workers form a buffer group between whites and blacks.

Undoubtedly there will soon be many more black foremen at National Acme. But black accession to middle management and professional jobs such as manufacturing, engineering, and accounting may be very much slower. Blacks will surely remain minorities in these occupations during the 1970s.

One final point: No urban company like National Acme can alone do what needs to be done. Its management will need to continue its cooperation with other power groups in Chicago and the suburbs and indeed with the powerless people too. All have a stake in the successful outcome: Mayor Daley's administration, black leadership, white leadership, and the "no-leadership" people as well. Dealing creatively with both the decision-makers and with the powerless is the challenge for National Acme management for the 1970s.

CHAPTER FIVE

Yankee management in Virginia

> *In order to do its job General Electric will have to operate in a community in which it can get labor of all colors and skills. It is going to have to have a community that is at peace, a community that is rational in regards to labor relations with people that are dedicated to good work, too.*
>
> Edward Cummings, GE–Lynchburg manager

The expansion of northern-based companies in the South raises important questions about minority manpower and community relations. What stance should management take regarding race, both within the plant and within the city? Should it accept local customs, as was usually done in the past? Should it insist upon its own "outsider" standards? How far and how fast should it move? How does management balance the needs of its Negro employees and community, the reactions of its conservative southern white workers, and its major task of manufacturing products at a reasonable profit? This chapter describes the experience of one company, General Electric, when it opened a new plant in Lynchburg, Virginia, and reactions of over 100 black and white people to whom we listened in the plant and in the community.

GENERAL ELECTRIC COMES TO LYNCHBURG

In 1956 General Electric moved its rectifier business from Lynn, Massachusetts, into a new plant on the outskirts of Lynchburg, Virginia. Lynchburg had a large labor pool, attractive wage rates, and low turnover and personal injury rates drawing a number of other northern companies such as Babcock and Wilcox and H. K. Porter. In 1958 the Communication Products Department of General Electric was moved to Lynchburg from various locations in upstate New York.

The Lynchburg Plant is now the world-wide headquarters for GE's Communication Systems Division. With about 4,000 people on the payroll, it is the largest employer to locate in Virginia since World War II. As a headquarters plant, more than 40 percent of all jobs are white collar with many highly technical positions in engineering, manufacturing, and marketing. The light factory work is primarily on delicate electronic components and assembly of mobile radios and fixed communication systems. Three-quarters of all the factory workers are women. The plant is modern, clean, and air-conditioned. By 1970, because of its size and employment policies, General Electric had become the major employer of Negroes in the Lynchburg area.

The city of Lynchburg is 180 miles southwest of Washington, D.C., on the James River in the foothills of the Blue Ridge Mountains. Although it is one of the most industrialized cities in Virginia, it is rather remote from other business centers. The present population of the city is 55,000; 80 percent are white. Greater Lynchburg—the labor market for the GE plant—has a population of 170,000 people. An amazing 99 percent of the Lynchburg citizens are American born. They boast of 96 churches, one for every 600 people. Lynchburg is a quiet city with one of the highest per capita incomes in the state of Virginia. Its people are generally gracious, warm, and hospitable, but there is a minority of staunch conservatives loyal to Virginia and the past, and a small circle of First Families of Virginia aristocracy. Lynchburg is called a "good place to raise children." There have been no riots or school disturbances and little crime.

At the same time there remain racial and economic problems. Although Lynchburg's white population does not have the racial feelings of the deep South, segregation has been a deeply established way of life. Change has been peaceful but slow and often reluctant. A Negro professional is still welcomed quite differently from a white. Total unemployment in 1970 was very low, ranging between 2.4 and 2.9 percent according to the Virginia Employment Commission. This affects black people more heavily, for in May 1970, while blacks were 20.1 percent of the population, they represented 36.7 percent of the unemployed. A 1969 Lynchburg College study[1] of six poverty target areas in the city found unemployment or, better, *under*employment affecting about a quarter of the target area's poor blacks and whites. Housing is largely segregated, and attractive housing for black professionals is only now becoming less difficult to find.

As for job opportunities for Negroes, the recent past was far from ideal. Melvin Warlick, a chemical technician at General Electric, described the job

[1] *Profiles of Poverty: Report of a Survey of Community Action Agency Target Areas in Lynchburg, Virginia* (Lynchburg: Lynchburg College Research Center, July 1969), pp. 8, 51, 52. This survey of 3,148 households and 10,112 persons is estimated to have covered 90 percent of the people in the target areas and 67 percent of the city's black population. It was done in the summer of 1968. Admittedly, its definitions are not the same as those of the Virginia Employment Commission. Still, it gives us a rough estimate of people not working up to full employment.

situation in the earlier years:

> The [employers] worked the people hard and paid them low wages. Actually Negroes were only given the most unskilled jobs, and there was nowhere for a Negro to go to advance himself. He could work and exist and keep his family existing. But to really make a living, there was no advancement for him.

In the past five years, conditions for Lynchburg's blacks have improved. But deep racial problems remain beneath the surface calm. How does GE management define its role in such a community?

LYNCHBURG MANAGEMENT DEFINES ITS RACIAL ROLE

A key member of GE–Lynchburg's top management team, Edward Cummings, defined General Electric's stance toward race relations in Lynchburg. Mr. Cummings has been very active in working toward changed attitudes and better relations between the races in the community. He saw racial progress as an important part of General Electric's larger goal: a healthy business environment.

> I'm not conscious of being in a crusader role. . . . I feel that I'm doing only those things . . . that I think are necessary so that the city of Lynchburg can stay a healthy community in which to run a competitive business. . . . How does Lynchburg have to move so that it can . . . be a city in which a corporation such as ourselves can operate in a competitive environment?
>
> I think that there are changes that are needed, but quite frankly, I think the city is getting well up on the ladder, on those changes. I think it has done it in a most sane and rational manner. I've been searching for that extreme middle and trying to see if we can't develop that.
>
> But I don't really feel like General Electric can come to this community with the job to remold the community into a new way of life. It has a job to do to run a business in behalf of the shareowners. Now in order to do that job it will have to operate in a community in which it can get labor of all colors and skills. It is going to have to have a community that is at peace, a community that is rational in regards to labor relations [with] people that are dedicated to good work, too. . .
>
> What we've been searching for is ways to bring the black and white communities closer together, because we're asking them to work together out here. And we feel that we're going to have to have access to both black and white professionals. To do that we're going to have to have a community that can attract both white and black professionals. In that area, at the moment, we're deficient. So there's still some more work to be done. But I don't think it has to be done overnight, with

104   *The local experience*

ultimatums, and things like that. I think that working with the real estate board, working with churches, which by the way, are now trying to develop some programs in open housing. . . .

Another manager, Thomas Hall, commented on the impetus for General Electric's increased hiring of black employees. He said that one of the major reasons was the initiative of GE higher executives, especially the strong and

Table 5–1. Profile of the Hourly Workers GE–Lynchburg, 1969*

	Black	White
Age		
29 and under	37%	24%
30–39	41	42
40–49	17	27
50–59	7	7
60 and over	0	0
Average age	32 years	36 years
Education (highest grade completed)		
Some College	10%	5%
High School Graduate**	76	40
High School 3 & 4	8	0
High School 1 & 2	0	37
8 grades or less	6	18
Average grades completed		
Men	11.4 grades	11.5 grades
Women	11.7	10.0
TOTAL	11.6	10.5
Birthplace		
Middle South	96%	90%
Deep South	0	6
Northeast	4	4
Residence		
City	65%	48%
Suburb	9	10
Outlying	26	42
Skill level		
Craftsmen		6%
Operatives	100%	94
Shift worked		
Day	59%	81%
Evening	27	13
Night	13	7
Date hired		
1956–1959	9%	11%
1960–1964	13	46%
1965–1966	22	24
1967	18	3
1968	38	16
Average years of service	2.9 years	5.0 years

* The profile and attitude tables in this chapter are weighted projections from the random sample.
** Until 1958, county schools both black and white graduated students after eleven years.

continuing interest and support of individuals such as Mr. Cummings and former vice president and division general manager, Dr. Louis T. Rader of Charlottesville, Virginia. Other reasons for change were the need for more employees and the efforts of the Lynchburg Community Action Program for the unemployed and underemployed. Still there has had to be a continuing sales effort by Employee Relations to get hiring managers to accept more blacks.

Regarding criteria for General Electric's success in its program to hire and promote minority people, Hall said: "First of all [the criterion is] the number of entry jobs filled by Negroes." He added that within two or three years the first priority would change to an upward distribution of Negroes higher on the occupational ladder. He also saw as a criterion of success the favorable performance of Negroes, compared to other employees, regarding quantity and quality of work, absenteeism, and turnover. He thought the acceptance of Negroes by other employees was encouraging.

PROFILE OF THE WORK FORCE

Who are the men and women who work on the factory floor at the General Electric plant in Lynchburg? In January 1969 about three-quarters were women, and 17 percent were black and 83 percent white. As we see in Table 5-1, the blacks were somewhat younger (thirty-two) than the whites (thirty-six). The blacks were almost entirely from the middle South, whereas a few whites came from the deep South. A few of both races came from the North. Blacks had one more year of formal schooling on the average than whites, with the greatest differences between black and white women. Since most blacks were hired much more recently, it is not surprising that more of them worked on the less desirable shifts.

Table 5–2. Annual Turnover, 1966 to 1969 GE–Lynchburg

	1966	1967	1968	1969
All Removals (Quits, discharges, layoffs, retirements, and deaths)	471	384	368	504
Average Work Force	3,397	3,168	3,505	3,766
Turnover Per Year	13.9%	12.1%	10.5%	13.4%

Turnover among the Lynchburg employees has been unusually low, as seen in Table 5-2. The turnover rate in the last several years varied from 10.5 to 13.9 percent per year. One fact here is worth noting: During the business dropoff in 1967, GE–Lynchburg laid off nearly 300 employees; about 20 percent of these were Negroes. While 68 percent of the whites laid off returned when they were recalled, 87 percent of the blacks came back, indicating one advantage for General Electric in having black workers.

EARLY HIRING

The doors at General Electric were open to blacks from its first day in Lynchburg. In the climate of 1956 and 1957, when traditional local employment practices were often unfair to blacks, this official policy of nondiscrimination was significant: it meant new job opportunities for some Lynchburg blacks at General Electric and it could influence other employers. But the number of blacks hired at the start was small. Pretty and light-skinned Diana Gilbert, who was hired early in 1960, said:

> When I first came here I think I was the fourth Negro girl here. Four or five, and it stayed that way for a while, you know. They'd hire maybe one or two every six months. Then all of a sudden these past two years, they've been flooding them in.

The earliest company records available show that by the end of 1962 there were 121 blacks on board, 5.6 percent of the hourly work force.

Inadequate communication may be one reason for the small numbers of blacks in the early days. When the Lynchburg plant opened, several Negro leaders were asked to refer qualified black applicants, but General Electric did not need to advertise widely in either the black or white communities. They were swamped with over 5,000 applications for just 800 jobs. Many Negroes, however, were so sure they would be turned down for factory work that they were not willing to make the attempt. Thirty-year-old Lois Livingston felt that Negro men especially became discouraged and gave up hope:

> I say men twenty-nine or thirty, you know, older, have just been from place to place tryin' to get these jobs. "Well, I'll call you back." [Or they get] laid off and not called back. They just get discouraged, and say: "Well, I'm just not goin' to do it." Or, "I won't get on there."

More vigorous communication would have been necessary to convince these blacks that there really were opportunities for them at General Electric. But in 1958 an emphasis on reaching out to skeptical or uncertain blacks had not developed anywhere.

With so many applicants General Electric could also afford to be very selective and apply its employment standards rigorously. Blacks, handicapped by a lack of industrial experience according to management, were less able to compete. Some blacks, probably realistically, felt that they could not meet early General Electric standards and did not apply. Twenty-nine-year-old Negro assembler, Brenda Withers, who was pleased with GE selection procedures when she applied in 1966, felt that the communications-confidence problem had kept her from applying earlier:

PURCELL: This Community Action Program here in Lynchburg, they are trying to get more people into jobs. Do you think that this is a good idea?

MRS. WITHERS: Well, I really haven't had much to do with that. But I really believe something should be done because it seems, I don't know, some people got the attitude "well, I'm colored . . . I can't get nothing like that. They won't hire anybody for nothing like that."

Because about ten years ago when I was working over at Lynchburg General [Hospital]. I think that's what held me back. I mean, I didn't come in sooner. A lot of the girls would say, "You all, you have to be so much this, and so much that, before you can get in at GE." And, really, I was afraid to even try, because the way they talked, you had to be way up there, you see, to get anything. And I think that's why I didn't come in sooner than I did.

There also may have been discrimination, unconscious at least, in employment office procedure. That, at any rate, was the perception of some of the older-service blacks. They felt that employment office standards were applied more rigorously to blacks than to whites in those first years, especially education requirements and credit checks. Management and black employees agreed that the first Negroes for certain positions were selected very carefully.

Let us listen to a few of the black employees. Jake Duncan, a college graduate who had been working at the plant since 1959, compared General Electric's attitude toward blacks then and now: "At one time, when I was starting out, I would say the opportunity for black people definitely was not here. But now, it's my feeling that the opportunity is here, if they are prepared, if they prepare themselves." Ella Walker, who had been at the plant since 1967, commented on educational requirements:

We know when the plant first came into Lynchburg, but we were under the impression for a long time that the work was extremely difficult. You had to have a certain amount of education, which is not true. You have a white girl here with six and seventh grade. Now they don't, but at one time, they wanted all Negroes to be high school graduates.

Diana Gilbert thought that a high school diploma was definitely required for blacks when she was hired in 1960. However, she felt that this had changed in later years and that there were Negroes employed at General Electric today who did not have a high school education:

Well, when I first came here, I had to have a high school education, and all the Negroes did. And there were a lot of the whites that did not have a high school education. I mean, it was really *mandatory* fo' a Negro to have this. Like George Logsdon was saying that he interviewed this woman for something and he had found out that she had only (this was a white woman), that she had only completed the sixth grade. He wondered how she managed to get over here. . . . Now I know there are Negroes out here that haven't finished high school, you know. Just like there are whites out here who haven't finished high school. So—it's better, you know, than it used to be.

Although a few blacks who did not graduate from high school have been at General Electric for some time, Negroes, especially the women, have clearly completed more years of schooling than their white counterparts. Our sample shows 86 percent of the Negroes holding high school diplomas while only 45 percent of the whites had graduated. Black and white men had roughly the same educational backgrounds, but 85 percent of the black women were high school graduates as opposed to only 40 percent of the white women.

A high school diploma was evidently never an inflexible requirement for a production job, but it was strongly preferred in the early days, especially for people without manufacturing experience. Thomas Hall of employee relations explains:

PURCELL: You never did have a high school requirement?

HALL: I guess that's right—not as a rockbound requirement. We preferred it for a number of years and now we don't even prefer it any more. It's a combination of our own experience with employees and an increasingly tighter labor market.

Other important criteria are the interview, manual dexterity tests, the physical examination, references, and a credit check.

The high school diploma may have been more frequently required of Negroes because they often had less previous factory experience. Sixty-five percent of the white women and only 30 percent of the black women in our sample had worked in factories before coming to General Electric. But almost all the black women with factory experience were also high school graduates while this was not often true of whites. The fact that black women were better educated may also indicate that some interviewers had higher standards for black applicants, perhaps unconsciously or perhaps in a deliberate effort to reduce white resistance by hiring the cream of the Negro applicants.

Another issue in the early days of hiring was the matter of credit ratings. Credit checks were applied to both blacks and whites, but perhaps hit the blacks harder. At any rate, Frank Gill, one of the community leaders interested in employment, stated:

> I find that in talking to a place like General Electric, they run a credit report.... This is why a lot of them were losing jobs. They wouldn't hire them, because I guess a place like General Electric, like any other place, didn't want to be bothered with garnishes and messing up their paperwork, so to speak. But I explained to them that the people cried to me: "Hey, how can we get out of debt unless people give us a job to go to work?"

Audrey Whalum had difficulty getting on at General Electric because of bad credit. She thought that a good credit record was required of Negroes, but she did not think that the same requirement was applied equally to whites in the early days:

> Like when we first got married, I couldn't work because we were havin' children, you know, one right after the other. We had some bills get ahead of us and what not. Now over here—I don't know if this holds true for whites or not—you could never have had any bad credit. Well, we paid off all our bills as soon as I could go to work. We got everythin' in tip-top shape.
>
> But when I was called over here, I knew myself that I passed the test. And I said, well, this [credit record] is the only thing that must be holdin' me out of this place, you know. So then I wrote them a letter, explainin' the whole situation and a year later, they hired me.
>
> But then again, since I've been here, there are girls whom you might work right beside, whose husbands have been taken into bankruptcy last year. Or such and such a one, she couldn't get any credit if she had to. And I listen to these things but I never say anythin' at all, you know. I'm just wonderin' how they could have gotten a job when I had to go through so much, you know.

(Management explains that no one once hired would be discharged because of bankruptcy in the family.)

A third problem of the early hiring days was what we call the "Jackie Robinson syndrome." Being in the South, General Electric was cautious in selecting its first Negro employees and the first Negro pioneers in certain departments. We do not judge whether management exaggerated or realistically appraised early white reactions. At any rate, General Electric felt that the first black employees should be "likely to succeed" when they came in to work elbow to elbow with southern whites. As a result, they often had superior qualifications. Wynell Bennett recalled his employment interview in 1961:

> When they called to interview me for the job before I was hired, I came in and I thought I was in court. This table! And they said, "Now look, we're going to tell it to you straight. Now you're the first we hired here." Now these are the exact words: "You are the Jackie Robinson of the Microwave Section." They as much as told me that what you do will determine whether we hire any more. So when I first came to work here (and not being interested in the racial thing anyway), it sort of put a strain on me. And the thing that really put the cork on it was, they said (and they emphasized this): "Don't bother the white women."

Once blacks were hired into a work group, management backed them up despite protests from white employees. Edward Loder, one of the employee relations managers, described an early confrontation:

> Shortly after I came here we hired some [black] female assemblers. All of a sudden, a spokesman for the white females (they'd apparently held their little kanagaroo court somewhere) came up to the foreman and said, "I'm sorry, but we cannot work. We are not accustomed to working with Negroes in our work group and we don't want them here."

110   *The local experience*

The foreman had been told what the proper answer was if this situation happened. So, he said, "I'm sorry. You are all good workers, and so is the colored lady. We are going to all work together, and if you find it unacceptable because of your principles, then I have no choice but very reluctantly to put through a removal from payroll for you and the other girls."

At that time our rates were substantially more than they could get making shoes, overalls, or children's clothes. They thought about it. And they decided that extra money was more compelling than to abide by their long-standing principles of not working with colored people.

Now I think we could have fumbled the ball; we could have placated these early people and said, "Well, we'll put her in another area." But I think we would have had the problem even today, if we had taken that route.

CURRENT HIRING

Beginning in the mid-1960s, General Electric's Lynchburg plant began hiring Negroes in greater numbers with sharp rises at the end of the decade. Thomas Hall, one of the managers in employee and community relations for General Electric, put it this way:

PURCELL: When did the plant first actively attempt to increase its Negro work force?

HALL: We've had some Negroes here right from '56 or '57. But it seems to me that we've made only moderate progress until like '63 or '64. And I'd say it's the last five years that we've really had the heat on to make a strong conscious effort. And, of course, the numbers have gone up dramatically. I think the statistics of the last four years—50 percent of the total net gain of employment has been Negro—is a pretty dramatic example of that.

With the Civil Rights Act of 1964 in effect a new stress was being placed nationally on outreach recruiting and the Negro percentage at a plant. The Lynchburg plant was also expanding and the labor market was tight. General Electric modified its entrance requirements: the stress on a high school diploma, strict credit ratings, and prior manufacturing experience. Recall that Mr. Hall also attributed increased hiring of blacks to the continued concern of regional top management.

As General Electric began to advertise, the Equal Opportunity Employer tag appeared in papers. The Virginia Employment Commission began referring blacks as well as whites to General Electric. And during 1968 a new poverty program recruited door to door. Figure 5-1 shows the increase in black percentages between 1963 and 1970.

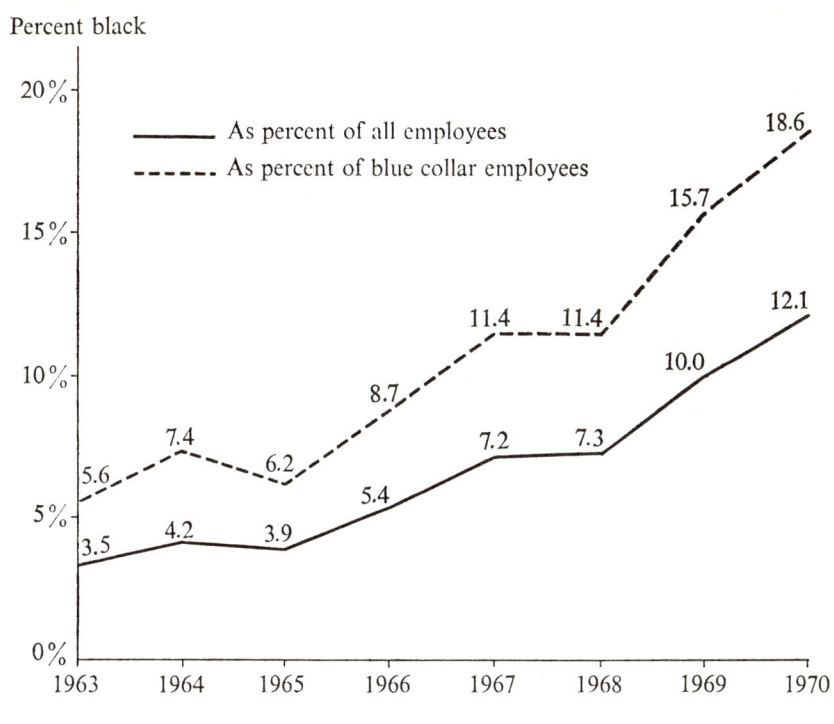

FIGURE 5-1. **Growth of Black Employment**
GE–Lynchburg
January 1963 to January 1970

Table 5-3 shows that between January 1966 and January 1969 the black percentage rose from 5.4 to 10. The number of blacks in blue collar work increased from 8.7 to 15.7 percent (Lynchburg is 20 percent black); 15.6 percent of all hourly paid women and 16 percent of all hourly paid men were black. Most of GE Lynchburg's blue collar jobs, being electronic assembly, were for women and therefore two-thirds of the black employees were women. Black craftsmen rose from 0 in 1966 to 2.7 percent in 1969. In the challenging white collar area, black employment rose from 1.3 to 2.6 percent; 5.1 percent of the clerical workers, 3.5 percent of the technicians, and 1 percent of the professionals were black.

It is not surprising that an overwhelming 95 percent of the whites and 92 percent of the blacks told us that the employment office did not now discriminate against blacks. Negro salaried worker attitudes were also favorable, although less so, with about 75 percent saying that the employment office did not discriminate. Significantly, only 6 percent of the white hourly employees felt that blacks received any preference in hiring.

We recall that Brenda Withers did not apply at General Electric earlier

112   *The local experience*

Table 5–3. Black Employment by Sex and Occupation GE–Lynchburg, 1966 and 1969

| | JANUARY 1966 ||| JANUARY 1969 |||
Occupation	Percent Black of All Employees	Percent Black of All Males	Percent Black of All Females	Percent Black of All Employees	Percent Black of All Males	Percent Black of All Females
Officials and Managers	0.0	0.0	0.0	0.0	0.0	0.0
Professionals	0.5	0.5	0.0	1.0	0.8	25.0
Technicians	2.3	2.4	0.0	3.5	3.7	0.0
Sales Workers	0.0	0.0	0.0	—	—	—
Office and Clerical	2.2	3.5	1.2	5.1	6.5	4.2
Total White Collar	1.3	1.3	1.2	2.6	2.2	4.1
Craftsmen	0.0	0.0	0.0	2.7	2.8	0.0
Operatives	9.0	12.6	7.7	16.4	18.7	15.7
Laborers	30.0	30.0	0.0	17.9	17.9	0.0
Service Workers	—	—	—	—	—	—
Total Blue Collar	8.7	11.2	7.7	15.7	16.0	15.6
Total All Workers	5.4	4.4	6.5	10.0	6.6	13.8

because she believed the work was too difficult. When she did apply in 1966, she was pleased with the selection process and orientation:

> PURCELL: The employment office—are they fair in the way they give their tests, and the way they select workers?
>
> MRS. WITHERS: I believe so because, let's see, I believe there were seven in all and four were white and three were colored and we were in the same class and everything together. We got the same treatment, the same tests, and everything. I think they really were, they really tried to be as fair as possible. I believe you'd be able to get whatever, you know, they think you qualify for. But me, not knowing anything about factory work, you see, I think they did pretty good in placin' me.

Black, thirty-four-year-old assembler, June Gordon, came to General Electric from doing household work. She said:

> I went up to the employment office and took the test and she told me I did well on the GE test . . . the Virginia Commission, you know. And of course, she asked me did I want an application and I told her, yeah. I didn't have anything to lose because I was looking for a job. . . . Within a week they called me . . . one, two, three, I was hired.

Another Negro assembler, Madeleine Anderson, came to General Electric–Lynchburg from the Lynchburg Hosiery Mill in September 1967. She had a very good performance appraisal rating by her foreman. About the employment office selection methods and testing, she said: "I thought it was quite fair. I think about twenty-four of us came in together at that time, when they were testin' an' all, and most of them that talked seemed to be right satisfied in the group that I was with, you know. I'm sure I'm satisfied."

Finally, here is Shipp Buford, a paint processor, who came out to General Electric directly from high school:

CAVANAGH: Do you think the testing and interviewing and all that you did when you first got your job with GE is all that fair, would you say, to everybody? Do you think everybody is given a fair chance at a job?

BUFORD: I thought the test was easy mahself. But I don' know. Different people have different ability. Actually I finished first. I think I was the first one out of the group to get a job as far as after the test.

COMMUNITY ACTION EMPLOYMENT PROGRAM

One of the primary sources of Negro referrals in 1968 was the Community Action Program (CAP) of Lynchburg, funded federally by the Office of Economic Opportunity. The CAP staff went out into the neighborhoods to find qualified men and women who might not realize that they had a chance for factory jobs at General Electric and other plants. It presented a new alternative to people who had grown up thinking in terms of part-time jobs and domestic work.

Some employees felt they would not have been able to get their jobs without the assistance of CAP. For example, high school graduate Lois Livingston got her job at General Electric through the help of CAP.

PURCELL: What do you think of the Community Action Program?

MRS. LIVINGSTON: I know at least twenty-five different people. I know they wouldn't have gotten a job unless the director had gone into these plants, talked to these people about hirin' 'em, and really gone out and worked to get these people.

PURCELL: How did he do it?

MRS. LIVINGSTON: He brought them in, and there was thirty-five of us, went to take this test. It was open to anyone that had a high school education. And they went from house to house askin' anybody who had high school who wanted to take the test. Well, I tell you really, the [CAP] got behind the employment office. [She means the Virginia Employment Office.] Because I have taken those tests at the employment office, approximately six different times. They always told me you made a good score, we will call you. And this is the end of it, and I never hear anythin' else about it. I had gone through the Virginia Employment Office and filled out three or four different applications for GE and even came to the gate, to put in an application which I never had heard. So I really feel the Community Action had a great deal to do with me getting on....

The CAP was also responsible for referring Edgar Watkins to a job at General Electric. Watkins was a twenty-four-year-old former hustler who had dropped out of high school in the ninth grade. He had been on the streets without steady work for three or four years:

> Well, I needed a job and I went to this poverty program thing that they had, about gettin' a job. I mean not that that was the way I wanted to do it. If I could have done it on my own, you know, if there was any way I could have got in to talk to people on my own, I'da come on in and done that. But really, the reason I went down there was so I could explain my wants of a job.

Right now Watkins is an exception. Most of the people CAP brought out to General Electric were high school graduates. Most of them might have been hired on their own, had they applied. The employees relations managers realized that General Electric had not yet begun to work with the really disadvantaged in Lynchburg. While no accurate records have been kept, General Electric believes it has hired about 100 Negroes through CAP.

General Electric was glad to have CAP's help in reaching members of the black community who might not ordinarily come out to the plant gate for a job. As a member of the employee relations department, Thomas Hall said:

> I want to give real credit to the Lynchburg Community Action Program, which has been a direct communication link with potential people, either unemployed or underemployed. And, by and large, I think the quality of these people has been tremendous.

The CAP employment director from his side gave General Electric much credit for cooperating with the Community Action Employment Program and taking on a goodly number of blacks.

A FINAL NOTE

Progress continued during 1969, although CAP was no longer an active source of black employees. By January 1970 more than 18 percent of all hourly workers were black. Four percent of the craftsmen, 6.4 percent of the clerical workers, 4.2 percent of the technicians, and 1.4 percent of the professionals were blacks.

VIEWS ABOUT COMPANY AND UNIONISM

Employees at the Lynchburg plant were generally pleased with their jobs. Work at GE–Lynchburg was light, and the pay was above prevailing local rates, with good fringe benefits. Employment had been quite steady. Written performance appraisals, a daily newspaper, monthly round table discussions between the foreman and his employees, and a counseling service which worked quietly behind the scenes indicated a particular concern for good employee relations.

One sign of blue collar workers' satisfaction is an index of employee attitudes toward company, supervisor, and work. Prepared by factor analysis of coded employee attitudes, the index includes eleven items on the job, training, foreman, chances for promotion, and the company.[2] With a scale from 1 (very unfavorable) to 5 (very favorable), Lynchburg whites had a score of 3.8 and Lynchburg blacks scored 3.6. Both groups were very positive toward the work situation but whites were significantly more satisfied. The question that brought the most unfavorable replies, especially from blacks, was on promotion opportunities. This will be treated separately in the next section.

Let's listen to a sample of employees' favorable comments:

MADELEINE ANDERSON, an older black assembler: GE is a nice place to work. And it's a challenge. You can learn so many different things.

ROSE LEE KRAMER, twenty-eight-year-old white assembler: We have a place to eat, a big cafeteria. We have ten minute breaks twice a day, thirty minutes for lunch. So really I guess it's a good place to work. I make a lot more than I did.

A white test technician recently hired: The company is very good. If you have some relations problems, you go to your foreman about it. If he can't answer it, he'll get you an answer.

EDGAR WATKINS, a black sheet metal worker: I never seen people get along so well.

DIRK PACKARD, white utility man: I think things are going better now as far as business is concerned. Everybody is getting promotions.

Another indication of employee satisfaction was the recent defeat of two union organizing campaigns. The IUE and the UE competed for representation in a forty-two month struggle beginning in 1965. There were no racial overtones to the campaigns. In 1968 the issue was decided: of the 1,900 votes cast in the September election, "neither union" was the choice of 74 percent of the employees, thus defeating both unions. The voting seemed to indicate a satisfied work force and effective communications.

Our interviews also showed most employees, black and white, opposed to the idea of having a union. Nevertheless, a larger number of employees voted in favor of the union at the actual election, perhaps due to a bandwagon effect. There was, however, a noticeable racial difference. While only 5 percent of the whites favored a union, nearly 18 percent of the blacks were union-minded, perhaps reinforcing our finding that black employees were somewhat less positive toward their experience in the plant than whites.

---

[2] A more detailed description of the content and construction of this index will be found in Appendix A p. 311.

THE SENSITIVE ISSUE OF BLACK PROMOTIONS

Promotion policies have always been a difficult area of personnel relations and are likely to become more so. Increasingly, blacks and whites alike are eager to advance and are critical of what they consider dead-end jobs or a slow pace for promotions. Yet promotion naturally depends on the availability of jobs at a higher level, on plant expansion or on turnover. Employee relations man Thomas Hall felt that promotion was a delicate and troublesome issue. It was difficult to set up fair standards for promotion and even more difficult to communicate fully:

> If you took a look at twenty personnel practices of various types and you were to poll the troops here, I think you'd get almost a unanimous vote that the whole promotion thing is *the* Achilles heel of the whole batch of practices, as compared with layoff, recall, hiring, testing—you name it.

Our interviews at Lynchburg showed promotion as the issue that raised the most discontent for blacks and whites. But there was clearly a greater dissatisfaction among blacks, and a strong feeling that race affected promotion chances.

The basic guidelines of promotion policy at GE–Lynchburg made seniority and satisfactory job performance the most important considerations for the less skilled hourly levels. Most women's jobs fell into this category. Promotions from assembly work to skilled jobs such as machinist or technician depended more on ability, with less emphasis on seniority. For promotion into supervision and highly technical positions, the main criteria were education and experience.

Tables 5-4 and 5-5 show many employees satisfied with promotion chances. Note that Table 5-4 treats an employee's attitude about his *personal* chances for promotion while Table 5-5 treats his perception of the chances of

Table 5–4. Perception of Personal Chances for Promotion
White hourly, black hourly, and black salaried employees
GE–Lynchburg

	Black Hourly	Black Salaried N = 13	White Hourly
Favorable	41%	75%	48%
Uncertain	18	—	31
Unfavorable	41	25	21

Table 5–5. Perception of Blacks' Chances for Promotion
White hourly, black hourly, and black salaried employees
GE–Lynchburg

	Black Hourly	Black Salaried	White Hourly
Favorable	45%	23%	95%
Uncertain	28	15	5
Unfavorable	27	62	—

the average black. There is a clear racial difference in attitudes toward promotion opportunities. Forty-one percent of the hourly blacks compared to 21 percent of the hourly whites were dissatisfied with their personal chances for promotion. The black hourly men were the most dissatisfied (50 percent). A special sample of black salaried workers (we have no comparable data for salaried whites) showed that 25 percent judged their promotion opportunities to be unfavorable. Table 5-5 shows that 27 percent of the black hourly workers and more than half the black salaried workers did not feel that blacks had a fair chance for advancement at the plant. Whites saw the situation quite differently, assuming that blacks were treated fairly. The whites saw neither discrimination nor preferential treatment.

Part of the reason for blacks' dissatisfaction was that in 1968 promotions at the less skilled levels (this included most of the women) were going to employees with about eight years' seniority and most blacks had been hired more recently. In addition, a lean business year in 1967 caused cutbacks, and people who had been downgraded had to be upgraded to former classifications before anyone else could be promoted. As Thomas Hall put it:

> The bombshell here can relate to this picture of service. In other words, at December 1964 about 100 [minority] people; today, about 400. But promotions are going to people with about 1960 service. Therefore, only 100 of the 400 minorities have any reasonable chance to move upward, so there's the time bomb thing that I mentioned before....

Another factor which may have contributed to a sense of discrimination, even though it did not necessarily indicate discrimination in promotion, was the distribution of blacks along the job ladder. As we noted earlier, only 2.7 percent of the craftsmen in the plant were black, 3.5 percent of the technicians, and 1.0 per cent of the professionals. At the time of this research, there were no black foremen.

Let us look briefly at the work performance of Negroes at Lynchburg before we listen to people who illustrate the statistics. When asked to compare work performance of black employees and white employees, foremen generally found the races equal in most respects. Every foreman interviewed said that there were no racial differences in quantity and quality of work, personality, or ability to learn the present job. But 11 percent had reservations about absenteeism, tardiness, and responsibility (growing problems), and 22 percent thought that discipline and promotability were somewhat lower among blacks. Table 5-6 shows the individual foreman appraisal ratings of the employees in their work groups.

Table 5–6. Foreman's Appraisal by Race
GE–Lynchburg

	Black	White
Poorer Than Average	0%	8%
Average	79	49
Better Than Average	21	44

But blacks did not always get the same informal help from co-workers as did whites. At the plant, 88 percent of the whites, but only 52 percent of the blacks, said that their fellow employees helped them to learn their jobs. This may have been a subtle form of discrimination. If it took a black person longer to learn how to do his job, he would not be judged to be so quick or adept, and not so promotable. Thus the rate at which he was promoted would probably be slower.

WHITES MOSTLY SATISFIED

Hazel McClintock, forty-five, had been with General Electric for six years. She had a ninth grade education and was then a mobile radio assembler. She was generally a very well-satisfied white employee.

PURCELL: Have you moved up since you have been here?

MRS. MCLINTOCK: No. You take it, so many girls have been here so much longer than I have and it goes by the years you've been here.

PURCELL: I see. And you'd have to wait until they move up, huh?

MRS. MCCLINTOCK: That's right, and really, I mean, I'm satisfied where I am. The higher you go the more responsibility you have. . . . If your name comes up for a high job they give you a chance for it if you want it. You can turn it down if you don't want it. They give you a chance.

Twenty-two-year-old Wilson Poultney, white, had been with GE– Lynchburg for only two years but in that time he had received five upgradings. When asked about his chances for promotion and upgrading, he said: "Well, there's always a chance, I guess. . . . I think I've done fairly well for the time I've been here. . . . I've got a wide variety of work. This job is the best one I've had yet. The people seem to be easy to get along with."

MORE BLACKS ARE DISCONTENTED

We saw that 41 percent of the blacks thought they had a good chance for promotion and an equal number were not favorable toward their promotion opportunities. This was a much larger proportion than among whites although some of the complaints blacks raised applied equally to whites. For example, Martha Cornell, forth-six years old, only a few years with the company, was generally a satisfied employee and a highly rated one. She recently got a VIP award for saving the company money. But Mrs. Cornell saw seniority as a problem:

> I don't think upgrading should be on seniority. I think upgrading should be on ability. If you have the ability to become a lead girl without being here ten years, I think they should let you.

> But upgrades are given strictly on seniority. . . . Sometimes you wait forever. I know people who have been waiting eleven years and they are still at 12 [skill level].
>
> And we have girls in our area, we have a new girl doing more work and better work than a girl who has been here ten years. And just because they are brand new, they gotta wait until they get seniority before they can move up. . . . I think seniority is good if they go on layoffs. Now they are very good on layoffs, because they are not going to lay you off if you got one more day than somebody else.

Twenty-year-old Shipp Buford had been in the plant seven months when we asked him whether he had a fair chance for promotion:

> I don't think I've gotten a fair chance so far, because I know two guys that came in after I did and already got promoted. . . . What bugs me is you talk to your foreman about promotion and all, or you go up to the office an' they tell you they don' have anything' open or may be your name's on the list or somethin' yet when I turn on the radio they've got this commercial on tryin' to encourage people to come on over and get jobs at GE . . . and I can't even get a promotion. And I've been here seven months. That's what gets me. Makes me mad.

Buford is angry but he did not blame his situation on discrimination. The interviewer asked whether the fellows who had been promoted were white. "One was white and one was Negro. So I don't really think you'd call it discrimination but I was there first an' I think I should get offered the job anyhow." Cliff Billingslee was hired in 1958 and had worked his way up to die case machine operator. He felt that he was then as high as he could go without more technical education. But in the first years he felt he was discriminated against.

PURCELL: You've been here eleven years? You must have been one of the early members of the black community to come in the plant.

BILLINGSLEE: Yeah, let me see, yeah, it wasn't too many here when I came in.

PURCELL: Do you think there was any discrimination in those days?

BILLINGSLEE: Well, in the particular area I was in, I believe it was. I know a man came in long after I did got a better job. I mean they might have qualified for 'em in some way but I know there's a lot of them that I could have did. But I didn't get the opportunity to. . . . Now, at one time I figured that I was overlooked for some reason . . . that was the first two or three years I was here, but since then, after I got in the area I'm in now . . . I mean I'm one of the top three men in the particular job. There's no higher I can go in that.

Todd Chisholm, another long-term black employee who had worked his way to a fairly high skill level, was dissatisfied because he had to work at an outside job to take care of his family needs. He also felt there was discrimination against black people in promotion:

> Once I answered one of the foremens back and I think that's what made enemies. Actually a guy had got a promotion which had less seniority, less education, and I was more familiar with the job. And I asked the unit manager what he go by in giving the promotion. He said education, job performance, and the seniority. So I think if he'd known what I was getting around to, he would of been altogether different. I asked him first how was I performing. Just how did he feel about it? He said I was doing a good job.
>
> Then I asked him about the promotion and I think I made an enemy, see, 'cause the guy he gave the job to, I had more seniority. Well, I had a high school diploma. I couldn't say I had any more education, but I did have a diploma and the other didn't. And he said I was doing a good job. So why didn't I get it? And so after I asked him that, I just made enemies I think.

CLEAR CRITICISM FROM BLACK SALARIED MEN

Three-quarters of the black salaried workers were satisfied with their current personal chances for promotion, but 63 percent, and almost all the men, thought that there was some discrimination in the general promotion process. Several of these men came up through the hourly ranks and had experience in the factory as well as the labs.

For example, thirty-two-year-old Melvin Warlick, a very able man who started as an hourly worker with the company ten years ago, said:

> I can't say that my rate of movement has been slow because I have moved within the company. But I think, well, usually I have seen and noticed that in order for a Negro to move within the company, he has to excel. Which I don't think is really appreciated by the Negro group because we have Negroes who can perform a job just as well as the whites. But in most cases when these jobs come up, and the manager or foreman is looking at the particular case, well, usually the Negro is given an excuse. Now this has happened. But more in the past than it has in the present. But it is still happening.
>
> Of course, I'm not talking about every manager and every foreman. 'Cause in every situation you have people who just don't feel as though a Negro should move ahead. And I think we have some people in that category here in management. If they have a chance to stop an advancement, well, the reason all the time doesn't have to be valid, I don't guess, as long as it's a pretty good reason . . . I'm not talking about top management. . . .

Warlick brought out the problem perennial to the whole matter of equal employment opportunity: how to get middle managers to carry out the objectives and goals of top management.

Walter Moses, another ten-year veteran technician, felt that the black man must be better than the white and the selection process was often a charade:

MOSES: I have found that in most cases, 90 percent of the time, that for the average Negro to move up, he's got to be three times as good as the man, the average white man he's runnin' against to get the job.

CAVANAGH: Is that right? Is this true even recently?

MOSES: Oh, yeah, even more so, because sometimes, I don' care how good you are, you aren't goin' to get the job if they don't want you to have it. Let's face it, that's the way it is. And I'll bet you on any average salaried job you go to, the first thing that they'll holler—if they don' give you the job—is that you didn't sell yourself.

CAVANAGH: Is that right? And that's what you've been told?

MOSES: You don' sell yourself. How do you sell yourself to a man who's prejudiced to start with? You might be sellin', but he isn't buyin', because he knows what he wants. When you walk in there and sit down, when he gets your folder and he's looked at your folder, he knows what he wants. And he's made his decision. I haven't been told this. But a lot of them have been told that I've already picked out the man that I want, but I'm just interviewin' because I have to. So why waste my time? I mean, why give me all those tests for somethin' I'm not goin' to get? Might as well just wrap it up there.

James Bailey, a forty-year-old black mail clerk, pointed out that promoting blacks could be an important influence in motivating younger blacks at lower levels.

> Personally, I would like to see some black men go into the administrative departments so that this would be a sort of incentive for the younger employee coming in here that this can be done. He has no motivation because he doesn't see—he doesn't have anybody he can relate to. He might have an engineer that he can relate to but he's a guy making $80 a week with three children—he'll never be an engineer, but he could be a load control clerk or purchasing clerk.

Bailey gave General Electric credit for promoting a lot of blacks to technical positions but he felt they were reluctant to promote blacks to administrative positions. Thus the black man whose aptitudes were administrative was discouraged, according to Bailey.

> And I'm saying that these fellahs have a great deal of ability and hidden ability—ability that is not allowed to be used.... If a guy has ability to do certain things—well, then he should be put in a position to do them and then this would motivate this other man that's coming along the line to do a better job of what he's doing.

We listened to Wynell Bennett, a forty-three-year-old black technician with two years of college. Bennett was not looking for discrimination but he talked of being passed by for more than three years for no other apparent reason:

> We have a new manager that came in and he recommended me for the job. He asked what did I think about it. And I told him I don't know, I hadn't given it much thought. So then he asked me: "What do you mean?" I said I hadn't been interviewed for any jobs for quite a while—three years or longer—and there were jobs opening up all over the place, you see, and I was just being passed over. If I had been given a good reason, well, then I would have been satisfied. But I'm not racially oriented as you might say, myself.

Paul Holmes was an eleven-year veteran who had been considered for a foreman's job several times, but was never chosen. The last time he was turned down because he was on the second shift and in management's view there would be no top- and middle-management people around to support him on that shift. He commented on the black man's opportunities for promotion:

> Well, frankly, up to a point I should say the opportunities have been fair. I would say—particularly being in the minority group—I don't think that they are anything as well as they should be. I feel that the Negro has to be about twice as good as the white person to get the same job. In many cases, he just doesn't get the job, period. Although he is better qualified.

BLACK FOREMEN

In January 1969 there were no black supervisors at GE–Lynchburg. One of the stated goals of the plant's Affirmative Action Plan was to have at least one black foreman by the end of 1969. (This goal was achieved.)

Most of the employees felt they could work well for a black foreman: 96 percent of the blacks and 77 percent of the whites. Significantly, 100 percent of the men, both black and white, felt favorably toward a black foreman.

There were some talented men in the Lynchburg plant who might well have proved to be good foremen. Middle managers said that most black prospects lacked education or experience. But as Melvin Warlick saw it, those explanations seemed invalid:

> Well, I know two fellows in particular that started about the same that I did, who moved into management several years before I was even considered for management. Incidentally, each of the fellows that was interviewed for this job as a foreman when I was interviewed for a foreman's job, have since become foremen.
>
> I have since got a promotion. But it's not direct responsibility over the people. Like when I was in manufacturing, I was working for a manager. He had told one of his white employees that they were opening up a new

job, and he told this employee that he would be given the job and he was interviewing people for his job. I had more seniority, more qualifications, more schooling, and everything of this nature, and so I went in and sat down and had a little talk with him. The first thing he said was "This man has been with the company longer than you have." I said, "Well, you get both of our folders on your desk in front of you," I said, "If you look you'll find that I have more time and grade."

So he looked at it and he said, "Okay, yeah, you've got six or eight months, that isn't a great deal." I said, "Okay," I said, "now how about qualifications, let's go back to that." So this man had only finished high school, and since I had come to work for the company I had completed technical school . . . and I had also taken company-sponsored courses here. So I sort of backed him into a wall on everything that he came up with. So he finally said, "Look, Melvin, let's face it, you just don't see Negroes supervising a bunch of white women."

Admittedly, the first black foreman would probably have to be more qualified than the average white foreman. Claude Proctor, himself a foreman, felt that any new foreman in an area had to establish credibility with his work group. For a black foreman, establishing credibility would be that much more difficult:

> Possibly people would be a little more prone to pick at—see flaws. You don't know how they're going to react to various things, you know. The foreman would be coming from outside the group, and he wouldn't have the credibility established. And trying to build this credibility if there was a flaw in the way he did it or if it were considerably different from the person ahead of him, he would meet an awful lot of opposition. Now, any new foreman when he walks into the area—you automatically see the opposition when you go in there and it's up to you to get around this. I think that the colored foreman will have more trouble getting around it. I think that that would be. Let's face it, the people feel that way, and it's up to the foreman and manager to dispel this feeling.

Most white workers in the plant seemed to feel that a few of their coworkers would have some initial difficulty accepting a black foreman, but they would eventually get used to it. The strongest personal reaction to the idea of a black foreman came from Suzannah Penton, who had never thought of it before and was a bit stunned:

CAVANAGH: I wonder what would happen if there were a colored foreman?

MRS. PENTON: Oh, I don't know. I hope that never happens! I don't know. I don't know how it would work. I never thought of that. You don't think there'd ever be one, do you? I don't believe there will. I don't know though.

CAVANAGH: How do you think the other girls in the group would feel about it?

MRS. PENTON: Well, I don't know, we had colored boys to work with us, and they do some testing and whatnot and everybody seems to get along very well. But I don't know how it would be if they got a foreman's job. I just don't know what they'd be like. I don't know. As long as I've been here, they're just testers and they have one that writes processes.

More typical of the white reaction to the idea of a black foreman was that of Shirley Haight. Before coming to General Electric she had prejudices against black people. But she had since become accustomed to working with them and felt that she would rapidly adapt to a black supervisor. In fact, a black might do even a better job than the whites:

> I don't think it would make any difference, I really don't. At one time I had feelings against the colored because of the way I was brought up. But since I've been working with them, it's a lot different. I don't think that having a colored foreman would make one bit of difference. I think he would show less partiality to the people too. I really do. I'm sure they have some intelligent fellows out there that could handle the job.

Just a few months after we left, Daryl Clinton, a black twenty-six-year-old technician who up to that time had not been interviewed for a foreman's job, but who had told us unequivocally, "I want to be a foreman in this plant," was promoted to foreman. He had joined the company on an entry-level job, and worked his way up to technician and process writer after intensive self-development. When Clinton was made foreman, some white women wanted to transfer out of his area. The company took the firm stand that that was not a sufficient reason for a transfer. In spite of threats, there were no resignations.

In addition, General Electric now has a small number of black college graduates who are trainees in its Manufacturing Administration Program. Several graduates have already been placed in responsible permanent positions.

EVALUATION

How shall we judge the sensitive area of promotion and upgrading for blacks and whites at GE–Lynchburg? Progress was slow in the early years of the plant in Lynchburg. Upgradings accelerated about 1965. But many blacks felt that their chances for upgrading were low and likely to be prevented by middle management. This frustration was especially true for older black men —the most critical of all our findings. Some of these men became bitter and discouraged, and ceased to try, or found their satisfactions away from the plant. Minority talent may have been wasted. On the other hand, we must admit that advancement plateaus in mid-careers also happen with white men.

Another factor working against advancement was the fact that blacks got less assistance from whites in learning their jobs than did the whites, who readily helped each other. (However, we did not notice any racial differential as to the amount of training given employees by the foreman.)

The year 1969 saw some improvements for blacks: About the same percentage of blacks (24 percent) received upgrades as whites (22 percent), even though blacks generally had less service. The major 1969 breakthrough of the first black foreman in the plant gives hope for the future. This was good, but slow in coming. As one black put it: "After twelve years!" Community housing and atmosphere will hinder bringing in many Negro professionals. It will take strong and continuing efforts to correct this imbalance.

HOW THE RACES WORK TOGETHER

The General Electric plant provided many of the citizens of Lynchburg with their first extended contact with members of another race. After the initial breakthroughs the strangeness and newness of working together wore off, and many of the superstitions that one race held for the other were dissipated. In this sense General Electric functioned as an integrator. Charles Seevers, twenty-eight-year-old electronic tester, compared the situation at General Electric with his first contact with Negroes in the military service:

> I mean, I never was around any Negro people until I went in the service. I didn't know what they were like and I was kind of scared to associate with them. I got over that real quick. Some of my best friends were Negro people. I expect you hear some people like I was that haven't had the chance to be around them and just reject them maybe. I don't know, it seems all of us back there working together—we're pretty aware of the situation. So we don't throw anything up against each other.

A twenty-five-year-old white utility man in one of the larger integrated labs who had not been in the military was more surprised when asked how the races got along at General Electric. "Pretty good. Better than I thought they would. Look like everybody get along good." A ten-year veteran at the plant, Grace Millmore, was also pleasantly surprised. Mrs. Millmore worked closely with other women on a conveyor line in a large but quiet assembly area: "When they first came in, I maybe felt a little funny about it. But as the colored come in an they're friendly and nice—they're not bigoted—they're easy to get along with. Well, you don't hear anything, and we just go right along together."

Madeleine Anderson, an older black woman, had her own booth to assemble materials but she was close enough to the girls around her to talk and become friends. She told of some of the misconceptions she held about whites that had been broken down by working together with them at General Electric:

MRS. ANDERSON: When you work with a friend, you find out you learn more about each other. And I think you learn to understand each other better.

CAVANAGH: What would you say you've learned?

MRS. ANDERSON: I have learned that they really aren't as selfish as maybe I had thought they were. And that all of them really didn't feel towards Negroes the way I had thought they did. It makes you feel better that you have been wrong, and I'm hoping they have found the same thing about us. I was happy to find out that I was wrong, and I found it out for myself just from working with them.

Assembler Shirley Haight, twenty-nine, told about the change that took place in the attitude of one black girl who came into her group. After a disagreement:

> My foreman came to me and wanted to know what it was all about. He finally straightened it all out. She was a very bitter person, and now she's one of the sweetest people you'd want to meet, rilly. But at first, when she came to work here, she was real bitter.

The great majority (see Table 5-7) of the employees and all the foremen interviewed felt that blacks and whites got along well at the GE–Lynchburg plant, at least while they were on the job.

Table 5-7. Perception of Black-White Relations on the Job
White hourly, black hourly, black salaried, and foremen
GE–Lynchburg

	Hourly Black	Salaried Black	Hourly White	Foremen
Favorable	87%	85%	96%	100%
Uncertain	7	0	4	0
Unfavorable	6	15	0	0

One of the first Negro women hired at General Electric, Dora Arnolds, felt very strongly that the company had been instrumental in changing race relations and attitudes in Lynchburg from what they were previously:

MRS. ARNOLDS: I think this company has done more to improve the relations in this community than any other company. I really feel this way. I think it's opened up more jobs in even downtown, and places like that.

CAVANAGH: How has the company done that, do you think?

MRS. ARNOLDS: Well, I think, before that, in a lot of industries that they had here, they didn't have very many Negroes in the type of work that we're doin' *together*. They had different type jobs, little separate jobs that they done.

> And I think since we've come here, they've learned to live together and to work together. And I think a lot of thoughts and superstitions, after they've come to work together, they just realize that this is not true. It's gotten around to other different companies, and I think they see that people can live and work together.

Wynell Bennett, who as a test specialist occasionally directed white employees in their work, felt that the company was neutral ground where personal prejudices were set aside:

> Here at General Electric, the people seem to me a little bit more mature than they are at some places. Although they may not like for you to tell them to do something, they are responsible people and they'll go ahead and do it. They sort of leave their personal likes and dislikes outside in most cases. And this plant here, whether they realize it or not, this plant has done a great deal toward helping white and coloreds understand each other.

Paula Crawford, a Negro contract specialist at General Electric, said: "Here I don't even know that I belong to a race, you know. I'm just a person." Randall Chafee, foreman, spoke of the girls he supervised on the conveyor—a work station that requires close contact with other assemblers: "If you couldn't see 'em and just listened to what went on out there, you would never know there was any difference at all." David Slater, a counselor at the Lynchburg plant, told of an instance when white women even went against a white co-worker who had insulted a Negro man: "But the thing that I was pleased to see was that other white women in the area were equally upset by the remarks and quickly came to his defense, you know, and came up to talk to me about it."

Employees also felt that their foremen treated blacks and whites fairly. No whites said that blacks received preferential treatment from the foreman and very few of the blacks thought their boss discriminated.

In the early years, the relationship between the races was not as amiable. The same Wynell Bennett, who felt there was not much personal prejudice in the company, told of how he was harassed by the white employees back in 1961:

> I worked on the bench there and they'd all gang up about, say six or seven of them, would come, they'd walk around. All of a sudden, they'd let out with a big "Hee HAW!".... I never even mentioned it to the supervisor, I just keep right on working. But you see what they didn't realize that I had been around and experienced at the very thing. They wanted me to explode, you see, so I just kept working, but after a year or so when they saw that I wasn't going to get rattled they stopped.

There were still instances of harassment in a generally friendly plant. When asked how blacks got along with the whites in their work group a perceptive and successful Lynchburg-born foreman, Ken Drumlin, said:

> They get along well. They're most likable, most of 'em. Mingle well—no problem there. And most friendly and cooperative, the ones I've had. In fact, sometimes the aggressiveness of their white counterparts will cause conflicts that they would never get into.

Walter Moses encountered this harassment when he moved into the salaried ranks:

> The other technicians were hangin' their coats up, and there was nothin' said, so I started hangin' my coat there. All of a sudden, one day, I came in and found this big note. "No factory workers' coats in the office." I didn't say anything, I just kept hangin' my coat there, because there was no signature on the note, so I couldn't question it. So one day I came in after lunch, and all the hangers were gone except the ones that had coats on them, so I simply reached into the manager's office and took an excess hanger off his rack, and hung my coat up. When I came back at four o'clock, I found my coat layin' in the corner on a box. So I marched around to Personnel. I said, this is the end. To avoid anyone gettin' hurt for puttin' hands on my personal property, I'll bring it to you. So that was the last I heard of that. I continued to hang my coat in the office.

These instances of harassment occurred particularly when a change of some sort was made. And it was not uncommon for white employees to request a transfer to avoid working with Negroes for the first time or to avoid taking directions from a Negro. But once the stand was taken, the work force seemed to adapt quite readily. Outside of these few incidents, the work relationship between black and white employees at General Electric appeared smooth and amiable.

Our finding that white workers at Lynchburg were quite tolerant of Negroes was further supported by factor analysis. Nine employee attitudes about interracial relations, including the acceptance of blacks as good co-workers and as possible supervisors, formed one "factor." With a scale from 1 (very unfavorable) to 5 (very favorable), white hourly employees at Lynchburg averaged 4.0, a very high score. It is not surprising that black employees, with a score of 4.4, were significantly more favorable to blacks. These findings indicate that white employees at Lynchburg are quite open toward working with blacks. Nevertheless, race remains a factor influencing perceptions and feelings.

BLACKS AND WHITES AT BREAKS AND LUNCH

While people had learned over the years to socialize easily in integrated work areas, blacks and whites still tended to separate at breaks and lunch. Less than one-third of the hourly employees, black or white, said that people of different races socialized on their own time in the plant—in the cafeterias, at lunch, or on breaks. However, both blacks and whites participated in the GEERA (General Electric Employees' Recreation Association) picnics, bowling, and basketball activities.

Thomas Hall, an employee relations manager quoted earlier, estimated attitudes that were very close to what we found: "I think 99 percent accept the day-to-day working relationship very well. But in social relationships, even as simple as going to a break together or having lunch together, and so on, the walls tend to rise in a hurry." Separation of the races in the cafeteria was common. It was an exception to see whites and blacks eating together, although this did occur on occasion. One of the authors received long stares from whites when he had lunch with hourly employee Shipp Buford and some of his black friends. Shipp Buford commented on his experience in the GE cafeteria: "I would be sittin' at the table all by myself and the resta the cafeteria's full. Some woman come down, standin' at the table lookin' all around for a place to eat at this great long table, an' she won't sit down." Salaried blacks may be more sensitive to this sort of think since they mentioned it more often: "Maybe you and two other fellows on the other side of the table, and then I come sit there, and then they move." Or, another: "You sit down and somebody pops up and moves, you know."

It seemed strange that people got along so well on the job at one moment and the next moment they were like strangers. Said Daryl Clinton:

> That's a funny thing; you see people laughing and talking and joking around the area. But when they go to the cafeteria, you'll see a group of people here, and then a group of people there, and they act like they don't know each other.

Clinton felt that the Negroes tended to eat apart because they were afraid they might be embarrassed by the whites and they felt more at ease with their own people, and that whites did not socialize with blacks from fear of what their friends would say. No one wanted to pioneer in interracial socializing.

A thirty-four-year-old black assembler on third shift, Irene Brewer, described that kind of harassment when asked if blacks and whites ate together in the cafeteria: "We don't rilly. But now we've got this one white girl that sits at the table with us. I was trainin' this girl. She's new. And they talk about her like a dog because she sat with us. Rilly, they do."

Separation has also continued to be observed by the employees at social events. Melvin Warlick, a ten-year veteran, a salaried black man, told of one such instance several years ago:

> As far as the relations go with the people at work and right at the stations, I would say it's fair. It's okay. Other than that I don't think it's real good. Like if they have a Christmas party or something for the area. Maybe the people in the area will get together and exclude the Negroes. In engineering it's a little better. Course we had the occasion there where they had a picnic and Paul Holmes [a black technician] put his name down. You know, they send a slip around. So they decided that, well, now we feel like—we work with Paul; we know Paul's okay and this and that—but we are afraid that the other people there might

> dislike it and there might be an incident. So they didn't want to go along with the picnic.
>
> At which point Paul wrote them a letter and told them that he would take his name off. I think he also sent a letter to Mr. Hall who told him that this sort of thing couldn't continue in the plant. He took the position that if the picnic was given, and if it was a company picnic, then Paul couldn't take his name off. He could, he *should* go. But I think the picnic folded and they didn't have it.

Forty-four-year-old assembler Linda Newell became good friends with a Negro girl with whom she worked at General Electric, but she too balked at the idea of what the neighbors might feel if her friend were to pay her a social visit at her home:

> I mean I would try to make her welcome. I don't believe in just you know, social visits, just going to her house just to be going to her house, or her coming to mine just to be coming. What I mean, I think you can get too close. Really I do. But as far as treating her nice if she were to come to my house, I'd be just as nice to her as I could. Course, I might feel a little funny you know, the neighbors see it. Not that, I don't mean that like it sound. But I mean as a social visit I would feel funny. You know because you just don't, that just don't happen, that I know of. Not here.

Much of the white's resistance to integrated socializing was based on his fear of interracial marriages. Said Valerie Ford, a native Virginian who had managed to accept many changes that had occurred in race relations since her youth:

> So far it seems like everyone has taken it as it comes, without too much of an argument about it. I don't know, myself, along with most everybody else, hate to see their children going to school with colored people. But, I don't think we should teach our children to look down on them, to work with them. I don't believe in mixed marriages or anything like that and I make that plain. I've got a little girl in the fourth grade now and I got two little girls that will be going to school and I try to talk to them about it. But I don't know how it will be when they do go into school.

MANAGEMENT ECOLOGY AND THE LYNCHBURG COMMUNITY

We have seen something of GE's policies and practices regarding race relations inside its plant gates. We have tried to understand the perceptions and emotions of the black and white employees toward those practices. Now we ask how management in the Lynchburg plant dealt with those issues outside its plant gates.

The business corporation of the 1970s is being called upon to deal in new and responsible ways with the people and institutions of its environment. This is especially true for the largest employer in a small or middle-sized city. Witness the case of Eastman Kodak's dispute in Rochester with the black coalition group FIGHT. These problems, if anything, become more complex when a national management with a northern background enters a southern community that welcomes jobs and prosperity but not outsiders' influence on its settled customs. Management will need to steer a balanced course between the company-store, company-town end of the spectrum and the corporate absentee-unconcerned stockholder end of the spectrum.

It is evident that General Electric has a stake in the Lynchburg community, in its peace and prosperity, if the company is to operate successfully. Managers are citizens of the city the same as anyone else. In a very analogous sense the corporation itself might be called a "citizen." At least it is an institution of major influence. GE management is concerned, of course, with the total community, white as well as black. But the focus of this section is on the black community.

THE BLACK COMMUNITY

There were about 11,000 black people in the city of Lynchburg and many blacks in the rural towns, hamlets, and farmland of the surrounding counties. Some blacks lived in poorer housing in the hilly, inner-city district; other in outlying sections of the city. In any case, unlike northern cities, the black communities and the white communities were often intermixed. There was not the strict geographical segregation as in Chicago, although blacks tended to be only on certain streets or one side of a street. Lynchburg had many poor blacks and some poor whites. There were also some middle-class, professional, and upper-class blacks in the city. The black community was not united and there were many different factions within it. There was no local chapter of the SCLC, CORE, or the Urban League. Some people said that the local chapter of the NAACP was an ineffective organization and not very militant; others saw NAACP as active, at least in integrating the schools. The new Black Lynchburg Action Council, BLAC, now claims to speak for the entire black community of Lynchburg.

During the 1970 campaign for City Council the black Lynchburg Voter's League endorsed four candidates—two blacks and two whites—who ran very well in the black precincts, indicating successful community cooperation. The two whites were elected. Equally important, a third black candidate was elected to the City Council, with substantial support from both blacks and whites. Mr. C. W. Seay, principal of Dunbar High School for many years and presently assistant professor of education at Lynchburg College, was the first Negro to be elected to the City Council. The newly elected mayor and vice mayor were a bit more liberal in outlook than the overall Council.

Black-white relations in Lynchburg seemed to be peaceful. There was resentment, however, beneath the surface and much will depend in the years to come on the leadership of both sides. In 1968 when Martin Luther King, Jr., was assassinated, black-white relations came to a boil. GE black employee, Henry Boyd, told how he took pistols from six armed Negro militants in the General Electric plant, right after the assassination of Dr. King:

> I took six pistols from six different Negroes in this plant because they had come in here hot as hell. . . . There was much talk that this plant won't be here tomorrow and this type of thing. And I don't agree with this. So I walked out of here with six pistols in my pockets. I know that the guard's going to catch me—no, he didn't catch me! And I carried them on out. And I put them in the trunk of my car and gave them back to them about a week or two later. They were mad as hell. They played the radio when the Kennedys were shot. But—they killed Martin Luther King—so what, this isn't important enough to turn the radio on. There were whites that complained about the fact that GE was flying the flag at half-mast when Martin Luther King was killed—openly complained. This is the type of situation that was here. And it was hot. It was boiling.

On the other hand, GE Manager David Slater said that he had been told that there was some militancy among the blacks at Lynchburg, but from what he had seen most of the Negroes were against it:

> Well, we are told by some Negroes that they [militants] exist. But they have not been able to get enough to side with them. And so we have not had any race problems here as such. We have not had any marches. We have not had anything of this nature. Most Negroes that I've talked with—that we have at GE—are frankly against it.

Both black and white young people were tending to leave Lynchburg, not to return. This was not primarily a racial question, but it had serious implications for the leadership of the divided black community. In 1967 Milles E. Godwin, Jr., governor of Virginia, said: "All too many of these young people have been leaving their home communities . . . to find more challenging environments, more job opportunities, more education." Godwin called this exodus "tragic," especially since it was going on at a time when, he said, Virginia was "making progress as never before in history."[3]

The Lynchburg College Research Center made a study of Dunbar High School students to discern why blacks were leaving the city. The reason given most frequently for the girls was to attend college, and for the men, to enter military service. The third reason was better job opportunities elsewhere. None of the students mentioned racism, or lack of recreational opportunities in Lynchburg, or marriage. The minority who intended to stay did not give many clear reasons for staying.

[3] *The News*, November 2, 1967, Lynchburg, Virginia.

A young senior in an Ivy League college, James Chamberlain, described his reasons for not coming back to Lynchburg:

> But I really couldn't see living here my whole life. I just couldn't see it. Well, socially and any other way. There's nobody to jam with. There are not too many cultural facilities and activities—you know, Fine Arts Theatre, well, you'd dig that. Personally, I don't think I could live permanently in a town under 500,000 to get everything I wanted out of life. . . .

Chamberlain also found the racial situation in Lynchburg oppressive: "Well, you don't have to leave Lynchburg to see racial attitudes. Conservative. I'd say most of the young people in Lynchburg—most people even though they haven't left—know that they don't want to live in Lynchburg. . . ." Chamberlain did not want to go back but feared the loss of leadership that he felt the black community would suffer:

> So few black kids who are in college want to come back here to live. You'd think in a couple of years, you'd just have a bunch of really old, bourgeois, mindless people in the black community and then you'll have a lot of just deprived people, but no real leaders. . . . It will be terrible really. There's no reason for a kid to come back here.

Garfield Corcoran, another black senior in an Ivy League college, was being considered for a position at GE. He talked about the community to which he might return:

CORCORAN: The problem as I see it is . . . a clash, a conflict between the middle-class blacks and the masses of blacks. When there is an effort to get the two together, the educated black has to be the leader. But as a result of the history of the conflict, the masses reject him automatically. . . . He has been Tomming too long with the white men. Although in some instances the masses of blacks are unjust in their accusations and their beliefs. Lynchburg has no [dominant] black spokesman. Now the only hope I see is for individuals like myself who go away and get an education to come back. Because the whole black community knows me, knows about everybody I graduated with. And they know exactly where I came from, how I grew up, my move from poverty to middle class, I guess you would call it. And I think only we would be able to provide the necessary leadership for Lynchburg. I don't know how many black students are interested in coming back. . . .

PURCELL: But that's a tragedy if they are losing all their black leaders.

CORCORAN: Yeah, but . . . what's going to happen to guys like the black individuals who don't want to come back? They're going to realize that the northern area, and the West Coast aren't the Valhalla that they were thinking about. . . . I'm in favor myself of coming back to Lynchburg . . . I've got high hopes about the possibilities of Lynchburg . . . I still think I could come back to Lynchburg and fight.

Many small cities, in the North as well as in the South, lose their young people who think that the larger city offers more opportunity or more excitement. They may well discover, as Corcoran said, that large cities are no "Valhalla." And as job opportunities grow in Lynchburg and as the general prosperity of the area develops, it is possible that more cultural opportunities will come about. But both black and white communities will need to find ways of holding their young people and getting them to return to provide leadership for the city.

We turn now to General Electric's involvement in several community issues which affected black employees and residents.

THE NEWSPAPER

Lynchburg has two newspapers, *The News* and *The Daily Advance*, both owned and operated by the same company. The two papers, termed by *Newsweek* are "shrill organs of archconservatism,"[4] were opposed to federal government intervention, liberalism, and the equality of the races. They deplored such things as social security, graduated income tax, and unemployment compensation. According to Dr. Nicholas Berry, formerly a professor at Lynchburg College:

> [The newspapers] tidy up their racism in verbiage and call it "race preference." They praise law and order and then attack our national government with the harshest language; they praise God and then condemn ministers who speak out, as Jesus did, on social affairs; they laud the value of education and lump college professors together under the "socialist-communist" label.[5]

The papers were founded by Carter Glass before the turn of the century. Carter Glass was Secretary of the Treasury under Wilson, one of the framers of the Federal Reserve System, and a Senator from the state of Virginia. Gunnar Myrdal quotes a strong racist statement from Glass in 1929. We print this statement simply to illustrate how far we have come in interracial attitudes in the last forth years:

> The people of the original 13 Southern States curse and spit upon the Fifteenth Amendment—and have no intention of letting the Negro vote. We obey the letter of the amendments and the Federal Statutes, but we frankly evade the spirit thereof—and propose to continue doing so. White supremacy is too precious a thing to surrender for the sake of a theoretical justice that would let a brutish African deem himself the equal of white men and women in Dixie.[6]

[4] *Newsweek*, May 8, 1967, p. 88.

[5] "Politics in Lynchburg," from *Ecco*, Summer 1968, p. 2, *Ecco* is a student-edited newsletter from Lynchburg College.

[6] Gunnar Myrdal, *An American Dilemma* (New York: McGraw-Hill, 1964), p. ccxviii. Compare Glass' words to the program of the Ku Klux Klan "for uniting native born white Christians for concerted action in preservation of American institutions and the supremacy of the white race." *Report of the National Advisory Commission on Civil Disorders* (New York: E. P. Dutton, 1968), p. 219.

Carter Glass, III, was the general manager of the two newspapers at the time of this research. Until recently, *The News* and *The Daily Advance* required Negroes to run obituaries as paid classified advertisements, whereas whites were given free obituaries. Marriages were listed separately for Negro and white. All Negroes were specifically referred to as Negroes, such as, "John Jones, Negro, was arrested." If a black committed a crime, it was usually printed in a prominent position, but a favorable item about a black was often buried.

Many citizens have echoed a Lynchburg department store executive, Harold G. Legget, when he said: "I don't think there's a human being with a mind who agrees with [Carter Glass'] position on race or almost anything else."[7] In spite of Mr. Legget's statement however, the consensus seemed to be that the newspapers had considerable influence on the attitudes of many Lynchburg people. One of the GE employee relations managers, Edward Loder, when asked about the newspapers' influence, said:

> I would say that the newspaper is very, very important. And I won't recount the problems we've had with the newspaper.... The open letter, the Dunbar incident, and the refusal to publish anything of achievement that they had accomplished. And I think that this is one of our big stumbling blocks now.

We do not wish to exaggerate the importance of the newspaper regarding race relations. WLVA Radio and TV have been moderating influences. At the same time, the newspaper has been a thorn in the sides of many.

In April 1967 seventy-one of the city's most prominent citizens, including Richard P. Gifford, then general manager of GE's Lynchburg-based Communications Products Department, and Robert C. Mark, manager of employee and community relations at GE's Lynchburg plant, sent an open letter to the people of Lynchburg. The letter deplored subjecting Negroes to 'repeated indignities" by the papers and accused the papers of contributing to the "frustration and bitterness" that is developing in the Negro community.[8] In an editorial appearing a week later in both papers, Glass denounced the letter as "scurrilous" and its seventy-one leading-citizen signers as "frightened dupes." But eventually the papers relented to the extent of printing some news about black Dunbar High School and an occasional integrated photograph.

These and other past pressures have apparently borne some fruit. After a reorganization, Carter Glass resigned as editorial director in 1969, to continue only in the background as secretary-treasurer of the corporations operating the newspapers. The papers are now printing black obituaries and more news about black citizens and their accomplishments. While they are still conservative and biased, there has been tangible improvement.

[7] *Newsweek*, May 8, 1967, p. 88.
[8] *New York Times*, April 23, 1967, p. 45. See also, *Time*, May 5, 1967, p. 78; *Life*, May 12, 1967, p. 4.

THE SCHOOLS

Lynchburg, like most southern towns, resisted integrating its public schools. Freedom of choice—allowing voluntary transfers to white (or black) schools—was the method chosen for eliminating segregation. The grammar schools were still largely *de facto* segregated in 1970. A movement on the part of the national NAACP for busing so that there would be 30 percent blacks in all elementary schools received insufficient support from either the black or white communities. Freedom of choice enrollment for high school students began in 1961. Some blacks were eager to move the children to the white high school. According to Ella Walker, GE assembly worker:

> Years ago, you know, our schools weren't like your schools, so therefore you shouldn't expect me to know what you know. I mean, it's a fact. A lot of people don't want to own up to it, you see. I know, 'cause I put my daughter in the white school here in junior high. And my two boys graduated from Dunbar. And now she's a senior at E. C. Glass. Well, I know the difference in her work. And I know how much more she knows than they do, the two boys.

But others were reluctant to move because they wanted to keep the values, unity, and support they had from their own school. Like black separatists in the North, they were caught between the benefits of integration and the value of separate identity.

By the late 1960s, 200 blacks had transferred to E. C. Glass and it was no longer feasible to maintain Dunbar for the 400 who remained. Mr. Gifford, GE's top executive, was vice chairman of the school board and worked toward solving the problem of integrated education. He said:

> Frankly, we have a real tough challenge. I don't think we can run the type of school which you could have pride in, if we continue it [Dunbar]. At the same time we've got to solve the problem of how to keep from losing pride in moving into a big school. So I said, "Let's see if we can't find a solution. Let's search for some things that could be maintained in an integrated situation, and maintain two choruses, two drama societies, even for a while. And let time erode these things."

> Provide an area for a Negro to be a Negro in among his own group if he wants, and have leadership in that particular group. Or if he wants to try for leadership among other groups, still provide opportunities there. We're going to have to find, somehow, a method of providing a path for maintaining and building pride, and at the same time providing a path for moving ultimately to a totally colorless society.

Finally ninth and tenth graders of both races were assigned to Dunbar and eleventh and twelfth graders attended Glass.

The new arrangement seemed to be working out well. General Electric's Robert C. Mark led the Mayor's committee in obtaining a Community College in Lynchburg and later served as chairman of the board of Central

Virginia Community College. GE management evidently saw the need and the opportunity for contributing toward building an integrated and improved educational system in Lynchburg.

THE HOUSING ISSUE

Housing for blacks in Lynchburg and also out in the counties tended to be segregated and often quite poor. Some black school teachers, doctors, and professional people lived in excellent homes but on segregated streets. Housing for the poorer blacks was often substandard, according to community leader Ronald Carter:

> I've seen people show me where they passed a housing code. They'll put a bathtub on the back porch. On the back porch they'll put some planks over and you can see cracks in there that wide. You've got a bathroom there with a bathtub and water. And you know, in ten-degree weather you take a bath in that and you are dead, man. . . . I have some statistics that over one-third of the housing in Lynchburg is substandard.

Haywood Robinson, Jr., Negro minister and executive director of the federally financed Community Action Group, said that housing is the most "visible" problem facing the community. Robinson challenged the City Council of Lynchburg to lead the way in finding a solution to that problem.[9]

Some progress may come from the newly established Redevelopment and Housing Authority, which is an independent agency separated from the City Council. A number of General Electric managers spoke before the City Council on behalf of the Authority. They were also involved with a housing group trying to improve the inner city housing.

The central housing problem directly affecting General Electric was finding housing for the black middle managers the company would like to promote or bring into the city. Thomas Hall of General Electric commented on the problem of attracting young Negro professionals to work in Lynchburg when they had options available elsewhere:

> I think a guy looks at the whole spectrum and he says: "Well, on the West Coast they're pretty liberal and I could live in a community that would let my kids associate with other professionals, be they black or white. And at least decent housing, maybe working and living within a framework of a professional black community anyway." And as they contrast that with things back here . . . they say: "Why fight it?"

Ten years ago the problem was much worse. Wynell Bennett, a black technician who moved to Lynchburg at that time, described the difficulties he had then in getting adequate housing:

> However, I must agree though that housing, decent housing, is a problem here. Because when I came from Norfolk I had to live in a house,

[9] *The Daily Advance*, August 2, 1969.

they've torn it down now, but it was the only thing I could find. I could actually see the sun rise through the floor in the morning and that was the only place I could get. And I was willing to pay, but there just wasn't any housing available at the time. But things have changed somewhat now.

How much corporate responsibility does General Electric have to push for housing improvements? Melvin Warlick felt that General Electric could break down the problem of housing and the segregation in the city if it really wanted to:

> I'll tell you what GE could probably do to help the community, and that is in the housing situation. They could find housing for them if they really tried to, but they would be in white communities. The housing in the Negro communities are pitiful.
>
> And the people who could come in and earn a salary commensurate with them moving into a good neighborhood—some of the people have come —and they have found housing very hard to obtain. They might get an apartment with somebody, or living with somebody, or I think they've got two apartment houses here for Negroes, exclusively. I think if GE really encouraged it, that they could probably move in with minimal effort.

Prior to, but especially since, Warlick's comment, General Electric has done much, perhaps more than any other company in the city, to open up new and better rental housing for professional blacks. In 1969 General Electric managed to help integrate four excellent apartment and town house complexes for its professional employees without incident. For a black to purchase a private house in a white neighborhood was still a problem in 1970. As GE executive Edward Cummings put it, "I've been pushing the real estate people trying to find ways to break that [the issue of housing for young professionals]! And there are some very cooperative members in real estate working on it."

CUMMINGS: At the moment all we can get is an apartment in the white community. They can get that. But they can't get let's say a $25,000 home in the white community. This is not yet possible. Usually they end up in some rural setup.

PURCELL: What if someone were to sell a house, which they could do legally?

CUMMINGS: I don't think there'll be as much problem as the older residents of the community would predict and might want to foment; ... generally they'll be moving into a young community. The young community is a much more mentally desegregated community.

PURCELL: Do you think there would be threats?

CUMMINGS: No, I don't think you would get physical threats or things like that in this community. . . . There's no legal problem about it. There's just a psychological problem. No, I think it would be just more through the press and so on.

THE 1969 COMMUNITY ACTION GROUP ISSUE

The Lynchburg Community Action Group, supported from federal funds, sponsored a program for underprivileged children at an abandoned local grammar school during the summer of 1969. The sanitary facilities in the dismantled rest rooms were inadequate, and an inspection by city authorities resulted in their closing the program "for sanitary reasons" on July 21, 1969. Members of the Negro community began a series of daily demonstrations with threats of worse (a sign, incidentally, of racial awakening in Lynchburg). The City Council sponsored a public forum to air black grievances at Dunbar High School on August 1, 1969. White supporters of the black demands at the meeting included GE's General Manager Richard P. Gifford. The City Council seemed reluctant to provide funds for sanitary facilities for the eighty children involved. Behind the scenes, GE offered some of its own funds to repair the building and enable the summer youth program to reopen. The City Council reconsidered and provided the necessary improvements itself, thus transforming the building into a very satisfactory community recreational center for the neighborhood families.

CONCLUSIONS

General Electric–Lynchburg opened its plant in 1956 on a nonsegregated basis. As a national firm, General Electric was in contact with the national winds of change—the incipient but growing governmental concern for fair employment. But perhaps more than anything, the leadership of its local management led it to make a voluntary decision to apply fair employment concepts in the South.

General Electric selected its first Negro applicants carefully, at least for jobs where management felt white resistance would be strong. Blacks were brought in despite some opposition, especially from white women. But actual white backlash was almost never so great as management anticipated. Harassment and prejudice were readily handled. Management stood firm behind its decisions and did not yield to white pressures. Employee relations managers felt strongly that this careful approach was necessary and was partly responsible for the success of the peaceful integration of its work force. Some blacks resented the fact that only the top level, the cream, of the black community was being hired. Progress for blacks has been rapid since 1965, doubtlessly influenced by the Civil Rights Act of the previous year and the changing American racial climate.

Blacks began at the bottom of the occupational ladder, and promotion, especially for black men, was slow at first. While most of the black employees were satisfied with their promotion chances, a number of the older black men felt blocked and extremely frustrated, although this was also probably true of some white men who had reached a plateau. Promotion was one of the prime problem areas. Advancement up the occupational ladder is coming at last and will be a challenge to GE for the 1970s. The promotion of blacks into supervision was long delayed, but a significant breakthrough came with the plant's first black foreman in 1969. Securing and advancing Negro technicians, engineers, and especially salesmen will be difficult, although four black professionals, including one field salesman, were hired in 1970. The professional area will continue to be a challenge. Housing and Lynchburg community atmosphere will need continuing improvement.

We learn from this story that management can successfully implement minority manpower policies, ahead of local customs, without creating serious friction between employees or with the community. General Electric might have been equally successful had it moved in 1960 as it did in 1968 and 1970—faster. Of course, between those years the national American climate changed, and so did federal law. With faster progress, valuable minority manpower and talents might have been more fully tapped.

As for the Lynchburg community, General Electric worked primarily through the leadership of its individual executives. Sometimes publicly, but more often privately, the executives used their influence to help Lynchburg overcome problems that might have made the city a difficult place for business to operate. Their leadership was liberal and progressive; indeed, they were called "nigger lovers" by some. Yet in a segregated city where management's social contacts are primarily with whites, or with the few blacks that have been accepted by the white community, there remains a constant need for understanding. Many blacks saw community problems touching themselves with a much greater sense of urgency than whites saw those problems. Expectations about the pace of change were often very different in the white and black communities. Blacks in Lynchburg, especially the young, shared the growing impatience of blacks nationally. We can hardly exaggerate the importance of this fact.

Could GE management have moved faster in the plant and in the community? Could it move faster today? The company's approach, while not aggressive enough in the authors' opinion, especially in advancing older black men into supervision and technical positions, seems to have been basically sound. This was borne out by our findings of unusual harmonious relations between whites and blacks while the black percentage in the plant more than doubled from 1965 to 1970.

During the 1970s other companies will move into the South for the first time or expand the southern plants they already have. Black neighborhoods in cities such as Lynchburg are cleaner and more of a community than Harlem or Hough. The same is true of white neighborhoods. Southern cities might help to relieve the impossible congestion of a New York or a Chicago if southern managements could deal creatively and firmly with racial relations, both inside and outside their plant gates. They have the opportunity to be the major agents of change in the South. Hopefully they may learn from this Lynchburg story.

CHAPTER SIX

Middle America and the blacks

The way I look at it today—I don't mean just the way the plant's run, but the way the whole country's run—they're discriminating against white people.
                                              Steven Grumbacher, white welder

This chapter tells the story of black and white working people and business managers in an average, middle-sized, northern city. Here are the ingredients.

Start with a manufacturing city of a half million or so people, a city with strong ethnic pockets. Bring in a major factory where a few blacks are employed from the start but do not gain many highly skilled jobs. Let the years roll on with some tranquillity and the factory's business be successful. Then add major changes: a threefold increase (since World War II) in the city's black population; the Civil Rights Act of 1964; growing black unrest that erupted in the 1967 riots; modest advances of black power in local city politics; and an increasing unrest among Middle American blue collar people from three predominant ethnic groups.

Suppose management finds it is not employing many blacks, at least in terms of the black percentage of the adjacent city. What is management's social responsibility in this case? Must it stage a balancing act between growing black demands for hiring and upgrading and latent ethnic resentments and fears? Is there a changing role for the local union? How do you carry out "affirmative action" in these circumstances? What should the black community itself do about its work opportunities?

This is the story of the huge Westinghouse plant in Buffalo, New York, its IUE Local 1581, and the white and black people who work there. The chapter is not dramatic and that is why it may be important, for there are many northern city plant situations like this one, and the absence of drama today does not preclude confrontation tomorrow. Further, a peaceful relationship, if it is dynamic and not static, may provide a solid base for improving, even rapidly, the working futures of both blacks and whites.

THE BUFFALO COMMUNITIES

Buffalo is the home of a wide variety of ethnic groups, and sometimes calls itself "The City of Good Neighbors." But Buffalo also shows the symptoms of the contemporary urban crisis. It lies on the shores of Lake Erie—a lake polluted by human and industrial waste—in western New York State. When the wind is southwesterly, the red dust from the Bethlehem Steel mills settles over the south side and central city. The city is undergoing rapid turnover as whites flee to the suburbs and leave the decaying central areas to the blacks. The suburbs, like suburbs anywhere, are sometimes unimaginatively close-packed, sometimes lush and beautiful.

Like most American cities, Buffalo was settled by European immigrants, many of whom were fleeing from religious and political persecution. The Irish, forced from their homeland by the potato famine of the 1840s, provided cheap labor for the construction of the Erie Canal. At about the same time, the Germans arrived. Since the Germans were mostly skilled craftsmen and artisans, they found good jobs. Around the turn of the century and into the twentieth century, Poles and Italians streamed into Buffalo. These new citizens were determined to guard and nurture their diverse national backgrounds. The result for Buffalo has been both rich variety and narrow chauvinism. Whenever one group brushed the shoulders of another in seeking employment and housing, conflict erupted. In the 1940s, antagonism between the German and Polish communities was so great that when the Poles went through the German neighborhoods to their jobs as laborers and unskilled factory workers, they needed to be escorted, so the story goes, by their Polish pastor, a certain Father Pitass.

Buffalo is unique among our four case studies in that ethnic identification is still a dominant political fact. Unlike Cicero, Illinois, where ethnic loyalties have diminished, Buffalo has retained the stable, closely knit, ethnic voting blocs that developed around the turn of the century.[1] Political power is still vested largely in the hands of the Italians and Poles who were traditionally excluded from the commercial and financial interests of the city. Richard Hannon, community organizer, disciple of Saul Alinsky, and staff director for the Buffalo ghetto organization, BUILD, says:

> Italians were forced by the Anglo-Saxons and the Irish into politics, organized crime, and food processing; once the Italians took control of these institutions in their own neighborhoods, they were able to move out into the suburbs.... The Poles, "further behind," are just now

[1] Lloyd Graham, *Buffalo: Metropolis of the Niagara Frontier* (Buffalo: Henry Stewart, Inc., 1967), p. 7.

using politics, union posts and lower level management jobs to move out in large numbers often to the suburban enclaves, such as Cheektowaga, outside Buffalo.[2]

In 1970 about 17 percent of the half million people in Buffalo were Negro, almost three times greater than their percentage at the end of World War II. Compared to the other ethnic groups, Negroes are relatively new to the city, since they first arrived in large numbers during the two world wars and the boom years of the early 1950s. Typical of any newly arrived immigrants, they had to compete for housing and jobs with the next most recently arrived groups, the Poles and the Italians.[3] Blacks are concentrated in three of the seventy-five census tracts in the city of Buffalo, where they constitute more than 80 percent of the population.[4] These areas have a 15 percent unemployment rate,[5] low median income, 30 percent dilapidated housing, and high crime and juvenile delinquency rates. In 1960, when blacks were only one in eight of the Buffalo population, one baby in four was black.

Blacks are now making a few political gains in Buffalo. Two black Democratic councilmen represent the black community. There are two black newspapers in Buffalo, *The Challenger* and the *Buffalo Criterion*. Dozens of community agencies are organized to fight the problems of unemployment, substandard housing, and poor education; among the latter are: Model Cities, Jobs Education and Training (JET), National Alliance of Businessmen (NAB), Concentrated Employment Program (CEP), and BUILD.

When the Irish and Germans and Poles look at these agencies working largely for the black poor, they are likely to point out that no one set up job training centers for them when they came to America as unskilled immigrants. For instance, no organizations helped the Italians to fight slumlords and secure better housing for their families. There were no industries in those days to help them secure better jobs and working conditions. But the ethnic groups often forget that they did not have the problem of being black skinned as well.

In his study of the origins of the 1967 Buffalo riots, Frank Besag says:

> There are almost certainly individuals in Buffalo of Polish birth who remember living, quite literally, in a barracks because no other housing was available to them. There are men of Polish birth who remember that they were employed because they were willing to work for less than the Germans, and who see or feel the threat of the Negro quite clearly.[6]

[2] Richard Hannon, "Split-Level Casbah" (unpublished paper, February 15, 1969), p. 34.
[3] Frank P. Besag, *Anatomy of a Riot: Buffalo '67* (Buffalo: State University Press, 1967), p. 7.
[4] *Tract Facts for the Buffalo Area* (Buffalo: Community Welfare Council of Buffalo and Erie County, 1964), p. 10.
[5] *Ibid.*, pp. 33, 34. The figures are averages for the three tracts.
[6] Besag, *op. cit.*, p. 8.

Ethnic resentment, however, is not a recent development in Buffalo. In 1863 the city experienced small-scale riots due to a combination of hostility to the Civil War and fear that Negroes would take white jobs.[7] At that time, it was the Irish who lived in the worst slums, and the prospect of the end of slavery merely sharpened the fear that Negroes, by providing cheaper labor than the Irish, would steal from the Irish the few economic gains they had made. Fears, protests, demonstrations, and even riots are not new to the American scene or to Buffalo.

Sociologist Besag paints a rather gloomy picture after the Buffalo riots of 1967:

> A basic problem seems to be that no one is listening to anyone else.... No one seemed to listen when [the blacks] tried to explain about the conditions.... There seemed no way to communicate with the power structure except through some extreme means....
>
> However, not only the Negro community remains unlistened to. The Caucasians, who express bigotry, are in reality expressing more than a dislike of Negroes. More significantly, they are expressing a fear of losing their status in life to another group....
>
> If significant positive communication does not increase [as one of his riot interviewees said]: "The real happenings haven't begun yet."[8]

This is meant to be a "listening chapter," listening to old as well as young, whites as well as blacks, foremen as well as workers, unionists as well as managers.

The Westinghouse white and black employees, who together number around 6,300, are a kind of microcosm of the city as a whole. Sixty percent of the hourly whites lived in suburbs and towns around the plant. Another third lived within the city of Buffalo but close to its borders, away from the central city ghetto. Sixty percent of the Negro hourly workers lived in two of the black central city areas, with an additional 20 percent in three adjacent neighborhoods.

According to thirty-four-year-old skilled wireman James Turesky, the failure of the melting pot leaves ethnic resentments in plant and city alike:

> In this plant, in this community, the ethnic feeling is very, very strong. You have the—if I might use the derogatory language—you have the Dago, the Polack, the Mick, the Nigger, I'm not going to pull any wool over nobody's eyes on that; this is definitely very strong. And you're going to have this coming out in our fall elections this year. You're going to have a racial backlash.
>
> Here in Buffalo, the majority of the registered voters are Polish. We're down to four hundred-some-thousand people. We're having a mass

---
[7] *Report of the National Advisory Commission on Civil Disorders, op. cit.*, p. 212.
[8] Besag, *op. cit.*, p. 83.

exodus into the suburbs, which is common in every city. But still the majority of the voters is Polish. Number two is the Negro, see? So you're going to have this friction. You're going to have this white backlash.

Community leaders for some time have been trying to join forces to promote understanding and reduce tensions. Westinghouse sees that it also shares that responsibility. It must deal with the traditional ethnic communities that are still the backbone of the plant. But management must also deal with the growing black community in an attempt to help bring about a solution to the urban crisis.

THE PEOPLE WHO MAKE THE MOTORS

The Westinghouse–Buffalo Electric plant is in Cheektowaga, a suburb bordering the city. Curtiss-Wright built and operated the plant during World War II for the production of tens of thousands of B-40 fighter planes and C-46 cargo planes.[9] As in Chicago, Cleveland, and Detroit, the aircraft plant was built right next to the municipal airport, so that as the planes came off the assembly line they could be wheeled onto the airfield and flown away.

A few months after the end of the war, Westinghouse purchased the plant and moved its Medium and Large Motor Division from East Pittsburgh to Buffalo. In 1948 the Industrial Control Division also moved from East Pittsburgh. The company brought along some of its own skilled people from East Pittsburgh, and also hired many of the old Curtiss-Wright employees.

In addition to large and small motors, the workers make a wide range of industrial equipment from controls for machine tools to complete systems to monitor and regulate the production of a hot strip steel mill. Most employees work at individual jobs not paced by assembly lines. Their pay is equal to or greater than most of the area firms, although perhaps slightly lower than the two other major factories: Bethlehem Steel and Chevrolet. Work at Westinghouse, however, is felt to be better—not so heavy, noisy or tiring.

As a division headquarters plant, Westinghouse–Buffalo has a heavy complement of engineering and technical professionals. Indeed, one-third of its employees are white collar.

Who are the Westinghouse factory workers? If we go by race and age, they fall into four groups: many older whites, a handful of older blacks, a small number of young whites, a handful of young blacks. Table 6-1 shows that nearly one-half the blacks had been at Westinghouse–Buffalo from its first days. In contrast to the other plants studied, the proportion of blacks and whites with high seniority was about equal, although this will change as more

[9] Graham, *op. cit.*, p. 113.

Table 6–1. Profile of the Hourly Workers Westinghouse–Buffalo, 1969*

	Black	White
Age		
29 and under	19%	17%
30–39	17	13
40–49	35	37
50–59	26	27
60 and over	3	7
Average age	42 years	43 years
Education (highest grade completed)		
Some college	3%	0%
High school graduate	35	53
High school 3 & 4	27	7
High school 1 & 2	18	24
8 grades or less	16	17
Average grades completed	10.7 grades	10.5 grades
Birthplace		
Middle South	6%	0%
Deep South	55	0
Northeast	32	96
North Central	7	0
Outside of U.S.	0	4
Residence		
City	90%	40%
Suburb	0	49
Outlying	10	10
Skill level		
Craftsman	6%	10%
Operative	74	90
Laborer	19	0
Shift worked		
Day	50%	60%
Evening	43	33
Night	6	7
Date hired		
1948–1949	48%	48%
1950–1959	9	13
1960–1964	9	12
1965–1966	13	20
1967	0	0
1968	0	3
1969	21	3
Average years of service	13 years	13 years

* The profile and attitude tables in this chapter are weighted projections from the random sample.

blacks are hired. Similarly, the age range for blacks and for whites was not very different. Almost two-thirds of the blacks and slightly more than two-thirds of the whites were over forty years old. About three-quarters of the employees were men—a significant factor since we are particularly concerned about jobs for black men.

Looking again at Table 6-1, we find two expected differences between the races. More than one-half of the blacks were born in the South, although a significant 39 percent were born in the North. As already noted, blacks came from the inner city, while 60 percent of the whites came from the suburbs or rural districts near the plant.

There were moderate differences in education but blacks and whites had both completed ten grades on the average. Whites were at slightly higher skill levels, partly because proportionately more blacks had been hired recently. With lower seniority, they had to wait for entrance to the higher skilled jobs.

As seen in Table 6-2, both quits and separations at Westinghouse-

Table 6–2. Annual Turnover, 1969
Electrical Industry, Westinghouse, and Buffalo Divisions
(In percentage of average work force)

	Electrical Equipment Industry	Westinghouse Corporation	Westinghouse–Buffalo	Buffalo Hourly
Accessions	49.5	21.4	11.0	12.0
Total Separations	49.2	20.6	9.0	8.5
Quits	28.5	13.0	6.0	6.5
Layoffs	8.3	2.7	1.5	2.0
Other*	12.4	4.9	1.5	—

* Retirements, death, discharges, etc.

Buffalo in 1969 were far below the averages for the electrical industry as a whole and well below the averages for the Westinghouse Corporation generally. Evidently the Buffalo employees do not often get into the kind of trouble that leads to a discharge. Further, when they come on the job, they intend to stay. Both of these facts give evidence of a satisfactory and relatively satisfied work force.

BEGINNINGS OF MODERATE AFFIRMATIVE ACTION

THE PAST

As we have seen, black men and women have worked at the Westinghouse-Buffalo plant since its inception in 1946. A number of the old Curtiss-Wright employees hired by Westinghouse were black and one of the men brought from Pittsburgh to instruct the new Buffalo workers was a Negro. About 125 of the Negroes still in the plant at the time of our study were hired in the late 1940s.

During the late 1940s when Westinghouse was rapidly building a large work force, Buffalo had a tight labor market. A veteran in personnel recalls: "If a man could walk, he got a job." It seems likely that this strong need for labor made it easier for black applicants to get factory work. Our study of the history of the electrical industry showed that blacks made most progress when labor was in short supply.

In the 1950s Westinghouse–Buffalo was already at peak employment, and due to the rather low turnover, hired fewer people. The employment office became more selective; it was often blacks who were screened out. One manager stated: "When we did hire a black, we researched him far better." Also during this time, top Westinghouse employment personnel were active in the Urban League. One early director of employment, Walter Dennison, served a term as President of the League. But, typical of many Urban League efforts at the time, emphasis was on jobs for a few very well-qualified Negroes. From today's vantage point, with emphasis on opportunities throughout the plant for black men and women with *average* qualifications, neither Dennison's espousal of black opportunity nor the Urban League's efforts seem very extensive: good intentions but little implementation.

Let us listen to some of the black old-timers reflect on the early days. Earline Mobley, a forty-six-year-old veteran stator winder, reported a disparity between the early blacks and whites hired:

> Now in the beginning, when I was employed in '46, the word went out to certain individuals: "Now we will hire a couple of colored girls. We want real nice colored girls. Intelligent girls." I mean there was a certain requirement, more so for us than there was for the white girls. In '46 the caliber of colored women and men that was employed on the whole was a higher degree than that of the Caucasian. Actually, we have to be, to get the same job. But now we are getting to the place where they are being selected on the basis: If they are good, okay.

Lillian Davis, forty-eight, also a stator winder, told of her earlier unsuccessful meeting with an employment interviewer in 1950.

MISS DAVIS: When I first came here, she did not want to hire colored.

PURCELL: You could tell it was that?

MISS DAVIS: Yeah, because you could sit there and she'd hire maybe fifteen white girls and one colored girl. So one day I just told her like it is. And I knew then that she would never hire me, as long as she were here. I told her: "How could you hire fifteen girls and one colored girl, and there's as many colored in here as there are white, not only girls but fellows too?" And she told me she knew her job. I told her, well, she sure did. But I understand they fired her. She'd been here for years and years.

Philip E. Hughes, of the employee relations department, has been at the Buffalo plant almost since it began. He admitted that in the 1940s and 1950s, the employment office had a reputation for being discriminatory. He commented on the woman who interviewed and screened Earline Mobley and refused a job to Lillian Davis:

> The girl that brought in most of the hourly and salaried girls ... had a discriminatory feeling about Negroes. I know that for sure. She was obvious. I think she was getting over it. But in the grain, she had it. And my understanding was that Westinghouse had a real bad name in the Negro community at that time, being a real tough place for a Negro to get a job.

Although it was Westinghouse policy from the opening of the plant that employees be hired at entry level and be upgraded without regard to race, several long-service blacks and foremen suggested that there was some discrimination.

Charles Tuggle, forty-seven, was a twenty-three-year veteran of Westinghouse. His first job at Westinghouse was as a janitor, even though he had had mechanic's training in high school and similar experience in the service. He had come to the plant in 1946, hoping to put his mechanical experience to use:

> Of course, I had my high school diploma, plus I had my service discharge papers. And right then I asked for machine work. Back when I was in school I had taken up machine work, mechanic, you name it and I had taken all that, while I was in school. And when I was in the service I was in engineering, a heavy equipment operator. When I came out, I was hoping to have gotten a machinist job

Tuggle was hired as a janitor but apparently told that he would get "first crack" at bidding on more skilled jobs as the plant expanded. However, it was several years, he said, after the plant was unionized, before he actually got a promotion. As he saw it: "I wouldn't lie to you, the only job they was giving me or any other colored folks was common laborer."

Roscoe Filkins, a black union steward, believed that opportunities for Negroes at Westinghouse were good in 1969 but when he first came to the plant in 1946 "mostly all the Negroes that were here, they had them as janitors. But as it grew, they began to get out of that."

Veteran foreman Len Jodka agreed with the picture both Tuggle and Filkins presented. He, too, recalled that in the early years Negroes were not allowed to operate machines:

> Years ago the colored were restricted. It was a bad thing that they've finally overcome. You never took a colored person on the machines twenty years ago. You never did; it was unheard of. Colored person come in, he was a sweeper, or a laborer, or a bench job, or elevator operator or something. You just never took them as a machine operator.

In 1953 a few Negroes at Westinghouse were promoted to more skilled jobs. Sal Patterson, who had been employed as a janitor and supplyman at the plant since 1946, became the first Negro electrician. He attributed his promotion to his own dogged persistence:

> There was a sign of discrimination when I first bid on this job here as an apprentice electrician's helper. Quite a few bid on it, and I guess there were some guys they had in mind that would get the job. But one thing, they were lacking in seniority. I had top seniority. But then they said, we will try it on experience. But they could not get through on experience, because I had the experience. I took training in school for electrical work, and besides I could put together circuits. . . . And there was no other way they could get around it at the time.

> Personnel did come to ask me, one thing I give them credit about. They said: "You know there is no other colored men downstairs in maintenance. Those guys could give you a hard time." I said: "Well, it would not be the first time. Just as long as they do not put their hands on me. Words do not mean anything to me. Just show me what to do, and I'll do it."
>
> That job was open for months. Nobody could get it. So I mean, when you get into something like that, the company, they got to make some sort of move. You have got to give and take in every field. So they said: "You want this job; we will give you that job."

The reaction of the work force to this innovation was at first hostile:

> When I first went downstairs, it was nip 'n tuck. Some guys thought I should not be there! You know? They said: "You want the job, you are going to do the job. We are not going to help you." I said: "So what? When I ask for your help, then you can help me. Until then, you stay out of my way, that is all."

But largely because of Patterson's perseverance, things in the department finally settled down:

> There were a lot of Polish people there; they had said a lot of harsh things in Polish. They thought I did not understand. So, one day one of the electricians spoke out of line.
>
> So I told him in Polish: "You watch your own mind and watch your filthy mouth, or else I will hit you in the mouth, see?" And that shook him right up. So he told everybody else that I told him in Polish: "He overheard me and he understands what I said." And from then on, the guys got a little more friendly.

THE EARLY WHITE COLLAR SITUATION

Black women in the early days were largely confined to factory work. It was not until 1955, just after Westinghouse headquarters began to reevaluate its racial employment practices, that attractive Mildred Farland was hired as the first Negro clerical worker. Progress for blacks into salaried work, however, continued to be slow, even after the initial breakthrough. Mildred Farland said that only recently had office work become fully open to Negroes. She added, "There's quite a few working here now. They have really hired quite a few. Whereas before, I was the only one here for about two years." Avery Hobbs, a forty-five-year-old, southern-born stockman, noticed the same change. He began working at the plant in 1947:

> Well, the biggest change I've seen here is, of course—I worked here for years and I never seen until six or seven years ago—I'd never seen a Negro working in the office here. And now, everywhere you look, you see 'em. They hiring 'em every day. This is probably the biggest change

that I've seen out here.... I worked here for years and never seen a colored person work a white collar job.

Freddy Dixon, sixty years old and a twenty-four-year Westinghouse veteran on a highly skilled job, said that a big problem in the early years was promotion into salaried jobs.

CAVANAGH: In the time you've been here, have you experienced any discrimination? At all? Would you say?

DIXON: Well, let's see. Some years ago, yes. I think that discrimination was in every plant that you could go into. Here included, absolutely.

CAVANAGH: How would you see it?

DIXON: Well, let's put it this way—you could probably better yourself out here in the plant as a hourly worker—you could go up through the labor grades. Never much problem there. But say, like going into something in the salaried thing. I think there was a little barrier there for a while. Yeah, definitely. Because I tried myself.

It didn't materialize but I didn't let it bother me too much. I stayed out here and I'm probably making more money. Because labor grade 12 is a pretty nice labor grade. But I'm saying if it was possible I would have probably gone into this thing at the time.

CAVANAGH: Okay. Is there any more of that, do you think, around here? That it's difficult for a guy to get into the salaried job?

DIXON: I will say it's much better now in this plant, and I suppose in more plants.

Phillip Hughes, who earlier spoke of the discriminatory feelings evidenced in personnel, agreed that the industrial relations department became concerned about bringing Negroes into white collar work in the mid-1950s. He described the reception of one of the first black clerical workers in 1955: "One of the first people we took in our own department here on the file clerk's job. I don't think we had any real problem, once people made up their minds

Table 6–3. Black Employment by Occupation Westinghouse–Buffalo, 1961*

Occupation	Percent Black
Officials and Managers	0.0
Professionals	1.6
Technicians	0.5
Sales Workers	0.0
Office and Clerical	1.1
Total White Collar	0.8
Craftsmen	2.9
Operatives	6.2
Laborers	5.0
Service Workers	10.5
Total Blue Collar	4.9
Total All Workers	3.1

*The positions included in each category in 1961, especially "Professional and Administrative" differ slightly from those included in the 1965 and 1970 tables.

152 *The local experience*

that we'd better hire some Negroes. I think the resistance dissolved pretty rapidly." But Hughes added that it was not until the early 1960s that larger numbers of salaried breakthroughs were made for blacks.

In summing up progress before the 1960s, we see in Table 6-3 that 3.1 percent of all employees and 4.9 percent of the hourly workers were black in 1961. Blacks were not represented in all the labor grades equally with whites. Nevertheless, a substantial percentage of blacks had moved up. Twenty-five percent of all blacks and 41 percent of all whites were in the hourly higher labor grades. There were very few blacks in white collar jobs.

AFFIRMATIVE ACTION IN THE LATE 1960s AND TODAY

During the late 1960s, in keeping with the changing national climate, Westinghouse–Buffalo made a more concentrated, systematic effort to recruit blacks and to be sure that selection procedures and upgrading were fair. During 1969, for example, 20 percent of the new hires were Negro. Westinghouse, however, was not hiring large numbers of employees—white or black. Turnover was low and the plant was not expanding. On two occasions, departments

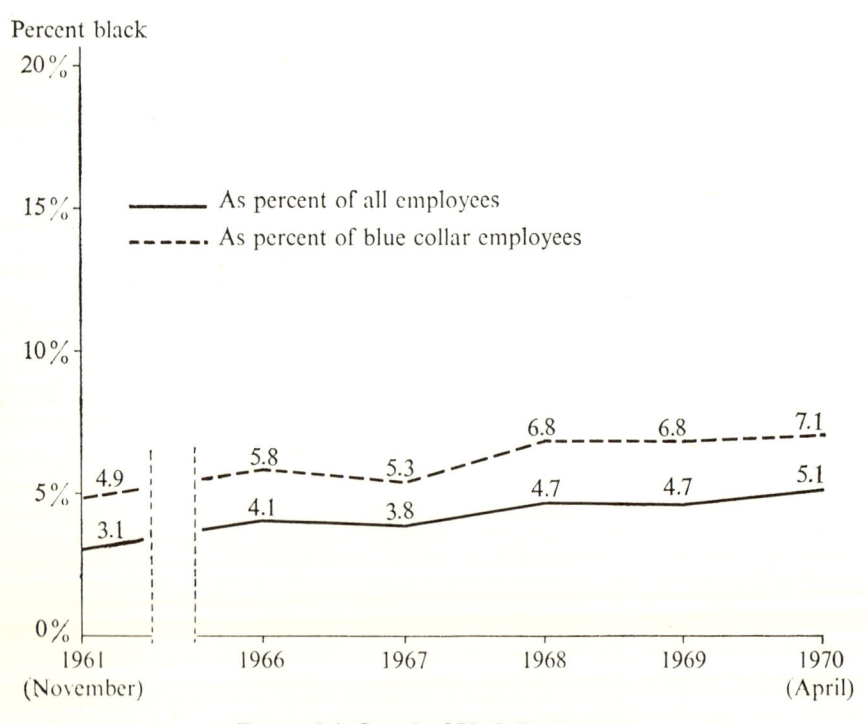

FIGURE 6-1. **Growth of Black Employment Westinghouse–Buffalo November 1961, January 1966 to April 1970**

Table 6-4. Black Employment by Sex and Occupation Westinghouse–Buffalo, 1966 and 1969

Occupation	JANUARY 1966 Percent Black of All Employees	Percent Black of All Males	Percent Black of All Females	JANUARY 1969 Percent Black of All Employees	Percent Black of all Males	Percent Black of All Females
Officials and Managers	0.5	0.5	0.0	0.2	0.2	0.0
Professionals	0.0	0.0	0.0	0.5	0.5	0.0
Technicians	0.7	0.7	0.0	1.2	1.3	0.0
Sales Workers	0.0	0.0	0.0	0.0	0.0	0.0
Office and Clerical	1.9	0.5	3.3	2.3	1.5	3.1
Total White Collar	1.0	0.4	3.1	1.3	0.9	3.0
Craftsmen	2.6	2.5	12.5	2.6	2.3	17.6
Operatives	5.8	5.3	11.1	7.9	7.2	12.9
Laborers	9.0	7.5	9.3	9.7	38.3	7.0
Service Workers	13.2	8.5	50.0	11.8	8.1	50.0
Total Blue Collar	5.8	4.7	10.0	6.8	6.1	9.1
Total All Workers	4.1	3.1	7.6	4.7	4.1	7.0

were moved out of Buffalo and, of course, no one was hired until displaced employees were resettled. Despite these problems, Westinghouse–Buffalo participated actively in the National Alliance of Businessmen (NAB) program for the disadvantaged. In addition to contributing executive time, they hired forty disadvantaged workers. (See Chapter 9.)

Figure 6-1 shows that the percentage of blacks in the plant grew slowly from 3 percent in 1961 to 4 percent in January 1966 to 4.7 percent in January 1969. There were some breakthroughs in white collar positions; Westinghouse appointed their first black foreman in 1965 and two more in 1969 and 1970; eight blacks were employed in professional and technical positions in 1969; and the number of blacks in clerical work rose to 3 percent, as seen in Table 6-4. But blacks were only 1.3 percent of all white collar workers in January 1969. In the year following our study further progress was made, and blacks made up 1.6 percent of the white collar workers. There is room for vast improvement, but the perennial problem of adequate qualifications will make it difficult.

Blacks in blue collar jobs at Westinghouse–Buffalo increased from 5 percent in 1961 to 6.8 percent in January 1969. As we said, blacks represent at least 17 percent of the Buffalo population and 8 percent of Erie County. Distribution of blacks through the hourly labor grades, controlled primarily by seniority, shows only modest increases in the middle labor grades. In January 1969, 9.0 percent of all operatives and 2.5 percent of the craftsmen were black. Again, 1970 showed some minor improvement with 2.7 percent of the craftsmen black. In some plants management has sought to increase the number of blacks in skilled jobs by recruiting them for training programs and then placing them on such jobs. Collective bargaining agreements at Westinghouse, however, require that all new employees start on entry level jobs, regardless of training or past experience. This provision makes it impossible to rapidly advance the number of skilled blacks in the plant since newly hired blacks will be concentrated in low skill jobs. However, it probably increases the long-range opportunities for advancement.

As for employees' attitudes toward employment, all the white workers sampled and most blacks were convinced that there was no racial discrimination in hiring at Westinghouse–Buffalo in 1969. Only 4 percent of the blacks thought that there was discrimination. (See Table 6-5.)

Table 6–5. Perception of Fair Hiring for Blacks
Hourly employees by race, Westinghouse–Buffalo

	Black	White
Favorable	77%	100%
Uncertain	18	0
Unfavorable	4	0

THE PERFORMANCE OF BLACKS

Now let us see in Table 6-6 how the foremen compared their black workers with the whites.

Middle America and the blacks 155

*Table 6–6. Job Performance of Hourly Blacks
Percentage of foremen who judge that blacks do as well as the
average worker, Westinghouse–Buffalo*

	About the Same	Worse
Quantity of Work	88%	12%
Quality of Work	100	0
Attendance	75	25
Promptness	88	12
Accepting Responsibility	100	0
Personality at Work	100	0
Discipline at Work	100	0
Ability to Learn the Job	75	25
Promotability	62	38

The Westinghouse foremen rated their black employees quite on a par with their white workers in work quality, responsibility, personality, and discipline. In five areas some of the foremen rated blacks as somewhat less satisfactory. Absenteeism and tardiness were among the less satisfactory tendencies, as we also found in our other plant studies. Concerning the ability to learn the job, promotability, and quantity of work output, some foremen also rated blacks below whites. In general, however, the Westinghouse black employees were rated quite favorably. Regarding the younger workers, we shall say more presently.

PROBLEMS OF UPGRADING AND PROMOTION

The opportunity for hourly upgrading was an important element with blacks at every plant we studied. At Westinghouse–Buffalo upgrading is by seniority in a "family" of jobs. Positions are offered first to employees in the line of progression within the family in which the opening occurs. Jobs which are not taken are then posted and are open to any employee. Thousands of employees are transferred each year. On-the-job training for the new position is provided for all employees.

Only 10 percent of the hourly blacks sampled thought that blacks as a group did not have a fair chance for upgrading (35 percent were uncertain). And only 17 percent of the blacks, compared to 37 percent of the whites, thought that they did not personally have a good chance for upgrading. Attitudes toward seniority did not vary along racial lines. These findings should perhaps not be surprising since almost half the blacks in the plant were hired in the plant's first years—the same proportion as whites.

It was the new, young, ambitious workers of either race who were most frustrated at their chances for advancement. Although they are a small minority, let us listen to some of the young. Strong-minded Wilbert Troy, twenty-four, said:

> First of all in the shop, there is no question, there are no chances for promotion. I am at the limit for the seniority that I have. Experience on

any other jobs? I don't have any. And I know that I'd have to be here a good twenty years to get the next labor grade, which is just an increase of four or five dollars a week. So, along those lines, there is nothin'.

Jerry Megget, twenty-seven, a black wireman with two years of college and three years in the plant, suggested that frustration with promotion leads to quits.

MEGGETT: One [young black] I know, he's sweeping in the section I work in now. He's constantly asking me to show him how to read these diagrams because he wants to get a better job. Yes, but this is what I mean: How is he going to get this better job? He has no seniority but he wants to learn. Eventually he'll get discouraged.

CAVANAGH: And what will happen, do you think?

MEGGETT: I think eventually he'll get discouraged and just maybe go back to the streets or whatever, you know. He doesn't have the seniority to bid on the better jobs, but he wants a better job.

Meggett himself had bid on jobs as a production clerk and draftsman, and had asked to take the foreman's test; but he heard nothing on his requests. He also said he saw his foreman and the general foreman, as well as personnel, but still had not been given the opportunity to take the exam. He was also discouraged.

Thirty-five-year-old Ira Patton was still young but had thirteen years' service in the plant. In his view management was making a special effort to upgrade blacks.

CAVANAGH: Do you have a fair chance for upgrading and promotion?

PATTON: Oh, they've been asking me that already, a couple of times.

CAVANAGH: Is that right?

PATTON: Turned it down. I like my job now and I get along with everybody. When you gotta go up higher, more responsibility, plus you got to lead the men and everything. And I said I just don't want to be with that now. But they tried quite a few times, got me in the office, just like you, sit down and talk to me left and right 'til they were blue in the face trying to get me to go higher. . . . So I'm telling you this is why I'm trying to say, if you've got the education, you believe me, nowadays they don't hold you back. They don't hold you back one bit. You can advance.

SALARIED POSITIONS

Speaking of blacks in salaried and more responsible positions, Earline Mobley, who gave us her views on the company's 1946 hiring practices, said:

There was a time that you would not see a Negro that smart or anything like that. And if you did, everybody would stare at him as though he had come from Mars. But now I notice that there are a few around here. Definitely there are new opportunities with Westinghouse.

College graduate Hosea James, twenty-four, a business systems analyst, was also optimistic:

> Still maybe not quite as many Negroes get hired as they should, but I think eventually they will. Because most of the college group now actually go to the companies that have a Negro hiring policy. And eventually they'll be in the top positions, too. And you can see it probably will get a lot better. As I've said, if there is discrimination, I can't sense it so.

On "breakthrough promotions" there is a fine distinction to be made on the question of how much the black person needs to be made racially self-conscious. Take the case of George Herman. He is a talented man about forty years of age with two years of college. He left the shop to become one of the first Negroes on a salaried inspector's job. Management was concerned about his reception, and Herman felt that the interview was painful and rather discouraging:

PURCELL: I think you mentioned that it wasn't—it didn't seem open and easy at your interview.

HERMAN: No, because the fact still remains that you are the only—"We never had a black inspector, and you will be the first one. What will be your reaction to whites, the people in the plant, if certain things are said to you?" He said: "I know you have the qualifications." It wasn't so much my qualifications. It was more my reaction of how would I speak out.

PURCELL: Do they need to ask all that?

HERMAN: For the job? No, I don't think so, because I don't think that the job entails that. I mean I'm not a public relations man. . . .

To conclude this section: Westinghouse-Buffalo is emerging from a sure but slow start in opening Negro job opportunities into a phase of moderate affirmative action. Black percentages have been gradually increased; doors have been slowly opened; breakthroughs have been made.

IUE LOCAL 1581 AND THE BLACKS

Workers at the Westinghouse Buffalo Divisions have been represented by the International Union of Electrical Workers (AFL-CIO) since 1949 when the UE was expelled from the CIO. The current president of the local, an able politician, held that office for almost twenty years until he was defeated in 1971.

The plant is a modified union shop, with all employees required to join within forty-five days of hiring. The union is therefore in a stronger position in regard to employment standards and upgrading procedures than at any of the other plants studied and is thus in a position to audit fair treatment of blacks and to help new blacks understand the way the plant operates.

WHAT WORKERS THINK OF THE UNION

Almost 90 percent of both races wanted a union in the plant. But there was considerable criticism of some union leadership. About one-third of the employees—black and white—clearly approved of the union leadership, with about one-third unfavorable and the rest uncertain and likely to split their ticket in an election. Some union officers were criticized for being cliquish. One ex-steward said that if you should decide to run against an incumbent union officer, you were his enemy for life. Other complaints heard several times were that the worker could not get a copy of the union contract from his steward, and that some union officers signed out on union business when they were campaigning for their own reelection. Significantly, we found no racial differences in attitudes toward the union or its leadership at the Buffalo plant.

The ethnic background of the union members plays a strong part in union elections and affairs. Veteran union steward, James Turesky, who earlier described Buffalo's strong ethnic chauvinism, told how a man with a Polish background capitalized on this to win the election:

> One of the reasons why is this John Czajkowski. Now I know him as John; he's always John. But he knows the sentiment of the people in the shop. He changed his name to Jan, the Polish version of John. That's right. As humorous as it is, that's a fact. It went over big with the old-timers that were Polish, you know. He knew that, you know.
> You take a look at the employment records here. I would say maybe three-fourths of the people in this place are Polish. Oh, maybe I'm exaggerating. Maybe it's 50 percent. There's an awful lot and you can see by the members of the union administration. The president is Polish, then you have an Italian vice-president. The chief steward now is Polish, and every once in a while you find an English or Czechoslovakian name. But 80 percent of the slate is Polish.

As in most ethnically oriented politics there was a conscious effort to include a few members of each group on union slates. Thus, there had been one or two black union officers from the earliest days. In the 1969 election of union officers there were two blacks on each of the twenty-six-man slates. But ethnic bias was evident. Blacks, both winners and losers, received somewhat fewer votes than others on their slates.

Bright and personable Quentin Goode, twenty-five, a new black union officer, questioned the wisdom of encouraging ethnic voting:

> When I was elected, I was told don't bother with any white fellows. Get to your Negro brothers and try to persuade them to vote for our slate. I didn't like the idea. Because that's not going to help relations at all.

> One reason was because if your name isn't -ski you have a hard time making it here.... And you ask people why.
>
> Ignorance—that is the way they were brought up: that black people are lazy and shiftless, and that Italians are no good because they're sneaky; and Polish people are no good because they're dumb and things like this. And it isn't true. Even though I might admit that within their own national origin or background, the person himself may be this way.... But you can't judge all by one. And I was astonished when he told me that.

Goode said that among the union officers there was no overt ethnic or racial discrimination because that would weaken the group, but "a lot of things are hush-hush" on the race issue. Although the officers said they were doing everything they could for the black community within the shop, nevertheless "to me I don't think that much is being done."

Local 1581 leaders placed great emphasis on seniority and fairness. They apparently processed grievances for blacks regularly, and seniority provisions have protected long-term black employees as well as Poles and Czechs. But the local strongly opposed any special treatment. A black, on his part, might be suspicious of a white steward. Draftsman Ray Jarvis' comments on the salaried union applied as readily to the plant union:

> Most people, when they first join the union, if they're black, they get the feeling, you know: well, I'm not going to a white man to tell him my problems. He'll just walk over me, and stuff like that. Give a big smile, you know, and a kick in the behind at the same time. If you find someone like your own race, you can sit down and explain it to them better. Feel more at ease.

In sum, it appears that Local 1581 was generally fair to its black members. But official union policy represented the white majority in opposing any special efforts to hire and promote black workers.

SOME EFFECTS OF RACIAL CHANGE

BLACKS AND WHITES GET ALONG ON THE JOB

There has been a moderate change in black employment at Westinghouse–Buffalo and greater changes in the general racial climate in the city of Buffalo. What effects did these changes have on the attitudes and feelings of the Westinghouse workers and supervisors?

Our first and major finding is that the whites and blacks generally got along quite well in their working relationships. Table 6-7 gives one summary of these findings.

Remember that Table 6-7 does not report a questionnaire statement, but rather represents the focused conversational comments of the employees

Table 6-7. Perception of Black-White Relations on the Job Hourly employees by race, Westinghouse–Buffalo

	Black	White
Favorable	79%	86%
Uncertain	17	10
Unfavorable	4	4

Table 6-8. Attitude Toward Working with Blacks Hourly employees by race, Westinghouse–Buffalo

	Black	White
Favorable	100%	80%
Uncertain	0	17
Unfavorable	0	3

about how the two races work together. The great majority of both races saw their interpersonal relations as good and satisfactory. Only a small minority disagreed. Another statistic will bear out this same point, as seen in Table 6-8.

Morris Wolodsky was thirty-one, white, and a thirteen-year employee. There were "quite a few" Negroes in his section. When asked how they got along, he answered: "Everybody gets along good in our section, that's one thing I can say. It's like one happy family in our section. Just my own personal opinion." Thirty-five-year-old Ira Patton, who spoke earlier on management's efforts to upgrade blacks, agreed that workers got along well on the job: "The group I work with? . . . Yeah. We don't have no problem here. When it comes, you know, little problems which everybody has. But none of this big stuff. We all together." Bill Larson, fifty-eight, white, when asked the same questions, echoed: "There's no problem there."

Some white employees did feel that it was difficult to get along with individual blacks whom they found "antiwhite" or "lazy." And some blacks felt that whites who were friendly on the surface remained prejudiced. In terms of behavior, however, blacks and whites could agree that the races got along well. We would not expect whites to be as open toward blacks as blacks were toward members of their own race. As in our other field studies, we constructed a "tolerance of blacks" index by factor analysis, combining the employees' coded attitudes toward how the races work together, issues of preferential treatment, black supervisors, Negro stereotypes, and so forth. On a scale ranging from 1 (very unfavorable) to 5 (very favorable), the Buffalo white workers scored 3.7. This is a favorable score, and is higher than those for Memphis or Chicago. However, the blacks were significantly higher than whites: 4.0. Evidently color blindness has not reached the Buffalo plant, any more than it has most American factories.

A FEW OUTSPOKEN, PREJUDICED MEN

A few white men in the plant were unfavorable to Negroes and showed some backlash. But they were not simply the old-timers, as we might expect. Some were young, articulate, and forceful. While only a handful, these outspoken, prejudiced whites could have considerable influence beyond their small numbers and it is therefore important that we try to understand them.

Listen, for example, to twenty-two-year-old Stephen Grumbacher. He is a welder, a four-year employee at the plant, tall, nice looking, and talkative and smiling. These qualities make his deep feelings more impressive:

GRUMBACHER: I don't hate 'em. But I'll tell you somethin'. I've dealt with quite a few of them, 'n the majority of them in my estimation are bad. Like I says, I've had a few run-ins with some of them, and I'll tell you: the majority of 'em I have no use for 'em at all. There's a few good ones. With a few of 'em, I got along really good. But most of 'em, not.

PURCELL: Right here in the plant? What kind of trouble would they cause?

GRUMBACHER: Well, it's like this. The foreman will give him the same chewing out that he gives me. This shine will yell "Discrimination," and hey! (whistles)—let's forget about it right now, right?

PURCELL: The foreman drops it?

GRUMBACHER: Right. I've seen a letter that come from the general manager of the division to every supervisor. And they said in it that no matter what, if this man's qualified or not, you hire him for the job.... I've seen them so dumb they can't read a yo-yo. [Management knows of no such letter but others mentioned it.]

PURCELL: I wonder how that works out?

GRUMBACHER: I don't know. But I still see 'em disqualify white people. And actually the way that I look at it today—I don't mean just the way the plant's run, but the way the whole country is run (bangs fist)—they're discriminating against white people.

A few minutes later, Grumbacher admitted that he very often went home on Friday half way through the shift, after getting his paycheck. The boss got on him, but rarely jumped on the blacks, who, said Grumbacher, took off whole days and did this consistently. When he was asked where he thought it would all end, he replied:

> It ain't gonna end. It ain't gonna end until they're in complete charge of everything. This is the way it is right now. And if everybody caters to 'em, I can't blame 'em. I look at all these riots; and when these people go beserk and they start burning these buildings up and the whole bit, I say: "Call in the Guard or get the police in there and start shooting them down." Hey! This is the only way to treat 'em. 'Cause this is the way that I'd expect to be treated, if I did this.

Gerald Drake, twenty-eight, is a stocky, young-looking coil former. He is a pleasant fellow, but he reacted quite negatively to any suggestion of special treatment for the poor or for blacks. He voted for George Wallace, and he said he was about to get himself a pistol. He felt that there were a number of people in the plant who were becoming increasingly prejudiced:

DRAKE: I think there's a lot of people that are more prejudiced than they were. There again because of the racial violence going on at the present time. And unfortunately, a lot of them condemn the whole race for a minority.

CAVANAGH: How many guys would do that?

DRAKE: Oh, I'd say at least 10 percent, maybe 20 percent of the people I associate with.

On the other side, a few blacks in the plant were also militant and clearly rejected whites. Harrel Dinkins, twenty-two, had been reading a lot of black literature during the last year and it had profoundly affected him: "The more they come out about what happened to us over all these 400 years and all that jazz, the less we like you people. And that's all there is to it." He later explained why he did not trust "whitey" and why he was impatient with the white liberal:

> Well, most of the kids in the colleges are now greater than what they used to be. But then you still have a few that are crusading for us. You know, they get carried away with their causes. So they say: "What's your problem?" White cat says: "What's your problem?" "You're my problem," I says, and they look at me. . . . The black man cannot trust the white man, because he's been stabbed in the back, you know, smiling face, stabbed in the back.

If there is this much frustration and anger in a man with a steady job for four years, what about the man on the streets who all his life has met with disappointments and failures?

Several older blacks were upset by the new climate Dinkins represents and by the reaction of white men like Grumbacher and Drake. For example, perceptive, affable, long-service wireman, Grady Harris, fifty-three, anguished:

> Things are so messed up nowadays. I don't know. I just figure, I just think to stay here, work my time out, retire as soon as possible. . . . Well, in fact, I think that Martin Luther King brought out a lot of things, and hoping. But he made it more—I don't know—it's more tense now than it was before he started, you know. There's more jobs offered. It's better, but it's a tense feeling all the time.

Harris would opt for a gigantic program of education for the poor: "Teach people so they can read, write, and vote right and all that stuff. . . ."

In our opinion, the white prejudices we found are closely related to the economic and social problems of the blue collar worker—the white "Middle Americans." These people feel threatened about their housing and their jobs. Taxes and credit buying are anxieties for them. They feel that they are being passed by in favor of the upper classes and of the poor and blacks. They have strong ethnic solidarity, and since they are still the majority race, they think they can voice their prejudices. The young, militant blacks for their part are also impatient; they want big improvements, *now*. To repeat, we found just a few whites or blacks at Westinghouse–Buffalo with such extreme views. Only the future can tell whether or not their numbers will grow.

PREFERENTIAL TREATMENT

Most of the white (and black) workers at Westinghouse–Buffalo did not observe or complain about any special or preferential treatment being given to Negroes. Nevertheless, 27 percent of the whites thought that blacks were given special breaks in the hiring process, as seen in Table 6-9.

Table 6–9. Perception of Preference for Blacks in Hiring Hourly employees by race, Westinghouse–Buffalo

	Black	White
Favorable	7%	27%
Uncertain	10	27
Unfavorable	83	46

As for blacks getting preferences in promotions, no blacks and only 10 percent of the whites thought this was happening. Finally, regarding preferential treatment given to blacks by their supervisors, again no blacks and only 7 percent of the whites thought this to be true.

Let us take another group of attitudes that indirectly throw light on whites' feelings about blacks. Although some whites and older blacks considered some poor people lazy, only 7 percent of the whites thought that the poor as a group did not want to work (58 percent were uncertain.) Even fewer were opposed to the plant recruiting more poor people. Yet 29 percent of the whites were opposed to Westinghouse *going out of its way* to recruit the poor.

Although few whites thought Westinghouse was giving blacks preference, many made it clear that they opposed such favoritism. They were critical of federal civil rights efforts for Negro hiring and promoting target quotas. Here are some representative examples:

FRED HOLMES, white, forty-two, father of eight: Now I don't feel Westinghouse should say: "We'll give you this job because you dropped out of school and you're too darned lazy to do anything else." ... I did not have them putting a rope around my neck and dragging me in here [saying]: "Either you work or you don't work today. You can just come into the plant and stand around for eight hours. We don't care as long as we have you on the payroll." This is certainly wrong.

JOHN LEODAS, fifty-nine, and a twenty-three-year veteran at Westinghouse: The thing I can't see is why these people should think that they should come in, you might say, on the top. Golly, you learn to walk before you start to run. You don't start way up the ladder because you might fall off; you have to learn how to climb that first. So why put a person on as inspector like that, instead of giving him some machine experience?

LAWRENCE HEBEMANN, forty-five, electric tester and a Westinghouse veteran: What does bother me is the colored getting the preference *because* they're black. This I am against. I say, I don't care what his color is. If he has the ability to do the job, he should get the job—not *because* of his color. They shouldn't hire 20 percent just because they're black. This is discrimination in reverse as far as I'm concerned. . . . If they want it, they can earn it like I did. I am not saying deprive them of something—not at all.

DEAN LOHR, forty-two, veteran grinder: Well, like my boy for instance. I think he should have the same opportunity. I don't have anything against it. I mean it's a good thing. But, I mean I don't think that maybe they should bring in somebody from the slum area that just doesn't have the capabilities, over some other person.

Some white people have come to fear as well as resent the black man. Listen to Edwin Holden, forty-six, a veteran wireman:

There has been a lot of discrimination against the white people here by the colored folk. . . . You had a few people up here that would push the colored folks in, where on the same job they wouldn't take a white person. Well, it's just turned out that the white people in here—a lot of them—are afraid of the colored folk and that's it. You take a white person in here is fired, you better believe he's fired. There's been an awful lot of colored fellows in here's been fired, is brought back in. Not once, but twice.

Foreman Thomas Burrell, forty-three, described his understanding of the slender line between legitimate preferential treatment and preferential treatment carried too far:

I know it may be hard on some of the people that are working here, but I think you're going to have to try to give him the easier, simpler jobs originally, and gradually work him into these other ones. I feel he should, after a period of time, come up to what the other people are doing. Or if he doesn't, I'd feel then that we have a serious problem. Because it's not fair to the other ones either then. . . . 'Cause they have feelings, the same as anybody else. And if they feel that this person is only doing one-quarter, and he's getting away with it. . . . I think this may even take a little bit of salesmanship of the foreman to explain to the people, if these questions arise.

The theme that seems to run through the comments of almost all of the whites and old-time blacks at Westinghouse is: be fair. Although they recognized that special effort and perhaps even training might be given the disadvantaged when they first came in, they ask that once the disadvantaged learn the job they be expected to produce just as much as any other employee.

Management has no simple path in this matter. As one manager put it:

> Well, we're walking a tightrope. To get a higher percentage of blacks as we move further into the program, it's going to get tougher and tougher. I really feel that if you show open discrimination [in favor of blacks], you lick the whole thing. All your standards drop. Everything goes to pot, everything you're trying to do. And so you have to maintain a uniformity. And yet we all know we have to discriminate a little bit, even to get the guy in, in the first place. You have to be a little bit more patient. You have to train a little bit differently, I think. It's a little more. . . .

The problem presented by white aversions for any kind of special treatment for blacks is this: if Westinghouse, or any other company for that matter, is going to accelerate its affirmative action to correct the imbalance of its black employees, it will have to make special efforts in both hiring and promoting. It will have to go out of its way to help black workers. We shall treat the whole issue of preferential treatment more thoroughly in Chapter 10. We simply note the problem here and the need for white workers to try to understand it.

OLDER FOREMEN FIND YOUTH CONFUSING

It was hard for many of the older Buffalo foremen to understand the new young workers—both white and black. Youth come in with demands for a good job and quick promotion. They have no desire to work long hours. They are different from the old-time Poles and Italians.

Summing up the perplexed attitudes of the older foremen was fifty-eight-year-old supervisor Glen Humphrey who had been with the company for twenty-two years:

HUMPHREY: This new generation coming in is a little bit hard to figure out, I'll be honest with you. I don't know what the young people today want. I don't think they do themselves.

PURCELL: Are they complaining, less desirous to put in a full day?

HUMPHREY: No. They don't seem to be complaining about the amount of work they have to do. It's just: "Why am I doing this much work? I'm not getting enough money for what I do." They don't seem to have the initiative that they used to have, of having a little pride in their work, and trying to keep up with the other fellow. They're clock watchers more or less.

PURCELL: Would that be men or women?

HUMPHREY: Men and women. I've found it in both sexes. This new generation, they think the world owes them a living, without giving anything in return. Where it's going to end up, I don't know. I shudder to think of what's going to happen.

A bit later, when talking about the black man, Humphrey's stereotypes perhaps give some indication as to why he finds it difficult to understand youth:

PURCELL: So the old-timers, they're....

HUMPHREY: They're steady; they're good workers. Oh, when you're talking colored, you know how colored are: happy-go-lucky type of person. They don't set the world afire, but they'll give you a day's work. You know what I mean, if you keep on 'em. And there's not too many of 'em that's got initiative to be a supervisor, or be a lead man or anything like that. But just do their job, and that's it.

Five or ten years ago, the men used to fight for overtime. Today, said foreman Len Jodka who earlier spoke of job discrimination, you're lucky if they'll work five days a week:

> Well, I'd say five, ten years ago, I had a group of people in there that couldn't possibly make enough money. The more money they made, that's the way it had to be. "If there's overtime, I want it. Not Joe over there—*I* want it. I have to check that he doesn't get any more overtime than I do. And I want to work every Saturday. And if you can't get the workload in here, and can't get the authorization for overtime for Saturday work, you're not a good foreman." And then when you get the class of people that we're starting to get in now, they don't even want five days a week. They're sure not going to tell you that they want a Saturday, or they want overtime.

Foreman Edwin Silverman recalled a young black who was a very good worker. He did a good job until one day he just did not show up. Silverman was dismayed and confused as to why he left, but he did admit that he found it difficult to communicate with him: "He's a hard fellow to converse with. He didn't want to say too much."

It is not only blacks who do not want to work; according to foreman John Cipriano some whites today are just as bad:

> Let's not pinpoint it only on the blacks. Now I'm going to be real honest with you. I'm not a lover of Negroes. I don't say I dislike them. I believe that they should deserve the same rights as we have. But let them earn it—that's all I ask. But the whites are just as bad. Your four basic nationalities that make up Buffalo are Irish, Polish, German, Italian—they're just as bad....
> I wish I could hire people over forty-five or fifty years old. The young element is very difficult to handle. You have to be a psychologist, more or less. You have to baby them. You have to get them on your side some way. And, well, if they don't like your looks sometimes, or you speak the wrong way, you've got problems with them.

An older black employee agreed that young people were very different from the older generation. He felt that they were eager to learn and that something had to be done to meet their expectations. Freddy Dixon, who had worked in the same plant making fighter planes, contrasted present youth with his own generation: "They all expect more. They're not willing to do like we did—or, I say myself, or the generation that are parents and grandparents now. So the only answer to that is to try to give them more jobs, so they can maintain themselves. And I think it will work out."

The supervisor is often caught in the middle between two types of workers. Those in the first group are around his own age and he is more comfortable with them and their "keep it to yourself" psychology. The older ethnics have strongly internalized goals. They expect the foreman to do his job and tell them what to do, and they will take it or leave it. Those in the second group, the young blacks and whites, generally expect more support from their foreman. They want orientation, training, and feedback from the boss on how they are doing. They want a boss who is approachable and open with them. These two groups are looking for elements in their supervisor that are quite different and may even be conflicting.

In spite of problems dealing with the young, the Buffalo foremen were remarkably well received by nearly all of their employees, as can be seen in Table 6-10.

Table 6–10. Attitude Toward My Foreman
Hourly employees by race, Westinghouse–Buffalo

	Black	White
Favorable	82%	87%
Uncertain	14	10
Unfavorable	4	3

Taking both young and old together, 73 percent of the blacks and 70 percent of the whites thought that their foreman was approachable enough so that they could take a personal problem to him, although older workers would rarely think of doing this.

REACTIONS TO A BLACK FOREMAN

The promise and reality of a black foreman was accepted much more readily at Buffalo than at any of the other plants. Buffalo is the only one of the four plants where not one white said that he personally would have difficulty accepting a black boss. Further, only 13 percent of the white workers said their work group would be uncomfortable with a black supervisor. More than 90 percent of the work force felt that the black foreman would eventually work out and could do his job effectively.

Stuart Orkin, one of the first Negro foremen, described his reception. It was better than either the company or Orkin had expected. But he did encounter some resentment:

> The last words that I had when I came out of the manager's office: "Well, there's going to be some things that we can help you with, and other things where you're going to have to weather the storm yourself."

> I had to work this out myself. As far as academic things, like your contract and insubordination, okay, that was cut and dried. I got as much support from the company as any other foreman.
>
> But I found I got opposition from foremen. . . . I even got opposition from some of my own people. I call this jealousy, because this is one of our bad traits. We don't band together as much as we should. What do you call it, clannish, like the Polish do? If you got a name, I mean, you got the support. But the Negro is a little different. They don't like to see their brothers get ahead, and they do their best to knock them, you know.
>
> And I got opposition from some of the union fellows, 'cause they figure I sold them down the river, you know. Company man. Not realizing that I had my own life to live. But, overall, the reception wasn't bad at all. As a matter of fact, the remark was made that I wouldn't last three months. And I'm still here.

Acceptance by his own people has been a difficult problem for Orkin. Quentin Goode, who earlier mentioned ethnic voting patterns at Westinghouse, talked of the black reaction to Orkin:

> I think he's doing pretty good. Like I say, the man has a job to do. And a lot of black people gave him a hard time. Maybe they resent that he was in charge of them, and he was black, and he was stepping on them, more than on whites. White people recognize that this man is here for a purpose, even though they were sort of sorry that he had to be black. But management chose him, and they're going to keep him there. But the black people in that department, at one time they ran circles around him: "I'm not taking orders from you." That sort of thing.

Goode felt that blacks are often a bundle of anxieties and ambivalencies. They are frequently prejudiced against themselves, and do not want another black to get ahead. Goode continued:

> We both have to be educated. You know what I found out? That Negroes are prejudiced to a great extent to their own. They despise white people and the reason is because, like I say, they are gullible. We were cheated out of this, or we were snaked out of that, because we didn't know any better. We thought we were getting a good deal there, and actually we weren't. And it looked like a real jewel on the outside, but on the inside it was rotten.
>
> We're prejudiced against ourselves because we can't stand to see one another of us get ahead. We're all in the same sort of boat, and we should all stay there. Well, I don't believe in that. I feel if I can help pull somebody out of that rut to come along with me, beautiful. I'd be more than satisfied.

Harrel Dinkins, who earlier expressed great job frustration, was a machine operator with four years' experience at Westinghouse and was one of the most militant young blacks interviewed at the plant. He was one of the blacks who was highly critical of black foreman Orkin, writing him off as an "Uncle Tom":

> He's tough and he's ridiculous. Like I lost all feeling for Stu before I ever knew who he was. Because, like they told me: "We got a colored cat out here as foreman." And I saw him, he had his white shirt and his tie on. Then this white woman came by and patted him on the head, and he grinned from ear to ear, you know. And I mean, that just blew my whole thing, right there. . . .
>
> When you get a colored foreman, they figure well, he'll give me a break, you know. But he has to look good to the *man*, see. And this is where Stu was going overboard. Now, he'll jump all over your back and all this. And he's a lousy foreman; he's a lousy foreman. I didn't have to work for him, but I just heard enough about him and watched him. . . .

Dinkins went on to criticize what he considered to be Orkin's lack of patience and sympathy in handling black disadvantaged workers: "Stu just wasn't altogether at all. I mean, he fired a few colored cats, you know, things like that. Well, there's just so much that a cat, just fresh off the streets is going to do, when he gets in here, you know."

For fear of showing favoritism to his own people, perhaps Orkin leaned over backwards for whites. James Winfield, thirty-eight, a black worker in Orkin's work group, understood his delicate position: "This first foreman that I had was a black man; he's the only one in the plant. He has to be awful careful, because all the eyes are on him. He'll get it from both sides. I believe that he's afraid that maybe he'd be showing favoritism or something." But Winfield, a good worker and a balanced person, felt that Orkin had been harder on him than on the whites:

> But I noticed there's some incidents that he will be a little more lenient with the white fellows than he could with me. In fact I was the only colored working in the department. And that could be because he didn't want to show any favoritism, you know for fear that they'd take his job.

Winfield thought that Orkin was poorly prepared for his job, that he should have had some foreman training to enable him to deal fairly and objectively with all the men in his work force.

Foreman Roger Putnam, fifty-nine, worked closely with Orkin. He felt that Orkin's biggest problem was his own self-consciousness at being one of the first black foremen:

> I think his biggest trouble is, he's trying to live down the fact that he's a colored boy. And I think he thinks that people resent the fact that he is. . . . I have heard some fellows say that they wouldn't work for a colored

man, but I just smile and say: "Well, if he's qualified, why not?" I think it's something that he has to overcome.

The delicate position that Orkin was in as a black supervisor was further underscored by Jerry Meggett, who had foreman aspirations of his own: "Well, no matter how we look at it, you've got to look out for your own, I believe, if you as a race, a people, are going to get ahead. And I think that this is the only way it can be done, that you're going to have to look out for your own." Meggett's point of view is certainly very common among the young black work force. It is probably true that various ethnic groups have done this over the years. To help a brother get ahead has always been considered a good thing. But Meggett felt that this sort of man would never be chosen as a foreman. He said that management was likely to choose "Uncle Toms":

> Well, you know how management is. Your foreman has to cater to whoever is above you, and so forth. And I think it's harder for a Negro when he's coming up. See, to me if you're an outspoken Negro, and you stand up for your rights, then they don't like you too much. I can say it to you: an Uncle Tom type character, and you're all right with them.

Meggett went on to underscore the great pressure that a black supervisor is under from both sides—either for showing favoritism or for selling out.

EMPLOYEES RESENT WELFARE RECIPIENTS

A significant minority of the workers we listened to in the Buffalo plant spontaneously brought up the matter of payments to people on welfare. The subject of welfare was not a direct part of our study since it did not concern racial relations at work. We did not probe for this attitude, nor did we code it. We present only our impressions, but these impressions are strong: welfare payments were a source of concern and resentment to more than a few Westinghouse–Buffalo workers, blacks as well as whites. They suspected cheating by those on welfare, and they thought that many recipients were young and able-bodied, and should be working.

Among the blacks, it was especially the women and the older men who were critical of welfare recipients. Ira Patton, the veteran stockhandler who spoke earlier of management's attempt to upgrade Negroes, stated the case graphically:

> A lot of our colored people out here don't want to work. They're so used to sitting down and doing nothing. It burns me up. Like one woman told me one time: "I'm gonna get a stove"—she didn't work—"but I'm gonna get this on your money." Kinda got to me. I know she's healthy, and she no more than twenty-five.

New York State welfare payments were higher in 1969 than those of most other states. To some workers, it appeared that the welfare recipients were making more than those who work. Said clerical worker Mildred Farland, whom we met in the beginning of this chapter:

> Those people on the welfare look like they are living better than me. I think they do! Some of them. Because John over there is on welfare, and he will buy a car in his cousin's name. You follow me? While he is sitting home all day, I am coming to work. And I do not have a car as good as he has. You see? And they really need to probe into some of these situations, because some of these people are really living good. This makes me as an individual rebellious, you see? I don't want to go to work, if I can sit around and get a car like him!

And again to quote draftsman Ray Jarvis who also resented misuse of welfare when he had to help pay for it:

> Most people just sit back and do nothing and get money. I was discussing this with my wife. Like her mother—I feel that anyone who can sit around the house and stuff like that, they can do housework, do anything they want to do, go get a job, you know. I didn't realize this when I was going to school, but now I see it, because that money they're getting is coming out of my paycheck, too. I was telling my wife, you know, your mother is getting part of my check.

Others criticized welfare because they felt it hurt the very people it was designed to help, breaking down initiative and rewarding bad conduct. Still others thought that welfare tended to make people lazy and irresponsible.

Generally, white attitudes were about the same as those of the blacks quoted above. Bill Larson, a twenty-three-year Westinghouse shipper, complained about his low pay: "If I don't work six days, I'm ashamed to cash my check." He compared his situation to that of the people on welfare, saying that some of those on welfare who had big families made more than he did working in a plant. "If they didn't support them like kings, I think they'd go to work so that they could get something. I don't say to let them starve, by any means. But this coddling them is doing no good." Larson said this was not the majority of those on welfare, but it was true of "quite a few of them." He cited an example:

> Well, now the other day here a fellow in our section said one of them cashed a welfare check for $99.00. That's for one week for food. Right ahead of him in the market. He said: "My gosh, I don't earn that. And I come to work every day. Here she gets that out of my tax money." He was really sort of bitter about it. But I think you'll find that true all over. That the people that are working and making an effort, they are a little bit—how would you say it?—down on these people.

What shall we conclude from listening to these people sounding off about welfare? We do not doubt that their complaints were often without full or accurate knowledge of the facts in each case. On the other hand, blacks, especially, live close to welfare recipients and can observe them. Yet we cannot judge the validity or the prejudice of such complaints. We know that some abuse exists. It is a commonplace that the welfare system in America is sadly in need of reform. The main conclusion we draw from our listening is this: many blacks at the Buffalo plant are as much a part of Middle America as whites. It is a conclusion worth thinking about.

CONCLUSION

What have we learned in this chapter about Middle America and blacks, and about the roles of management and the union in such relationships? We found that quite a few Westinghouse–Buffalo Negroes could also be called Middle Americans. We found that Poles, Italians, and others had few feelings of backlash toward blacks, in spite of the strong ethnic ties still existing in Buffalo. We found very few blacks with racist hatreds for whites. In a word, the two races worked well together in the plant, even though neighborhood socialization after work was quite rare.

Few whites claimed that blacks were actually getting preferential treatment, for blacks were a small minority and whites did not feel threatened. But the Westinghouse workers we listened to felt strongly that hiring and promotion should be equal and fair. When any real or imagined evidence to the contrary is uncovered, it is quickly communicated and can become a battle cry. For example, many resented the welfare recipients who took a slice of the workingman's pay check, because they felt these people were taking advantage of the welfare system. This regard for fairness motivates the work force to favor giving the poor a chance at a job but also to oppose any preferential or special treatment for blacks in hiring or in promotion. Westinghouse management and Local 1581 leadership take the same position: neither blacks nor anyone else should be specially helped to come to the plant and to move up in the plant.

But in our opinion the central problem is this: blacks are going to need some form of special help if the present racial imbalance is to be corrected. Negroes represent about 17 percent of the total Buffalo population. While not all of these blacks are of working age, let us say that a target in the Westinghouse plant of 17 percent black is a reasonable possibility. Since the plant is now about 5 percent black, and since this minority improved by only 1 percent from 1965 to 1970, it would take roughly sixty years at that improvement rate to bring the black population up to 17 percent. Now there are several assumptions here (such as the ones we discussed in Chapter 3) and we do not suggest that our predictions are precise. But it remains a possibility. Sixty years would be a long time to wait. In our opinion, both management and the union will need to work together toward the goal of improving the black growth rate at Westinghouse Buffalo.

If both management and union adopt policies aimed at more aggressive affirmative actions on behalf of Negroes, will they be walking a tightrope between blacks and ethnic whites? They will have to balance opposing demands, but the tightrope analogy seems to be exaggerated. We saw much good will between both black and white employees. A solid base for accelerated integration is already there. Furthermore, older workers tend to respect a strong stand taken by management, especially if racial policy is reasonable and supported by federal law. In all our listening and observing, we found that white workers generally would accept blacks, even many new blacks, provided management takes a strong stand. Whites may not like it; but they will not quit. And in time many will adjust. Even in a northern city such as Buffalo, a plant like Westinghouse remains perhaps the most powerful agency for racial mixing and socializing change in the entire city situation.

Blacks have always been present in both the plant and local union. But they remain few. They will want fellow blacks to join them and they will want advancement. The threat of white resentment about preferential treatment remains, but it is far from an insurmountable obstacle, if ingenuity and persuasion are utilized. Westinghouse management, in our opinion, can run a profitable motor and controls making business and at the same time contribute significantly to a major social problem in Buffalo: jobs for black men.

CHAPTER SEVEN

Racial change in a deep-South plant

> *The first Negro girl that came to work out here was named Katie. They really gave her a hard time—all of the ladies in the lounge and in the bathroom. I think that if she hadn't stayed out here and put up the fight that she did, that others of us wouldn't have had a chance. But she stuck it out, and she's still here.*
>
> Anita McCray, black production helper

Opening an industrial plant to black workers once a pattern of segregation has been long established is no easy task for management—especially in the deep South. Careful planning is essential, yet management must also have the courage to begin acting before they have all the answers. This chapter, in part, is the account of how one management in the South was able to bring black employees into its work force after fourteen years of all white existence. Once a breakthrough is made, what is the present status and likely future of race relations in the plant? Our story concerns the Fairbanks International* plant in Memphis, Tennessee.

First, we shall look back to the change from white to black-and-white. The lessons of history can be useful for managers who have yet to make this change. Some plants have barely gone beyond token integration. And for years, in both the North and South, there will be many areas of factories or occupations where blacks will work for the first time. This chapter has something to say about opening racial doors. The recent past also provides a contrast for seeing the progress Fairbanks–Memphis has made.

Present race relations at Fairbanks are of particular interest in our larger study of management and the black worker because in this chapter we are listening to people from the deep South, where some might expect to find deeply ingrained feelings among both blacks and whites.

* Fictitious name.

MEMPHIS: YESTERDAY AND TODAY

Memphis, in the extreme southwest corner of Tennessee, sits high on a bluff overlooking the Mississippi River and the surrounding flatlands. The delta cotton country extends south into Mississippi, a bit north into Tennessee, and west into Arkansas. Memphis grew as the center where cotton bales were sold, loaded onto river boats, and shipped on down the waterway.

With almost 500,000 citizens in 1960[1] Memphis is the largest city in Tennessee, Mississippi, or Arkansas, and is a growing commercial and industrial center eclipsing its past of *The Blues*, catfish, and gambling. Modern multistoried buildings overlook the ancient and wandering Mississippi River. Firestone, RCA, International Harvester, General Electric, Fairbanks International, and other industries have settled into Memphis' history, traditions, and labor force. Memphis has been a stopping-off place for black and white migrants from the cotton and soy bean farms of the Mississippi delta: only 56 percent of the population of the city was born in Tennessee, and more than one-quarter have lived in Memphis less than five years.[2]

With its city limits bordering Mississippi, Memphis is a part of the deep South. It lies directly southwest of Fayette County, which received national publicity as recently as 1961 when black tenant farmers' attempts to register to vote resulted in mass evictions.[3] Reverend Jimmy Grant, now director of a training and employment program in Memphis, led a group of would-be voters to form a tent city. Grant can even remember a lynching in adjacent Fayette County in 1940:

> I can remember the lynching of '40. I remember my father saying, "We don't go out of the house for the next day or two. We don't go down town. If anyone knocks on the door, let me answer." And he had his gun behind the door, and he would always peep out before. Because everybody was frightened and leaflets had been circulated saying, "We got Elbert Williams. Who will be next?" [Williams had organized an NAACP meeting.] And when they found him it was a hideous thing. I didn't know what lynching was, and I questioned my daddy. He said, "A man was killed. And you just don't bother, if you don't understand it. I'll tell you later."

Memphis maintained its tradition of segregation until the early 1960s. The demonstrations and sit-ins of 1961 led to the desegregation of public facilities, the "colored" and "white" rest rooms, and drinking fountains. The

---

[1] U.S. Census 1960. U.S. Preliminary Census figures, 1970, estimate 700,000; no estimate of racial breakdowns is available yet.

[2] James Harry Kellow, *A Study of the Structures and Functions of Public Employment, Retraining and Welfare Agencies in Memphis and Shelby County, Tennessee* (Memphis: Tennessee Department of Employment Security, 1968), p. 11.

[3] *Time*, January 6, 1961, p. 22. Also *Ebony*, March 1961, pp. 61–67.

Shelby County school system was not desegregated until 1963, and in most cases desegregation was token. As late as 1970, 77 percent of the public schools were judged *de facto* segregated.[4]

Although the business community in Memphis has not had the liberalizing effect it had, for example, in Atlanta, business executives did participate in a Human Relations Board during the early 1960s and founded a Plans for Progress Merit Employment Association to take the initial voluntary steps to end discrimination in employment. A top manager of Fairbanks, Roger MacGregor, participated in both these projects, which brought white decision-makers into contact with intelligent and critical Negro representatives. But, as in other parts of the United States, whites were still far from recognizing blacks as equal partners in planning for change.

Southern-born Fairbanks foreman Thomas May, forty-four, told us: "We got prejudice up to the eyeballs around this part of the country." He suggested that the equality enforced in the Fairbanks plant was not generally supported outside. Talking about a white girl who habitually taunts Negroes, May said:

> But you'd be amazed at how the colored girls handle this girl. They just stand up to her. They found out she's loud and opinionated. And they find out they're in a *semiprotected atmosphere*, and they can express their opinions without—see, they can get away with something in here that they can't outside. You take for instance if somebody were to go downtown here, and some colored person made some sort of a snide comment—boy! They'd have the police on them just like that. You just don't do that.

When the authors lived in Memphis in early 1969 there was limited interracial visiting among some church and civic organizations but little joint membership in integrated groups. In 1970, however, Willis Wing, a black active in the community, reported that "Memphis is really progressing in interracial socializing among the young and the middle class."

THE BLACK COMMUNITY

About 40 percent (200,000 people)[5] of the total population of Memphis are black, with 33 percent at the working ages of eighteen to sixty-four. Following the national pattern, more neighborhoods near downtown Memphis are becoming black, while new all-white suburbs such as the appropriately named and affluent Whitehaven spring up around the city.

Walking through a black neighborhood just east of the Fairbanks plant, one sees that working people with moderate incomes occupy attractive single-

---

[4] Figures are from a report of the unanimous decision of the Supreme Court that Memphis schools must integrate. *New York Times*, March 10, 1970, pp. 1 and 24.

[5] *Social and Economic Conditions of Negroes in the United States* (Washington, D.C.: Bureau of the Census, 1967), p. 47.

family homes with small lawns. In 1960, however, 13.7 percent of the housing in the portions of Shelby County where blacks reside was classified as dilapidated, while this was true of only 2.1 percent of the white housing.[6] Other figures show a large gap between the income levels of blacks and whites. In Shelby County, for example, over 57 percent of the Negro families had incomes below the "poverty level" of $3,000 in 1960, while only 13.8 percent of the white families were that poor. Unemployment in January 1969 was estimated at 2.6 percent by the Tennessee Department of Employment Security. Black unemployment was over twice as high, and employed blacks are overrepresented in the unskilled and laboring positions. Marshall and Van Adams put the basic cause of the Negro's disadvantage in "institutionalized discrimination" affecting both the demand for and the supply of Negro workers:

> On the supply side, Negroes suffer from skill disadvantages, inadequate knowledge of job opportunities, and limited access to the same training and employment channels used by whites. On the demand side, white employers, like whites in general, have regarded Negroes as inferior people not suited for higher level jobs and, therefore, have either neglected blacks or discriminated against them when seeking skilled manpower.[7]

The median educational level of blacks over twenty-five years old in 1960 was 6.7 years, while the median white had completed 11.1 years of school.[8]

Negroes are not represented in city government in anywhere near their proportion of the population. In 1968 three of thirteen city councilmen were black; 5 percent of the members of all city boards but none of the Memphis School Board members were black, although two nonvoting black advisers to the Board were appointed in 1969. The then mayor of Memphis was not popular in the black community. Listen to Fairbanks employee Marian Scruggs:

> Have you heard of our mayor, Loeb? I say it's the best thing that could've happened to a Negro here. I tell you the reason why. Because if they had elected a man that they felt was for the Negro, he would have paid off to the first two Negroes. They wouldn't have said anything. But Loeb comes out and tells you that he don't want you. He don't like you. And then this will give you something to go from... with Loeb, can't nobody compromise with him. He don't like it, he let you know he don't like it, and this brings things out.
>
> But just like Nixon, all the colored people don't like Nixon. But it's the best thing that can happen to the world, because he'll bring out the

---

[6] Donald D. Stewart, *Poverty in Memphis and Shelby County* (Memphis: Memphis State University Bureau of Social Research, 1966), p. 47.

[7] F. Ray Marshall and Arvil Van Adams, "Negro Employment in Memphis," *Industrial Relations*, Vol. IX, No. 3, May 1970, p. 322.

[8] Stewart, *op. cit.*, p. 46.

same thing. Then you will have something to go on. But as long as you have a person who cover up, cover up, you never will get anywhere.

Civil rights activities reached a climax in Memphis in early 1968 with the black garbage workers' strike. The grievances, through the action of Dr. Martin Luther King and local leaders, helped to galvanize the black community into a cooperative, unified, and forceful group. Setting aside personal and ideological differences, a new unified civil rights group was formed: Community on the Move for Equality (COME).

The garbage piled up while the black community resorted to marches and demonstrations to publicize the demands of the garbage workers. Many white citizens backed the mayor in his adamant resistance to the pressures of the strikers, saying that the strike was unwarranted and King was an irresponsible rabble rouser. It was inconceivable to many Memphians that local blacks could harbor the bitter and intense frustration that had shown itself in the riots in northern cities. The best way to handle the unprovoked strike was by being firm and inflexible. Many other whites did not support Loeb, but most were silent. Garbage continued to gather along the routes of the police-escorted garbage trucks.

Rev. Martin Luther King was shot on April 4, 1968 at Memphis' Lorraine Motel. The bitter disputes and gross misunderstandings that surrounded the strike, plus the totally divergent views that blacks and whites had of Martin Luther King, collided violently that night. The rift between the black and white communities and the resulting riot was not limited to Memphis: many U.S. cities experienced riots on the night of April 4.

In Memphis, as in other U.S. cities, community organizations function best when their activities are focused on specific, urgent grievances. After the garbage workers' strike was settled, unity and cooperation in the black community began to fade. The black community again united in the fall of 1969 when two new issues appeared: a hospital workers' strike and demands for immediate black representation on the all-white School Board. The continued conservatism of the city government and its rejection of some of these demands provided the occasion for renewed cohesion and militancy in the black community. Whether Memphis has entered a period where progress for the black community will come only after confrontation and turbulence, or whether black and white moderates will speak up and give leadership for rapid but peaceful change, remains to be seen.

Other civil rights groups range from the Urban League and the National Association for the Advancement of Colored People, once a leader, to the newer Invaders. The Invaders are a small, loosely organized group of young black militants. They speak loudly and have some influence, but have little in the way of a program. As with other newer black groups, the Invaders want to build black political and economic power and pride in black manhood, although one white Fairbanks union leader said that "their militancy and disregard for all law is creating the exact opposite effect."

The more conservative elements of the black community were perhaps best represented in the Memphis black schools. Most of the black principals and teachers felt that their purpose was to prepare their students to live in a largely white society, where color supposedly made no difference. Their goal is full integration. Other observers indict the schools for spilling youths out onto the streets without real values or with too little parental control. As for the young blacks, a good number drop out of what they consider to be an irrelevant school.

FROM LILY WHITE TO BLACK AND WHITE

Fairbanks International began manufacturing in Memphis early in 1947 with 100 employees producing electronic components such as attenuators, head phones, and condensers. Similar product lines were soon added, increasing the work force to 500. In the late 1950s and early 1960s operations from several other Fairbanks plants were consolidated at Memphis. The plant expanded rapidly until 1966, when it leveled off with a total work force of over 1,200, spread almost equally among three full shifts. In 1961, near the beginning of this period of expansion, the first Negro was hired.

THE STRATEGY OF DESEGREGATION

When asked why the plant began with white employees only, Mr. Kenneth Smith, one of the managers who opened the Fairbanks–Memphis plant, told us that it had not occurred to management in 1947 to bring in Negroes. The common practice in all industries at that time was to conform to southern custom and practice. Roger MacGregor, a current manager, described the management's position during the late 1940s and 1950s: "I think the social conscience was there over the years. We were fighting the problem of the general overall situation in the South, and we weren't going to crusade." MacGregor attributed the decision to hire blacks at the Fairbanks–Memphis plant to encouragement from the corporate and divisional levels, which began in 1958, to a gradual change in the racial climate in Memphis and to beginning community acceptance of such desegregated facilities as cafeterias, drinking fountains, and toilets.

Earlier, in the 1950s, local civil rights leaders had approached the Fairbanks management asking that Negroes be hired. Neither these civil rights leaders nor MacGregor felt that their efforts influenced the decision significantly. One of the local men described his visit to the plant with Mr. Augustus Fox of the National Urban League, who had been consulting with Fairbanks at the corporate level:

> Mr. MacGregor told us emphatically that the plant was not built to accommodate Negro employees [it did not have separate rest rooms,

> lounges, and locker rooms for blacks] ... and he definitely so stated. And Augustus Fox asked: "What do you mean, wasn't built for, wasn't conducive to employing Negroes?" And Augustus could use some stronger words than I could. He said: "They all do the same thing. Where do these people go to?" It wasn't humorous. It really was a dark picture. And we began to send in committees from here.... But when the change really came was when the compliance officials of the Federal Government [began to be active].... The reason for this change, like many, was not civil rights movements, not marches, not demonstrations, but government contracts.

MacGregor remembered his meetings with the Urban League as friendly.

Nor was the need for labor a major consideration in Fairbank's decision to desegregate. The pay at Fairbanks compared favorably to that of local industry and the plant management had no difficuty recruiting an adequate number of employees from the all-white labor pool.

The Fairbanks plant was organized by the Electrical Workers of America* (EWA), Local 40, AFL-CIO. Although the local reflected the segregationist feelings of the majority of its membership, it was not a significant factor, positive or negative, in the decision to desegregate. On the national level, the EWA had taken a stand in support of Negro workers but with no apparent effect on the local.

Once the decision was made, management made its position clear to the foremen, most of whom were southern. Charles Thayer, another manager, told us of some of the preparations:

> I can remember when the decision was made: We will hire a Negro. This was brought up to the total plant at a foremen's meeting. And the plant manager, MacGregor, said: "This is the right thing to do, and we are going to do it. We are not here to discuss the pros and cons of it. We are here to say that this is what is going to be accomplished. And I would like each of you to come down and tell me, if you were plant manager, how you would do it. And give this to me in writing."

By 1961 the idea of working in the same plant with a Negro was not totally foreign to the people of Memphis, but the prospect of using the same rest rooms, locker rooms, and eating areas was strongly resented by many. Top management was firm in insisting that the new Negro employees be accepted and that they use the same facilities as the whites. Said Catherine Stagg, fifty-two, who had been at the plant since its beginning:

> Of course, when they brought them in out here, you know, they told us that we'd have to learn to accept them. They would use our bathrooms, use our water fountains and everything, you know.... We'd just have to learn to accept it. Of course, we didn't like that either, too much, drinking after a Negro, like that. But the men that come around and

---
*Fictitious name.

clean up, well, they'll always wash the water fountains good, and everything.

NEGRO PIONEERS OF THE PAST

The first black employee, Mrs. Katie Fuller, was very carefully chosen after three interviews, the last being with the assistant plant manager, the personnel manager, and a general foreman. A bright high school graduate, then twenty-one years old, Mrs. Fuller had successfully held three previous jobs, including one in the North in an integrated group. Fairbanks management was aware of possible hostile white reaction, given the Memphis racial climate in the early 1960s, and scheduled Mrs. Fuller to work the same hours as office and management staff, rather than the normal second or third shift hours new hires usually worked. She was given a regular job, but one that required close contact with only one other girl, and that girl, young and sympathetic, was hired at the same time. Mrs. Nora Larkin, who had been with the company since 1948, explained on what conditions she agreed to break in Katie Fuller on her job:

> When they brought the first one in here, I said I would train her. I didn't have to do it, but my foreman asked me if I would train her. I said: "Yes, I will train her under two conditions: first, I will train her just like I would train a white girl. I'm not going to give her any whip because she's a Nigger." And I said: "Then the second thing: I am not her buddy either. I do not go on break with her." I said: "If you meet them two conditions, okay."

The harassment and personal abuse that Mrs. Fuller and the girl who worked with her endured were intense; however, the assistant plant manager did keep in touch with her, asking her how things were going. Mrs. Fuller found it reassuring that management was "keeping an eye on her," as she described it, but it did not reduce the day-to-day suffering:

> I didn't know I was the only colored person. I thought they had hired a bunch of them, you know. [Management had explained that she was the first Negro in the plant. But Katie evidently thought there would be several pioneers.] And when I got out here—nobody but me and the good Lord know what I went through. But I just pray. I asked God to help me. I said: "Help me, Jesus, I got to work somewhere. . . ."
> And they would have to come down this certain aisle going out. See, they would be getting off, while we would still be working. They'd get off at 3:10, and we'd be working almost to 4:20. And they come through here hollering "Nigger," and talking all kind of ugly talk. Cursing. And I would look over to the side, to the space next to me. And I thought these people were crazy. And I'd look at 'em and I would laugh. I'd kinda smile. It took a whole lot out of me, you know. And I never worked with anybody like this before. A whole plant of people in here were—I don't know how to describe it. Devil action!

"Nigger Katie"; "Katie, you're from the Congo"; and other insulting names and phrases were scrawled on washroom doors. Anonymous calls threatened that her house would be bombed if she did not quit. She found a small doll with a hangman's noose around its neck on her locker. And a group of employees hid and peeked around the corner of the lockers to watch her surprise and fear. She would constantly hear laughs and snickers directed at her.

Katie Fuller felt that her first foreman was prejudiced and tried to get her to quit:

> I used to hate the man, he was so mean to me. He would say: "If you don't like this, you know what you can do." I was doing a good job; I know I was, and I was told that I was by the manager in personnel, by the big wheels. I was told that I doing an *especially* good job.... But my foreman, he would get with the employees and they would laugh and snicker. You know when people talk about you. Like you and I getting together and we're talking about (she whispers), "Nigger this and Nigger that." And they start laughing real loud. And this was happening right here in this plant, and I would keep right on working. I wasn't supposed to do anything about it.

But later, when working for another foreman, she had to ask for help. She got help:

> One night this girl got on my nerves so bad, I went and told my foreman. I said: "Looka here, I've taken enough! I'm not going to work out here, and all this hollering and snickering and all. No job in the world is worth it. I'll leave tonight, if I got to work under these conditions, and I mean it!" So he [the foreman] asked me who was bothering me, and I told him. And I went and got the girl, and she went and got her union steward.

> And the foreman said: "I don't care who you bring in here. Katie is doing her job, and you are pestering her. And she is going to work out here, even if you don't." And that girl had been out here a good while. "You see, I heard complaints on you," he said. "People have told me that you have been pestering her." From that day to this, she hasn't bothered me.

The strong position taken by this foreman was effective. The white girl continued to be prejudiced and difficult, according to Katie, but she stopped harassing her. But one might ask why the foreman had not done anything sooner if he knew that Katie was being harassed.

In August 1961, two months after Katie Fuller was hired, Bernard Ivy was employed at Fairbanks–Memphis as a janitor. Then thirty-four years old, with experience at a variety of jobs, Mr. Ivy was a thoughtful, patient, and capable man who has since become a friend and spokesman for many of the black employees in the plant. According to Alfred Magner, turned down in

1961 but now a mechanic and union official at Fairbanks, twenty-one black men were interviewed for this one janitorial job. The fact that blacks of Ivy and Magner's caliber were eager for a janitor's job revealed a lot about the job discrimination that a black man faced in 1961 both in Memphis and at the Fairbanks plant.

Bernard Ivy did not encounter as much resistance as did Katie, perhaps partly because he was a man, but especially because he held a position often assigned to Negroes:

> I haven't had too many problems in the plant as a whole, for the simple reason because I was already on the bottom of the totem pole. You understand? You don't get any problems when you are already a floor sweeper. That's why I didn't have the problems that another individual would have.

We recall Catherine Stagg's remark that in 1961 whites did not like coming to a water fountain and "drinking after a Negro." Ironically, Ivy was assigned to wash the drinking fountains. With amusement, he told us about his efforts to challenge this ancient southern taboo. Speaking of a white fellow janitor who shared the responsibility for cleaning these facilities, Ivy said:

> And I noticed that if he were going to the water fountain or something, If *I* stopped, he'd stand way back in the corner and go to another water fountain. So the next day I come into the plant I said: "Well, I'm going to make sure that he's going to drink out of one of these water fountains behind me." Because every water fountain I came to, I stopped and had a drink (laughter).... We didn't have any conversations, just a staring conversation. And I was about to bust, I was drinking so much water. It sound comical, but it's true.

The Fairbanks plant was fortunate to have Negro pioneers who were able to cope with the difficult transition period. The hopes and aspirations of other blacks and the success of white-black relations for the larger society depended on their persistence, courage, and maturity. Anita McCray, twenty, a production helper, said that it was due to them that she and the other Negroes had been given a chance: "The first Negro girl that came to work out here was named Katie.... I think that if she hadn't stayed out here and put up the fight that she did, that others of us wouldn't have had a chance. But she stuck it out, and she's still here."

Aside from the personal qualifications of the Negro pioneers, another reason for the success of the Fairbanks plant desegregation was the careful selection and planning by management, and especially the support of top management, although desegregation took place at a time when the small management staff was already taxed by rapid expansion, and Roger MacGregor was not able to devote as much time to it as he would have liked. If we may "Monday morning quarterback," two problems are apparent now nearly ten years later: while Fairbanks top and middle management strongly supported the Negro pioneers, some first-line management did not consistently do so. It is true that, in fear, the victim of harassment may well not tell her foreman about it. Admittedly, it is often difficult for a foreman to know what is really going on among his work group. Yet foremen have a serious responsibility to support such pioneers and top management needs to check up on the foremen.

One might ask if it would have been advisable for Fairbanks to have brought in several blacks at the same time so they could give one another moral support. On the other hand, one of our black consultants said that if Fairbanks had brought in a dozen or so "it probably would have caused a great deal of fights between the races." There is no simple answer.

Happily, the desegregation transition was successfully made. White workers at Fairbanks–Memphis eventually began to accept the new black employees. Manager Charles Thayer remembered it this way:

> By about the third or fourth one that they got in here, they couldn't keep doing it. I don't know how long it lasted. It was six months, nine months, something like that before it settled down. Yes, there were repercussions. It's not an easy transition, but by the same token I think we overcame it very well. We didn't have riots or fights or anything like this.

Alfred Magner was the second black man to be hired when he began as a warehouseman at Fairbanks in 1963. He, like Bernard Ivy, ran into much less resistance than Mrs. Fuller. Magner, a distinguished-looking man with slightly graying hair, put it this way:

> There was no *major* problems. But fellows let me know. As a matter of fact, one fellow told me point-black that he didn't think I should have been here. He said he didn't particularly dislike me, of course. But there wasn't any love lost between us . . . and that is about the only problem that I've had, so far as people are concerned. . . . Of course, having been around this place quite some time, you can tell if people want to be around you or not. And I have some very good relationships particularly after I came up here [to his new mechanic's job].

In addition, some young Negro women coming to Fairbanks at that time found little trouble. Dolores Hemphill, for example, hired in the fall of 1963 after two years of college, said she had a "real good" trainer and although she had some trouble with one of the mechanics, found most of her fellow workers receptive:

CAVANAGH: No trouble, no discrimination . . . ?

MRS. HEMPHILL: No. I have never had any trouble getting along with anybody, anyway. I have heard some of the other girls every now and then say that they had a little run-in, but then some of those girls are girls that

I know have had run-ins all the time, too . . . in fact, all the girls in our department seem to be just real regular. There doesn't seem to be any hostility between the girls at all.

And Iantha Asbury, twenty-seven, hired in 1964, the first Negro woman steward in the plant, also had just a little trouble:

When I first came here I was the first Negro on the capacitator line. And I didn't have any trouble with the girls, on the whole. It was another young lady that I had a little trouble with that worked on the other side, in circuits. . . . And I really ignored her. And after a while it was all right.

Regarding Mrs. Katie Fuller she said:

Oh-h-h, she had it . . . but Katie's got the personality where she handled it. And it was all right. She's still here . . . and I could understand their point. But I also could understand Katie's point or the other girls that hired in. And it was hard for both of them, really. That's the way I look at it. . . . When I see that both of them are trying, then I say: "Well, it's not because they dislike Negroes or they dislike whites. It's because they've never been around."

By 1964 the most difficult transition years at Fairbanks International had passed, although tensions would inevitably rise with each new breakthrough— the first Negroes in new departments, the first black mechanics, and so forth.

HIRING AND PROMOTING BLACKS

PROFILE OF THE WORK FORCE

Who are the people who work at the Fairbanks International plant? The typical employee was a middle-aged white woman. Two-thirds of the employees were women working at machines that produce small, delicate components. Their work was light, quick, repetitive, and well paid. As can be seen in Table 7-1, there were some very dramatic differences in background between the white and black employees: the blacks were much younger and more recently hired; with less seniority, they tended to have less skilled jobs, and were also more likely to get the less desirable night shifts. One of the biggest differences between the races was in education. Practically all the blacks had a high school diploma, while one-quarter of the whites did not. Even more importantly, only about 7 percent of the whites but 33 percent of the blacks had had some college. Since the educational level of whites in the area was considerably higher than that of blacks, it seems that the blacks coming to Fairbanks were the best of the black community. Whether or not

186   The local experience

*Table 7–1. Profile of the Hourly Workers
Fairbanks International–Memphis, 1969**

	Black	White
Age		
29 and under	82%	26%
30 to 39	16	27
40 to 49	2	31
50 to 59	0	17
60 and over	0	0
Average age	25 years	38 years
Education (highest grade completed)		
Some college	33%	7%
High school graduate	65	67
High School 3 & 4	1	10
High school, 1 & 2	1	13
8 grades or less	1	3
Average grades completed	12.3 grades	11.4 grades
Birthplace		
Deep South	99%	97%
West	0	4
Outside of U.S.	1	0
Residence		
City	95%	80%
Suburb	0	7
Outlying	5	0
Skill level		
Craftsman	4%	28%
Operative	95	68
Laborer	1	4
Shift worked		
Day	21%	43%
Evening	39	27
Night	40	30
Date hired		
1940 to 1949	0%	23%
1950 to 1959	0	13
1960 to 1964	15	23
1965 to 1966	39	20
1967	11	10
1968	35	10
Average years of service	3 years	9 years

* The profile and attitude tables in this chapter are weighted projections from the random sample.

they had had better education (Negro schools in Memphis and the counties are seriously inferior, perhaps about two grade levels behind white schools),[9] the marked differences in Table 7-1 at least indicate a strong educational motivation on the part of the blacks.

We have seen that integration began slowly at Fairbanks International's Memphis plant with the careful selection of a few pioneers. As seen in

[9] "One estimate by the Memphis Superintendent of Schools based on achievement test scores was that an eighth-grade education in a predominantly black school was roughly equivalent to a sixth-grade education in a predominantly white school. The gap probably widens at higher levels of education, as has been found to be the case in other school systems." Marshall and Van Adams, *op. cit.*, p. 314.

Percent black

* As percent of all employees **

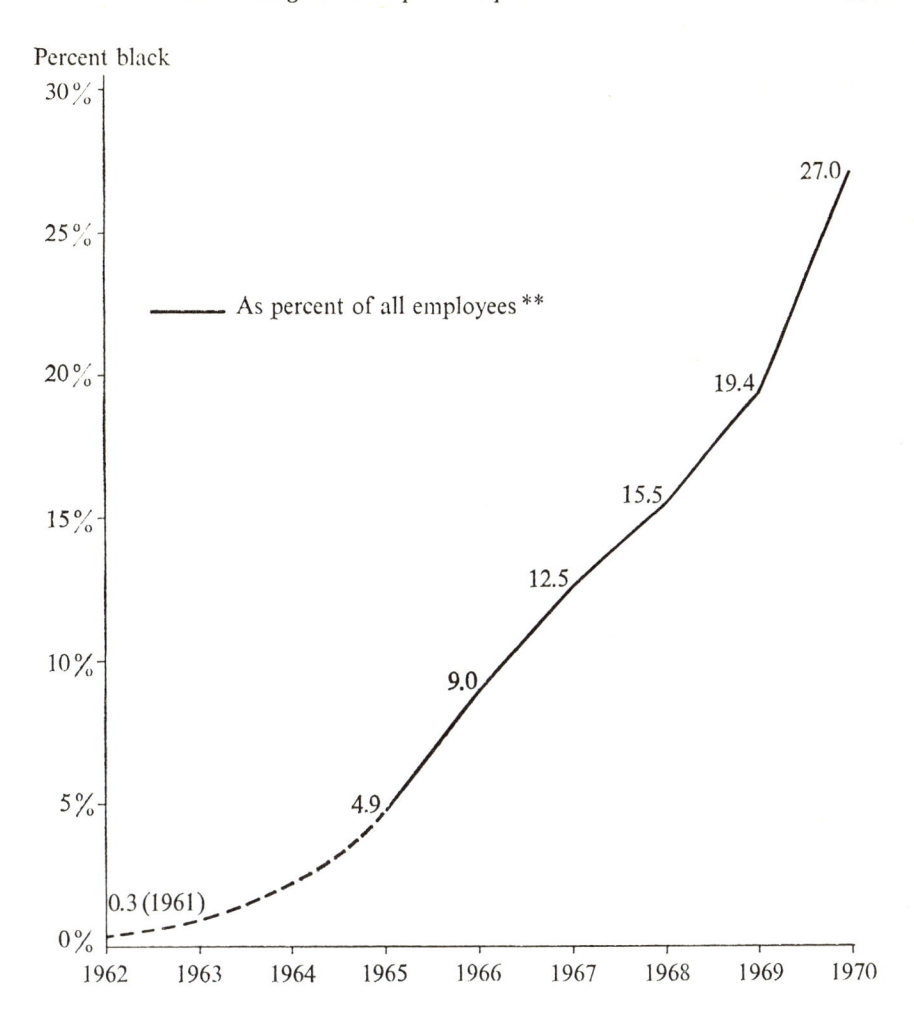

Values on curve: 0.3 (1961), 4.9, 9.0, 12.5, 15.5, 19.4, 27.0

* Broken line indicates estimate.
** The percent black of blue collar employees is practically the same

FIGURE 7–1. **Growth of Black Employment
Fairbanks–Memphis
January 1962 to January 1970***

Figure 7-1, less than 5 percent of the hourly work force was black in January 1965, despite a 33 percent minority labor market. However, in 1966, 9.7 percent of the hourly workers were black, although there were no black craftsmen or white collar workers. January 1969 saw more improvement with 19 percent of all employees and 21 percent of the blue collar workers black. Seven black craftsmen, a black technician, and a black clerical worker had been hired. Fifty percent of the women hired during 1968 were black. Also, by 1969 Fairbanks had hired fourteen disadvantaged people in fulfillment of a National Alliance of Businessmen pledge. (See Chapter 9.)

Yet almost a quarter of the black men and women we interviewed thought that there was some racial discrimination in hiring, often at the Tennessee state employment office. And 27 percent of the blacks thought that there was discrimination in promotion.

BLACK WOMEN AND TENNESSEE EMPLOYMENT SECURITY

Fairbanks had done most of its hiring of hourly employees through the Tennessee Department of Employment Security (TDES).

The only exception was the men who applied for a mechanic's job; they came directly to the plant to be interviewed and tested. All others were screened first by the state agency. Dave Rodgers of personnel explained what they did: "The employment center has a certain set of criteria. If they meet these norms, if they have a high school education or the equivalent, if they are between the height limits of 5'2" to 5'9" and they're over eighteen, they can refer them out here." Tennessee Employment Security also administered a test for Fairbanks and automatically eliminated those who did not come up to the Fairbanks standards. Those who met the criteria were then referred to the personnel office at the plant for final selection. Tennessee Employment has had, and still somewhat retains, a reputation for being discriminatory. Until recently TDES maintained two segregated divisions. Daniel Flaherty, presently in line management but formerly in personnel, recalled that until 1965 he had to call one office for black workers and another for whites:

> They had two different offices up there. This nearly floored me. You have to call the black office and the white office. How they got away with that for as long as they did! We had no other way to get Negroes except to call what they considered their farm labor or something like this. But if you called the one on Poplar Street, you could get blacks.

Civil rights leaders and employees described the tactics that they believed Tennessee Employment Security used to thwart blacks trying to get a job. Said black leader Rev. Jimmy Grant: "The Tennessee Employment Security might sit on this job order for one or two weeks. The position had to be filled. There are plenty of qualified people around. But they will take the order and say, 'We can't find a Negro.' Then Fairbanks can put it on their record that they tried." Reverend Hadley, also concerned with employment, described another apparently discriminatory practice:

> We have had some complaints at Fairbanks that Negro girls go there [TDES], and they don't get referred back to Fairbanks. They said: "I came for a test for Fairbanks." They [TDES] want to send them to

> some other little place, you know, where the wage scale is even different and everything else.

Tennessee Employment's main office assisted people over twenty-three years of age, whereas those under twenty-three got help through the Youth Opportunity Center. For Rosemary Venson, twenty-two, failure to refer her to Youth Opportunity meant a long delay in getting a job at Fairbanks: "Every time I go to the Tennessee Employment Office, they kept saying I wasn't old enough, and I was twenty-one when I tried. They kept saying, 'You're not old enough. Come back when you're twenty-three.' And I just didn't know what to do." She finally obtained her job with the assistance of the employment and training project run by Reverend Jimmy Grant. Others were told by TDES that they were "too tall" or "too short." Mollie Coleman, twenty-three, worked at Fairbanks but she first was told that she was too short:

> I carried a friend of mine down to the employment office, and she was trying to get an application for Fairbanks. They told her that she was too tall. And I asked 'em to give me one, and they told me I was too short. They say you had to be 5'4". So the next day I went back down, and I was 5'4", so they gave me an application.

Despite these problems, however, Fairbanks was able to increase the number of blacks in the plant. The state employment agency was under federal and local pressure to place more blacks, and to place them in better jobs. Dave Rodgers, who spoke earlier about the employment center, suggested that the large number of black referrals to Fairbanks in 1968 and 1969 was largely because of these pressures. Also, as the number of black women in the plant increased, more black women had applied because they had friends at Fairbanks. This referral procedure, plus the grapevine, is one of the most effective ways to recruit new employees. By 1970, a year after our interviews, 37 percent of all women operatives at Fairbanks were black.

JOBS FOR BLACK MEN

The story of black men at Fairbanks was not nearly so bright, and the problem was much more difficult. At the beginning of 1969, there were sixteen black men in a plant that employed 390 white men; black men were 3.9 percent of the total male work force in a city with a 33 percent minority work force. Stockhandler Richard Ellington, twenty-nine, suggested that these numbers in themselves had led some employees to wonder whether blacks were still discriminated against at the Fairbanks plant:

> When I first started here, which was two years ago, there was only seven Negro men working here. But now we have, they hired one last week, we have may be seventeen or eighteen. That's all. So there would have to be some unfairness, because it would be more. At one time they

claimed the Negro didn't apply for these jobs, but we know definite people we had recommended to come out and take these tests. But I do feel that they are improving their hiring practices.

Part of the reason for the low number of Negro men is that 90 percent of the hourly paid positions open to men are jobs as mechanics, operating and maintaining complex machines. Management has had difficulty finding Negro men who they feel have the aptitude and skills necessary to do the job.

But it seems that Fairbanks management only recently began looking for black mechanics. A single black laborer was hired in 1961; a second black man was hired as a material supplier, a semiskilled position, in 1963. Both these men had sufficient mechanical aptitude so that they were later promoted into the mechanical craft but not until 1966 and 1969. The first black mechanic was hired from outside and another was promoted in 1966, five years after desegregation. Apart from the shortage of qualified applicants, the delay may also represent apprehension about the reaction of white workers. Black janitors and stockhandlers were common enough in Memphis and, more important, their work did not bring them into close contact with many other employees.

Alfred Magner, who we said was the second Negro man hired by Fairbanks, felt strongly that management was reluctant to make a black man a mechanic and did so only when they could no longer avoid it:

> From the time that I got here, I was asking: "What's the problem that you cannot find any Negroes?" And they said that the fellows that were qualified, they were on other jobs; and they didn't believe in taking anybody off of another job. There was just a scarcity; they couldn't find Negroes that were qualified. I know that was just an excuse and I'm sure everybody else knew that was just an excuse. something to justify not doing it.

Magner went on to say:

> I haven't seen a job in this plant that I don't feel that they could find some qualified Negro man to do it. I've been around here, and I've seen the plant in operation. Even now on this particular job I'm on now [mechanic], I was led to believe that it was so tough. But it's not the case.

Management's view was that hiring or promoting mechanics required some caution. Dave Rodgers explained:

> So what you're talking about—you're talking about hiring a man in, and you're going to give him responsibility for a piece of equipment that's maybe worth $200,000. That's a big risk. Not to mention training time, which averages two years before a man is fully productive.

Fairbanks management used flexible hiring criteria, balancing scores on both mechanical and dexterity tests with an appraisal of previous work. They were able to be most flexible, they felt, with the black men already in the plant whose performance could be observed on a day-to-day basis. Personnel official Bill Phillips explained how it worked for one man who was promoted:

> I can pick one out, Eric Fraley, a Negro man who was on material handling. He is now elevated to a mechanic. Why is this so? Well, he demonstrated a certain level of mechanical ability and comprehension. Looking at his total background from a mechanical angle, I guess you wouldn't give him an opportunity. But we were able to look at this man from his performance. We gave him an opportunity.

But there were still very few black men at Fairbanks, and the problem promises to remain critical for some time to come. Five black mechanics were hired in 1968, and management had set a goal of bringing in seven more during 1969. At seven mechanics a year, assuming the total number of mechanics to remain the same and the new blacks to take positions formerly held by whites, it would take about thirteen years to bring the percentage of black skilled craftsmen up to 33 percent, the percentage of blacks in the Memphis working population in 1960.

As of June 1970 Fairbanks International had seventeen minority mechanics. Management said that it would be happy to hire more if they could find the qualified applicants. The primary source will have to be men hired in as mechanics, since there are few unskilled and semiskilled positions from which black men with mechanical potential might be promoted, as Ivy, Magner, and Fraley were. Despite new approaches which included advertising in the black newspaper and contacting poverty, civil rights, and community agencies, Fairbanks was having a very difficult time finding qualified applicants for these skilled mechanics' jobs. There was no question that vocational education for Negroes in the Memphis area had been poor for many years and that opportunities for blacks to gain experience as mechanics had been limited. Some kind of compensatory education is going to be necessary if Negroes are to obtain and hold the mechanics' jobs available at Fairbanks. Fairbanks management did not then feel able to undertake such extensive training themselves, even with federal funding. The management staff felt they were simply too few to carry out this kind of project. But some kind of intensified recruiting and training will be necessary if black men are to take their part in the work force.

ARE BLACKS GETTING PREFERENTIAL TREATMENT?

In 1968 over 34 percent of all hires and 50 percent of all women hired were black. Many whites said that management was leaning over backwards to hire blacks and 11 percent thought that blacks were definitely getting special breaks in promotion, while 22 percent thought they might be.

In just nine years the number of blacks in the plant had risen from zero to almost 300, and the number had increased much more rapidly recently. Foreman Paul Tate, forty-nine, who thought that the company has gone "hog wild" in hiring blacks, saw employees' reactions like this:

> There's been two ways of it. There's been almost a complete change of attitude. Because I think the people have accepted the fact that this is coming. Fact is, I had a little girl working for me one time, first colored girl we had here, she hid behind boxes over there, and they cursed her, and threw water on her, and everything else. And now she's working right back there with 'em, and fitting in fine.
> But then we got this other thin line that's begun to form, that they think—not all of them, but there's a segment of them—that thinks that the company is leaning over backwards to increase the number of Negro employees.

Some whites did see the broader implications of trying to help minority people. Mississippi-born white mechanic Idell Jemison, forty-four, who had been in the plant for twenty years, felt that the white work force was not much bothered with the preferential treatment issue:

> Well, maybe momentarily or something. But they seem to realize the position that the country is in, and all this pressure, you know, from the recent loss and stuff [the King assassination]. We realize, you know it hasn't been no problem on my part—because I feel like this had to be. Just take time to make the adjustment.

Other whites found preferential treatment more difficult to understand, such as the view expressed by a white mechanic, Reginald Dalton, forty:

> I don't know, it's just like they got a couple of mechanics upstairs, colored fellas; oh God, they've trained one of 'em, I think it's been four months now. A white person, they wouldn't do it. I mean, they go out of their way. Well, like I say, there's always two sides to it. Somebody like that, I mean, they do need extra help.
> I know that somebody like that, you say, who's at a disadvantage to begin with, why I do think they do need extra training and so forth.

We feel that the issue of preferential treatment—what it means and whether or not it can be justified—deserves further analysis and we shall do this in Chapter 10.

EMPLOYEES DISCUSS THEIR WORK

Did we find any racial differences in blue collar employees' attitudes toward their working situation at Fairbanks? We shall use here the same indicator of worker satisfaction that we described in Chapter 5: our index combining eleven attitudes toward the job, training, foreman, chances for promotion,

Racial change in a deep-South plant 193

and the company. On a scale from 1 to 5 (5 is high), the Fairbanks blacks and whites both scored 3.4. This meant that they were moderately satisfied with their work. Interestingly, there was no difference between the races. Table 7-2 pinpoints one specific attitude.

Table 7-2. Attitude Toward My Job
Hourly employees by race, Fairbanks-Memphis

	Black	White
Favorable	57%	63%
Uncertain	38	30
Unfavorable	5	7

Once again, we found the majority of the employees favorable, with no important racial difference.

Table 7-3 shows another important aspect of work: the employees' attitude toward the foreman. This attitude was also one of the components in the general factor mentioned above.

Table 7-3. Attitude Toward My Foreman
Hourly employees by race, Fairbanks-Memphis

	Black	White
Favorable	74%	72%
Uncertain	20	17
Unfavorable	6	11

The foremen appear to be generally quite well received by their employees, with little difference between whites and blacks.

Before we leave the area of job satisfaction, let us see how Fairbanks foremen evaluated their black and white employees. While the foreman can sometimes be prejudiced, he is perhaps the one person best qualified to evaluate an employee. Quantity of output is a significant work virtue and the employees were rewarded for it on an incentive system. According to Table 7-4, all the foremen saw blacks equal to whites in production. Quality was also an important issue and each employee was held to account for any rejects. Almost all foremen said that the quality of blacks' work was good.

Table 7-4. Job Performance of Hourly Blacks
Percentage of foremen who judge that blacks do as well as the average worker, Fairbanks-Memphis

	Better	About the Same	Worse
Quantity of Work	0%	100%	0%
Quality of Work	0	87	12
Attendance	12	62	25
Promptness	12	75	12
Accepting Responsibility	0	62	37
Personality at Work	0	100	0
Discipline at Work	0	100	0
Ability to Learn Job	0	62	37
Promotability	0	62	37

* May not always equal 100 percent because of rounding.

Because of more difficult living conditions and often because of greater transportation problems, it may not be surprising that 25 percent of the foremen rated blacks less satisfactory in attendance. Ability to learn the job and promotability are closely related and again may simply reflect here the newness of the young black workers. Over one-third of the foremen rated blacks lower in these qualities. All the foremen rated the blacks equal in personality and discipline at work.

BLACK-WHITE RELATIONS IN A DEEP-SOUTH PLANT

Eight years after desegregation, race relations at the Fairbanks plant were generally good. There were still some incidents of harassment, and racial barriers tended to rise at lunch and breaks. But in the work areas most whites had adjusted well. Blacks and whites worked elbow to elbow with little friction and often in genuine friendliness.

Foreman Thomas May, forty-three, described his pleasure and surprise at the ease with which this had happened:

MAY: I was amazed at how well they got along in this plant. Because the plant that I came from had no colored at all. Completely segregated. And I just didn't know how I was going to handle this kind of situation. What their reactions were going to be.

CAVANAGH: When did you come up here?

MAY: In '65. And I was quite amazed. It's hard, your not having come from this part of the country, you don't realize. It's hard to realize that you can take a colored girl and a white girl and set them side-by-side on the job, and they're both doing the same thing. And they'll work together nicely. I mean, this is just something you don't do in this part of the country. For crying out loud, they don't sit together on buses down here; they still don't, if they can get away with it. But they'll come down here to work, and they'll work with them.

CAVANAGH: How do you explain that?

MAY: I don't know. I really don't know. I'm just happy that it is. *I think it's because they know that they've got to. They're forced into a situation that they would not try themselves!* And they found, well, for crying out loud, they're another human being.

Employees agreed that blacks and whites got along well on the job. While workers at Memphis did not describe race relations quite so positively as the employees at our other locations, Table 7-5 shows that three-fourths of the blacks and 80 percent of the whites felt that the races got along well on the job. Very few felt they did not.

Racial change in a deep-South plant

Table 7-5. Perception of Black-White Relations on the Job Hourly employees by race, Fairbanks–Memphis

	Black	White
Favorable	75%	80%
Uncertain	19	17
Unfavorable	5	3

Emily Meadows described the changes since she came to the plant in 1963 when there were still only a handful of blacks in the plant:

> But when we first got here, they told us not to pay 'em any attention. Sooner or later they would get used to us being together, working together, eating together; and sooner or later it would change. And it took about a year or two. You might hear somebody say something about you, where you just go on about your business and didn't pay 'em any attention, it would change. So that's what it is, two or three years later, everybody got to be everybody's friend. I mean, we have Christmas, we exchange gifts. We laugh and talk together and everything. It's really nice now.

Many blacks were not so enthusiastic as Emily, but most agreed that they could talk and laugh happily on the job.

An index constructed by factor analysis also indicated a generally tolerant work force. It combined coded items reflecting employees' attitudes toward blacks personally, toward a black foreman, and toward preferential treatment. On a scale from 1 to 5 (again, 5 is high), Fairbanks whites scored 3.4, slightly below the whites in other case studies, but clearly on the tolerant side.

WHITES LEARN FROM BLACKS

Clearly most blacks were received very differently in 1969 from the way they were when Katie Fuller and Bernard Ivy were hired. Yet many of the white employees were the same people. What happened? As Thomas May observed, white attitudes seemed to have changed primarily because people had been put into a position where they could not avoid associating with one another. The employees at Fairbanks had grown up in a city in which total segregation was customary, and segregation in schools, colleges, and public transportation was required by law.[10] Although the racial climate had been changing, there were still rather few places in Memphis where black and white adults met as equals. And there was probably no place where so many blacks and whites spent so many hours in close contact as they did in the plant.

White employees described the influence this contact had on them. Rosalie Johnson was thirty-six years old with ten years of service in the plant

---

[10] *Tennessee Code: Annotated Official Edition*, 1956; and *Cumulative Supplement*, 1969 (Indianapolis: Bobbs, Merrill, 1969). On separate schools, see Vol. 9, p. 265; on public transportation, see Vol. 2, pp. 720, 768, 769.

when the first black employee was hired in 1961: "It's been a big change. It has. And especially for us older ones that thought we'd gotten to the place we wouldn't have to do it. But when you see you're gonna have to, you might as well go on and do it." She went on to explain why she would be willing to train a Negro girl yet showed that she still held some stereotyped views:

MRS. JOHNSON: But I certainly wouldn't mind training one, and showing them everything I can. I would much rather them be out here working and making an honest living, than the way most of them make it, and us having to pay the taxes.

PURCELL: The welfare?

MRS. JOHNSON: Yes, sir. Now I get real tired of that.

The first Negro employee, Katie Fuller, whom we met earlier, described the change in two white women who once disliked her. The first was Catherine Stagg:

> They say she used to hate my guts. I heard that she used to just talk about me. They talked about stringing me up, pulling with my privates, you know. One girl I worked with told me this. She said that Catherine —this woman I'm telling you about—she planned to do this to me, and how she hated me and all. And now we talk. She [Catherine] and I talk. She's been just like another colored person to me. I don't know how she feels in her heart, she hasn't divulged it you know. . . .
>
> But the girl I work with, she used to hate me too. And she told me when she first started working with me she had never been around Negroes. She lived in a small town in Mississippi where there weren't too many Negroes and they didn't come in contact with them too much and she didn't know how to take 'em, you know. And she's one of the best friends I got out here.

When we spoke with her, Catherine Stagg felt that blacks and whites were getting along well:

MRS. STAGG: Well, I think it's working out, you know, real well. I think it is.

PURCELL: The girls feel that maybe too many of them are coming in, though?

MRS. STAGG: Well, some of them does. But after all, they gonna have to hire them, we realize that, you know. And when they first came out here, of course the girls didn't like it, or the boys either. They didn't like it at all. But it was just the idea of us not being used to working with them, I think. But after all they're human, just like we are. They've got their place just like we have.

PURCELL: You've got some over where you work? Do they get along?

MRS. STAGG: Right on the machine next to where I work. And I think the sooner everybody realizes this, you know, that they've got their place just like we have, that you know we all work out. It takes time, I guess. But I think, out here though, it's worked out real good.

Young people too had met black people on equal terms for the first time in the plant. Joyce Henderson, twenty-three and on second shift, came to the plant in 1966 when 17 percent of the women were black:

> Well, I like 'em all down there personally. I mean I never been around—my father was from Mississippi—and I was raised kind of here in the South. I never worked around colored people before, until I came out here. But after I got used to 'em, I like 'em all. Took me a little while to get used to it.

Mrs. RosaLee Myers was only nineteen years old when she came to Fairbanks in 1961, and she was totally unprepared for integration. She described her initial reaction and how the whites and blacks got along at the time of the survey:

> I think they get along real well. I was here when they first started hiring colored people in. And at first it was a little, I guess, it was a shock.
> I was always raised with little colored people, but I wasn't really taught to love 'em. And I resented it at first. When they first told me they were hiring colored people in, I just threw a fit. I said: "Boy, if they ever put one with me, I'll quit. I won't work across the table with one." And they got to teasing me about putting a colored girl on the other side of me. And I just said: "No, I'd refuse. I wouldn't work across the table from a colored girl."
>
> But really it wasn't very long and they had one sitting down over there (laughter). She turned out to be the best person that I had worked with. Maybe it was because she was colored and knew that I might resent her, I don't know. I think it is mostly 'cause she is just that type of person. But she helped me in just lots of ways.

Meeting face to face in the plant tended to break down racial superstitions and generalizations. Mrs. Nancy Brigham, forty-three, on first shift and a real old-timer in the plant, found that at least some blacks did not fit her stereotype:

MRS. BRIGHAM: Well, I tell you. I didn't like the idea of their bringing the Negroes out here in the first place. But since they have, I've gotten along very well with them. I guess the reason is that most Negroes that I had seen were unclean, and had such an odor. And that was one of my biggest objections, because it's awfully hot in the summertime upstairs. And I didn't know how that would turn out.

CAVANAGH: How did it turn out?

MRS. BRIGHAM: Turned out well. Because I think they try to pick people that are educated and take care of their bodies.

Veteran foreman Paul Tate, forty-five, had been carefully observing his work force all during the period that the blacks came into the plant. He underscored the initial shock, and the final acceptance:

> Now you know you get some people who talk a lot. I don't think they really mean what they say: "I won't work with them." Then when you put a colored person with this particular person, she says: "Well, she's different." You'll see them going and helping them. I have some real nice girls, colored girls. If I'm after them about production, white girls are down helping them. And you see it in reverse. You might see a white girl who is low in production, and you'll see a girl over there that'll be helping her. It's wonderful.

There were exceptions of course. Several women described problems with their mechanics. A woman working on production is paid according to the quantity and quality of her production. When the machine is down or running poorly, she cannot make her ordinary pay; hence she is vitally dependent on the mechanic. Arlene Holley, twenty-five, had a mechanic whom she found to be prejudiced against blacks:

> I was put on this new machine. And the mechanic they gave me, you know how you'll hear, "He doesn't like Negroes. And he talks and acts real ugly to them." So I made up my mind when I got over there, that I'm not going to let him bother me. Just going over there and do my job. Well, I took it pretty good for a time. I would ask him to do certain things about the machine. Or if it was running bad, I would tell him. He got to the point where he wouldn't answer my light, if he's not close to the machine. And if I'd tell him something was wrong, he'd say: "It looks all right to me," and go on about his business.

Arlene took this problem with her mechanic to her foreman and was disappointed by his reaction.

> Finally, I told the foreman about it, and he didn't seem to do anything about it. And it just kept going on and on. And the tubes were running bad on the machine and this was costing me money. I was real upset; and I kept on trying to talk to my foreman about it, because I figured if anyone could do anything about it he could.

The foreman did not get the mechanic to fix the machinery to Mrs. Holley's satisfaction, and she filed a grievance for discrimination.

Monroe Webb, forty-seven, a black warehouseman with a reputation for being a militant, also reported incidents but gave his manager, Roger MacGregor, credit for listening to black grievances and improving the situation:

WEBB: I have talked to him about a few things that were going on here, and he has stopped those.

CAVANAGH: What kinds of things were those?

WEBB: Well, when they were having that trouble here in Memphis.

CAVANAGH: During the sanitation strike?

WEBB: They were making a lot of cracks, and things like that. And people were getting too offended, every break and like that. So we go to him and we never hear no more.

Generally on-the-job relationships were good at Fairbanks. And the daily constant contact most often led to a change in white attitudes toward blacks. The plant has functioned as a social equalizer: Both blacks and whites were doing the same jobs with equal pay, respect, and pride. It was a forum where they met each other as equals for the first time.

BLACK COPING IN A WHITE ENVIRONMENT

As a rule, whites have little idea of how a black person feels when he moves into a hostile situation and of what it demands of him. Blacks cope with the situation in a variety of ways. Some expect very little from their white co-workers, and thus describe as "good," working relations that a more demanding person might resent. Tony Longfield told us that he got along well with other mechanics in his work group because he shared their interest in fishing and hunting. But this was true at least partially because Longfield was very careful not to alienate his white co-workers:

LONGFIELD: Because these people out here are funny. They all know each other. They've been working out here fifteen, twenty years, and they're tightly knit. And you need only to turn one against you.

PURCELL: And you turn them all?

LONGFIELD: That's right. And you might as well walk out clean. Because they can really make it hard for you. If I was difficult to get along with, or did some of the things that they might resent, I wouldn't know the first things about those machines because nobody would help me.

Again illustrating a willingness to accommodate to the rudeness of some whites is twenty-five-year-old Jacob Kingwell. He described an incident that he rightly considered petty but that might have evoked a very different reaction from an angry, frustrated man. Kingwell is a big man (6′6″, 250 lbs.), and came from a very poor black Mississippi school where he did not even learn to read and write. He worked as a janitor and was very happy with his work at Fairbanks:

KINGWELL: Here I'm full satisfied. I'm satisfied with the pay. I know that I'm living 100 percent better. And I haven't had a word with anybody out here. You know, like someone's trying to start something.

CAVANAGH: Do they treat you differently as a black person, than they would in Mississippi, do you think—here in this plant?

KINGWELL: Well, not exactly. Fifty percent of them say this is something that they got to work with and deal with, so they go along with it. But you can't blame a man for not coming up to you, speaking to you, every morning. They walk by you, won't speak; but that's not anything.

Like the time, well, there's one fellow here, I was combing my hair in the washroom, and when I finished he say: "It's still standing up." I said: "Thank you."

CAVANAGH: Was he being smart or . . . ?

KINGWELL: I think so. I think he was trying to be smart, but. . . .

CAVANAGH: Does that make you mad?

KINGWELL: I looked over it. I'm not easy to get mad. I'm just the type of guy it takes a whole lot to make me mad, and I'm easy to please. So on a small thing, I can look over, you know. Like a lot of guys, they would have said something about. And then we could have got into a fight, could have lost my job, over a small thing.

Negroes have often been taught to cope with prejudice by not challenging white people. This is true even of the young. Deidre Oatis, a twenty-year-old Fairbanks employee, an inspector on the second shift, commented: "My sister tells me to keep my head up and whatever they say, don't pay no attention to them." Remember Mrs. Meadows said she received similar advice from Fairbanks management when she was hired in 1963.

On the other hand, interchanges where blacks feel free to defend themselves or to challenge white behavior and assumptions can be healthy and productive for whites as well as blacks. And some blacks now feel free. While a Negro woman was apt to be tentative and reserved on the first shift, she could better demand basic respect on the second and third shifts where there were many more blacks. Mrs. Mollie Coleman, thirty-three, commented on an outspokenly prejudiced white girl who was about to be transferred to the third shift: "They'll straighten her out on third. They don't take the stuff on third, or second either, like they do on days."

The authors sat in on a special meeting of a black caucus of Fairbanks employees. At the meeting, Annie Gale was relating a conversation with a white fellow worker: "And I said, 'You talk to me the way you want me to talk to you. Other than that, you don't say *nothing* to me.' " This is merely ordinary courtesy, but it has not always been possible for blacks to demand it.

BLACK-WHITE SOCIALIZING

While a large majority of all employees felt that blacks and whites got along well when working, a quick glance at the cafeteria and lounges showed that a racial barrier arose when employees were on their own time. Groups of women chatting freely at the work place would most often separate on racial lines when they entered the lounges. None of the whites and only 12 percent of the blacks in the plant felt that the races got together at lunch and at breaks. And not one person reported any significant interracial contact with fellow employees outside the plant.

The races separated themselves partly from choice, partly from tradition, and partly from fear. Said Linda Sue Garrett, thirty-seven, a second shift inspector:

> Like this colored girl works with me, we're good friends; we really are. We can talk about anything, and we don't get mad, you know, and she said, "Say, Linda, I wouldn't want to come and sit down in your group and talk. We don't talk the same language. It's not bad. But nine times out of ten, you wouldn't want to come and sit with us, because we have our little get-togethers, you know. And we talk and laugh. You wouldn't enjoy being among these." And I agreed with her.
>
> But I think people can get along, I mean any race. Because, like she said, they really don't want any part of you any more than you want any part of them, you know. It's the idea that you can go so far; you can be friendly.

Said black third-shift inspector Virginia Fay, twenty-five: "I guess we never did sit together, you know. You can discriminate yourself as much as the other person can discriminate you, too. So, no one ever sits together; that's just the way it's been."

Unfortunately though, a more basic reason for separation of the races is not choice. It is fear: the black man's fear of embarrassment and rejection, based on a history of rejections. One better educated black had ceased trying to socialize with whites:

> People may be friendly while they're working together, then after they leave their area, it's two different ways; it's a different thing. I mean I was confronted with this by the people that I was working with when I first came. So after I saw this, I wouldn't try to keep my association as close as while doing my work.
>
> That's just like the feeling a person may get if he sees someone that he knows, and various people around, and you speak and the person says nothing or gives you a funny look. Well, this is the problem that the people here are concerned with. They are mostly afraid. They don't know the reaction.
>
> So I would not attempt to do anything like this again. I guess in a way, this is why we have the situation now about lunch and everything, because people are afraid.

Iantha Asbury, who was pleased with her reception back in 1964, had seen similar changes in her co-workers when they left the job and it hurt. They might be nice and friendly individually, but when in a group they feared that they might be alienated from their friends:

> Yes, because I've left the plant, and I've met a girl that worked here. I've spoken to her. I've had quite a few incidents like this happen. And now I've gotten in a shell, because I'm afraid to say, "Hi, Jean; Hi, Grace; Hi, Margaret," out in public, because they won't speak to me ... and I've grown in a shell, because I'm afraid to speak to her, because she might do the same thing to me the other girls did, and then I'm sitting there, standing there, all embarrassed....
>
> It's other people, the influence of other people. This girl could be altogether feeling differently, and just—there she is in this group, and she says, "Well, if I do this, they might do this, or they might...."

Eric Fraley, a mechanic, was convinced that it was this same group pressure that underlay the harassment of blacks in his department: "There are some people up there that actually tries to do what they think is right, I believe, in their heart. But they are so loyal to each other, and so loyal to each other's ways."

For either blacks or whites, crossing the racial barrier might result in anything from name-calling to total ostracism. The Negro who socialized with whites might be called an "Uncle Tom"; the white who associated with blacks might be a "Nigger Lover." Richard Ellington, the black material supplier concerned about the small number of Negro men in the plant, said:

> We have lots of people, they want to do right; they want to associate. But, if I got two or three friends that is against it, [I think]: "What will they say about me? Will they recognize me as their friends?" See, this is the type thing that they have in their minds.
>
> Otherwise, as far as the heart is concerned, they have no difficulty; they have no problem mixing. But it's: "What's my friends going to say?" So, in order to associate with my friends, I'll do what my friends think.

A group of young factory girls, black and white, had a different experience working in the warehouse. They ate together and went out together. Unfortunately, when they transferred to the main plant, taboos and traditions made this interracial relationship uncomfortable, if not impossible. Said young Brenda Luckey:

> When I was working over in the warehouse, we were sort of like a family. And at lunch time we'd go across the street to this little restaurant, and all of us would eat together. And some of the girls said they hated to come over in the big plant, because it's traditional that they separate. Over in the warehouse they felt free to do as they liked. And we would eat together, talk together, and the day would pass by. And before we knew it, it would be time to go home; and there was nothing to it.
>
> And when I came over to the plant, I did see it was different. And it's not as close over here as it was over there. Well, Susan worked over in

the warehouse, and then she came over. And she says: "You know, Brenda, I wouldn't mind eating lunch with you and I'm not prejudiced. But they're so different over here. I would be picked out by the rest of them. I—you can go along with this, but don't let this end our friendship." And one day, she comes up to me and says: "I don't care what they say, I'm still going to be your friend."

Blacks as well as whites can make one of their race uncomfortable for attempting to cross the barriers. Said twenty-four-year-old Zita Woodyard:

> I've had a lot of Negro girls tell me, "You sit up and talk to the white people all the time." So I tell 'em, I say, "Well, I'm out here working on a job. I like to be friendly with everybody. I talk to the Negro girls." But see, I've got a job that doesn't compel me to stay in one place, and I have to work around these people. I don't see why I should just walk around and say nothing.

> I don't know if a whole lot of people know it, but it's a lot of prejudiced white people out here. But it's a lot of prejudiced Negroes out here, too. And I think each person has his own outlook on what he wants to do. But, just like I told these girls: "Don't tell me how to run my life."

Many white employees, aware of change in themselves and their city, recognized that traditional separation was breaking down. But they found that their attitudes, reactions, and habits were deeply ingrained. They did not know how much change they would be willing to accept. Nancy Myers, the young woman who was surprised to find that she could work with a Negro girl, explained that this friendship could not yet continue outside the plant:

MRS. MYERS: But I learned to really love her and appreciate her. But I don't think I could have asked her to come home with me. I haven't been able to accept it *that* far yet. It's the intermarriage that bothers me. I think in a public place like this, I have to be nice to 'em; and I'd be nice to 'em should they come to my home. But I couldn't with an easy conscience, or at ease, invite 'em for a social or something.

CAVANAGH: What would be the problem, would you say?

MRS. MYERS: I don't know. I guess it's just that I'm not used to it. I've never done that. It used to bother me to see 'em in a cafeteria or a cafe. But now I—it's seen more often, and it doesn't bother me. I used to think I'd never eat at the same cafe with one, but I've learned to like 'em now, and get along with them a lot better. I don't know. I guess it's the way I was brought up, that I can't really invite 'em in. And I certainly can't go along with interracial marriage. I just don't think it was planned that way.

Supervisor Daniel Flaherty recognized these same deep feelings in many employees:

> We do have some deep-rooted segregation feelings. They practically tell that that's the way they were born and brought up, and nothing is going

> to change them. I've had different hourly people tell me that their feelings outside the plant, who they want to live next to and socialize with, are strictly their own business.
>
> Usually they'll agree that a person should not be denied a job based on the color of his skin. I just kind of put that to them. But you can still see that, "Well, it's okay to give them a job, but they still ought to stay in their places." The familiar saying. I don't think we're going to change them at all, the really deep-seated. It will be the next generation before you see a change in some of their attitudes.

Anything done explicitly to change these basic attitudes would meet with deep resentment, according to Flaherty. He said: "Anything that we did in an overt way would make the situation worse. Like if we gave it publicity, or something."

There were signs, however, that traditional social barriers were breaking down. Individuals like Zita Woodyard stepped across them. An employee of one month, Essie Colbert, said that segregation had gone out of style:

> I don't think anything about that, because that's gone out of style. That's old stuff. If you're tired, you just sit down. And just to be honest, I haven't noticed anyone that wouldn't want me to sit down with 'em. Because I figure like this, everybody's out here to work, and they know that we're going to be in contact with them. And they're going to be in contact with us. So the best thing for you to do is to leave your feelings at home. So, I just never pay any attention to anything like that.

New employees such as Essie Colbert were much less inhibited than were their fellow workers of even five years ago. In their youthful enthusiasm they set a more open tone for the interracial relations of the plant. Foreman Kevin Crowley charted a change in the attitudes and habits of the work force over the last decade:

> I think they work pretty smooth together. We had a Christmas party up there, the girls all brought in their food, and everything, the last night of work before Christmas. They invited myself and the other foreman up there to set at one of the tables with them. And we went in and sit down, and I look around and there were two colored girls sitting at the table with us. White girls, colored girls, you know, mechanics, and I thought to myself: "Ten years ago I never would have believed this." Of course there was one table over there, the biggest majority of 'em at that table were colored. But it was by preference; and they had brought all their food to eat together. But I think any time you got something like this, you got to think we're making progress.

What role did company and union policy play in informal race relations? Both had stopped sponsoring parties at the time blacks came into the plant. The union held several private all-white parties in the early 1960s. The company's Family Days (plant tours) in 1963 and 1968 provided some social interaction, and company baseball, golf, and bowling were open to all employees. In 1969 the union set up a Human Relations Committee to consider social as well as job-related problems. More company-sponsored social activities would seem to make sense as a sign that the company did not agree with the southern taboo on interracial social events and was not afraid of interracial socializing. The union, of course, could have made the same move. But Samuel Grant of Local 40, of the Electrical Workers of America (EWA), AFL-CIO, felt that it would be easier for the company to begin the move in this direction:

> I've approached the company several years ago . . . at least twice now. We've taken the position, maybe it's wrongly so, "You first." Because anything we do has to be done by consensus. Again you get to the matter of the company can do as they durn well please in these areas. . . . They were afraid of it among other things, but I figured that if they did it the first time, then this would get into it.

The company did not have quite so much freedom to encourage better interracial relations as Grant implied, but it is probably true that it would be easier for the company to take the initiative since it does not depend on a membership vote, and since employees expect management to exercise leadership even though it must do this within carefully defined limits.

MODERN PIONEERS

Negro mechanics were relatively new to the work force at Fairbanks in 1969. The first black mechanic had been hired just three years before. The number of mechanics had increased to seven, still too few to be widely dispersed and accepted in a plant employing 314 mechanics. The reception of the first black mechanics gave cause for both hope and concern. Several moved easily into a job that is demanding and that brought black men into close contact with a white group for the first time. Alfred Magner was particularly fortunate in being assigned to Francis MacCauley for training. For Magner pioneering was not difficult:

> I just come up, and started to work with this guy. They got some real good people out here, too, you see. Because this guy Fran MacCauley . . . he's a mechanic in the tube department. And he was really all right with me; he gave me the best he had. He did. He would just show me. He said, "Go over and go to work on it. Play with it as long as you want. If you run into a problem, call me." He'd bring in his book, the mechanic's book that we used for our department, and he would show me the different parts of the thing, you know.

On the other hand, Eric Fraley, also promoted from material handling to mechanic, found so much resistance that he was certain that white fellow workers were trying to force him to quit:

> Like I say—it's a conspiracy. They got it like they want it; and they intend to try and keep it like that. They try to keep it like that just by doing you bad enough to make you want to quit. And in this process of doing you bad enough to make you quit, they can get you hurt.

The black mechanics often found the first few months difficult. But with perseverance they gradually won the acceptance of their white co-workers. We heard Tony Longfield, a new mechanic, say that he now got along well with the whites, but the first few months were rough:

> I think after they found that you're not overly excited by the sight of blondes, you're no threat. Then they accept you. That's a big part of it. Well, I couldn't last very long out here if I was.
>
> When I first came out here, they used to do little things to my machines. When I would come in, there would be the wrong size buttons in my hopper, and they would get hung up. And it would keep me running all night. Things like that.
>
> Someone planted over $1,000 worth of swivels on one of my machines, in a hopper. I had never seen a swivel. I didn't even know what they were. They looked like little .22 bullets to me. But the guy who's training me found them, and he turned them over to my foreman. He said that someone was probably trying to set me up. Someone come along and say: "What do you have in the box?" Dumb me would say: "Buttons." And they'd look in the box, and I got $1,000 worth of swivels. So I go out the door. Guys out here have had things put in their lockers, stuff like that. I think they're getting used to seeing us around here now, and I guess they say, "Well, maybe they're not so bad after all." I don't have any trouble [now].

Longfield was successful partly because he went out of his way to be agreeable. We saw above that he felt that if he were difficult to get along with he "wouldn't know the first thing about those machines." He also received real help from his trainer. General Foreman Daniel Flaherty placed Longfield under this mechanic because the mechanic had actually asked to train a Negro:

> He could see the day was coming when we'd be putting Negro mechanics on the groups. And he said, "Give me a good, sharp Negro and I'll train him and make him one of the best mechanics in the area. These other so-and-sos who aren't doing their job will see what he's accomplishing, and due to their feelings toward the blacks, their pride will make them do as good or better." And to him it was going to be a motivation.

Longfield praised his mechanic trainer: "I mean you have a lot of help; everybody's real nice about helping you if you have something you can't handle. And you learn a lot faster that way, because, well, you have someone over you constantly."

Edgar Dolan, twenty, was a remarkable success story. He was hired as a disadvantaged NAB pledge in early 1968, and before the end of the year he was promoted to mechanic. He also had a hard time when first promoted: "When we first came they kind of gave us a hard time, those ladies did. A lot of criticism, laughing, you know, about different things we didn't know how to do. Which actually make you feel like, you know, well, 'I'm just going to quit.' " But he reported that this lasted only about four months and then the situation improved: "It's really nice. I like it. If I have any problems, I go to the other mechanics. They're usually nice about it, telling me, you know. I tell them my problems and they come over and help me." More than one-half of the new black mechanics whom we interviewed were satisfied with their reception and training. But the quite different experiences of some are significant.

BLACK MECHANIC WITH WHITE OLD-TIMERS

Eric Fraley, quoted above, met the most resistance. The reaction of the work force could probably have been predicted since he was working on the day shift in a department that was preferred by white old-timers with seniority. The unit had a reputation as anti-black. One of the few black women who worked there at that time said: "They work like they want to, do like they want to, and treat you like you're not a human being. Because I'm taking it daily." This group was cohesive and powerful enough to give management a hard time. It is not surprising that they tried rough tactics on Fraley; and, unlike Longfield, Fraley received no help from his trainer:

> I remember one morning there I was putting on a gasket. And after I jerked my hand from under my machine, *then* the mechanic told me, "Oh, I meant to tell you that you had to cut the machine off."
>
> I think that would have been the first thing that would have dawned on my mind if I meant you right, to tell you the danger in what you were going to do.

Fraley, like other mechanics, was responsible for keeping several machines in good operating order. When a woman was having trouble with her machine, she turned on a light that notified the mechanic. Fraley found himself at the mercy of these women machine operators and found that learning a demanding job in this hostile environment was very difficult. Mechanics refused to answer his questions, and the women who operated the machines would call him away from another job when nothing was wrong or would refuse to tell him what kind of problem they had with their machines. And the harassment sometimes took a physical form in requests that he pick up tubes that he did not know were red hot, or in glass put in chairs so that he could not sit down:

> ... and oh man, I just didn't think people could be like that. I just can't really tell you; you would have to be around. I been up there about six months now, and I be willing to bet there hasn't been a night, hardly, out of the six months, that I haven't had a bad dream about this place and that job. And that's just how much it has been on my mind and how hard.

But Fraley rarely took a problem to his foreman. He was convinced that the white work group would be rougher on him if he did:

> If you get to telling on people down there, it'll spread all over the plant like wildfire that you're a tattler; you tell things. On either shift you on, you going to catch it. They let you know that before they really come down on you.

> You know yourself it's best for you to say nothing. If they can be that nasty to you, and you haven't done anything to them, there's no telling what they would do if you tell on somebody. So you just have to try to do the best you can. And try to treat them as kind and proper as you can. And try to make them like you. That's all you can do. That's *all* you can do!

And Fraley also assumed that the harassment was obvious enough so that his foreman did not have to be told. "He knows exactly what's going on, and if he meant right, he would stop it himself. He could stop it."

Fraley's foreman, Daniel Grogam, was *not* aware of the harassment that Fraley was receiving. Grogam thought that Fraley was getting along fine and did not need special help, although he did feel that Fraley was not so mechanically inclined as some mechanics. Perhaps Fraley did not have as good a mechanical aptitude, but he may also have been prevented from learning by the hostility of his co-workers and by the strain of the relationship. Fraley recognized that Grogam had taken time out to teach him, and he said that Grogam was a good man personally. But he also felt that Grogam had not really laid down the law to the trainer to make him teach Fraley thoroughly.

BLACK MEN AND WHITE WOMEN

Some white employees acknowledged that relationships with the new black mechanics were not easy, although none mentioned harassment. White long-service worker Kathleen Pritchett, fifty-two, felt that difficulties existed because the black men were new to the plant and because any relationship between a white woman and a black man was taboo:

> But the colored men, they're just now starting to hire a bunch of them. I guess in time we'll get where they feel the same way as they do about the women. But right now the white girls do not like the idea of having a colored mechanic.

> I think it kind of worries me too, because I feel like sometimes there might be some trouble. Because you know, down here, for a colored man just to say something, make a pass at a white woman, that's just unspeakable. You don't even talk about things like that. And then I don't agree with, I don't like it either. I don't think it's right.

Foreman Kevin Crowley, thirty-eight, himself formerly a mechanic, noted that the black mechanics had been very careful to avoid close contact with the white women:

> That's like the mechanics we have up there now, the colored mechanics. They're real careful. They have to pull components over these white girls, and they're real careful not to touch one to cause anything. They know. And we've had real good results with it, and we haven't had any problems. But if you get someone that doesn't care, you know, then he could just upset the whole apple cart.

The extreme circumspection expected of black mechanics was in sharp contrast to the familiarity, joking, and sometimes even physical contact seen between the white mechanics and the women. Black men were not being asked to conform to the established white norms but to respect a very deep, traditional barrier between black men and white women.

SALARIED BREAKTHROUGH

Just one month before we (the researchers) arrived, Calvin Green had been promoted from mechanic to quality technician. Twenty-six years old, with three years of college and mechanical training, Green was the first Negro to hold a significant salaried job. Employees were full of gossip about the promotion. Some reported jealousy or hostility but many were impressed by Green's qualifications and found him personally clean cut and well educated.

Here we have another example of a successful recent breakthrough. Many employees had accepted the fact that blacks would be hired on all levels, but another reason for the moderate reaction to Green's promotion may have been that he did not have to work in close association with many hourly whites.

ELEMENTS OF SUCCESS IN MANAGING BREAKTHROUGHS

The clear stance of top management is crucial in achieving acceptance of racial breakthroughs. The choice of a department, a foreman, and a trainer are all important. And the first-line supervisor must *clearly* indicate his support for the new black worker.

Daniel Flaherty had three black mechanics working in his units on second shift. One of them was Tony Longfield who was so pleased with his trainer. Flaherty felt that second shift was better because there were more blacks working then and, in addition, the whites were younger, with less service, and were more open to change. Said Flaherty: "It just seemed to work out better, but eventually it will move by the natural process to other shifts." Flaherty went on to indicate how he made his choice: "When the first Negro mechanic came in—you try and be a little careful who the first one is, what type of man he is, and then where you put him. These are just kind of stacking the deck a little bit for success." Management must keep a fine line between reasonable precaution and confining blacks to certain jobs and shifts. Even where care is used in selection and placement, conflict may arise.

Both the favorable and critical comments of the workers at Fairbanks–Memphis pointed to the foreman as a key person in controlling conflict. Of course, foremen cannot be aware of every personal confrontation that takes place in their department, but they must learn to be alert and recognize them. A few foremen spoke of taking whites aside and reading them the "facts of life." Listen to Foreman Scott:

SCOTT: I feel like it's real hard for some of the white people to accept the fact that it's [integration] here to stay. It's going to be.

CAVANAGH: What do you tell 'em, just that?

SCOTT: That's right. You have to accept it. Part of the job is working with other people. You have to cooperate. You have to get along.

CAVANAGH: How do they take that, the whites, when you tell them that?

SCOTT: Well, some of them know this. And some of them are realizing the fact that it's here and it's here to stay. And they accept it. Some of them are just hard-headed, and it goes in one ear and out the other. And they do continue to—there's some animosity—or they just ignore the colored. I think it's getting better. I don't see a whole lot of this.

Getting this message across effectively is difficult. It takes time, persistent effort, and skill, even when a foreman is totally committed. Foremen at Fairbanks received a clear statement of company policy in 1961, but there was no core of experienced industrial relations men to help them with desegregation. The 1960s were a transitional learning period for foremen, managers, and corporate staff. And plant expansion sometimes diverted attention from integration in the early years. As the corporate program developed more fully, personnel men from headquarters reemphasized company policy to the foremen. At the 1969 annual review meeting the headquarters manager spoke out strongly for continued hiring of blacks and sensitivity to their needs. Also in 1969 Fairbanks–Memphis foremen went through a racial sensitivity session that followed the Bell and Howell format and that was run by a young black industrial relations officer from Division headquarters. The experience of the foremen and managers at Fairbanks can in turn be helpful to others who face racial breakthroughs now.

THE BLACK FOREMAN ISSUE

An important element in management's efforts to make breakthroughs in racial relations is getting blacks into line supervision over both whites and blacks. White employees at Fairbanks had no experience with black supervisors, and were more hesitant about accepting a black foreman than the workers at any of the other three plants reported on in this book. Most of the work force, however, expected that a black foreman would be named in the near future.

Fifty percent of the whites and slightly more of the black employees thought that a significant number of their work group would be uncomfortable with a black foreman, but Table 7-6 shows that only 21 percent of the whites and 12 percent of the blacks thought that having a black foreman would not work out, *in the long run*. Two-thirds of the white employees felt that they personally would have no trouble working for a black foreman, but 20 percent said that they would not be able to adjust.

Table 7–6. Perception of a Black Foreman's Chance for Success Hourly employees by race, Fairbanks–Memphis

	Black	White
Favorable	76%	72%
Uncertain	12	7
Unfavorable	12	21

When asked how they thought white employees would accept a black foreman, employee responses varied:

REGINALD DALTON, forty, white mechanic: I believe that they'll accept it. Like now, they see the first black engineer on the job. I mean they expect that it's coming. It just depends on what kind of foreman he is.

ALFRED MAGNER, forty-three, black mechanic: I believe they would. If management says: "This is the way it's going to be." That's it. Now he [a white man] might be ever so hostile, but I don't think he'd mess up a good thing just because he had a Negro supervisor.
You'd probably find some people who would really give you a bad time. And they could possibly do it by slowing down on production and this type of thing. You'd really have to be up to handling the situation.

ARLENE HOLLY, twenty-five, a black woman hired in 1964: I think that they would accept it. I think that at first it would be highly resented. Because too many people out here need these jobs.

DONNA HILLMAN, thirty-five, white: I think it would be pretty hard to take right at first. Now we might get used to it, I don't know. Things like that come a little bit easier than you think they would.

ERNEST SCOTT, white foreman: To start off with they'd object to it a good bit, but I think if he handles it properly, they'd accept it. I think people learn to accept a lot of things they hadn't accepted before or had to accept before.

The authors also found some more articulate resistance to the suggestion of a black foreman, although this was very much a minority position. Here are three white workers, all with twenty or more years of service:

MRS. KATHLEEN PRITCHETT, fifty-two, brings up the sexual fears of white women: No, there's too many single women and widows working out here.... And they have, a foreman has a chance at your record: where you live, your phone number. And no white man needs to let a colored man have that. Not a single person. You don't know who they'll give it to.

MRS. CROSSWELL, fifty-eight, when asked what would happen if a Negro were made foreman: Oh! I don't think that would be right.... I don't think putting a Nigger in a white man's job like that, I don't think that's right. No. I draw a line there. That's too much for a man to be over a white woman.

ROBERT ANDREWS, forty-nine, material supplier, would not take orders from a Negro: I can't answer for the other fellas, I'll answer for myself. I'm going to tell you something. I don't think I'd work under him. I really don't. I just don't think that I would care to take the orders from him.

It was the same people who said they would personally refuse to work for a black man who also felt that a black foreman would not work out at the plant. They were a small minority of the work force, were among the oldest employees with the most seniority, and a disproportionate number were on the first shift.[11] Because seniority is needed to obtain a secure position in the preferred units on first shift and no Negroes were hired before 1961, workers there had the least contact with black fellow workers. They were entrenched and secure in their jobs, and thus also had the greatest sense of power as a group in resisting management initiatives.

Management was only too well aware that the appointment of the first black foreman would meet the resistance of many white employees and that the foreman would require its clear and unambiguous support. Management also felt that the first black supervisor would have to be a superior individual. Charles Miller, a bright liberal manager at Fairbanks–Memphis, said:

I think the right Negro can get the job done, and I think it would take an awful lot of support from the plant manager to get that job done. And I think we're going to have to be prepared for a concerted effort to make him look very bad. I think he's going to have very severe problems.... I think he's going to have a hell of a hard row to hoe. But I think it can get done.

[11] Of the seven who were extremely negative on a black foreman, six (86 percent) had been in the plant more than fifteen years, one (14 percent) was under forty, and five (71 percent were on the first shift. Compare this with the total white work force: 37 percent had more than fifteen years in the plant, 53 percent were under forty, and 43 percent were on first shift.

It seems likely that adjustment to a black foreman at Fairbanks will take the same pattern as adjustment to other pioneers: shock, resistance, and resignation. Foremen and management all were convinced that eventually a black foreman would be accepted and work out. But the foremen knew from personal experience how difficult it is for a new foreman to win the cooperation of his group; and they expected a black to have a much rougher time. Yet extremely sharp negative reaction would probably come only from predictable individual work groups: those composed mostly of entrenched white old-timers. It would take a very capable black to stand up under the pressure and, most important, he would need considerable support from management, but it was certainly possible that a black foreman would be successful.

In January 1971 the Fairbanks plant appointed its first black foreman, Calvin Green, who as we saw earlier had been the first black quality technician. Mr. Green's appointment as supervisor was a very important breakthrough for Fairbanks. As we went to press, Mr. Green appeared to be succeeding.

THE BLACK CAUCUS: UNITY SECURITY ASSOCIATION

In 1968 a formal black caucus, the Unity Security Association (USA), was formed by black union members at the plant. The USA grew out of black discontent with the practices of, and the representation they received in, EWA Local 40. The USA goal was to strengthen the position of the blacks in the union and in the company; this was in the classic pattern of minorities organizing to achieve more power within the established institutions. This aggressive black organization was a distinct break with, and a threat to, the traditional southern pattern of white dominance. But there is no evidence that it was a separatist or extremely militant organization.

THE UNION LOCAL AND THE BLACKS

Local 40 never officially resisted integration of the Fairbanks plant, but neither did it support the move. The local was slow to seek black members and might even have excluded some of the early black employees. An international representative of the EWA recalled providing a union card for a black after he was unable to obtain one from his steward. In those days the union had a reputation of being riddled with officers and stewards who were members of the segregationist White Citizens' Council.

The local's orientation until just a few years ago was an affront to blacks. Two dramatic public incidents made dominant racial feelings painfully obvious to all; both involved the use of union funds to support southern white resistance to desegregation and black equality. In 1957 when public schools in Little Rock, Arkansas, were closed to avoid complying with the Supreme Court order to desegregate, Local 40 voted to send $150 toward the support of private schools for whites. When civil rights leader Medgar Evers of Greenwood, Mississippi, was killed in 1963, a special meeting of Local 40 authorized a donation of $500 to defend the accused slayer of Evers. When this second incident received wide publicity, the president of EWA in Washington was furious. One of the key officers of Local 40, Sam Grant, felt that it was the officers' responsibility to carry out the wishes of the majority. His defense of the donation was that it was to support the judicial system:

> He was accused of having shot Medgar Evers, and a group of people down in Mississippi got up a defense fund for him, and got some publicity. And I received a petition for a special meeting to discuss helping this defense fund. And frankly, I wasn't too unsympathetic, I'll be truthful with you. Because it was a defense fund, and I've never really been convinced that the man—although he may have known who did it —I don't think he did shoot him. And of course it was never proved in a court of law.

> But we did donate, as a matter of fact. The membership voted $500 to be used in his defense fund. And we sent delegates. Well, Jimmie Floyd and a couple of other fellows that were instrumental in getting up the special meeting, took the money down there. They took the money down there the next day.

> Well, of course this was a big deal, here in the South, you know, five hundred bucks. And they got a front page picture in the newspaper down there in Greenwood. But in any event, I took a firm position as far as I was concerned. Here was the defense of a man, which to me, there was nothing wrong with this.

As the number of Negro employees in the plant increased, black union membership grew, and in 1968 Negroes made up approximately 20 percent of both the hourly work force and the union membership. Many of the new black employees were at least vaguely aware of the above incidents in the prosegregationist history of the union. Some black women were relatively satisfied with the present activities of the union; although like most employees, many knew very little of it except that an individual steward or officer was a nice person. Many others, and half of the black men, were dissatisfied with the union's operation and leadership.

White women, too, were not positive toward the union in January 1969. The local had supported a number of strikes over unsettled grievances. Many women, less union-minded to begin with, resented losing a day's pay over what they considered frivolous complaints. Table 7-7 shows only 30 percent of the blacks and 39 percent of whites favorable to the 1968 union leadership. The greatest support for the union came from white men, 80 percent positive. In the 1969 union election the incumbent president was defeated.

Table 7-7. *Attitude Toward Local Union Leadership Hourly employees by race, EWA Local 40, Fairbanks–Memphis*

	Black	White
Favorable	30%	39%
Uncertain	29	30
Unfavorable	41	31

While blacks probably shared the concern for pay lost in the walkouts, the issue had racial overtones for some. Said black checker Dolores Hemphill, twenty-seven: "We walked out quite a few times for them. I don't know of any cases, and that's in five years, that they have ever walked out because of the grievances we file. And I know that they file quite a few. So I don't know exactly how that goes." Intelligent and perhaps overly sensitive Estel Walker, twenty-nine, agreed:

> For one thing, they have us outnumbered. We can't ever get anything. Just like maybe a Negro girl files a grievance for some reason about her job. Well, that is the end of that. She just files a grievance. It's never pushed. Never. And they never walk out for anything that a Negro has filed a grievance on. You never hear any more about it. Bring it up at a union meeting: "Well," they say, "it's being worked on," or [they say] "It's at second step." And that's it. Whereas for the white, we walk out for the least little thing.

Arlene Holley, twenty-five, who had at least a full year of college before coming to work at the Fairbanks plant, said:

> Basically, I don't think they are representing the Negro in the union. I mean, as far as in any official capacity. And you have so many people who really don't care for Negroes. I feel there should be one in there to speak for our side of the thing. No, I don't think they are representing all of us.

By 1968 a few black union stewards had been elected, usually by informal and unpublicized efforts of blacks in a particular work group. But the three black union stewards represented less than 10 percent of the total, and blacks still felt they were at a serious disadvantage.

In the spring of 1968 the sanitation workers in Memphis, almost all of whom were black, went on their history-making strike. EWA Local 40 received a petition from fifty black employees that a special meeting should be called to discuss supporting their fellow workers financially. As is quite common in attempts to organize workers, the strikers received support from other unions all over the United States, including some Memphis locals.

At the special meeting of Fairbanks employees, a motion to send $1,000 was overwhelmingly defeated. The vast majority of the union members at the meeting were white, and they saw the strike as a rallying point for a new black militancy. They considered it a racial rather than a union matter and voted down the proposal. A few felt the amount was too high and that black leaders had undermined their chance for success. Blacks were particularly disappointed and angry at the massiveness and unanimity of white opposition, since they had expected some support from white friends.

A black active in union affairs, reflecting on this experience, argued the inadequacy of blacks trying to operate only through the white-dominated union local:

> I tell you what you can expect, when you do make gains within the union. Anything that happens here [any black success], you'll see the change in the local constitution next time around. For instance, like when we called a special meeting. It took fifty signatures. The next change in the constitution called for 200 signatures before you can call another special meeting. . . . Not only that, I mean I could name several constitutional changes which have been made to combat the black people. I mean it's just that simple.

An EWA international official, acquainted with Local 40 union activities, also recognized that whites tended to vote racially:

> You've got to understand the background of this local on this whole segregation issue. There's so many die-hards that all you got to do is tell them that you're going to do something with integration, and they come to that meeting. And they won't come to another one.

Another black active in the USA agreed: "If it were publicized that one of us were running for office, the ones that don't ever go would come that day. And they'll come out just to defeat us."

Sam Grant, a union leader, said that the union had always tried to be color blind in processing grievances and that by the time a person got to the second step, officials usually did not even know whether that person was black or white. He felt that part of the problem was that many Negroes were new to union procedures and did not understand the processes or that they filed grievances that would not hold up. He also pointed out that the union actively supported the first promotion of a black man from a semiskilled position to mechanic in 1966. In addition, the local had set up a Human Relations Committee at the suggestion of the international office.

In spite of Grant's protestations of color blindness, and in spite of the new Human Relations Committee, there remained a credibility gap for the black workers. Whether it was misunderstanding or discrimination, experiences like those quoted above contributed to dissatisfaction and to the conditions under which the black employees felt that a separate black caucus was necessary.

BLACK UNITY

The Unity Security Association was organized in 1968. It arose from the desire of the black employees for a greater share in decisions that affected them and for more effective black participation in the union. The defeat of their proposal to help the sanitation workers organize underscored their feeling that they were alone. They could expect little help from their white co-workers on most of these issues. To the blacks this dramatized the need to educate and organize themselves if they expected to achieve a proportionate say in union and company affairs. Bernard Ivy, a founder of the Unity Security Association, said:

> What we set this organization up for was to try to inform these people of their rights, and bring it to light. And then we got to take affirmative action on protesting these things in a legal way. I mean, that's the only way you can do it. And then you got to educate them on their rights in the local's affairs: what they can do within the union. That's what you're looking for. It's not, I mean, that's all we can do.

The purpose of the USA regarding the union was to make Local 40 more aware of its black members and to provide them with their share in policy-making. Bernard Ivy continued: "We couldn't do much without the union. But you've got to make the union realize that you're going to become active in the union, you know what I mean. And you're going to demand some of the things they've been refusing to do for you."

The officers of the USA felt that the union had not represented the black workers' grievances adequately to the company. Thus another objective of the black caucus was to deal directly with the company on these issues. Another black leader explained:

> We were going to the union for help; and we wasn't getting any help. So the men, the colored men who worked, we all decided we were going to try to do something about our own colored. So we got together. We met about six months before we brought it to the other people who were working here.

> And we decided we would just try to get together, and get us an organization. And try to deal with the company firsthand. And we have. And we have got some results from this.

> Matter of fact, we have got more results in the last five months than the colored have got over-all since we've been working.... We're not guests. I mean we're not guests any more.

The USA gave discontented blacks an alternative to opting out of the union. Mrs. Mollie Coleman explained this attitude: "That's why at one point they were talking about—all the girls wanted to get out of the union. The colored girls wanted to get out because they weren't getting any representation." The leaders of the new group urged blacks to participate even more in union affairs. Said Eric Fraley:

> We tell people from the first, we want them to join the union. We don't talk against it. We want them to join it. Join the union and join us....

> Anybody with common sense, if they was to stop and think, well, it's a
> help to everybody as a whole. It's a help to everybody.

The founders of the USA stopped what might have been a mass exodus of blacks from the union in the summer of 1968. The USA was also a center for discussion and education in union procedures and processes. A clear understanding gained there could lessen frustration at apparent mistreatment and could also provide a channel for redress of legitimate grievances. The officers of USA also worked to persuade blacks to take a more active role in the union: to run for steward and to attend meetings. Education and motivation came slowly. But the union president noted a distinct increase in black attendance at union meetings.

A brief look at the leadership of the USA reinforces the view that although the organization was aggressive, it was still moderate, constructive, and institutionally oriented. The founder was then forty-two years old with eight years of service in the plant. He had served capably as union steward and had been able, according to the local president, to win support from whites as well as blacks. He was in contact with both the union officials and top plant management even before the organization of USA. A key officer of USA had received two promotions since coming to the plant in 1965. He had a frustrating experience as a pioneer mechanic, but had the persistence to last it out. Another officer was promoted to maintenance mechanic after persistent efforts; in June of 1969 he was elected vice president of the union local, and he apparently had good relations with both whites and blacks in the plant.

Tactically, the USA helped to elect a black vice president of the union in the June 1969 regular election. Also at that time one Negro was elected as a trustee and two were made permanent delegates to the Memphis AFL-CIO Council. In addition, two liberal whites, who had long been active in the union and were among the first members of the Human Relations Council, were elected to union office. In the fall of 1970 the union president resigned and Vice President Alfred Magner was elected the first black President of Local 40. Both whites and blacks appeared to be responding to his leadership. However, in 1971 Magner was defeated by a narrow margin and only one black was elected to the Local 40 Board.

CONCLUSION

What did we find at Fairbanks International? First, we look back ten years to the decision to desegregate. We found a strong stand on the part of top management, with inconsistent acceptance by first-line supervision. Some foremen were helpful to the first blacks; others seemed unaware of the pioneers' real problems; still others were hostile. Foremen sensitivity programs are now becoming more common and have been used at Fairbanks–Memphis plant. This chapter shows the need for these programs, not only as industrial plants go beyond token integration, but as larger numbers of disadvantaged workers come into already integrated plants. Clearly, the foreman is central to the success of racial relations. When we say this, we do not exclude the role of the union steward who is also in a position to help.

Second, great credit must be given to the black pioneers themselves—especially to the three or four men and women who made the first breakthroughs in 1961, 1962, and 1963. Their patience, maturity, humor, and steadfastness were major reasons for the success of the desegregation move at Fairbanks International.

Looking to the present, we see tranquil, even good, working relations between whites and blacks in the plant, as well as equal job satisfaction. Although we find but the barest beginnings of off-plant socialization, it is encouraging to see both races changing in their attitudes and emotions toward one another—and this is in the deep South. Fairbanks and some other plants like it—perhaps more than Memphis schools and churches—have been meeting places for the two races as well as significant agents for social change.

There has been a rapid growth in the number of black women at the Fairbanks–Memphis plant. Jobs for black men are becoming available very slowly and, because of the technical abilities required, present a much greater challenge to management's ingenuity both in training and in stimulating the inadequate Memphis vocational school system. High hurdles still to be surmounted are more black breakthroughs into line supervision and middle management.

We said at the beginning of this chapter that we would have something to say about opening racial doors, at craft and management as well as entry levels. What have we learned?

- We learned, first of all, that management must want to open those doors and must communicate its stance to all, especially to its foremen.
- While careful planning is essential, a learning period wherein mistakes are made may be inevitable.
- We learned that taking a new look at traditional testing and promotion criteria often discloses abilities among blacks (and, for that matter, among whites) that hitherto were hidden.
- Prudent, although not scrupulous, selection of black pioneers is important.
- The candidates' own sturdy qualities are especially essential to success. Not everyone wants to pay the price of being a pioneer!
- Finally, we learned that continuing management support for breakthrough employees is needed, at least for the first years, and that top management must assist and check on line supervision.

Given the above ingredients, there is hope for continuing improvement, particularly for more *rapid* change, in deep-South plants and, indeed, in northern plants as well.

PART THREE

The issues

CHAPTER EIGHT

Making minority policies effective

> *Such a goal can only be achieved by a systems-wide application of the corporate commitment.*
>
> General Electric policy statement

The national and local experience of black people in industry show that only a massive and systematic planning approach will provide solutions to American racial problems before it is too late. The theme of this chapter is that the success of any organization in improving its employment of minority people will depend on top management commitment, on consideration of equal employment goals when planning *all* aspects of the business operation, and on a reorientation of the standards by which management and company success are measured to encompass this new thrust.

Management commitment begins with policy. Many people are suspicious of policy statements on any subject, but black Americans are especially suspicious of minority policy. The contrast between the ideals expressed in policy statements and everyday practices is often too evident. General Motors had enumerated "continuing product improvement" as a basic management policy more than ten years before Ralph Nader.[1] But this "product improvement" did not stress safety standards until public pressure was applied. Corporations with long-standing policies of nondiscrimination have operated southern plants on a totally segregated basis. We recall Ralph Waldo Emerson's statement: "What you are speaks to me so loudly, I can hardly hear what you say."

Yet policies and statements of ideals *are* important. In his classic study of prejudice, psychologist Gordon Allport warns that "official doctrines do not

---

[1] Stewart Thompson, *Management Creeds and Philosophies* (New York: American Management Association, 1958), Research Study No. 32, p. 111.

always correspond to the actual views and practices of the adherents." But he continues: "Yet [ideals] are psychologically important, for where they exist they inevitably point the minds of group members in a common direction, and present norms for their behavior."[2]

Policy by itself certainly does not guarantee implementation, but implementation without policy is unlikely. There will be no equal employment responsibility assigned, goals set, or progress measured without first having top management commitment in clear policy. The very effort to formulate policy influences the thinking of top management because it requires management to clarify its assumptions and goals. It is especially valuable if evaluation of policy is a continuing process. In 1958, the American Management Association made a study of 103 companies, asking them for statements of their company creed and what they thought about it. Many of the respondents said that one of the big advantages to written policy was the process of formulating it.

Since written policy (and also unwritten policies) is central to a company or to any organization, it is worthwhile to look at two examples of corporate equal employment opportunity statements. First, Westinghouse as of July 1967:

> It is the continuing policy of Westinghouse Electric Corporation to afford equal employment opportunity to qualified individuals regardless of their race, creed, color, national origins, or sex and to conform to applicable laws and regulations.
>
> This policy of equal opportunity comprehends all aspects of the employment relationship, including (a) hiring of new employees, (b) upgrading, transfer, selection for training opportunities, wage and salary administration, and application of service, retirement, and seniority policies to already hired employees.

General Electric's 1970 policy restates its position on nondiscrimination and then adds a strong statement on affirmative action:

> In addition, while it is the policy to apply appropriate job related standards to the conditions of employment and to maintain such standards at a level consistent with the healthy growth of the Company's business in a highly competitive economy, it is also the policy to take affirmative action to seek out individuals at any level of the organization whose potential has not been fully utilized, with the objective of assisting them to reach their full potential and meet job standards. Affirmative action will include finding additional sources of applicants who can become qualified, utilizing appropriate training which will assist these individuals toward full qualification, and developing programs to assure upward mobility for qualified individuals, regardless of their race, color, sex, religion, national origin or age.

[2] Gordon W. Allport, *The Nature of Prejudice* (Garden City, N.Y.: Doubleday Anchor Books, 1954, 1968), pp. 92, 93.

> A major goal of the Company is also to become a civic leader in programs and activities which enhance equal employment opportunities for all citizens within the various communities in which the Company operates throughout the nation. Programs and activities include fostering fair and open housing in the communities where the Company operates, assisting in the solution of transportation problems, and working with educational leaders to develop relevant curricula in preparing people for jobs.

Policies like this, which are still unusual, have come a long way from early statements such as RCA's in 1919: "Employment opportunities are open to all qualified people solely on the basis of their experience and aptitudes. Advancement is based entirely on the individual's achievement and potential for promotion."[3] How different black participation might be today had this policy been adopted and carried out in 1919! Hindsight perhaps?

SYSTEMS PLANNING

If equal employment policy is to be effectively implemented, a systematic approach is necessary. In the so-called hard sciences such as electronics and space research, systems engineering has had remarkable success. Here are three examples: the development of microwave radio relay systems, the Nike Ajax surface-to-aircraft missile, and the Telestar satellite. We could add the outstanding example of the pioneering Apollo Mission to the moon. In these cases, the preliminary systems planning was often done even while essential physical knowledge and technology were lacking.

The systems approach has also been used successfully on the "hard" side of business problems in manufacturing, finance, marketing, and others. Applying it to "softer" areas such as urban problems and minority manpower planning is more difficult, but this is getting more attention as something important and feasible, at least with larger corporations.

Central to the systems approach is an analysis of the interaction between individual units and the whole, in order to coordinate units and achieve greater effectiveness. Planning within the company will be coordinated. Management will consider minority manpower objectives in financial planning, research and development, facilities planning, economic and social forecasting, and so forth. Similarly, management will consider the impact of minority manpower programs on all other aspects of the business. The company is also part of larger social and economic systems. But first, a few examples of the importance of internal coordination.

Hard-core training programs must be related to economic forecasting. Because of seniority rules some major firms had to lay off recently trained hard-core workers during the 1970 recession. If the possibility of a recession had been seriously considered by the training program staff and by top

---

[3] "Equal Employment Opportunity," an RCA booklet dated 1961.

management, contingency plans might have been developed. Another example: it is no use taking on large numbers of the so-called New Work Force unless foremen are helped in coping with and understanding them, and are rewarded for doing so.

We have already noted the importance of plant location. A company may make a serious commitment to improve the number of blacks recruited, but if all new plants are located far from Negro populations, little improvement will be possible.

Careful analysis of trends outside the firm are also necessary. Companies deal with different parts of the country—with suppliers, customers, unions, civil rights groups, the labor market, federal, state, and municipal governments, foreign competitors, and foreign governments. The corporation should seek to understand these outside systems to see how it might relate to them for, let us say, the next ten years.

For example, should a firm be concerned about the quality of education that its local school system provides? Traditionally, this has not been a "business" problem. Yet a corporation pays taxes that support education and then often finds that people are not adequately trained to work in its plants. The company either has to retrain such potential workers itself, or use government training grants, also partly financed by corporate taxes. One executive of the companies we studied puts it like this:

> As a result of getting involved [in a hard-core program], managers get into the whole question of "people economics."
>
> Why can't we get in and deal with the problem way back at the grammar school level, the educational level, and the environmental conditions that have led to the drop-outs, that have led to the hopelessness and what not? As businessmen become involved with this little piece of the problem, you know, they begin to ask themselves what can we do to avoid all this extra cost that's involved.
>
> Then they have to go back to the beginning to understand how did this problem develop to begin with. You keep it in a business focus, it forces them to go back and look at the sociological aspects of it. But they're looking at it from the point of view of dollars and cents, efficient work force, disruption in the cities where the plants are, the plants being engulfed by neighborhoods that will set you up as the first target.

This executive brings up another point: the corporation cannot operate efficiently in a neighborhood where riots are likely. The firm has a stake in correcting patterns that breed resentment, alienation, and violence.

Let us take an example, one very pertinent to the 1970s, which requires both careful coordination within the company and an understanding of the larger systems outside the company. Should a given corporation move a plant *from* the inner city or *to* the inner city? By systems planning, this decision will take into account not only short-run economic benefits, but the long-run benefits to the community as well as to the corporation. It may be costly for a company like Western Electric to operate a plant in Newark, but if in time this plant can build up a satisfactory work force, it will help both the company's labor need and the city of Newark. And if the plant's work force helps build a better consumer's market in Newark for Western Electric products, Western Electric will further benefit.

In its influence outside the plant gates, the corporation needs to consider the effects on racial opportunity of its purchasing power, its bank deposits, and its persuasive influence on the community schools and housing. The limits to a systems approach need not be rigidly fixed, but should be expanded as necessary. The system is open to new inputs as needs change.

One of the most concise corporate statements of the importance of systems planning in equal employment and minority relations is the following from General Electric:

> There are two characteristics of the EOMR (Equal Opportunity and Minority Relations) program which virtually demand that any program, or solutions must, to be adequate, be preceded by a systems analysis of the problem. In the first place, there is virtually no part of the company's operations that is untouched by its impact. Because it is a "people" problem, it pervades every function and every location. Second, there is a strong and necessary connection between the external and internal aspects of the problem. Because the problem originated in society at large, the search for solutions cannot stop at the plant gate but must extend into the community....
>
> Clearly, such a goal can *only* be achieved by a systems-wide application of the corporate commitment: it can not be achieved by a single staff component nor even by a limited number of operating components, no matter how energetic and valid these efforts may be. This is why the implementation phase of this systems approach is so critical.[4]

SIX WAYS TO IMPLEMENT POLICY

Let us look now more closely at applying the systems approach to minority management within the firm (or within any large institution). Of the six methods we present, measurement is by far the most important.

1. *Locating responsibility.* Concern for racial advancement within the corporation is certainly everybody's business, but unless this concern is also the major responsibility of specific men and specific departments, it will get no one's serious attention or it will be the interest of only a few dedicated people.

A significant management development of the late 1960s and early 1970s is the rise of central corporate departments whose main function is to see that

---

[4] "General Electric's Commitment to Equal Opportunity Minority Relations, Case Study of a Systems Analysis Approach to Social Responsibility Programs," GE brochure, Corporate Industrial Relations, April 1970, pp. 10, 19.

the corporation advances the cause of minority people. From the early days of American business history, there were basic corporate departments of finance, accounting, marketing, manufacturing, purchasing, and law. The scientific revolution added the research department. Worker unrest and moves toward unionization about the time of World War I led to the industrial relations department. As community relations became more challenging, this too received a corporate staff.

Now, our urgent racial unrest points to the need for a corporate officer or department concerned primarily with minority workers. This is required of government contractors by the 1970 Order No. 4 of the Office of Federal Contract Compliance: "An executive of the contractor should be appointed as director or manager of company equal opportunity programs. Depending upon the size and geographical alignment of the company, this may be his sole responsibility."[5]

A corporate equal employment opportunity department is especially important for long-range planning and coordination with other company programs. It also has a crucial role in developing policy, reviewing its implementation, appraising the effectiveness of new programs, and developing criteria, measurements, and needed communication.

Nuances of line-staff relationships will vary with every company, but operating managers need to have the ultimate responsibility for implementation since they have the power to allot resources and set priorities. As one equal employment opportunity executive said, "Our job is to be a catalyst. We put the responsibility out in the line organizations. If *we* had the responsibility, that would be the end of performance."

2. *Communicating policy.* The problem of communication has received much attention, but difficulties remain whether we look at the differences between races, generations, or nations.

In the field of equal employment opportunity, communication checklists have been developed which include traditional procedures such as the circulation of policy to all levels of the organization, issuing standard procedure instructions to management personnel, inclusion of nondiscrimination clauses in union agreements, notifying all employment sources and community agencies, and the use of the equal opportunity emblem in all recruiting advertising, feature stories in company papers, and others. Obviously, particular methods will vary with the size and management style of the corporation. There is no one right way. The purpose of such checklists is to encourage a systematic and thorough use of all available means.

One of the most important elements is communication of top management's position. Some companies hold conferences for both line and staff management on the significance of equal opportunity effort. These conferences typically include a speech from the president of the company or a movie in

---

[5] See *Federal Register*, Vol. 35, No. 25, Feb. 5, 1970, Sec. 60-222.

which he stresses the corporation's commitment to the program. Communication (if possible on a person-to-person basis) must continue down to the foreman who deals with the day-to-day human relations aspect of the company minority policy. The seriousness of management's intention will *best* be communicated by effective measurement and rewarding of progressive equal employment efforts at all levels.

Equally important is communication between corporate departments, as we saw in our discussion of systems analysis. The major electrical corporations now often consider minority manpower objectives along with other business elements in their regular management goal-setting activities and evaluations. This provides an opportunity for weighing EEO objectives with other business goals, and coming up with feasible plans. It allows input from EEO planners and financial and engineering people at the same time.

Western Electric's management meets regularly for "President's Discussions," finding discussion of black employment in this context one of the most effective ways of changing management behavior.

GE has set up three panels to consult with its Equal Opportunity and Minority Relations Department: line and staff executives to make recommendations, top corporate executives to review these recommendations, and, significantly, a minority panel of sixteen professionals, mostly black, to evaluate policy and program recommendations from the minority viewpoint. These panels allow two-way communication with managers. A balance of field, corporate, and minority inputs should help give the resulting recommendations credibility and therefore better acceptance.

Communications outside the firm are also necessary. Even if equal employment policy were fully understood and implemented, communication of this fact would still remain a challenge. The greatest problem is reaching young blacks in the ghetto. The credibility gap there is hard to close. Young blacks simply will not believe that a corporation has good jobs for people who want to work. More innovative communication will be needed.

3. *Identifying problem areas.* Another aspect of implementing policy is making periodic depth studies of specific minority manpower problems of a given component or plant. Is the major problem hiring, promotion, all-white departments, the union's behavior, the neighborhood? What about apprenticeship for craftsmen jobs? Is there backlash? Is there any conflict between minority groups such as Spanish-speaking and blacks? What are the most important elements in a given situation?

Identifying the problem may not be so easy as it sounds. For example, "underutilization" of minority people is clearly a national problem. But how do you define it in relation to a specific plant? The Office of Federal Contract Compliance defines underutilization as having fewer minority members than would be "reasonably expected by their availability." But "reasonable availability" is a complex standard. The percentage of minority people in the plant compared to the percentage in the community, local minority unemployment, the availability of minority people with the skills that are needed, the number of promotable employees within the organization, and the availability of training institutions or programs are all relevant factors. What relative weight should a company give to them? What responsibility does a company have for developing skills when a large number of people are available but not qualified? This kind of careful and difficult questioning will be part of all depth studies.

4. *Establishing goals and timetables for minority programs.* Every manager knows the importance of having a goal or target for next year's sales plans or cost reduction. Without a target, or with only a vague target, policy will rarely be implemented.

Managers need concrete goals about the number of blacks they expect to have in each position, if they want to succeed in hiring and upgrading larger numbers. These quantitative goals are easy enough to handle. But it is also necessary to set up measurements for qualitative aspects of equal employment programs as far as this is possible. If not a precise number, at least a pointed evaluation can be made of a manager's answers to such qualitative questions as these: What is a brief summary of the minority situation in your community during 1971? What are the major priority needs in your community? What role is the company playing? How does our company's performance compare with that of other major employers in your community? What are some of your innovative approaches to affirmative action?

Setting numerical employment targets for blacks requires a careful assessment of what can be reasonably attained with vigorous and innovative efforts. There is real danger in adopting goals that are too high. The Office of Federal Contract Compliance Order No. 4 of 1970 was applied in the spring of 1970 first to the McDonnell-Douglas Corporation in St. Louis. The result was a negotiated affirmative action settlement agreement that may well have committed the corporation to goals that were extremely ambitious and perhaps unattainable. At any rate, exaggerated goals and timetables will disappoint the black community and will be a cause of annoyance to management.

On the other hand, it is important not to set goals that are too conservative rather than taking some risks with innovative ways of recruiting, training, and promoting. The policy of the Department of Defense seems to be that of stretching the system without breaking it.

One company is experimenting with the possibility of setting two targets: an affirmative action plan for the federal government that will meet minimum requirements and not raise aspirations beyond levels the company is sure it can reach, plus an internal plan with higher targets. This practice is directly parallel to adopting a departmental budget as a reasonable target but privately trying to do better than that target.

5. *Developing programs to meet local plant targets.* Innovative programs will be necessary to reach reasonably ambitious targets. An initial step, now required of government contractors by executive order, is an evaluation of

current recruiting, selecting, training, and promoting to eliminate any tests or practices which may unintentionally screen out qualified people.

Beyond that, new sources of minority employees need to be sought. Many plants discover that they can expand their recruiting programs or find among their minority employees some with hidden potential for promotion. Special programs are necessary to orient employees for entry job levels, and to provide them with the skills they need. Current research into the effectiveness of new programs will help to reduce the risk of experimentation and to spread successful techniques. But imagination is still needed at all levels.

A by-product of these new affirmative action efforts is that improved techniques can apply to white employees as well as to blacks. If better orientation helps blacks to adjust to the job and stay on it, better orientation will help whites to do the same thing. Sensitivity training helps a foreman deal better with all his employees, both black and white.

6. *A system of measurement and sanctions.* The keystone in the arch of policy implementation is measurement of EEO performance and the use of sanctions to encourage desired behavior. Every manager, including the foreman, has many competing responsibilities: production to meet sales, quality of output, profitability, and so forth. It is unfair to ask a man to act in a whole new area in ways that could adversely affect this other work without reviewing the whole measurement-reward system. The new "rules of the game" must be clear and the manager and the foreman must have an opportunity to learn them.

A sophisticated measurement system is necessary. Standard criteria are needed to compare this year's performance with last year's, and also to allow comparison of one manager with another.

Complete evaluation needs to include at least the following analyses: minority participation at each job level classification and in hiring and upgrading; local community and labor market minority percentages; the social and human relationships between the races in the plant; the civil rights climate; major community problems and priorities. Such analyses obviously must be qualitative as well as quantitative. But we suggest that quantitative criteria can also be applied to areas such as human relations and support for community programs.

An example of a new and comprehensive measurement system, that of General Electric, brings out our point: In 1970, as part of the annual review of manpower planning, every GE plant and division manager was required to make a report on the following items:

1. *Analysis of community climate*
    - present and projected population growth by race
    - unemployment by race
    - summary of priority needs of minority community; individual and company leadership involvement, minority organizations and assessment of leadership

- support to minority business in purchasing dollars and in making deposits

2. *Management leadership and involvement*
   - reports how well corporate policy was communicated, whether EEO goals were included in budgeting and planning, how well EEO responsibility has been assigned, manner of auditing and measurement, and EEO special training programs.

3. *Minority recruiting*
   - numbers and percent interviewed and hired
   - evaluation of special recruiting programs

4. *Employment placement and orientation*
   - statistical analysis of racial composition by job category, current and projected
   - current and projected number of disadvantaged and their retention rate
   - listing of funding and number of trainees for government-company training programs for disadvantaged

5. *Developing and upgrading*
   - current and projected proportions of minority in exempt positions
   - special programs to identify, train, and upgrade all minority people

6. *Reports with findings and recommendations of*
   - any government review, and/or
   - discrimination complaint

The central problem in the equal employment opportunity measurement system is the balancing-of-values issue. How shall the company weigh the values to be placed on these facets of management performance as opposed to others? There are no neat answers, but some effort toward value balancing must be introduced into the system.

Ultimately how much weight will be given to equal employment opportunity will depend upon a firm's top management. Top management will certainly consider the equal employment opportunity area when dealing with managers in plants dependent on the New Work Force near the inner city. At least a few companies have announced that performance in the minority area will be an important evaluation ingredient for all management personnel as well.

To have the mighty improvement needed in black employment and promotions during the 1970s, we shall need top management commitment in vigorous policies, a systems approach to all aspects of the problem, plus practical methods for policy implementation such as measurements and sanctions to guarantee effectiveness. One major issue will continue to confront systems management: the poor and disadvantaged candidate for a job.

CHAPTER NINE

New opportunities for the disadvantaged

No man can live with the terrible knowledge that he is not needed.
Elliot Liebow

"Screen in, not out" and "Hire first, train later" became slogans of the new National Alliance of Businessmen (NAB) during the late 1960s and 1970s. Key business leaders, concerned about the conditions underlying the riots, worked to persuade employers to provide jobs for men and women supposedly unemployable—people who were called (often quite rightly) "disadvantaged."

There was enthusiasm; there was skepticism. Thousands of jobs were pledged but were the numbers real or inflated? Factory employment offices and foremen found themselves confronting people—mostly black and mostly young—from another world, that of the American urban ghetto. Management asked: Will these young disadvantaged people become good and steady workers, producing quality products? How do you motivate, teach, keep them? The ghetto people asked: Does the "Man" really mean it when he says there is a good job for me if I want it, one with a future?

This chapter is neither an extensive national analysis, nor a how-to-do-it manual. Instead it offers insights from five situations studied in some depth. Three are noncontract NAB pledges from plants we portrayed in earlier chapters: Fairbanks–Memphis, Westinghouse–Buffalo, and National Acme–Chicago. Two are intensive orientation and training programs in plants we have now to present: Westinghouse–East Pittsburgh and Raytheon, near Boston. The latter two programs are subsidized by the federal government through Manpower Administration contracts, which reimburse private employers for the extra costs of training the disadvantaged.

We shall give enough facts about the programs to show what they are doing, plus statistics that are reasonably hard. But mainly we introduce the people involved who ought to be heard in a "listening book."

"The white manager, or, for that matter, the black manager living in a middle-class culture, will never understand the rejected hard-core black man merely by reading finely reasoned analyses or executive summaries. He will learn only by confrontation—by hearing these ghetto people out—with enough humility to believe that he has something to learn as well as something to teach."[1]

WHAT ARE DISADVANTAGED PEOPLE LIKE?

The definition of the U.S. Department of Labor regarding disadvantaged people is well known: "*poor* persons who do not have suitable employment and who are either under 22 . . . or over 45 . . . handicapped, or subject to special obstacles in employment."

How do hundreds of disadvantaged people from our five plants fill out that definition? A glance at Table 9-1 shows that the people hired varied with the program. Some were hardly disadvantaged, but most were young black men, often born in the Deep South. Usually they had not finished high school. Sometimes an arrest record excluded them from employment. Often they had been unemployed for months before their job as an NAB pledge.

But statistics cannot show the impact of a poor education, limited opportunities, and an often inadequate family life. We need to listen to the disadvantaged themselves and to their friends. Each man is an individual but each can tell us something that is true for other people as well.

"I WAS SO CONFUSED WHEN I FIRST CAME HERE"

Coming from the ghetto world to the industrial plant world is a transition as difficult as that of the average white man trying to fit into a group of black men on a street corner in Harlem.

A young Fairbanks NAB worker, Essie Colbert, was a high school graduate; but when she came into the Fairbanks International plant to learn to be a machine operator, it was tough:

> I was so confused when I first came here! The people move so fast. I mean the first few days. I would be the only one at the bus stop, and I say: "I know somebody else got to be riding the bus, but everybody gone but me." They move so fast, and I be so confused.

[1] Theodore V. Purcell and Rosalind Webster, "Window on the Hard-core World," *Harvard Business Review*, July–August 1969, p. 118.

Table 9–1. Profile of Disadvantaged Workers
Five plants

	Fairbanks–Memphis N=10	Westinghouse–Buffalo N=42	National Acme–Chicago N=30	Raytheon–Boston N=12	Westinghouse–East Pittsburgh N=112
Race: percent black	100%	85%	82%[a]	92%	90%
Sex: percent male	20%	76%	94%[a]	83%	100%
Age (median)	20 years	25 years	24 years[a]	24 years	26 years
Education (median)	12 years	11 years	10.5 years	10 years	10 years
Birthplace					
South	90%	36%	50%	50%	—
Northeast	10%	64%	0	42%	—
North Central	0	0	36%	8%	—
Outside U.S.	0	0	13%	0	—
Arrest record	—	12%	12%	—	78%
Previous unemployment span (average)	—	5.5 months	3.5 months	—	15.5 months[b]

[a] From the total population of 466 NAB pledges. The other figures are from a random sample of 30 NAB pledges.
[b] Includes time spent in prison.

> I couldn't find my card. I couldn't do nothing. And I would go up to my foreman, then was Duggins. I would go up to Duggins and like I had a problem about the clock every evening. But finally I learned my clock number, and he beared with me. I had the wrong card. My downtime wouldn't be right, or something. . . . I got it, but it took me about a week.

Mrs. Colbert moved from the welfare rolls onto the payroll of Fairbanks: a success story for herself, the plant, and for society as a whole. But she said she never could have done it if she had not been given a chance by the plant and also given some special support by her foreman.

HE FIGURED THE NEXT MAN WAS OUT TO BEAT HIM, TOO

The young disadvantaged worker may come to the plant with a deep distrust of anyone in a position to make decisions, especially white people. Roger Green, a Raytheon–Boston Job Training Center graduate eager to get ahead, showed this clearly when he described his first reaction to Raytheon's program:

> You know, I figured the next man was out to beat me just like anybody else. And that if anyone offer me something I know there must be a catch to it. So I went to the school, I say: "I'm gonna see just what these people are putting down," you know. And at first I didn't like it, like I told you, I didn't like what they were putting down, so I had a talk with Mr. Sampsen and he say: "Well, look, things are gonna change. Stick it out." And Mr. Griggs told me the same thing. So I stuck it out and after a while it started straightening out.

Without special encouragement from Mr. Griggs and Mr. Sampsen (both black), Green might have quit the program before he had really given it a chance—even though it promised an education and a job that he wanted.

Leroy Dawson came to Raytheon's Job Training Center after he finished high school in the South and completed a term of service in the Army. He was ambitious, willing to work, and aiming for promotion. He probably did not need the Training Center preparation. He was doing well on his job, was respected by his foreman, and had been promoted since being hired—partly in response to his own pressure. Yet he too felt: "You have to know what is going on to survive—see, you got the guy who'll be good to your face, and then talk about you behind your back. So you don't know who to trust." According to Dawson, a good supervisor is one who is straight: "McAvoy is about the best. He's straight. You know he don't lie to you; at least he hasn't lied to me. Maybe he have, but I haven't found out about it yet. But he been straight so far." There is wariness even in his vote of confidence.

Although management may be fully committed, it will still have to deal with a long period of testing and suspicion, but this suspicion is not irrational.

The disadvantaged man knows that people have been paid to attend skill training sessions that did not result in a job. He knows people who have been laid off just before they became permanent employees. He knows that companies have advertised special job opportunities for disadvantaged Negroes but hired only a few of the most qualified.

Because of this distrust, misunderstanding may appear to be lies and alienate an already suspicious employee. Recall the bitterness (Chapter 4) with which Elliot Tompkins, a disadvantaged employee at National Acme Electric–Chicago reported a misunderstanding about pay: "They're not holding to their promises." William Fleck, also at the Chicago plant, felt the same way: "I thought I'd be makin' about $3.15 an hour, *but I see that was a whole lot of baloney.*" Recall, too, the warning of John Clay in Chicago: "If a guy has a high expectation and feels that he is cheated by the organization, *then that organization as far as he is concerned is useless.*" It is difficult to work with an employee who feels that the company has cheated him.

"THEY'RE AFRAID THEY CAN'T MAKE IT"

For some young disadvantaged people, fear of failure contributes to anxiety about the job. Learning a new job can be a threat even when the job is relatively simple. It means a new challenge and another risk of failure. Russell Simpson complained that assembly work was monotonous at National Acme–Chicago, but he did not like being put on a new job without preparation:

> You might be here for maybe two or three years, and you want everybody to think you can do everythin', although you really can't do it. You be doin' this job and then they put on this new job and you fall down on the line. They got to stop the line and wait on you. And they [the workers] don't want to take the chance of bein' put on something they can't do.

Simpson probably would not tell his foreman he was afraid. It is more likely that he would become belligerent about his "right" to stay on his own job. In a new situation he might show his fear by reluctance to ask questions that might reveal his ignorance. Or he might even walk off the job without saying why.

The problem of fear can be even more intense when skill training is involved. But the rewards are great. Roger Green described his reaction to skill training at Raytheon's Job Training Center:

> It gives a man an opportunity to feel that he's—what do you call it now—able to do something on his own and he can do it. That he don't have to sit around doing nothin' just because he's afraid. That's the main thing right there. A lot of people are afraid they can't do it. Like when I first started. I said: "Electronics? I don't know the first thing

about it; I might not be able to do it." That kept going in my mind. Then they started talking to me, you know. And I started looking and reading and I said to myself it wasn't as hard as I really thought it was. Although it gets harder as you go up. But I said to myself it wasn't as bad as I thought it would be. So then I started thinking: "Well, heck, I can do it if I put my mind to it."

"YOUNGER PEOPLE AIN'T GOING TO TAKE JUST ANYTHING"

Young blacks, like young whites, are becoming more particular about the kind of job they want. Higher aspirations and discontent with menial dead-end jobs will continue to grow. Leroy Hutchins, an aggressive young man at Raytheon–Boston, told us that people he knew cared about the reputation and status a job brought, as well as the work itself. Hutchins, a leader among the trainees at the Bedford plant, had a full Afro haircut and slight goatee. We asked him whether he thought the people in Roxbury (Boston's ghetto) really wanted to work:

> Yeah, I mean you know you gonna find some that don't want to work but the majority of the people as a whole, they want to work. But they want something nice. They want a nice job, nice atmosphere. They don't want no janitor's job. They want something they can tell their kids when they grow up about being this at Raytheon or I did this in such and such a place... an' this is the main thing people are lookin' for, especially the younger people. The younger people ain't going to take just anything nowadays.

Chicago-born, twenty-two-year-old black assembler, Chester Favreau, made the same point in relation to Acme–Chicago: "Evidently, they wants to work, but they not *pleased* with their work. If they didn't want to work, there'd be no use 'n filling out the application. So I would say, if they were *pleased* with their work. Inquire to see if they're *pleased*."

Young blacks are also eager for quick promotion. Hutchins liked to brag about working at Raytheon in "electronics" but he was angry that he had not been promoted more rapidly. He also felt that no one in his department had the kind of opportunities he really wanted.

The high job aspirations of blacks are related to their new pride. Ken Pruett, twenty-four, a cable maker at Raytheon, was working with six other blacks in a predominantly white department. He was asked if his white co-workers ever gave him a hard time:

> They don't give us a hard time because they gathered from when we first came here that we don't accept no hard time. During the times of our mothers and fathers, they would accept things. But like with this generation that I'm in, and the one younger than me... they really don't take a lot of junk.... This younger one will not take nothing from nobody. You can see that the way that things are today.

"WHO DO YOU BLAME?"

Let's listen also to Lawton Pierce. Mr. Pierce is a middle-aged, respected craftsman and one of the few long-service black men at the Acme–Chicago plant. He was in trouble himself as a young man. He told about the home and school background of the disadvantaged he knew so well:

> ... Did he miss something in his elementary years that prevents him from understanding or comprehending what's going on in the seventh and eighth grade? I say yes. Because if he could keep up, he would stay there. And the only reason he doesn't stay is simply because he can't keep up. And his classmates are possibly laughing at him, making fun of him. They will pass a test and walk out in fifteen minutes, and he stay there two hours trying to complete a test. So he gives up.
>
> And he might be from a family—possibly his mother and father were drop-outs. They couldn't help him with his homework. Well, that's another burden on him. I'm speaking of the hard-core black now, but this is what I know.... I don't say he dropped out, he got pushed out. Do you blame the school? All right, so the school can't do what the people should have done at home. Who do you blame? Society? I don't think it's fair to blame society. I don't know who is to blame. But it's a problem. How do we eliminate the problem?

And there aren't enough jobs, according to Pierce:

> Nobody wants to be poor with their hands stuck out. Give them a chance to go out and make an honest living. They'll go out and earn it. But we all know the work is not there. We are creating jobs as we go along, we all know this. But we're not creating them fast enough.
> We have guys today. They don't care. They've never had anything They don't look for a bright future. They don't feel like they'll ever have anything.

They aim for a big car instead of a home.

> You see more Cadillacs, more Buicks, than Chevies and you wonder why. Here's a guy who, the money that he makes and the outlay that he has to have for an inferior living, he can't look forward to a new home. He can't look forward to it. So he tries to get the best he can get with the money he's making. And the far'est he can look forward to is a decent piece of automobile to drive. He can't look forward to joining the country club....

And without a job, or with a poor one, they cannot fulfill responsibilities to their families.

> It's a situation where you take one man. He's not employed. He's got a wife and two kids, and he feels like he can't find a job. He can't feed the kids, so what can he do, you know? They might be better off if he left and they accepted some type of restitution from one of the agencies.

A broken home again. So what causes a broken home? Is it society or is it the man? Who's responsible?

Elliot Liebow develops this same theme in *Tally's Corner*.[2] A man who does not have the earning ability to take on long-term adult responsibilities will continue to find his greatest satisfaction in spontaneous day-to-day living, and these attitudes make it more difficult to get a job. And with few responsibilities there is less need to work regularly. It is a vicious circle; it is also a realistic adjustment to an economic environment. But Liebow concludes: "Before [the Negro man] can earn a living he must believe that he can do so and his women and children must learn to believe this along with him."

"NO WAY OF GETTING ANYTHING BY KEEPING THIS JOB"

Most men in the ghetto do work—irregularly—but the important point is: The jobs they get do not encourage the habits and attitudes toward work that are necessary for steady jobs that pay well.

Too often the small employer near the ghetto exploits the habits of his workers. He invests little time in training, makes few demands, and pays low wages. Layoffs are frequent, and hiring may be done on a temporary basis, even daily. There is no union mechanism for working out grievances. If a man clashes with his boss, he quits or is fired. In this kind of situation there are no rewards for working regularly, being punctual, or trying to work out problems.[3]

Willie Montgomery, draftsman trainee at Raytheon–Boston, is a slight, soft-spoken Negro who looks you directly in the eye. Twenty-four years old in 1969, he had come to Boston from Alabama at nineteen and held a series of temporary jobs, supplementing his income by hustling. When he joined the training program in early 1968, he was angry and very antiwhite. He had never worked more than four months at one job. When we spoke with him, Montgomery had been with Raytheon eighteen months. He had married during this time and his wife was expecting their first child. Montgomery hoped it would be a son. He described his old way of life and one of his former jobs like this:

> I was, what you say, like just a guy on the streets trying to make it any way I can. Doing anything I can for money. If I get it, I just get it. Like I had a part-time job. There wasn't no future in it, nothing like that. I had no way possible of getting anything by keeping this job. Just a job working to survive here in Boston.

This job did little to teach Montgomery good work habits.

[2] Elliot Liebow, *Tally's Corner* (Boston: Little, Brown, 1967), p. 224.
[3] Peter B. Doeringer and Michael J. Piore, *Internal Labor Markets and Manpower Analysis* (Boston: D.C. Heath, 1971).

"IS A JOB REALLY AN ADVANTAGE?"

For others a job may actually create short-term economic problems. Richard Ross, former director of the Westinghouse–East Pittsburgh program for the disadvantaged, said:

> The way we look at a job, the way most middle-class white people look at employment and education—it's an escape from the position where they are. But to these people many times a job was a disadvantage to them because they owe bills. One man wasn't working and he owed hundreds of dollars. As long as he wasn't working people wrote off the fact of collecting any money; now when he gets a job, his creditors are pushing in. Now his friends, now he's working, he has to support them and you know, a job is not an ally to this guy.

Ross counseled many of his trainees on handling these difficulties and helped them to see the long-term advantages of employment.

AND THEY FOUND OUT THAT HE HAD BEEN ARRESTED

A substantial minority of disadvantaged people have arrest records. When they look for a job they are turned down. Eugene Kelly, twenty-eight, told how he was turned down at Westinghouse–Buffalo in 1965:

> They were hiring like crazy. I passed their test at that time and got a good score, supposedly. I made the mistake, you know, of being honest with them. Well, see when I was a kid, when I was seventeen, I got into some difficulty. I wasn't living at home. Subsequently I was put in a reformatory.
>
> I had left the question blank on the questionnaire, see. And so I already gotten my work shoes, my glasses and everything. I was going to start work that minute. He says: "Oh, we noticed one question was blank. Would you mind answering that?" I said: "Sure, what was that?" He said: "Were you ever arrested for anything other than minor traffic violations?" I said: "Yes, I was." And he says: "What?" And I told him: "Back when I was seventeen, I was jailed for—actually, you know, burglarizing a package out of an automobile." He tells me to wait, and he goes back into the office, and he says: "I'm sorry we can't use you."

When asked about taking men such as Kelly into the work force, Charles Eliot, a respected Acme Chicago black foreman, said:

> You can get good guys like this, you know. And there's no way of knowing anything until you try. And in the best family, you got the worst kind. So you can't pick out and say: "Well, this guy is not going to be any good because he was, he is a criminal." You can't say this guy's going to be no good because there's something wrong, a broken home. Or you can't say this guy's real good because his father took care

of him and brought him up. He may be the worst guy. He is really worse than the guy that hasn't had the education, that hasn't struggled enough, because he's had it all his way.

And Kelly was doing well at Westinghouse in 1969.

"WHY COULDN'T I GET A JOB ON MY OWN?"

In spite of the fact that poverty program agencies like the Concentrated Employment Program are willing to help, we must remember that it is not always easy for a disadvantaged man to wait in line and be a "case." Jesse Byrd, for example, twenty-two years old, came out to Westinghouse-Buffalo and put in an application on his own. He heard nothing. He then went down to Buffalo's CEP. He was classified as "disadvantaged," although he did not know this. His application for a job was accepted. Byrd is a high school graduate with a good record, and he did not understand why he could not have gotten a job on his own:

> There I was on my own, which a person should in getting a job—is come down on his own to try to get it. And that's the only reason I—I hated to go down there [CEP]. But I had no alternative, really. So I went there, and they got the job for me. And I was kind of hurt because I couldn't get it myself.

A director of a training program underlined this point. "Who's really hard core?" he asked. "Maybe it's the company who sets hiring criteria unnecessarily high and excludes people that could do the job. Maybe it's the foreman who can't adjust to black workers. Maybe it's the white guy on the line whose sense of security is based on being better than blacks."

Special programs for men and women who need them are good but it is also important to accept people who are already qualified.

THE NATIONAL ACME-CHICAGO NAB PROGRAM

The National Acme plant in Chicago pledged 200 jobs as soon as the NAB program was announced in April 1968 and hired 466. For Acme, hiring the disadvantaged was no experiment. As we saw in Chapter 4, the racial composition of the neighborhoods around Acme had been changing and by 1968 the majority of their applicants were young and black. The early Acme experience with the hard core was not very different from its experience with the New Work Force, described in detail in Chapter 4. Indeed, 80 percent of the NAB pledges were designated disadvantaged *after* they were hired. (Classification, as in many other cases, was based primarily on residence in poor ghetto neighborhoods, since checking an applicant's income was difficult, expensive, and not always reliable.)

National Acme Electric's involvement with the hard core is especially important because of its size. If Acme can develop effective methods it will have an impact on hundreds of men and women. Acme hired 466 NAB pledges in its first fourteen months. On July 1, 1969, at the end of that period, 165 were still working at the plant. This was a 64 percent loss. But more than half of *all* the people hired at Acme during 1968 left before the end of the year—white, black and Spanish-speaking alike. Similarly, absenteeism was a problem with the New Work Force, whether classified NAB or not. Our conversations with the disadvantaged in the plant, their co-workers, and foremen suggested three major problems—a special need for orientation, a need for good relations with the foreman, and frustration with assembly line work. These issues were discussed in detail in Chapter 4.

The quality of foreman support depended on the sensitivity and initiative of the individual foreman to whom they happened to be assigned. This varied greatly. One NAB employee, Earl Pratt, was pleased with the orientation and the extra time that his foreman gave to him:

> When I first started, they took me around, showed me around, showed me a few different parts, and let me work with another guy. They show you the main points. And they just don't take you and shove you over and say: "Here, go!" you know. They put you down with another guy, a guy that's more experienced with it, and he'll work with you for a while. Then after that, they'll come back and ask you: "Do you think you can work it?"

Pratt was high in his praise of his foreman and of the way his foreman helped him become acclimated to the job:

> I didn't know anything about the job. So, he stuck with me. And he showed me how to do it, showed me some of the numbers. Which, I know he believes as well as I do: you can't remember everything at once. As far as me, I don't think I'm better than anybody else. He'll be right there if I need him, if I get kind of pulled or anything.

Another NAB worker, William Fleck, was much more negative. When asked if he was given much help in learning his job, he replied: "No. They just put you there. They show you a few things, let you go. They work with you for a little while, ain't no more said to you."

While all whites and 86 percent of the older blacks were clearly favorable to their foreman, only 38 percent of the young blacks were, and 25 percent indicated that they did not get along with him.

With the problem of low tolerance for monotonous repetitive jobs, Acme Electric faces a special challenge. Almost all entry jobs are on the assembly line. While this makes it easy to absorb a person with few skills, motivation on the assembly line has been a long-standing problem. It is even more difficult with the hard core.

Here we present some additional data bearing directly on the disadvantaged who left the plant and those who stayed. Company-formulated reasons for leaving most often do not touch on basic motivation, but they can be instructive. Table 9-2 shows the reasons or circumstances for leaving for those 301 NAB pledges who were no longer at Acme in July 1969. Note that absenteeism, as at Westinghouse–Buffalo and Raytheon–Boston, was a major problem, but that discipline problems were minor.

Table 9–2. Disadvantaged Employees' Reasons or Circumstances for Leaving, Acme–Chicago, 1969

N = 301

Fired	Percent	Voluntary Departures	Percent
1. Excessive absenteeism and tardiness	26.2	1. No report (after 5 days absence)	22.2
2. Couldn't adapt	6.3	2. Resigned	11.6
3. Falsification of application	3.3	3. Left for another job	7.6
4. Violation of shop rules (abusive language, drinking, etc.)	2.3	4. Walked off job	3.3
5. Refused job assigned or to follow instructions	1.7	5. Didn't like job or pay; personal problems related to job	3.3
6. Not qualified	.7	6. Personal problems, or home duties, not job related	2.3
		7. Never started; or worked one day and didn't return	3.0
Total	40.5		53.3

Other: Moved away; returned to school; military; laid off; deceased; unknown: 6.3

We took two samples of the Acme NAB employees: those who stayed and those who left. (See Table 9-3.) To our surprise, we found very little difference between the two groups in sex, age, marital status, number of dependents, arrest record, or race. But we did find two significant differences: first, pay upgrading. The previous pay for those who dropped out was $2.49 an hour and their starting rate at Acme was $2.34, a job rate that incentives might raise by 20 or 25 percent to $2.90 or $3.00 an hour. The previous pay for those who stayed was only $1.97 an hour and their base starting rate was $2.45 (plus incentives). For those who stayed, Acme pay meant a big step up. For those who left, Acme pay was not a big increase.[4]

The second significant difference was place of birth. Retention was lower for people from the North. Only 20 percent of those who stayed but 45 percent of those who left were born in the North. This may mean that the men with more opportunities are more mobile; they know where they can go to get another job. It could also mirror the frustration and militancy of the northern-born black. Men born in the South are more thankful for their job. They

[4] The same finding is reported in Fredrick Herzberg, *Job Attitudes: Review of Research and Opinion* (Pittsburgh: Psychological Service of Pittsburgh, 1957), p. 107. See also Bertram C. Shlensky, "Determinants of Turnover in NAB-JOBS Programs to Employ the Disadvantaged," unpublished Ph.D. dissertation, Sloan School of Management, Massachusetts Institute of Technology, September 1970. Shlensky found that for six NAB-JOBS federally funded training programs in New England, turnover was highly related to being young, male, and black. Wages were also a factor.

Table 9-3. Profile of Disadvantaged Employees Who Left vs. Those Remaining, Acme–Chicago, 1969

	Drop-outs N = 20	NAB Pledges Still on Payroll N = 10
Sex	96% male	90% male
Age (median)	23 years	25 years
Marital status	65% single	70% single
Education (highest grade completed)	10.7 grades	10.2 grades
Rate of pay at previous job	$2.49 per hour	$1.97 per hour
Beginning rate at Acme (not including incentives)	$2.34 per hour	$2.46 per hour
Arrest record	15%	10%
Place of birth		
North Central	45%	20%
Middle South	0	10
Deep South	45	50
Outside of U.S.	10	20
Shift worked		
First	47%	70%
Second	42	20
Third	11	19
Number months unemployed before Acme job	3.6 months	3.4 months

may work hard and hope to get ahead. The northern-born man may be less satisfied with monotonous, hard assembly work. Roughly 50 percent of the drop-outs and 40 percent of those who stayed worked on assembly or conveyors. More drop-outs worked on the less desirable second shift.

Acme did not originally provide any special orientation or training for the NAB hires, or any foreman training specifically aimed at dealing with the disadvantaged worker. The employee relations department instead directed its tentative efforts toward the entire New Work Force. The employment office tried to develop criteria predicting which men and women would stay on the job. Despite a number of experiments described in Chapter 4, few tools were found to aid the employment interviewer in making a decision.

In the more important areas of orientation, foreman training, and counseling, Acme–Chicago experimented on a small scale. Special counseling was provided for about a year for the worst absentees in one plant; fuller orientation was used in another. Don Keith, who had been in charge of hiring at Acme Electric for a number of years, attempted to find out what the potential employee really liked and why. To him as an employment man, there was little difference between operating a punch press or a shear, but it could make a great deal of difference to the new employee. Keith often took the new man out into the plant to see the various jobs, and asked him which job he thought he would like. He found that this, coupled with a thorough orientation, helped to reduce turnover. But there was neither time nor staff to use this personal approach with many new employees.

Seeing the need for innovation and more support for the New Work Force, Acme Electric began a special vestibule orientation and training program in mid-1969. A federal MA-4 contract provided about $1 million for training 400 disadvantaged at a cost of about $2,300 per man.

The program involved nine weeks of classroom training, subcontracted to the Chicago Opportunities Industrialization Center (OIC), a black-run group originating in Philadelphia under the Reverend Leon Sullivan. The trainees were on the Acme payroll from the first day of their training.

Counseling and support were an important part of the program. The man's regular foreman was also expected to act as a counselor, and to be understanding of the background out of which the man came. To ensure this, all of the first-line supervisors and higher level managers attended a special minority relations sensitivity training program, conducted by the staff of OIC. Acme realized that an investment in these men might result in lower operating expenses, especially for turnover, absenteeism, and tardiness. Acme management was encouraged by the early results of the program—by the end of 1970, retention was about 64 percent.

THE WESTINGHOUSE—BUFFALO NAB PROGRAM

The Westinghouse plant in Buffalo also joined the National Alliance of Businessmen job pledge program in the spring of 1968. According to the directors of Buffalo NAB, Westinghouse provided one of the better teams of company officers whose job it was to convince executives of other corporations of the importance of hiring the disadvantaged. Of course, Westinghouse itself promised to hire disadvantaged workers during the remainder of 1968. In the following fourteen months, Westinghouse employed forty-two formerly hard-core unemployed. Most of the disadvantaged were certified hard core and placed through the local Concentrated Employment Program (CEP). The CEP in Buffalo services the mostly black Model Cities Area. Certification as hard core or disadvantaged was based simply on residence in the Model Cities Target area. Said Reginald Nichols, a director of CEP:

> Our qualification for CEP is that you come from a target area. That's the ultimate need, there is no financial criteria. You see, the original criteria that they had for some projects was that if you made over $3,500, you can't participate. This is not realistic.

The CEP and the New York State Employment Service screened applicants for Westinghouse security requirements. But the purpose of the NAB program, said Theodore Hunt, a Westinghouse employment officer, was to screen *in* rather than screen *out* the "substandard" employee.

> Screening has to be very limited. Because, you know, they've been fired here, they've been arrested here. And the whole concept of the NAB program is that these are people who are not good applicants to begin with—people who can't be checked out, or people whom you normally would not hire for one reason or another. Now, from the quality of applicants, the very nature of the persons being Model Cities residents makes them almost entirely substandard.

But are they? Substandard to Hunt meant that previously they probably would have been refused employment at Westinghouse. Until 1968, people with arrest records and high school drop-outs were almost automatically turned down by the Westinghouse–Buffalo Employment Office. Some Westinghouse NAB workers could have met those criteria. The NAB pledges hired in the first fourteen months averaged eleven years of education and less than 15 percent had arrest records. For background data on the disadvantaged at Buffalo, see Table 9-1.

The NAB workers, as with all new hires, were placed in low job grades. The Westinghouse policy of filling the more skilled jobs by promotion in order of seniority assures the disadvantaged worker a fair chance of moving up eventually, but also means that he will spend his first difficult months on a job he may not respect.

An interesting and unusual feature of the Westinghouse NAB program is its work with deaf mutes. Four of the NAB pledges were deaf mutes. A large and very good institution, St. Mary's School for the Deaf, is located in Buffalo, and for many years Westinghouse has provided job opportunities for these deaf people. There are now about fifty deaf mutes on the rolls. Although it is unusual to have so many physically disadvantaged working, Westinghouse found that these men tended to be very stable employees. They did good work, and they were pleased and thankful to have a job.

How shall we evaluate the Westinghouse–Buffalo NAB program? First, let us look at the number of disadvantaged workers who have been retained on the job. For the first phase of the Westinghouse–Buffalo program, retention was rather good. Twenty-eight of forty-two workers hired between September 1968 and June 1969 were still on the job at the end of that period. A year later sixteen of these men and women were still with Westinghouse. Half of the thirty-four pledges hired between July 1969 and May 31, 1970, were still on board at the end of that period.

Another way of evaluating the NAB program is to listen to the foremen who deal with the NAB workers. Before the first NAB workers were brought into the plant, the issue was brought up with foremen at the training seminar. The foremen's reaction in early 1968 was described by Arthur Sanford of the industrial relations department:

> We got some pretty sharp questions. Such questions as: "Are you going to have special training programs? Are you going to bring in a group

and teach them to read and write and this type of thing, or are you going to integrate them into the work force?"

And that raised the question about anxiety. Were they hopeful that we would do this? Or fearful that we might go way beyond what we have done with others? And I think the general feeling was one of anxiety rather than hope, because of the fear that they had about having these disadvantaged, no matter how much training they had gotten, being part of their work force.

Management asked the foremen to notify industrial relations of any special problems that arose. The department could then ask the referring agency to counsel the worker. Foremen were to be told that an employee was hard core before the initial interview. Some foremen did request special help with problems of their hard-core workers, but, in talking to the foremen in the spring of 1969, we found that the majority did not know who their hard-core employees were until we asked about them.

We interviewed twelve of the NAB pledges and eleven of their foremen. In *every* case, the foremen thought their disadvantaged employees were doing adequately in quality and quantity of work! Thirty-six percent judged the pledges to be doing better than average. Their major reservation was absenteeism. Sixty-four percent of the foremen considered the disadvantaged to be poorer than their co-workers in coming to work regularly.

As can be seen in Table 9-4, these relatively favorable findings are quite different from the impressions of Buffalo foremen who did not supervise NAB workers. Fifty percent of the foremen in the regular sample said that the

Table 9-4. Foremen Ratings of Individual Disadvantaged Workers Westinghouse–Buffalo

	Better than Others	Same as Others	Poorer than Others
Quantity of Work	36%	64%	0%
Quality of Work	36	64	0
Attendance and Promptness	27	9	64
Acceptance of Responsibility	54	27	18
Personality at Work	45	36	18
Discipline at Work	73	18	9
Ability to Learn Job	64	18	18

disadvantaged did not work as well as the average employee and several were not sure. Eighty-seven percent were ambivalent toward the statement: "Most poor people want to work."

Foreman Bart Resnick described one of his NAB workers, Willie Baxter, who fits the rating profile described in Table 9-4.

He turns out work like crazy. He's very capable. And he has the intelligence. Unfortunately, he is the type that money will hit him. After pay day, in fact there were instances on Thursday night, he would ask the foreman if he could leave after lunch for no other reason than just

New opportunities for the disadvantaged 249

personal reasons. He's got the bug, see? You've heard people having money in their pocket that burned a hole? Well, he's probably the type. But it's unfortunate because he is a good capable worker. When he's here he does a tremendous job. He needs very little supervision, picks up quickly, learns very quickly.

There's only one problem. If we could circumvent that, he'd be a good man. But you're left with the feeling, will he or won't he be in? You're never too sure, you know? And there's nothing worse than to have the feeling about a person, will he show up or won't he?

Terry Marlow, an old-timer in the plant and foreman for almost fifteen years, had had several hard core in his unit: "And I'm reluctant to say that all of those fellows I've had to discharge." He told about his last attempt to straighten out a NAB and his absentee problem:

To me it appears that these fellows like to be paid every day in the week, and come to work whenever they want to work. It seems as though there was a pattern to the way they worked. They were off on Friday; they'd be off Monday, and they had more excuses why they wanted to be out. I think they just spent more of their time trying to figure out how they could stay out. And they got these jobs, probably, through some agency on the outside.

I did talk to the benefactor of this one boy. He was a nice boy. I was interested in him when he first started. I thought maybe we could get him straightened out. She said that she had talked to him and told him he had to be aware of the fact that there was a job that he had to do. And if he wasn't there, the job wasn't being done. And she gave him all those facts and everything, and he agreed. But lo and behold, two days later, he's back out again.

Marlow was not successful with the disadvantaged. Yet he was a good, conscientious supervisor who tried. But one might ask: How skillfully did Marlow really exert himself to understand and to communicate with these men? For example, why didn't he raise those crucial questions with the employee himself? Why did he leave it to a third party to build rapport and allegiance for him? Did he feel that he couldn't possibly communicate with this new, young, disadvantaged worker?

One clue to absenteeism may lie in the NAB pledges' relations with their foremen. The NAB pledges at Westinghouse–Buffalo were much more

Table 9–5. Attitude Toward My Foreman*
Hourly employees, disadvantaged, blacks, and whites
Westinghouse–Buffalo

	Disadvantaged N = 11	Black N = 30	White N = 30
Favorable	36%	82%	87%
Uncertain	27	13	10
Unfavorable	36	4	3

* Random Samples

estranged from their foremen than were other employees. Only 22 percent felt that they could take a personal problem to their foreman. Tables 9-5 and 9-6 show the attitudes of the disadvantaged toward their foremen as compared to those of other blacks and whites in the plant.

Table 9–6. Attitude Toward Taking a Problem to My Foreman*
Hourly employees, disadvantaged, blacks, and whites
Westinghouse–Buffalo

	Disadvantaged	Black	White
Favorable	22%	73%	70%
Unfavorable	78	27	30

* Random Samples

Yet research has pointed out that the retention of the disadvantaged worker depends to a great extent on his relations with his immediate supervisor.[5] If there is an open, human, understanding relationship, a disadvantaged person is much more likely to stay on the job.

Clarence Nason, an officer in the NAB program in Buffalo, agreed that pretraining is crucial to the success of hard-core employees. But he found that many employers who were willing to hire the disadvantaged did not want to invest time and money in extra training. He felt that the success of the hard core depended on such a program:

> This is one of the real difficulties: Most of the employers do not want to get involved in any extraordinary training.... They want to avoid it if they can. And many of them say: "Look, I'll take them the way you send them to me, and I'll try to do what I can with them. But I'm not going to sign up for any extra training. Because I just don't have the time to fool with it." And of course we're saying that the training is necessary for retention, not only so that they can hold the job that they enter at, but so that they'll have upward mobility. So they'll want to stay for that reason, so they know they can grow in the company, like the other employees in a given company.

But all of the top managers in industrial relations at the Westinghouse–Buffalo plant made it quite clear that they were not in favor of any special "vestibule training program" for the disadvantaged: a program that involved basic education, discussions, and attempts to build motivation. In part, they felt such a program might be preferential treatment. Phillip E. Hughes, one of

---

[5] See Allen R. Janger and Ruth G. Schaeffer, *Managing Programs to Employ the Disadvantaged* (New York: National Industrial Conference Board, 1970), p. 21; Lawrence A. Johnson, *Employing the Hard-Core Unemployed* (New York: American Management Association, 1969), p. 166; Theodore V. Purcell and Gerald F. Cavanagh, "Alternate Routes to Employing the Disadvantaged Within the Enterprise," *Proceedings of the 22nd Annual Winter Meeting, Industrial Relations Research Association, 1969*; and Theodore V. Purcell and Rosalind Webster, "196 Men Get Another Chance," in Peter B. Doeringer, *Programs to Employ the Disadvantaged* (Englewood Cliffs, N.J.: Prentice Hall, 1969).

the personnel managers at Westinghouse whom we met in the previous chapter, said:

> I definitely felt from the beginning that we would try to treat them as much like other employees as we possibly could, not set them aside and make them feel like they're different. And we're quite opposed to classroom instruction, getting them together as a group of different kind of employees.

Hughes feared that if they were brought together, they might stay together as a little closely knit group that would eat together and perhaps even disrupt things. If they were treated the same as the rest of the employees, he believed they would form friendships in an ordinary manner with others in their work group.

Westinghouse–Buffalo has continued to pledge and hire the disadvantaged. The subject is discussed in depth several times a year at foremen sessions. Theodore Hunt, an employment supervisor who earlier spoke of screening *in* the disadvantaged workers, believes that acceptance for the program is growing. A foreman who might have complained: "Dammit, Ted, my father and mother were Polish. No one helped them when they arrived," is now likely to say, "Geez, I've done everything I can think of and I still can't get through to this guy. Can you help?"

To sum up, Westinghouse–Buffalo's work with the disadvantaged is a moderately successful part of Westinghouse's affirmative action commitment. The program is small, because Westinghouse is not hiring extensively, but it has provided jobs for men and women, some of whom might otherwise have been unable to get a job at a company like Westinghouse.

THE FAIRBANKS–MEMPHIS NAB PROGRAM

In 1968 the Fairbanks International plant in Memphis pledged to hire ten hard-core unemployed as part of the National Alliance of Businessmen's JOBS Program to bring the disadvantaged into industry. By February of 1969, the plant had surpassed its self-imposed goal and had fourteen disadvantaged on its payroll; six came from the Job Corps. Most of the hard core hired at the plant were able to meet the standard hiring requirements. Nine of ten women were high school graduates, and they all successfully passed the employment tests. For the men, Fairbanks waived some hiring requirements—three had less than an eighth grade education and the fourth had a juvenile prison record. All four have worked well. Indeed, one was later promoted to condensor mechanic. A fifth man was fired for excessive absenteeism. Most of the NAB pledges had been in the plant only a few months at the time of our study but retention to date was excellent, and 80 percent of these men and women were still employed at the end of 1970, almost two years later.

The company's decision to choose motivated people made hiring the disadvantaged relatively easy at Fairbanks. Said Dave Rodgers, a personnel manager:

> One of the reasons it's successful is that we're not taking the hard, hard-core person. Actually the person that we're taking in the NAB program is the person whose only problem is that he needs a chance. There's a lot of difference between the two. We're taking the one that does want to come to work, primarily.

The foremen were generally very satisfied with the disadvantaged workers that had been sent to them. Foreman Tracey Ober, who had three pledges working for him as janitors, said: "You might call it preferential treatment, but we're getting our money's worth out of it. I mean, we're not getting inferior people. We do some careful interviewing. I think hiring these people is fine as far as my department is concerned." In spite of their low educational achievement, Ober said that he would gladly take additional men of their caliber.

Dave Rodgers described the reaction of one foreman to the NAB girl in his department: "The girl started on Tuesday, and we went to see the foreman on Friday to explain to him that this was a NAB girl, what the NAB program is, the whole business. He said: 'Well, I never would have guessed that this one was in NAB. She's doing great.'"

Fairbanks required foremen of NAB employees to fill out monthly evaluation forms. While such formal procedures do not guarantee supervisory support, they do indicate a continuing management interest in the new workers —something which is often lacking in NAB programs. Several people hired as part of the NAB program at Fairbanks were enthusiastic about the opportunity and support they had been given. We noted, however, that some were not getting adequate feedback from their supervisors as to how they were doing.

Because of its careful and successful selection, the Fairbanks plant had to cope only once with the more serious and time-consuming problems of hard-core motivation. (Despite the effort, it was not able to keep the one poorly motivated man it hired.)

To make a significant dent in the hard-core unemployed of Memphis would probably require a formal training program and a larger staff to provide the necessary support. At that point, Fairbanks Electric did not feel able to assume the expense even if it had a government contract. And, as Dave Rodgers pointed out, there were still many people who could be helped without this additional commitment:

> I feel that if you're going to hire the really hard-core person, you're going to have to go on with special programs and special people to work with them. There's still plenty of hard-core people around. We can take these people and work with them and do something productive anyway.

As for the *general* problem of aiding the Memphis disadvantaged, Marshall and Van Adams say:

> The sizable numbers of employers cooperating in the voluntary programs of the NAB and MEA [Memphis Employers Merit Employment Association] were in sharp contrast to the smaller number participating in the OJT and JOBS programs, programs which dealt with skill and cultural disadvantages faced by blacks. As of July 1969, only 18 employers held MA-4 JOBS contracts.... Slightly over 30 employers participated in the OJT programs with jobs available for 400....
>
> Thus as several employer interviewees confirmed, the "cream of the crop" was helped and the "true hard-core disadvantaged" was left behind in many instances.... Most [employers] are motivated by profit maximization and therefore are not likely to do much to help the really hard-core unemployed (or underemployed) unless public policy or general business conditions make it profitable for them to do so....
>
> In Memphis the steps taken thus far to resolve the employment problems of blacks have only touched the surface. Change can be described as neither pervasive nor extensive; in most instances it has been token. The deeply entrenched problems faced by blacks in achieving economic equality will require greater efforts and more comprehensive programs.[6]

RAYTHEON—BOSTON JOB TRAINING CENTER

Raytheon is a large electronics firm, heavily committed to defense contracts. The company was 96.8 percent white in 1969. Most of its plants are located in small New England towns where few blacks live. A high proportion of Raytheon employees are engineers, professionals, technicians, and skilled craftsmen.

In February 1968 the Raytheon Company opened one of the first industry-run training programs for the disadvantaged. Technically part of the President's Test Job Program, a predecessor to the MA contracts, the program (called an MA-2 program by Raytheon), was largely financed by a $600,000 grant from the Department of Labor. It was followed in 1969 by an MA-4 contract.

Raytheon's Job Training Center, located in Waltham—a Boston suburb —trained disadvantaged men and women in four skills that were needed at Raytheon and in the Boston area: drafting, cablemaking, clerical, and keypunch. Trainees also received job-related remedial education and individual

---

[6] F. Ray Marshall and Arvil Van Adams, "Negro Employment in Memphis," *Industrial Relations*, Vol. IX, No. 3, May 1970, pp. 322, 323.

counseling, and attended group sessions on "social survival techniques" (SST). This latter aspect of the program was designed to help trainees overcome suspicion, frustration, discouragement, and defensiveness—at least to the point where they could cope with the demands of the job and form constructive work relationships. At SST sessions, the trainees had an opportunity to discuss themselves, their problems with work, the experience of the black man in America, and the kind of behavior that the industrial system required. Training varied in length from two and one-half to four and one-half months, depending on the skill.

Trainees were on the Raytheon payroll from the first day of training, a very important aspect of the program. But contrary to later federal stipulations, trainees could choose to leave Raytheon for another company, following training.

Trainees were recruited by neighborhood employment centers in Boston, with a deliberate attempt to avoid selecting the "best" of the disadvantaged in terms of work record, education, or even motivation. (See Table 9-1 for background data on the twelve trainees at the Bedford plant.)

During its first fourteen months, the Job Training Center accepted 259 trainees and graduated 170. This 34 percent drop-out rate during the training seems high, but a Labor Department official estimates that it is slightly better than the national MA-2 average. Raytheon records show a variety of reasons why the disadvantaged leave a program, as seen in Table 9.7.

Table 9-7. Reasons for Leaving Raytheon Job Training Center During Training February 1968 to April 30, 1969

Higher paying job	12
Job Corps	2
Left for other program	2
Military service	5
Day care for children	16
Left state to help family	6
Domestic problem	2
Illness or pregnancy	8
Medical termination (overweight)	1
Terminated by Raytheon	2
Lost interest	33
TOTAL	**89**

Retention of those who successfully completed the program is hard to evaluate. Forty-five percent of the 112 JTC graduates who took jobs at Raytheon left during the first year, most saying they were going to better jobs. If these dropouts are still employed elsewhere and using their new skills, the program can be considered quite successful. (As in all early NAB tabulations, retention figures include all hires, both those who had been working many months and those who started work the day before the tally was taken.)

Two special factors made retention more difficult at Raytheon. Its plants are all quite a distance from the Boston black community in Roxbury (although Waltham is somewhat closer), and most are not served by public transportation. Second, clerical and keypunch skills in particular are in great demand in nearby downtown Boston. To ease this problem Raytheon negotiated a Jobs-70 contract to recruit and train disadvantaged people—blacks and Spanish speaking—many from small cities, such as Lowell and Framingham, nearer their plants.

How successful was the Job Training Center? Did the trainees really develop marketable job skills? Did their attitudes change in a direction that was beneficial to both their employer and themselves? What did their foremen feel about the competence and job performance of the trainee graduates? What did the graduates themselves have to say about it? To answer these questions we made a field study of a Boston-area Raytheon plant at Bedford and listened to about fifty people, the twelve JTC graduates, a random sample of their fellow workers, and all their supervisors.

SKILL TRAINING

The Raytheon school was the only one of the programs we looked at that recruited disadvantaged men and women for relatively skilled jobs. Despite educational handicaps, this aspect of the program was quite successful.

The managers and foremen who supervised the disadvantaged workers at the Bedford plant were favorable toward the program. We found particular enthusiasm in the drafting department. Drafting is difficult and on-the-job training was necessary, even after weeks of classes at the Job Training Center. Yet the manager of the drafting section, Henry Beliard, was very positive:

> I'm in favor of the program, by the way, 100 percent. I've been to the Training Center. I know the instructors there, and they're doing a good job. They're taking someone with a limited education, and getting him to the point where they're coming in here. Okay. I'm not saying they're the best draftsmen in the world when we get them. We call them trainees. I do ask my supervisors to provide some special instructions. But it's working. Most of the people who come from the program can make it.

Jeffrey Morgan, who worked under Beliard as a section manager, was closer to these men. He saw both the challenge and the problems in more detail:

> We want to see them make it. And if their attitude is good, they'll make it, because we want to be patient with them. And we'll see that they make it. But it's a long process. I have to be honest with you. They don't pick it up as fast as the other guys. I think at first a lot of it was mental block because of acclimating themselves to a whole new environment for them. And we understand this, so we kinda make it as cordial as possible for them.

A supervisor in cablemaking, Michael Lazlo, was very pleased with the training the disadvantaged had received. In keypunch some graduates needed a little extra help at the start.

The graduates themselves were enthusiastic about skills training:

LEO PRATT, describing why he went to the Center: This is something new for me, I thought. If Raytheon is going to be training people I guess I better get into this because this is something I've been waiting for.

ELVIN SANBORN: That give you a start, you know? Like I was in hospital work. I went to the Training Center. They give you a chance to better yourself, to get out in the world and make money.

JOE MADDEN: It's the skill of the future, I'll tell you that.

PEARL TENCO, keypuncher, implies that she now has a marketable skill: Like Raytheon they place you. If you don't want to stay with Raytheon, they find a job for you with the telephone company, city hall. I know a lot of girls that went to the school. They're holding good positions now.

MOTIVATION

But what about attitudes? Were these men and women who needed only training? Eight of the twelve we talked to had a history of job hopping and/or part-time employment but had been at Raytheon more than a year—a record for each of them. Why did they stay?

For some trainees the SST discussions on racism, black identity, and poverty were very important. One man, Willie Montgomery, who spoke earlier of his previous hustling days, felt he had changed greatly as a result of SST:

You wouldn't believe that I'm the same guy that went to that school, if you didn't see me at that time. Because I didn't care nothing about life. I didn't particularly care about people. I didn't care how people feel when I tell them anything. It wasn't no difference to me, you understand. I was walking around with a chip on my shoulder, and I didn't even know it. 'Til I got out there and Mr. Watkins [one of the black instructors at JTC], he gave me a long talk, and I never forget it.

Another young man, Leroy Hutchins, who told us of the frustrations of his Roxbury black brothers trying to get good jobs, looked on these discussions and talks as a pleasant although not always profitable interlude. But he did point to a new insight in his own attitude toward whites:

I found out that some white people were nice. 'Cause I had the attitude that I didn't care about any of them. You know, I found out that all of them wasn't alike. I really did; I found that out. Once a white man likes you, he'll do anything he can to try to help you. I learned that too.

In this context, perhaps even more important is his new attitude about work:

And as far as me working for a dollar, I changed that attitude. And I started working. Whereas I wouldn't work. I just refused, you know?

But it [JTC] really helped out in quite a few ways. I think a lot of other fellows feel this way when they really look into it.

Hutchins had been very successful as a hard-core nonworker. After finishing eleventh grade in Alabama, he lived in New York City until things got too hot. He spent a year and a half in Boston without working, although he supported himself rather well. The Training Center looked like an easy stipend, so he joined with no intention of taking the job after graduation.

When we spoke with Hutchins, he had been working at Raytheon for eighteen months. His foreman found him very competent and self-confident, and a good worker except for his absenteeism. He deliberately took time off to enjoy life, but he found the work easy and not unpleasant. Why did Hutchins stay? Because he got interested. It seems that there was enough enjoyment and satisfaction in the total experience to keep Hutchins on the job.

Generally, the supervisors evaluated the graduates' work and attitudes as satisfactory. But absenteeism continued to be a problem for many. Some were absent often enough that their foreman thought they were not progressing as well as they might and were consequently hurting their chances for promotion.

Both the disadvantaged and their supervisors considered transportation the primary reason for missing work. Commuting to Bedford by car from black Roxbury takes thirty-five minutes to one hour; public transportation takes two hours, costs at least $10 a week, and leaves the worker a mile from the plant. A special bus from Roxbury to some of the plants along Route 128 was run during part of this period but did not stop at the Bedford plant. The transportation problem clearly must be solved. Since a major investment has already been made in each of these workers, it would seem wasteful to allow serious absenteeism to continue for lack of additional counseling or assistance.

FELLOW WORKERS TALK ABOUT THE PROGRAM

Although their fellow workers were more critical of the graduates than were their supervisors, they were still generally quite favorable about the graduates' work performance and attitudes. A minority said that some disadvantaged were lazy, moody, and irregular in their work performance. A more common complaint was that they often seemed to have a chip on their shoulder when they first came on the job. They seemed to be suspicious and defensive. The peers also criticized the graduates' attendance.

There was, however, almost no resentment about special training for the disadvantaged. White employees commented: "Well, it gets them off the streets." "It's a good investment for the country." "We owe it to them." The following conditions influenced white acceptance of the program: (1) No preferential treatment in salary or promotion was given; (2) several employees had received free training themselves under other programs; (3) free training after work was available to all employees; (4) the average length of service in these departments was very low (perhaps new employees are more open to change); and (5) there was no threat of a large influx of blacks. The program was on a small scale and blacks were less than 1 percent of the plant (and about 3.2 percent of the total corporation).

The Raytheon Job Training Center had brought hope and work to a limited number of Roxbury black men and women. Yet problems remained.

CRISIS OF CONTRACT CUTBACKS

In October 1969 defense cutbacks caused layoffs of many regular workers at Raytheon, affecting among others the Bedford plant, where seven of the twelve JTC graduates were laid off. Three of the seven had bumping rights at the Lowell plant. Because of the distance between Lowell and the black community, it is not surprising that these men did not use their rights. Their immediate reaction to the layoff was mixed. Roger Green, who told us earlier of his JTC training, spoke for several who were quite upset:

> That really make a lot of people feel bad, you know? Not only that, it makes a lot of people think. About, well, we got this far and we could only go as far as they wanted us to. And now we're right back where we started from. And people start getting that attitude back again. When they had built up hopes that they were going to get some place.

On the other hand, a few claimed they were not disturbed: It was time for a change; they didn't want to continue in cablemaking anyway. Only one man thought it would be difficult to get another job. The crucial question, however, is the long-term impact of the layoff. Will these men really find good jobs and stay with them?

Defense cutbacks also made it difficult to find places for new trainees just graduating at the time. Raytheon offered to these men and women additional training, temporary assignments in departments where openings were available, or arranged to have them work for other firms while remaining on the Raytheon payroll. These firms in turn paid Raytheon as they would a temporary help agency. Some graduates found these alternatives unattractive and left.

This crisis, however, raises the question of whether it is wise for companies so dependent on defense contracts to attempt to train the disadvantaged, unless they can convert to civilian products or train in skills that can be used elsewhere. Job security at all levels is now a number-one priority in company thinking.

THE WESTINGHOUSE–EAST PITTSBURGH OCCUPATIONAL TRAINING SCHOOL[7]

There were riots and frustrations in Pittsburgh's Hill District in 1968. The Westinghouse Occupational Training School (OTS) is the story of how 316 people—mostly black—from the Hill District, Homewood, Braddock, Hazelwood, Turtle Creek, and East Pittsburgh at last found a chance as persons and as workers at the huge East Pittsburgh works of the Westinghouse Electric Corporation.

SELECTING THE TRAINEES

The pasts of the trainees varied, but most could not meet customary employment requirements—that is, a high school diploma, absence of a police record, and so forth. In fact, Table 9-1 shows that OTS trainees were much more disadvantaged than participants in the other programs we studied. More had been arrested, fewer had graduated from high school, many had been out of work for a long time. But in two important ways they were quite employable. They were motivated and capable. They had the desire to work.

Former OTS Director Ross spent a great deal of time listening and questioning. He could not afford to jeopardize the program by hiring men who did not want to work or who were enmeshed in such serious problems that they could not work steadily. But Ross did not use traditional criteria to assess motivation:

> What to some people might have been a disadvantage, to me I saw as an advantage. A man who's been in a penitentiary, he's been in a different type of environment. I thought that was a positive factor, if he could adjust properly, didn't create a problem, and was smart enough to accept that situation, and deal with it until he got out. And I thought he could go into a plant where you're placing some people with hostile situations. And he'd be better equipped than say, an eighteen-year-old high school kid, who had an IQ of 110, who could pass a Wonderlic test in the right percentile. I'd rather work with this man with a criminal record. He'd probably had a family and he needed to be successful. He had a purpose.

Or again:

> If a man would get up and spend the money to come out to East Pittsburgh, catch two buses to seek employment because someone told him

---

[7] The Westinghouse–East Pittsburgh OTS was originally financed in April 1968 under a two-year Department of Labor MA-3 contract for $375,691. One hundred and sixty-five were hired under a target of 196. There followed an MA-4 contract for women clerical workers. Twenty-eight were hired under a target of thirty-six. Subsequently an MA-5 contract was negotiated for the factory men. Up to October 1970, 116 were hired under a target of 150. A Jobs-70 program was then contemplated.

he had a chance, knowing he didn't have a high school diploma, knowing he had been arrested, knowing he had been turned down many, many times. He's motivated!

Ross' selection techniques worked particularly well in the case of Tom Mitchell. Thomas Mitchell is not typical; rather, he is unusual. Yet most of the problems he faced, at least taken separately, are the problems any hardcore man has faced. Tom Mitchell is large, impressive, and intelligent. He used to be a drug pusher—at one time he was making something like $3,000 a week. Miraculously, Mitchell cut loose from his own drug habit some years ago. At OTS he became the leader of his training group. The trainees listened to him and many followed his lead. Mitchell told us that Ross was the first employment person who believed him when he said he was no longer using drugs and wanted a job:

> That's the first person—the first person, you know—that just accept me at my word, when I told him about I was hooked, and what I had went through about being in jail, and about my record and everything. And I told him that *I hadn't used no stuff in six years* and that all I wanted was a chance. Somebody had to give me a chance, somewhere. Yeah, and I told him: "Well, like if you don't give me no job, this doesn't mean that I'm going back to narcotics, you know, because I'm not going to be. I'm not going to let you or nobody turn me around to this point where I go back to this. So if I don't get a job here, well, I'll just go someplace else. I'll just keep on looking."
>
> But he said: "All right, I'll take a chance on you." And he's given me a job, and I intend to do everything I can to prove to him that he didn't make a mistake, and to help the program. Because I know there is a lot of other people out there, you know, that would really appreciate this.

The demands of the job were clear from the beginning. Ross made every applicant aware that he must be willing to accept any position assigned to him, even sweeper or janitor; that no absence or tardiness was allowed; that the trainee was to be an example to his community; and that the success of the program was dependent upon the success of each individual.

THE PROGRAM

The trainees started immediately as employees of the company at $2.64 an hour for a month of orientation and motivational training. The program was developed after it was under way, flexibly responding to the trainees' needs. Basic educational instruction in reading, arithmetic, writing, and speaking was provided, rather than formal training in work skills. Central to the training program was instruction in what is to these people the new world of work, represented in this instance by Westinghouse. The trainees began at once to learn the importance of getting to work on time and not being absent.

For the first time in their lives, they were encouraged to talk out their feelings and problems, to exchange ideas and experiences, and to receive a unique type of group support. In addition Ross and his staff worked long days, far beyond the hours and confines of OTS itself, following up the trainees in many plant areas, going to the ghettos and the homes of the trainees, securing bail, arranging credit, fixing marriages, persuading, being tough when it was needed, encouraging, supporting, and, more than anything else, believing in the integrity and possibilities of the men they selected for the school.

A man like Tom Mitchell could probably have started on a job immediately and adjusted well. Other men, although they wanted to work, really needed this month of orientation. Let us listen again to Mitchell:

> I'm really devoted to the program, and everybody here is devoted, everybody here. Like *some of the dudes when they first, when the program first started on, they had, like I said, militant attitudes, attitudes that "if you say something to me, you're picking on me,"* so.... But they're coming out of this, they're all adjusted. And they see the importance of the program, and they're—like me and Wayre and the group leaders. We try to talk to the dudes every chance we get. And try to make them see that we're older, and the things that these younger boys got to go through, a lot of the things we've been through already, you know. And we try to make them see that if you don't do something now....

TRAINEES IN THE PLANT

Once in the plant the trainees no longer had the strong morale and esprit de corps of their OTS director and peers. Responses of the Westinghouse foremen to the program were varied. Most reactions were lukewarm, neither favorable nor unfavorable. The foremen received only a brief explanation of the program and occasional visits from Director Ross and his staff to help them cope with their new employees. The foremen we interviewed found that they had to spend more time counseling the hard core than their regular employees. However, all said that they would give the same time and advice to any of their workers. Preferential treatment was over, and the hard core, like all employees, were subject to company rules and regulations and were expected to meet company standards.

Foreman Hennessey was pleased with the two disadvantaged men he supervised:

> I've put a lot of time into Richard. I've worked hard with him and I feel like I've accomplished something. Right now, he'll stay away but he'll be disciplined. And I'll come up and, what I tell him to do, he'll do, regardless whether I tell him to jump off the building.

> I don't think Richard ever had anybody in his life who he could put any faith or any trust in. I think from the time that he's been a kid what he's had, he's had to hang for himself. I don't think anyone was ever willing to help him or talk to him....

> One day he come in here, and he said—and I believe he was telling me the truth—he didn't have but about an hour's sleep that whole night because he couldn't get into his bed. He tried to sleep in a chair and then when he did get to bed about six o'clock in the morning, he slept. And, as a result, he was late getting here. And I was giving him heck about coming in late, you know. This is the thing you've got to impress on them . . . they're never going to get out of the hole and they're never going to better themself. . . . The only way they're going to get money is by coming in and working.

Other foremen were not nearly so open to the new employees. And fellow workers were sometimes resentful. Hennessey continued:

PURCELL: Did you prepare the rest of the people who work here at all for these people who were coming in?

HENNESSEY: No. No. You can't do that. Cuz the minute you say to the other people: "Now, this is a hard-core fella that we're bringing in here." . . . The more you can have the other people forget about it and treat him as another employee, another person, the better off. . . .

PURCELL: Have you had any problems with the other people?

HENNESSEY: Yes, we've had problems with the other people. There's going to be people who's going to resent. And one of these reasons: Some of the people had the idea that these people were here and the government was paying their wages. And this wasn't true. But this was something, the government was paying their wages; as a result, they were getting special privileges.

Trainees, like all new hires, were placed on low-skill, entry level jobs. But these were not dead-end jobs, and a number of the graduates began getting promotions. In July 1970 Westinghouse was challenged by a United Black Protest Committee saying that OTS graduates were not being promoted. But a plant study compared the 165 disadvantaged people hired from July 1968 to April 1970 with those (121) hired through normal channels during the same time period. These people were also unskilled and hired for the same types of entry level jobs. Fifty-seven percent of the OTS graduates received at least one upgrade during the period, with a total of 149 upgrades. Of the regular hires 57.9 percent got at least one upgrade, with a total of 111 upgrades. In sum, the disadvantaged workers were promoted as well as the regular hires.

ATTENDANCE AND RETENTION

During the first months of the program, OTS trainees had an excellent record on the lack of absenteeism, tardiness, and turnover. A growing percentage of men were involved in both tardiness and absences once they left the protected environment of the school. This is understandable since they no longer had the encouragement of OTS emphasizing the importance of their individual roles. Nevertheless, their records compared favorably with the other employees at the East Pittsburgh plant.

As for retention, the Westinghouse Occupational Training School had the high rate of about 90 percent retained in its first six months. We made a follow-up of the first 112 men who went through OTS from July through November 12, 1968. Six months after their starting dates, 87 percent of the trainees were still at Westinghouse; after a year, 64 percent, and after two years, 46 percent. Among those who left, one man died; some went on to better jobs; one joined the White House police force; two went to college; and some entered the Armed Services.

When the results of the MA-3, 4, and 5 are put together (plus seven NAB pledges not in the contract program), out of 316 hired, 170 were still working toward the end of 1970. This is a retention rate of 53 percent. While doubtless some of these people were recently hired, others were at Westinghouse for nearly two years. If we add to this amount the people who stayed with the company at least six months before they left (the new NAB criterion for "permanence"), we get 233 out of 316, or a retention rate of 74.9 percent.

In this whole matter of retention, it is not fair to compare the percent of disadvantaged retained with some ideal of 100 percent retention. Westinghouse made a control group study of the 292 men hired for entry level jobs through normal channels during the same years. One year after their respective starting dates, 82 percent of the nondisadvantaged were retained; after two years, 73 percent. The record of the OTS graduates is not as good (46 percent as opposed to 73 percent), but it looks much better than if compared to an unreal ideal of 100 percent, and it compares well with other programs for the disadvantaged.

In addition to insightful selection, sensitive program, and the dedication of Ross and his staff the Westinghouse Occupational Training School owes much of its success to the commitment of top management. Westinghouse President Donald Burnham took a strong public stand both in theory and in action on the need for business to involve itself in the affairs of the ghetto and the city. Foremen, employees, and union representatives knew that the company wanted the program to work.

FROM DISADVANTAGED PEOPLE TO EFFECTIVE WORKERS? SOME INSIGHTS

If a man is really disadvantaged, it is not enough merely to show him to his job and expect him to be there every day to do his work. There is a gap of understanding and motivation that must be bridged. A number of mature, older black men, particularly at National Acme Electric–Chicago and Westinghouse–Buffalo, made clear their opinion that the young disadvantaged workers they observed needed more support.

Eric Tunstal, forty-three, a plater, had worked at the Westinghouse-Buffalo plant for twenty years. Himself a black man from a poor family, he understood the problems of the disadvantaged entering the work environment and the necessity of providing transition from ghetto to plant:

> Industry will definitely have to bend a great deal. Some of these people haven't had the opportunities. But strange enough, it seems the jobs themselves that requires so much qualifications, doesn't even require that much mentality to do it, see? And once a person gets on the job and gets familiar with the work, and also the time element—about fifty hours a week—coming to and from work and then putting the forty hours in work. Now that'a a lot of time out of an individual, especially when an individual hasn't been familiar with putting in any time any place. So this presents a big problem. But once they become adjusted to this, then the problem of them adapting to a job is no big thing.

If the disadvantaged are to succeed and stay on the job, the company must supply them with additional support and training, according to veteran black employee and union officer, Roscoe Filkins, also at Westinghouse:

> Let's say we have four or five kids here that have been in trouble. This company should, if they're really trying to help these individuals, consider having someone here that's like a counselor over these kids. If there's something wrong, let me know about it. Because first of all, we've got to remember now, we have kids that are, well, we can say they are mentally disturbed in a way of speaking, they're off the track. Now if we had someone here that was—now, my job is to stay with this group here. I make sure that they're here. Like if they're due here at seven o'clock, now it's my job to see that those kids are there. I want to know the reason why, if Joe wasn't here this morning. I think that if we had someone following these kids up, you would find that we would get along. You would be able to bring a lot more into your society where they should be.

A number of older blacks, like respected and competent NAB pledge Franklin Bosworth, did a little informal counseling on his own. He recounted taking aside a less serious fellow worker for a heart-to-heart talk at the Acme plant in Chicago:

BOSWORTH: We had this one fellow, he liked to take breaks all through the day. And so, I got him off on the side one day, and talked to him. And I told him, I says: "One fellow cannot do his job, and that would shut us all down. You're gonna have to do your part, so we can begin to do ours. And everything's gonna work out." So, he's doing pretty good now.

PURCELL: That's the thing, Mr. Bosworth, if somebody is in late, then that hurts the other guy.

BOSWORTH: If you is doing parts, and I got to put my part on it, and your part is not finished, then it got to come to me. Then I can't do it because you're not finished. And I got no idea how to do your part. And then mine's got to go undone. Then the other fellow can't do his. And that's gonna throw the whole thing off. So, if everybody do his job, and do it right, then that'll keep the whole thing going.

He spoke strongly and convincingly of the importance of teamwork and cooperation among the line workers. Bosworth was convinced that when people know each other and work together, it lessens absenteeism, turnover, and tardiness.

Cyril Ford, forty-three, a respected black with considerable service at Acme and much human wisdom, emphasized the importance of continued communication after the new young worker is on the job:

> There's something that really hurts this section in here. The employees and the 'ministration, they don't seem to have a way they can communicate. I mean when I say communicate the way they do things. And I think that would cut down on a lot of resentment and this agitation and what not. . . . Talking to each other, be able to understand why this is this and that and what not. Lot of fellows don't understand management and business. Like I say, when these guys come to them, and they say this is the way it's got to be, lotta guys, you know, they balk.

Everlee Singleton, twenty-two, a bright black engineer, felt that his company had made little effort to retain the disadvantaged. He stressed the importance of personal relationships on the job:

> I have the impression that when they hire guys like that, they may be a little bit too eager to get production out of them. You know what I mean? And it's pretty wild. It gives the impression that these people [management] really don't care. They're just doing us a favor so they can get their names on the book as equal opportunity employers. And all they want to do is get us in there, teach us a little bit, and let us go. I guess if you can establish a personal relationship between the guy and the people he's going to be working with, then he might like the idea. I mean you might actually get a guy to *want* to come to work. Because if the situation at home isn't that hot, like most black people, they have a tendency to want to do something else. That's why they turn to the street, maybe. So if they made the job an attractive place, some place to come to, it might serve two purposes.

DISCIPLINE CAN SHOW YOU CARE

Black supervisor Johnny Clay of National Acme Electric–Chicago felt strongly that fair, straightforward discipline was an important part of foreman relations:

> I would like to see supervision, people in management, working a little bit closer with these people. When an employee comes in and people in supervision are told these are hard-core employees, the fear is there. I don't want to tell this guy that he's not performing his job. I don't want to tell this guy: "Well, look buddy, you can't use this abusive language here because it's against company regulations." Because I fear you. I know you're black and you're hard core. This is what I would like to see eliminated.
>
> Not two standards, you know. Don't let the black employee do it because he's black and you expect it of him. See, because the white employee is not allowed to do it, the black employee's not allowed to do it either, because the regulation says so.
>
> This is what I would like to see: more on-the-spot corrections. Don't be afraid of getting slugged in the jaw. This is what I would like to see. And I think if we did this, there is a possibility that we would have less termination of these kids, hard kids, poor kids, kids that we have here. Because no one has been big enough, and brave enough to stand up to this kid and say, "Now look, you've got to get in here on time. And when I tell you to do this, I intend for you to do it."
>
> Don't be afraid of them. Forget about what you see on TV. Don't be afraid of this guy. Tell him. Make the on-the-spot correction. And I think we could do a lot on this. And I would like to see it.

Because he cared about the young people, Clay wanted more discipline. He knew new approaches might be necessary and that caring was very important, but reducing standards tells the young worker: "We don't care whether you ever adjust to the routines of plant life."

FRIENDS FOR NEW GUYS

We observed that relationships with fellow workers were important for the young disadvantaged. At Acme, NAB pledge Elliott Tompkins, twenty, a transferman, felt the lack of any real relationship with his peers. On his own initiative he offered some of his own small suggestions to make up for this: "Well, maybe they have some kind of arrangement for everybody, like on break or something, maybe take a few minutes for everybody to introduce hisself, get together. Maybe this would improve the relationship to people." Tompkins' suggestion is minimal and halting, but it illustrates his own felt need.

Support for the importance of getting along with co-workers came from white Hank Clifford, Acme–Chicago, after complaining about the monotony and frustration of his work as an assembler:

> Probably it all depends on the people around you again. I like to associate with people, you know. Get to know 'em, talk, you know. Have a little fun while you're working, too. That always comes in handy, as long as you're being careful about what you're doing. Because you can't work, you know, isolated from everybody.

White in a predominantly black area, Clifford felt rejected and was able to make it through only a few weeks. More often it is the black who is alone in a "sea of white."

Drafting manager at Raytheon–Boston, Henry Beliard, who earlier spoke with enthusiasm about JTC, described the sensitive reactions of the first black draftsman in his department:

> Amos Brook was one of the first colored boys we had out of this Training Center, and he found it very difficult. I spent a lot of time with him talking over the problems. One of the problems that we talked about was that he felt that people were talking about him. He felt that nobody was talking *to* him....

> Well, the breakthrough came one time when the supervisor was coming down the aisle and one of the fellows was fooling up front. And the only remark from Amos Brook was "Here come the Judge." And from that time on he had no problems with the people, and he mixed in.

There are numerous examples: A trainee was doing very well in a group of young people he liked, but his work and attendance deteriorated when he was moved to a group of older men. Some black cablemakers with a strong sense of group identity stayed on the job despite strong resentment that they were not promoted as quickly as they thought they should be. The social atmosphere on the job is certainly one important influence on job satisfaction.

FOREMAN-DISADVANTAGED RELATIONSHIPS: SOME CASES

In all five case studies we found the relationship between the foreman and his disadvantaged worker to be vital. The young worker meets the company most directly in his boss. It is from the supervisor that he learns what the company really expects of him and what it thinks of him. The foreman must be supportive, helpful, and fair. He must know his disadvantaged as men as well as producers. He must be honest and consistent, but firm in discipline. All of this has been said before, but it may be a new challenge for a foreman who is supervising people who do not share his values or his perceptions of the company and society.

268   *The issues*

We present here in greater depth several individual foremen-disadvantaged relationships. Most of them are drawn from Buffalo where we systematically interviewed NAB workers and their own foremen. We feel, however, that the same kinds of relationships could happen in any plant.

THE ERROR OF WATCHDOG TACTICS

We have seen that Foreman Cipriano found the New Work Force a new and disconcerting experience (Chapter 6). He went on to explain some of his fears and problems:

CIPRIANO: I should be able to leave this department for a half hour, an hour, and come back and things be going well. But I can't. I have to be there eight hours a day. Father, let me tell you something. I go to the john maybe once a night, maybe twice if I have to. Because I just can't leave them.

PURCELL: If you left, what would happen?

CIPRIANO: Well, if you leave, you come up and you find two talking. You find three talking.... People just don't want to work. In a day work shop such as this, like I say, you've got to draw it out of them. You've got to make them work. We shouldn't have to make people work. People should want to work on their own free will.

When asked for his evaluation of Roland Farmer, a disadvantaged worker under him, Cipriano responded that Farmer was a good worker on all counts but:

Farmer did need a little pushing.... He's just one of these kind of guys that you have to keep prodding a little bit. But basically—he did have a little problem at the beginning of being a little absent or a little late, but I think now that he's on days, I think this will clear up. From the reports I've gotten from the daylight supervisor, there's no problem.... So you try corrective criticism, let's put it this way. Roland needs just a little bit of prodding once in a while.

From his side, Farmer volunteered his opinions on what makes a good foreman. He said he had an excellent foreman at his previous employer:

FARMER: The foreman would tell you what you had to do, and then he'd go about his business, and let you do the work. And you probably wouldn't see him until it was time to quit. And he might come through and see if you're doing the job. But he wouldn't stand around or anything. He'd go about his business.

CAVANAGH: Is that different than here? Does the foreman here....?

FARMER: Oh, yeah. It's a whole lot different. It seems like the foreman, I don't know, he pushes a lot.... He sits. Most of the time he'll sit right there, and be watching you, you know? As if this is going to make you work faster, or work harder or something, I guess.

Close help and support for the disadvantaged does not mean the sort of impersonal watching and prodding that Cipriano apparently used. Cipriano's method probably took more of his time than would the establishing of closer relationships with his workers. The fact is that Cipriano was ill at ease with the New Work Force, and the members resented his constantly looking over their shoulders.

One unintended result of this sort of close watching can be a lessening of voluntary cooperation. Farmer explained how he came into the unit open-minded and later settled into the customary and defensive pattern of controlling production:

> This other fellow would tell us to go slow. . . . Well, he was right. See at first I thought he was just doing this just because he was lazy and didn't want to work. But I found out later that he was right because the more we did, the more motors we did, the more motors he wanted.

Cipriano did not seem to recognize that a little effort in encouraging his workers and in recognizing their good work would probably go much further in boosting his production record than did his watchdog methods. And it seems clear that helping a young disadvantaged worker adjust to the plant demands better personal relationships with his workers than Cipriano was at the time able to achieve.

COOPERATION

A much more favorable foreman-disadvantaged relationship was described by foreman Bart Resnick. When asked how NAB pledge Jesse Byrd was doing, Resnick replied:

> He started to have a little bit of an absentee problem, but it seems as though it's not one that's going to continue. Because I talked to him before I hired him and told him I had checked his attendance record. And I told him I wasn't very happy with an employee on probation to be taking as much time off as he has. . . .
>
> He looks like a cleancut fellow. He's never dressed sharply, you know what I mean? Pretty neat, and he's obedient. And he listens to me. He does his work. He's picking up speed. I haven't got him on standard rate yet. But I encouraged him. I try to encourage him, because after all, what I make out of my people will be to my benefit. 'Cause the better worker I get, the easier my job is.
>
> So I always try to get people in the right mood, the right feeling. I like to have them mingle with my people so that there's no barriers between them, personal barriers or otherwise. He works in a group of four men, and there's nothing worse than to have someone sitting at his machine and not talking to the other three. If I notice that these people aren't mixing, then I try to find out why, and maybe talk to the others and encourage them. . . .

But Jesse is working out very well. I think he's gonna turn out all right.

Jesse Byrd, twenty-two, graduated from a Buffalo high school although he was born in Alabama. We described earlier his confusion and disappointment when he apparently needed the help of a community agency to get his job at Westinghouse. Byrd described his first foreman as demanding and unsympathetic, but he was high in his praise of Resnick:

> To me he's far better than this other foreman in concerns of my work. Because I feel as though every worker should have a boost of morale in some way and pride of what he's doing. So he could know which is best for him. If he's good in his field, or if he's good where he's at. And this foreman, every now and then he tells me that I'm doing satisfaction or I'm doing good. And this foreman over here, the one that I had before, didn't seem to notice. He just didn't seem to want me to get on the ball in some way where I can see myself.

And a bit later Byrd praised Resnick's abilities with his workers even more succinctly: "As far as him being a foreman and doing a job that a foreman does, he's all right because he shows his workers that he's concerned about the person's work. And he'll tell you if you're doing a good job or not."

FAILURE OF A SENSITIVE EFFORT

Edwin Silverman had an absentee problem with one of his NAB employees, Rodney McCoy. Silverman hoped he could straighten it out with patience and a better explanation of what was expected, but he failed:

> And I said, maybe I can straighten him out. So we leaned over backwards and let him put in the sixty days, and then we really had problems with his absences. But still his attitude toward people was good. He wasn't overly ambitious, he got kind of lackadaisical in his work, and spending more time away from his machine. But then the Friday before he didn't show up, I said: "Now Rodney, I'm depending on you. I need you here. This fellow that's working with you is going on another job Monday. You'll be all alone here. Promise me you'll be here every day next week. I need you. You're very important to the company."
>
> I always try to make a person feel that they're important. They are. Because you can't do without them. Let's face it. You put a machine there, and nobody to run it; we're out of luck. So, he said: "Yeah, I'll be here. I'll be here." And lo and behold, Monday he didn't show up. He said he'd be late. I said, well, at least he'll be in. So Tuesday morning somebody else called up, said he was sick, wouldn't be in. Well, we haven't seen him since.

SPECIAL HELP

Edgar Dolan, twenty, began in the plant as a common laborer just a year ago. He had finished tenth grade and served time in a reformatory for burglary and assault and battery. Dolan is a very straightforward and sensitive person. He explained that as a teen-ager he hung around the pool halls: "When you look at a man and he's got a $30 sweater, and he says, 'Only suckers work,' you want to be a big man too. You want to kind of model yourself after him." And he sees now that this is where he went wrong.

After getting out of the reformatory, Dolan spent a year with the Job Corps. He was high in his praise of what that year did for him. Just the opportunity to live with and get to know Chinese, whites, and Mexicans, for example, Dolan found to be extremely important in broadening his horizons. He was a new man, determined to do well on the job, and he gave a great deal of credit for his success to his foreman, Daniel Grogam.

DOLAN: He's always taken care of me. You know, you can talk to him. Person to person. He's caring about the personal problems you might have, and things like that. He gives you good advice. I believe he's got strong judgment.

CAVANAGH: Is he a help to other guys, too?

DOLAN: He's nice to everybody. I mean, you know, he'll go out of his way for you. He lets you do your work and go along. He seems to talk to everybody. Everybody seems to like him. He's a real likable person.

CAVANAGH: Does he help you both as a person, and to do the job? Or would it be just to do the job?

DOLAN: He helps me in all ways he can. He used to be a mechanic, and he would tell me things. He wouldn't hold back anything. I think he's about one of the nicest foremen here.... You can't hardly do anything, if you've got a foreman, you think: "If I make this mistake, he'll be against me. Get me fired or something."

Dolan has done very well, especially considering the lack of mechanical experience in his background.

Foreman Grogam, from his side, found Dolan highly motivated and conscientious. To Grogam self-confidence was the essential ingredient to success in the plant:

> There's some guys can do just about any job in the house. But don't overload a man, because that's going to actually hurt himself. As you say: "Let's run these high speed electronic complicated machines." Well, he gonna be no good. He's going to be scared to death. When I first hired in, and I saw the machine, I was ready to go back home. I didn't want it. But they're not as bad as they look. But you build up some confidence in himself, and eventually he might just get along.
> I think it's [self-confidence] more important for these [hard core], because I feel that they probably need it worse. Because they have come into surroundings where someone might say: "Well, what's he doing here?" And if the guy's got the confidence that, "I'm here because I can do just as good as you can," if they feel that, then it's good.

CONCLUSIONS

What is the value of the National Alliance of Businessmen's programs we have seen in these five case studies? The programs varied considerably in the number of disadvantaged hired, the degree of disadvantage, the extent of help provided, and the amount of success, judging by retention and by listening to both management and workers. The three noncontract programs, of course, differed greatly from the two contract programs. What light can our five case studies throw on the major questions asked about the national NAB effort?

Were the job figures misleading? The National Alliance of Businessmen program was launched with glowing press releases reporting thousands of new job opportunities for disadvantaged men and women. But were the men and women hired really any different from workers who would have been hired normally without any NAB fanfare?[8] Further, did the companies "cream" their disadvantaged applicants? The Occupational Training School at Westinghouse and the Raytheon Job Training Center—both contract programs hired people clearly more disadvantaged than their other applicants. Westinghouse–Buffalo changed its hiring criteria so that disadvantaged applicants could meet them. Many (though not all) of the NAB pledges at that plant would not have been able to meet earlier Westinghouse criteria. At the Fairbanks plant in Memphis, on the other hand, hiring requirements were waived for a few but many of the NAB pledges met regular standards and were, in fact, hardly disadvantaged at all. The Acme–Chicago pledges raise a new question. Most of the men filling the Chicago pledge were disadvantaged but they would have been hired anyway. Acme needed men. The Acme–Chicago jobs did not generally mean new opportunities for the disadvantaged. But as we saw, most of these employees soon left their jobs. Therefore we consider the 1969 manpower training contract awarded National Acme–Chicago important because by improved orientation, support, and supervisory training it aimed to keep the disadvantaged on the job.

What jobs did the disadvantaged get? At all our locations except Raytheon, disadvantaged men and women were hired for unskilled or semiskilled jobs, though opportunity for upgrading was promised. The jobs were not dead-end jobs. The Raytheon Job Training Center successfully taught clerical, keypunch, drafting, and cablemaking skills, for jobs offering more dignity and satisfaction.

The major difference between the voluntary noncontract programs and the MA programs we studied was in the amount of orientation for the disadvantaged. There was no special orientation for NAB pledges in the three noncontract programs and normal orientation was sketchy. In contrast, the

---

[8] For early evaluations of the National Alliance of Businessmen efforts see Sar A. Levitan, Garth L. Mangum, and Robert Taggart III, *Economic Opportunity in the Ghetto: The Partnership of Government and Business* (Baltimore: Johns Hopkins Press, 1970), and chapters by Herbert Striner and E. F. Shelley in *Business and the Cities*, ed. Neil W. Chamberlain (New York: Basic Books, 1970).

Westinghouse Occupational Training School and Raytheon's Job Training Center provided intensive, long-term orientation emphasizing strong personal relationships with the training staff and fellow trainees.

Did the men and women who received this special orientation do better on the job than those NAB pledges who went directly to work? It is significant that foremen found the quantity and quality of work done by most of the disadvantaged satisfactory in all five case studies—contract and noncontract. But problems of absenteeism, tardiness, and retention were common. And many disadvantaged, especially the young black men at Chicago and Buffalo, felt estranged from their foremen. Although the extra orientation given by the contract programs did not solve these problems it did help greatly. At the Westinghouse OTS, attendance, promptness, and retention were extremely good during training, better than the records of regular employees in the plant. While problems increased when the trainees began work in the plant, their record remained remarkably good. At Raytheon attendance and retention were not so good since they were aggravated by a severe transportation problem. Yet most of the Raytheon graduates spoke of warm relationships at the Training Center, and several said that their training experience had greatly helped them in getting along with their fellow workers and foremen.

What more is needed? Even with good orientation, many disadvantaged men and women need continued help once they are on the job. A major part of this responsibility falls on the foreman. Yet none of the programs we looked at, including the contract programs, gave the foreman much help. Foremen generally seemed to feel that top management did have a special interest in NAB workers but many foremen did not know how to cope. Nor were they sure that their efforts with the hard core would be taken into account if productivity fell.

Counseling was also used very little. Graduates of both training centers were free to go back to their centers to talk and many did. Training staff could also go out to the plant for special problems, but there was no regular follow-up either with the graduates or with their supervisors. More extensive foreman training and more on-the-job counseling seem important additions to the orientation already used in the contract programs.

A special question about support programs for the disadvantaged is this: Do such special efforts really help the trainees, especially in their motivation? Or are the candidates already motivated, only needing a chance for a job? We found both types of trainees in the contract programs, but many trainees had known little success with their past jobs or school experiences. For these people a mere job was not enough. They needed the motivational support provided by their programs. Only a minority of the trainees would have been able to develop good work habits without the extra help they received.

How important is retention? The National Alliance of Businessmen goal of 500,000 job placements was surpassed in late 1970, but less than half that number are still on their jobs. This retention problem was apparent, in varying degrees in three of the five programs we studied. Retention is a significant criterion in evaluating the success of programs for the disadvantaged since it guards against a plant's merely channeling disadvantaged persons through entry level jobs with no attempt to make the job worth holding or to help the person adjust. But retention cannot be the only criterion. People who leave may have learned something during their time on the job; they may move to jobs previously not open or known to them. The staffs at both Westinghouse–East Pittsburgh and Raytheon–Boston claimed that a number of their drop-outs left for other jobs. Such persons merely follow the trend of young people of any class in moving from job to job to explore the range of possibilities open to them.

Are programs for the disadvantaged costly? Programs like those at Westinghouse–East Pittsburgh and Raytheon–Boston are not inexpensive. While some companies, such as Western Electric–Newark, have set up programs at their own expense, most others will need financial assistance as an incentive. Government contracts are one way to induce management to make this effort. Also some urban plants compete with plants in rural areas with no disadvantaged nearby; to be competive, the urban plants need financial assistance for dealing with their disadvantaged. In any case, the costs seem modest as opposed to the costs of welfare, crime, and idleness.

The numbers of men and women in NAB programs like these seem small when we consider the thousands who have no jobs. One could say that such programs are only a drop in the bucket. But a drop is better than nothing. The lives of even a few people are valuable. Moreover, the programs affect more than the men and women directly involved. Each employee is a member of a family and of a community. His new job indirectly affects the people with whom he lives.

Equally important is the fact that increased attention to the disadvantaged has meant a learning process for all concerned. Some disadvantaged people have learned that there can be a place for them in industry, at least in plants not hit by a recession. Managers have learned more about both the problems and the possibilities in hiring the disadvantaged and the need to plan their programs more carefully. Some foremen have begun to understand their disadvantaged employees. A time of learning and experimenting is necessary and some failures should be expected.

Of course, the point Ray Marshall makes about Memphis is applicable to much of the American urban industrial scene: We have "only touched the surface.... The deeply entrenched problems faced by blacks in achieving economic equality will require greater efforts and more comprehensive programs." Since problems of housing, transportation, family life, and political power also affect the disadvantaged person's ability to get and hold a job, business alone cannot solve the problem of urban jobs. One must not oversell what business can do but neither should we underestimate its responsibility. We have seen that these programs can be successful. The need is greater than ever.

CHAPTER TEN

Equal versus preferential practice

> *All animals are equal but some animals are more equal than others.*
> George Orwell

If management sincerely undertakes vigorous affirmative action to correct the underrepresentation of Negroes not only in entry level jobs but especially in the craft and white collar management jobs of American industry, it will need to think through and deal firmly with a second major issue: the controversial matter of preferential practices.

Whitney Young described the "Domestic Marshall Plan" adopted by the National Urban League in 1963 as a "special effort to bring [the Negro] into the central action of our society. The effects of more than three centuries of oppression cannot be obliterated by doing business as usual."[1] Young advocated deliberately including Negroes in all phases of American life and choosing them over whites when necessary. He warned that trigger phrases like "preferential treatment," "reverse discrimination," "indemnification," and "reparations" can mislead "unsuspecting, unthinking and uninformed Americans."

Preferential treatment is clearly a loaded and provocative phrase, seemingly undermining American ideals of equality and merit. Yet preferential treatment can often be justified. Equally important, many practices labeled as preferential do not in fact prefer blacks over whites but rather allow blacks to compete. The latter we call "equalizing practice." The distinction is no mere academic exercise, since equalizing practice is easier to justify.

Equalizing practice means spending extra time and money simply to make current opportunities equal in recruiting, hiring, training, and helping

[1] Whitney M. Young, Jr., *To Be Equal* (New York: McGraw-Hill, 1964), pp. 27, 32.

to promote Negroes. There remain very real perceptual, motivational, and communication blocks in employment and promotion processes. There is still much discrimination, usually subconscious, by plant staff, as well as a credibility gap with blacks. Many apparently nonracial practices actually favor whites more than blacks. Special efforts to overcome these problems do not give the Negro an advantage over the white person, but merely make equal competition a realistic possibility. We shall give only one example now, but more later: If an employer makes a greater effort to recruit at Negro high schools than at white high schools, this merely corrects communications blocked by decades of racism; it brings to Negro high school students only a knowledge of job opportunities that white high school students have had for years. Such special efforts do *not* give Negroes specific advantages over whites. They are not preferential but rather equalizing practices. They merely let blacks know that they are welcome to join in the competitive race for jobs.

Preferential practice, however, does mean giving a qualified black, precisely because of his race, specific hiring, promotion, or disciplinary *preference over one white person or over a group of white persons*. We shall give several examples later, but let one hypothetical case suffice for the moment, as proposed by Whitney Young. If a business has no Negroes or very few in its offices or plants and "two equally qualified people apply, it should hire the Negro to redress the injustice previously visited upon him."[2]

In the case of *both* equalizing and preferential practice, our discussion makes this important assumption: The black person who receives either equalizing or preferential attention *is either adequately qualified now for the work required or can become qualified after a reasonable time*. To be helped merely because of one's identity with a certain race, with no reference to ability, is demeaning to a man's personal dignity. It would actually be a kind of paternalistic racism in disguise. Surely a black man, or any person, wants to be hired or promoted eventually because he is valued as a person who can do the job.

We must make a further qualification: We do not propose the need for equalizing or preferential practices for Negro Americans at work as something necessary forever. Hopefully such special attention, indeed even the very gathering of statistics about what jobs are filled by Negroes as opposed to whites, will become unnecessary in American industry. In time we should not have to notice a man's race in looking at hiring or promoting in business. But it is very doubtful that this ideal will be realized in our life time. By the year 2000, a chapter like this ought to be an anachronism; in the 1970s it is vitally needed. In looking at the matter of equalizing or preferential practices, we should never forget the place of *individual* attention to any person at work. Apart from race, sex, age, or length of service, the employee is an individual person. Ideally management will look at him as an individual and as far as possible deal with him as an individual.

[2] *Ibid.*, p. 29.

Equal versus preferential practice

The rest of this chapter should help to clarify our definitions and the important distinction between them.

THE CONTEMPORARY CLIMATE

Some Americans feel that preferential practice or even equalizing practice for Negroes in this country is basically un-American, unconstitutional, impractical, and conducive to racial unrest or white backlash. It seems to be an attempt to punish today's white workers because yesterday's were not fair. It appears to be discrimination in reverse and would be opposed by many employers and union leaders, the latter fearing that the seniority so vital to their members would be destroyed. Writing in *The Evening Star*, Washington columnist Richard Wilson says:

> On the face of it [government] agencies have adopted the sociological doctrine that centuries of bad treatment entitle the black to restitution in the form of preferential treatment....
>
> The effect, it is argued, is to impose quotas of black employment contrary to the intent of the Civil Rights Act and at the risk of denying to the whites their equal opportunity for jobs *because they are white*....
> The problem here is one of equal justice for the white as well as the black worker.[3] (Italics ours)

However, there are many varied components making up the American climate. Charles E. Silberman in his *Crisis in Black and White* writes:

> Most of the discussions of Negro demands for preferential treatment, and for "reverse quotas" have missed the essential point. The object is not compensation, in the sense of making up to the Negro for past injustices; it is to overcome the tendencies to exclude the Negro which are built into the very marrow of American society.... A formal policy of non-discrimination, a policy of employing people "regardless of race, color or creed," however estimable, usually works out in practice to be a policy of employing whites only.... As soon as we agree that special measures are necessary to overcome the heritage of past discrimination, the question of numbers, of *how many* Negroes are to be hired, in what job categories inevitably arises. Not to use numbers for a yardstick for measuring performance is, in effect, to revert to "tokenism."[4]

Labor economist Ray Marshall writes:

> Special programs for Negroes need not take the form of quota systems and need not deprive whites of existing rights. For example employers

---

[3] Richard Wilson in *The Evening Star*, Washington, D.C., June 4, 1969.
[4] Charles E. Silberman, *Crisis in Black and White* (New York: Random House, 1964), p. 241.

and unions that have not recruited among Negroes in the past, that have no Negro employees or members might make special efforts to recruit Negroes, or to help them acquire training. This would involve special efforts to include Negroes in the recruitment pattern, but it would not be preferential treatment because it would extend to Negroes benefits which whites already enjoy.[5]

To Marshall, efforts to rectify injustices resulting from the past are not necessarily preferential practice, as would be giving current advantages to one race over another.

Political scientist Charles V. Hamilton comments on the Urban League's domestic Marshall Plan which urged "special efforts to overcome serious disabilities resulting from historical handicaps": "This is not racism, it is not intended to penalize or subordinate another group; its goal is the positive uplift of a deliberately repressed group."[6]

Before we give our own justification and concrete examples of equalizing and preferential practices from our field studies, let us see if giving preferences is really so uncommon after all in American life.

When we look at the myths of equality or rewards by merit in American society, we are reminded that "all men are equal but some more equal than others." The American economy, although predominantly one of free competition, is riddled with instances of government intervention to improve the economic condition of one group or another, to favor one group at the expense of other groups. Often this preferential treatment is thought advisable by most Americans for good reasons; sometimes it is won by the sheer political power of one or another group or region of the country.

There are many examples of government subsidies: land grants to the railroads; federal depletion allowances to extractive industries such as the oil production business; subsidies to farmers; tariffs favoring certain American firms over others or over foreign producers; the Social Security program with weighted benefits to give a larger return to the low wage rather than to the high wage contributor; civil service preference to war veterans; immigration laws that in the past favored one nationality over another. Government intervention in the market place and in our social life may not be characteristic, but neither is it alien to American life.

Second, among private groups preferential practice has often been the rule: for example, law firms that prefer a Harvard or Michigan law school graduate over others equally well qualified but from less prestigious schools; craft unions that give membership preference to sons or nephews of union members; reciprocal purchasing agreements between firms that favor the parties to the agreement over outside competitors; WASP company managements that prefer executive candidates because of family ties or name and

[5] F. Ray Marshall, *The Negro Worker* (New York: Random House, 1967), p. 142.
[6] Charles V. Hamilton, "An Advocate of Black Power Defines It," *New York Times Magazine*, April 14, 1968.

exclude Jews, Catholics, Italians, or women; non-WASP firms that exclude WASPs; and, quite aside from private clubs, many American business and labor organizations have for years been giving preferential treatment to persons they deem "suitable," sometimes with reason but often with little concern for the qualifications of the "unsuitable." Equality and rewards for merit are not nearly such common practices in American life as the myths would have it.

THE LAW AND PREFERENTIAL TREATMENT

The Civil Rights Act of 1964 neither requires an employer or labor organization to give preferential treatment nor does it forbid it, except insofar as the entire tenor of the law is equal treatment with respect to race:

> *Nothing* contained in this title shall be interpreted *to require* any employer, employment agency, labor organization, or joint labor-management committee subject to this title to grant *preferential treatment* to any individual or to any group because of the race, color, religion, sex, or national origin of such individual or group *on account of an imbalance which may exist with respect to the total number or percentage of persons of any race*, color, religion, sex, or national origin employed by any employer, referred or classified for employment by any employment agency or labor organization, admitted to membership or classified by any labor organization, or admitted to, or employed in, any apprenticeship or other training program, *in comparison with the total number or percentage* of persons of such race, color, religion, sex, or national origin *in any community*, State, section, or other area, or in the available work force in any community, State, section, or other area.[7]

However, the Office of Federal Contract Compliance, which supervises the equal opportunity practices of government contractors (under Executive Order No. 11246), goes far beyond Title VII of the Civil Rights Act in its Order No. 4 of January 30, 1970. Order No. 4 requires that the government contractor remedy any *underutilization* of minority people in his firm. Underutilization means having fewer minority workers in a given job category "than would be reasonably expected by their availability." Expectations are formulated by looking at the minority *population*, the minority *unemployment*, and the minority *work force* in the area, including the degrees of skill that could be reasonably recruited, and finally by looking at the promotability of minority people already employed. The contractor is also expected to deal with outside training institutions and consider what training he could reasonably provide

[7] The Civil Rights Act of 1964, Section 703(j). (Italics ours)

to build up his minority work force guided implicitly by percentages of available people in the area.

Order No. 4 makes no explicit mention of preferential practice. It does not set inflexible quotas but rather uses targets as one measurement of the "good faith effort" applied to an affirmative action plan. The directive also asserts that it is "not to be used to discriminate against any applicant or employee [presumably whites] because of race, color, religion, sex, or national origin." (Sec. 60-2.30) But we think that the order implicitly calls for a certain amount of preferential practice.

JUSTIFICATION OF EQUALIZING AND PREFERENTIAL PRACTICES

Equalizing and even preferential practice, in our opinion, can be justified by both sociological and ethical reasoning. The reasons for both are the same, with one caution regarding preference. Our reasoning is based on two grounds: the needs of Negro people and the need of the total American society.

First, preferential practice may be justified because of the needs of Negro people. Past experiences of discrimination and segregation have separated Negroes as a group from the rest of American society, leading to lower per-capita income, often inferior education, and a whole constellation of sociological and psychic disabilities for many, although of course not for all blacks. Collectively, Negro Americans have been alienated from the rest of American society not by any innate inferiority but by white racism.

Because man is a social being, inevitably shaped by the social and economic structures within which he lives, justice is not achieved simply by assuring the rights of persons as individuals; it also requires just socioeconomic institutions. When encrusted patterns of education, employment, and housing put one group at a disadvantage, we are obligated to change those institutions. It is reasonable that individual citizens should participate, according to their ability and position, in group action designed to make the institutions of society conform to the common good of all citizens. The dominant white group must come to grips with itself and perceive reality with a greater objectivity. Quite contrary to the Bill of Rights and the Constitution, the white group and its collective psyche have permitted the existence of institutionalized patterns that are patently unjust to minorities such as blacks. Whites have a moral obligation to help reform those institutions to make them open to all Americans.

Now for our caution: Since preferential (not equalizing) practice gives a specific advantage to a black person over a white, each situation will need to be looked at carefully, balancing the needs of the parties concerned. There might be cases where the white worker would have such a great need for a certain job or a certain promotion that the previous argument on behalf of

Negroes would not prevail. On the other hand, there will be cases wherein a Negro's right to preference will prevail. And, of course, there will be a number of highly qualified Negroes who will have no need for equalizing or preferential attention.

Our second approach is broader and involves American society as a whole. Our reasoning is not merely in terms of Negro rights but in terms of the needs of our total society—particularly its need for peace and order under justice. Very practically, the choice before us may be rapid integration and upgrading of Negroes in jobs, education, and housing, at times by preferential privilege, or an escalation of the turmoil, conflict, and polarization of the 1960s and early 1970s. Unless radical racial change takes place, blacks and whites may grow farther apart, splitting the very fabric of American life.

This reasoning is not intended to be a mere "law and order" argument, since it is more important to have a just social order than to have a peaceful one. Life in the old plantation days of slavery was tranquil enough, but it also represented a shocking violation of the human dignity of almost half its citizens. The point of our reasoning is that peace under justice involves not only Negroes but *all* Americans; our entire American community is entitled to the peace and order necessary for a stable and happy society.

These two lines of reasoning regarding both the rights of the black community and the rights of the total American society satisfy us that equalizing and even preferential practice in one degree or another are morally as well as sociologically justifiable. A clearer behavioral description of preferential practice and how it differs from equalizing practice is necessary, and to that we now proceed.

BEHAVIORAL EXAMPLES OF EQUALIZING AND PREFERENTIAL PRACTICES

RECRUITING

CASE 1: Plant X had a large number of craft positions but very few qualified black applicants despite a large minority population near the plant. Management had no difficulty finding a sufficient number of qualified white men. But spurred by the stance of the EEOC, they set a goal for increasing the percentage of black craftsmen. They stepped up their recruitment program, making several trips to predominantly black high schools and conducting a plant tour for guidance counselors from those schools with opportunities to speak to black employees. They spent considerable time to discover which referral agencies were most effective in reaching the black community. They placed advertisements in the Negro weekly (though not in white neighborhood weeklies), stressed to the state employment service their desire for minority referrals, and attended school board meetings to encourage the city's vocational education system. All these efforts were aimed at the black not the white community. Management was moderately successful and a number of blacks were hired.

One manager questioned the value of investing so much time in a black recruitment program when whites were available and when several whites with qualifications resented being turned down in favor of blacks who might not have applied on their own. He called it preferential treatment.

There is no question that management spent extra time to reach blacks precisely because of their color and not for traditional economic reasons, but the action was hardly preferential. The intensive recruitment program merely brought to black students knowledge about job opportunities that white students had had for years. It showed blacks that jobs were open to them in industry, a fact that whites never had any reason to doubt. If whites lost out because of increased competition this was not preferential treatment for blacks but the end of special privilege for whites. However, if Plant X hired blacks in place of whites with *superior* qualifications this would be preferential. Assuming that such blacks were at least sufficiently qualified or qualifiable, we think that such practice is justifiable.

HIRING STANDARDS

CASE 2: The Westinghouse East Pittsburgh Occupational Training School (OTS) for the disadvantaged accepted applicants who did not meet selection criteria used for other employees at that time, such as a high school diploma, absence of major police records, and certain entrance tests. After training the trainees were expected to meet ordinary work standards. The program clearly gave a limited number of disadvantaged people, mostly black, hiring advantage over other applicants. Yet the Westinghouse equal employment opportunity policy explicitly disavows: "Lowering of job requirements or performance standards for the purpose of favoring any employee or applicant on the basis of his or her race, creed, color, national origin, age or sex."

Ninety percent of the Westinghouse OTS trainees were black. If not technically, yet practically, blacks received preferential attention over employees (mostly white) who were not hired through OTS. This is justifiable preferential practice, and it might well lead to changed selection criteria for all applicants as in the following example.

CASE 3: In the Westinghouse–Buffalo plant, cut-off scores on employment tests for hourly workers were lowered to make it possible to hire disadvantaged workers, but the new cut-off score was used for all applicants, regardless of race, and was found to be adequate.

This is neither equalizing or preferential practice; it merely represents a change of standards occasioned by the coming of the disadvantaged.

CASE 4: For years Westinghouse Buffalo gave preference for summer employment to sons and daughters of employees. In 1969 and 1970 the company decided that 20 percent of the summer hires should be black. (Buffalo is 17 percent black.) As usual, management had more applications from employees' children than jobs available, but they recruited black applicants from a local state teachers college, the Urban League, and the Concentrated Employment Program (CEP).

Preferential? Certainly. Solely because of their race, black young people were given an advantage over whites who also wanted the jobs. However, the former practice was also preferential since 95 percent of Westinghouse employees were white.

TRAINING

CASE 5: Foreman Grogam at Fairbanks International in Memphis found that some new black employees needed more help learning the job than he usually gave. Grogam felt that a person whose background did not prepare him for the plant needed an extra boost during the first months. Some older white employees resented this extra attention and claimed that blacks were getting preferential attention.

We agree with Grogam that people who need extra help should get it. This attention to individual needs is not preferential so long as whites who need help also receive it. This is "individual treatment."

CASE 6: An executive of a large New York insurance company describes this problem: One of their departments employed male clerks who did supportive work for computer programming. A certain competent white clerk, Bruce Becker, resigned. His place was filled with two black men, one from the outside and one from the same department, partly because work was expanding but especially because the company wanted to have more black employees.

Paul Smith, a white man working nearby, noticed the change. He also noticed that after being on the job for a while, the two black employees together were turning out about the same amount of work that Becker had done alone. The salary for this type of clerical job was $100 a week.

Because Smith was doing about the same amount of work as Becker, he complained to his supervisor that he should now be getting $200 a week, since the two Negro clerks were each getting approximately $100 for the same amount of work that he (Smith) was doing. Smith's supervisor tried to explain the needs of socially deprived people, how they needed better chances than others. Smith replied, "That's not my fault. I didn't cause them to be deprived. Don't put that monkey on my back!

Either I get extra pay or I slow down." The supervisor was able to get Smith a small raise that was far short of the amount Smith demanded.

Any new employee might be slower than a veteran. The insurance company probably expected that the two black men would be able to speed up with time, if not to Smith's rate, at least to the point where the discrepancy would not be so obvious. But taking the facts of the case as they are given the insurance company's action would seem to be preferential.

DISCIPLINE

CASE 7: When Westinghouse Buffalo began its NAB pledge program, the Industrial Relations Department asked that foremen discuss all discipline problems involving the disadvantaged with their general foreman, and if necessary with the Industrial Relations Department. Westinghouse foremen were accustomed to handling discipline on their own, and some felt that this special provision for the disadvantaged set up dual standards giving preferential treatment. The Industrial Relations Department believed that discipline should be firm. But they also knew that foremen might have more difficulty establishing rapport with their disadvantaged employees and that some foremen might be affected by prejudice, conscious or unconscious.

These special discipline procedures are not preferential if they are merely used to help foremen develop skill in supervising the disadvantaged. Fairness does not require treating all employees exactly alike but rather assisting all employees to meet the same standards. If there is reason to believe that foremen will need guidance with new responsibilities, they should get it. And if there is a chance that prejudice might bias a foreman, it would be negligent not to guard against it.

CASE 8: A white employee at Fairbanks International: I was with two white girls and we came back from lunch about two minutes late. The foreman gave the two white girls a warning notice for coming back late. And two colored girls came back after the white girls. He gave the white girls a warning notice and didn't say anything to the colored girls.

If true, this is preferential practice that we do not think advisable because it could harm both blacks and whites. Of course, it is possible that the Negro girls were reprimanded privately.

PROMOTION AND UPGRADING

CASE 9: Management at GE–Lynchburg made special efforts in 1969 to make sure that blacks were included in lists of candidates for promotion and upgrading.

Is this preferential? No; it is merely equalizing practice to make sure that qualified black men and women are not overlooked because of subtle race prejudice. A foreman, when recommending an employee for upgrading, may automatically look for personal characteristics typical of the white employees he has recommended in the past. But these characteristics may not be job-related. Or, as one manager suggested, a foreman may tend to recommend people similar to himself.

An employee relations man at GE–Lynchburg discusses the issue:

> I think this is mainly to give us some check that we just aren't overlooking some good bets. Again our problem is one of utilization of people in a relatively small community; so if we've got some talent around we want to know it, independent of EEO or Affirmative Action or whatever.

He continues later: "These two people are equal, but we promote the black one and not the white one. I think we're saying we'll do that.... But to the best of our knowledge, our selection is still pretty objective. We don't have double standards." Even with a single standard, which both races achieve, choosing a black over a white would be preferential.

CASE 10: At the National Acme Electric plant in Chicago, a young black having trouble with attendance claimed that his attendance would improve if he were given a job with more responsibility. Satisfactory attendance was usually required for a promotion, but personnel made an exception and moved him to a better job. His attendance did improve dramatically.

The technique worked, and both company and employee benefited. But is this preferential? The same thing could also have been done for a white. Management's action might better be called "individual treatment."

CASE 11: A black hourly employee at the Westinghouse–Buffalo plant reported that he had been urged repeatedly by both his foreman and the personnel office to accept a promotion for which he was qualified and to which he was entitled by seniority. To the best of our knowledge Westinghouse management would not have made this special effort for a white employee who was hesitating about a promotion.

Is this preferential practice? By seniority the black employee was qualified and had a right to the job if he wanted it. (His seniority would have continued.) He was not being given an advantage over a white fellow employee who might also want that job. This was not preferential but rather equalizing practice. Because of his background, this man may not have fully understood his opportunities or he may have needed confidence to tackle a more responsible job. There were few blacks at this job level, and it seems quite justifiable that management should make this special, equalizing effort.

LAYOFFS

Layoffs can be a major problem for company programs aimed at aiding the

286   *The issues*

disadvantaged. When men and women coming from disadvantaged backgrounds get special chances at a job but are later laid off, they can easily become suspicious, bitter, and frustrated, and the company loses people in whom it has made an investment. Yet layoffs by seniority are an established pattern of American industrial life. Some plants have made special provisions for the disadvantaged during layoffs.

CASE 12: In a certain plant, management anticipated a layoff affecting its government contract training program graduates working in a certain section of the plant. As far as possible, before the layoff occurred these men were transferred to relatively "safe" job slots in other sections of the plant.

In later 1969 and early 1970 another plant with a federal manpower training contract had to lay off employees. But trainees still in the company's training center at the time were given extended training or temporary placement on jobs still open. Others were kept on the company payroll while they worked with other outside firms on a "temporary help" basis.

A Westinghouse training center in Baltimore placed trainees in a subsidiary even though they were laying off employees at their regular plants.

These examples appear to be preferential practice for disadvantaged people, mostly blacks. Nevertheless, barring new facts that might change the examples, the company actions in these cases seem to be justifiable.

CASE 13: An executive of a major electrical manufacturer described this problem: Because of government contract cutbacks, the company had to lay off several engineers in a certain department. The least productive engineer was a black, Peter Roberts, age thirty-five. Roberts, a graduate of a fairly well-known technical institute, had been with the company two years. Recognizing some technical deficiencies in his education he was studying at home in the evenings and seeking special help from a fellow engineer. Roberts was very well motivated; his work was adequate and improving; but he was not yet able to compete with the other engineers in his department.

One reason for this was the fact that the department was engaged in advanced product development and had some highly skilled engineers. Had Peter Roberts been working in straight production engineering, he would have been able to compete. But with engineering layoffs throughout the company and highly competent engineers available everywhere due to the 1970 and 1971 cutbacks in government contracts, the company saw no transfer openings for Roberts. Management was trying hard to build up his confidence and abilities.

Pressed to cut budgets, the head of the department dismissed two engineers and kept Roberts. If efficiency alone had been considered,

Roberts would have been the first to go. The manager wanted to keep some mix in his organization. He did not want all his engineers to be prima donnas and he could use a man who would be satisfied with more routine work. He also wanted some racial mix as well.

Should management have kept Roberts when it was under pressure to trim the department?

GRASS ROOTS ATTITUDES ABOUT PREFERENTIAL PRACTICES

If minorities such as blacks get equalizing or preferential attention, what will their white fellow workers say? This seems to be an urgent question for many management people who sometimes see themselves as walking a tightrope between black and white discontent. In different degrees we report both equalizing and preferential practice for blacks in our four field studies. Yet few whites complained about this, or even noticed it. All the same, it is important that we listen to those few dissatisfied whites regarding black hiring, promotions, and dealings with the foremen.

Table 10-1 shows that the majority of white employees at most plants thought that blacks were not being given preference in hiring, although a minority did think so.

Table 10–1. Perception of Preference for Blacks in Hiring
Hourly white employees, four plants

	Chicago	Lynchburg	Buffalo	Memphis
Positive	22%	6%	27%	*
Uncertain	25	10	27	*
Negative	53	84	46	*

* Insufficient response. However, our strong impression was that a significant minority of Memphis whites claimed to see preferential treatment.

Since we discussed the actual hiring practices of each plant in Chapters 4 to 7, we shall summarize them only briefly here. At National Acme Electric in Chicago there were very few blacks in 1961. During the 1960s the labor market from which the plant drew its employees changed radically. Selection criteria were also changed. By 1969 most applicants were black, leading to a work force then 27 percent black. When Spanish-speaking workers were also counted, more than half of the hourly work force consisted of members of minority groups. Preferential treatment, if practiced at all, was given to the few white applicants. The white perceptions of preferential treatment that we found were doubtless a response to the rapid increase in the number of blacks rather than to actual preferential practice in the employment office.

In the GE–Lynchburg plant the number of blacks increased steadily throughout the 1960s. By 1969, 16 percent of the hourly work force was black.

Selection criteria were high and no dual standards were used, but the proportion of blacks among new hires was higher than 20 percent—their proportion in the Lynchburg population. It is therefore surprising that so few whites felt blacks were receiving preference in hiring.

The Westinghouse–Buffalo plant, 5 percent black, was making deliberate efforts to increase the number of black applicants and in 1969 had hired forty-two disadvantaged workers, most of whom were black. Cut-off test scores, as mentioned earlier, had been lowered for all, but some whites felt that lower standards were applied to blacks.

The percentage of blacks in the Fairbanks plant in Memphis grew rapidly in the 1960s—from zero in 1961 to 27 percent in 1969. In 1968 more than half of the women operatives hired were black. Selection criteria were not changed but were applied equally to blacks and whites. Nevertheless, management was deliberately trying to build up its percentage of blacks.

We listen now to some of the feelings of white workers who believed, rightly or wrongly, that blacks were being given preferential attention.

GERALD DRAKE of Westinghouse Buffalo saw it like this: They should be treated equal by all means. They're human beings. I don't care if they're black, white or yellow. But I don't want to see anybody treated special. . . . But they [management] say: "Well, we're going to hire you because we have to hire so many [blacks]." And that I really don't like. Because I had to search for a job myself and no one said: "You're white. We'll hire you," or somethin' like that. You know, they just went by what was I qualified. . . . I think they [blacks] should be treated equal, not better.

TURESKY, Buffalo IUE union leader, agreed: Now they come to the front door and say: "Lower your standards now." These people can't get a job. They haven't got an education. Nobody will hire them. Fine. Beautiful. I'm all for it. But on the other hand, if my daughter doesn't get a high school diploma, I want her to be considered in the same line . . . even though my daughter has a bank account and she's not from a hard-core area, or she might be driving a used car at my expense.

Even foreman Dale French was upset by what he sees as a national trend:

FRENCH: I don't go along with the theory that the colored should get the preference. . . . My opinion of that is whatever this country is, if there's 14 percent of them colored and the other 86 percent are white, you ought to hire fourteen and eighty-six, not all black. That's what they're trying to do, to make up for the wrongs they've made since 1865 to whenever they started this.

PURCELL: Are they hiring more blacks now?

FRENCH: That's all they hire any more. That's all they hire anywhere as far as I know. I mean they [blacks] get the first chance. That's our *national* policy. That's no Westinghouse policy.

On the other hand, William Prezioso of Buffalo was not very upset by quotas:

PURCELL: Do you think the company is leaning backwards on this thing or are they just being fair?

PREZIOSO: As far as race goes? Well, I don't know, Father. They may lean backwards a little bit; on hiring I would say. I don't know for sure, but I think it would be a little easier right now for a colored person to get a job. They have a quota, I'm pretty sure. But I don't know, I think they're pretty just and fair around here.

Barbara Pierce, a fifteen-year employee at Fairbanks International, felt resentment was growing:

PURCELL: It seems they've gotten more colored people in here in the last few years? [The interviewer used the word "colored" because that was Mrs. Pierce's word throughout the interview.]

MRS. PIERCE: Oh, definitely. That's about all they hire now. [Actually, one in three employees hired the year before this interview were black, and one of every two, women.]

PURCELL: Well, I was wondering, how does that work out? How do people feel about that?

MRS. PIERCE: Well, the people naturally, a lot of them are a little resentful because they know of people that are trying to get in and say: "They won't hire a white girl, and they will a black girl."

Peggy Small, also of Memphis, said:

MRS. SMALL: Lately, they just been bringing in a whole bunch [of blacks]. In fact, I can't think when they've hired a white girl on third shift.... You probably know more about it than I do, but anyway the government's making 'em go according to the population in the county; so we've had twelve or thirteen in the last couple of months.

PURCELL: Has this caused any feeling of anxiety, I wonder?

MRS. SMALL: Well, I think like I said, they're having to hire them and maybe someone's relatives are wanting to get on and they have to take a colored person. But it seems to be working out pretty good.

Coming next to the issue of upgrading and promotions, we listened earlier to a number of blacks who felt that they were being passed over. While special attention was often given to blacks in the four plants, we noticed little preferential practice. What did the white workers think? Table 10-2 shows that very few whites at any plant thought that blacks received preference in promotions. At Lynchburg and Memphis the scores may be lower because the majority of the employees were women who do not normally expect many promotions.

Table 10–2. Perception of Preference for Blacks in Promotion Hourly white employees, four plants

	Chicago	Lynchburg	Buffalo	Memphis
Positive	16%	0%	11%	11%
Uncertain	9	5	10	22
Negative	75	95	79	67

The low score at Memphis is particularly interesting since the first black technician had recently been promoted from being a mechanic. Many people mentioned this promotion during their interviews, but few complained of preferential treatment.

Nora Larkin, twenty-year white employee, was strongly opposed to preferential practice, but felt this particular man was well qualified.

> If they don't try to exclude other races—I mean, the big thing now is to advance the Negro—okay. I'm all for it, if he's willing to work, if he wants to work, and better himself, right. But I can't see *giving* them things just because their fathers and mothers and ancestors did without. They just don't get through to me to do that.
>
> We got a new boy—he's not new; he was here about three years ago and went to the service—came back and they've made him a technician now, which—boy, quite a few people talk to me about that, you know. The boy's got a good education; he seems to work hard, so I can't see that it's wrong. Because I'd rather see them take a man that's qualified and give him a job, than one just because the government says we have to have a Negro supervisor. So . . . I don't say that it's wrong. There are a lot of people that raise Cain about it.

Winthrop Hall, in Lynchburg, has the same standards: "When they come around to give a guy a promotion when he wasn't qualified, then I would start to gripe. As long as they keep it on a qualified basis, I don't see where they have any problems."

Table 10-3 shows that the vast majority of white employees at each plant do not feel that their own supervisors give blacks preferential attention. Some thought that blacks might receive preferential attention from *other* foremen. At Buffalo only 5 percent of all Westinghouse employees were black, and half of these were older men with many years' seniority who were likely to have easy relations with their foremen. These facts affect white attitudes in Buffalo. It is particularly interesting that the Chicago score is as negative as it is (70 percent), since the absence and discipline problems of its New Work Force were often found among blacks. The Fairbanks plant is in the deep South and has many new black employees. Hence it is not surprising that a greater proportion of its white employees think that their supervisors favor blacks.

While the great majority of whites see no preferential attention given to blacks, it is worth our listening to those who do complain. At times a few vocal people can spread discontent.

Table 10-3. Perception of Preferential Practice by Their Own Foremen
Hourly white employees, four plants

	Chicago	Lynchburg	Buffalo	Memphis
Positive	15%	0%	7%	27%
Uncertain	15	0	17	9
Negative	70	100	76	64

DEAN LOHR, twenty-two-year employee at the Westinghouse–Buffalo plant, said: Well, I'd say that they're leaning a little bit backwards, 'cause I know some [blacks] that get away with murder and they let 'em get away with it. Because I used to be a union steward on B-line for a couple of years. Boy, if I went to the foreman and told him I was going to put a grievance in for discrimination [laughs]—he didn't want any grievance in for discrimination. Of course, this was a lever and I think it's being used quite a bit.

MARY ANN CLEAVER, twenty-two-year-old assembler at Fairbanks–International, described one foreman as afraid to discipline blacks: 'Cause he told me on several occasions that the NAACP was putting pressure on him. And I couldn't understand where they should have any say-so in the plant. I mean this is Fairbanks and you do what they say to do, not what some outsider says do. We used to get pretty hot about that. We'd get mad at him 'cause he would take the white girls off and make them do another job and let the colored stay on their own, which wasn't fair.

STEVE MICHNER, veteran white mechanic at National Acme Electric, was also resentful: I think they're too easy with 'em. You take a colored guy. If he does anything wrong, he won't be punished for it like a white guy. The white guy, he'll git it right away.

NORA LARKIN, whom we quote again, was particularly bitter: I don't begrudge them a job. I mean, if they can come in here and do the job, well and fine. If they pass the dexterity test, and the intelligence test, and go pass the interview. They want equality. They want to be as good as you are. Then they should come under the same rules and regulations we do. You cannot have two sets of rules in the plant, one for white people and one for black people....

And let me tell you that the Nigras is gittin' it, and that's the reason there's so much confusion and bitterness. Now there's bitterness out there, you make no mistake about it. I'll be just about as bitter as any of them about it, because I never thought I live to see the day that Fairbanks–International would make that, because they have always been strict. You cannot carry somebody around. Well, that's exactly what they're doing up there.

However, according to Nora's foreman, Thomas May, most of the negative feelings toward the Negro are not legitimate resentment of preferential practice but simply racial prejudice:

We got prejudices up to the eyeballs around this part of the country. And they don't have to have any reason, that's a big part of it, too.

> And this is basically where you have the colored situation, the racism. Now you get a white one in here; they don't criticize so much on a white person as they do on a colored person. In other words, they are not looking for the good they can find in somebody. They're looking for the faults, and heck, we've all got them.

Thomas May's observation applied, of course, to prejudiced people in the North as well. Other complaints, however, are based on fact.

Some foremen do seem hesitant to discipline blacks who charge discrimination. Others find that some black employees need special help in learning the job or in coming to work regularly and on time. Many foremen look at it as a matter of giving individual help rather than racial preference, and even then they insist that the employee meet the ordinary standards in a reasonable amount of time. Listen to Daniel Grogam, who supervises Fairbanks–Memphis employee Edgar Dolan:

> I don't really agree with preferential treatment. I mean, not beyond a point. The average man, unless I knew more about him, I wouldn't give him the treatment that I give Edgar, or some of the other colored people that I have. 'Cause I think this situation is a little bit different. I mean, their background, they don't really know what's going on, or how the plant operates. 'Course I feel that we should give them preferred treatment to get him started. But then we're starting off level. From now on, I believe in being even all the way.

We occasionally found evidence that first-line supervisors sometimes tolerated behavior, especially absenteeism and tardiness, on the part of the disadvantaged and blacks that they would not accept from white workers. While double standards might be temporarily applied for new and young employees, all foremen agreed that black employees eventually should be required to meet the same standards as the rest of the work force.

Communication is an essential element in moderating backlash. Racial resentment feeds on rumor, exaggerations, and false reports. For example, several employees at Westinghouse–Buffalo insisted that they had seen a paper directing the supervisors to give black employees preferential treatment on the job. These employees insisted that they had *seen* the instruction; but careful inquiry showed that there was no such directive. When foremen clearly understand company policy on equal employment and are open men interested in their employees, they will be able to effectively communicate that policy. Their employees will then feel more free to check out rumors.

CONCLUSION

One major concern in undertaking vigorous affirmative action for employing and upgrading black people in American industry is the issue of so-called preferential practice. We found that much of what is labeled preferential practice is really equalizing practice or special effort—practices that do not in fact give black people an advantage over whites but simply make equal competition with whites a reasonable possibility. We did find some examples of sheer preferential practices, but we propose that these are sometimes necessary, and we have shown the sociological and ethical justifications for such practices.

A second concern is the reaction of whites to special or preferential attention given to blacks. We found only a small proportion of white workers complaining about, or even perceiving, preferential practices regarding their black fellow workers. To be sure, affirmative action in most of the plants we observed was rather moderate. But it is encouraging that black employees can enter plants so rapidly and begin to move up occupational ladders through receiving equalizing, and at times preferential, help without antagonizing many whites. The equalizing and preferential help needed for more rapid racial change in American industry is both justifiable and practical, if management understands it and learns how to apply it.

CHAPTER ELEVEN

The beginnings of some answers

We will not have progress until the thousands of lone human beings who make the decisions for the private sector decide to bring the money, managerial skills, and jobs at their disposal to bear on the problems of poverty and race relations.

Whitney M. Young, Jr.

As we come to the end of this book we return to the seven specific questions we asked at the start and also to our one overarching general question: What is the past and future of the corporation's social responsibility toward blacks?

In addition to thick files of reports, plans, and statistics, the hundreds of people we listened to in executive offices and on factory floors provide us with at least the beginnings of some answers. The specific questions are easier, and to those we proceed first.

SEVEN SPECIFIC QUESTIONS AND OUR ANSWERS

Do white and black workers differ in the way they look at their jobs and supervisors? Is there any difference in the work performances of whites and blacks?

Our answer is based on what the workers told us in four different plant situations: National Acme–Chicago, GE–Lynchburg, Westinghouse–Buffalo, and Fairbanks–Memphis. In certain plants we found differences between blacks and whites; in others no difference at all.

Race is, of course, not the only factor influencing a worker's view toward his work environment. His age, sex, the type of work he does, and his home neighborhood are also factors. If we lump attitudes toward the job and the company into one factor, we see the races differing in Lynchburg and

Chicago, with blacks at those plants being less satisfied than whites with their work situation.

Suppose we break down that factor into the crucial area of a worker's views about his foreman. Here, in three of our four plant studies, blacks are clearly less satisfied with their foreman relationships. To the credit of the supervisory forces at all of the plants, the vast majority of both blacks and whites said they got along well with their foreman and respected him. But fewer blacks than whites felt that they had these good relations. At Chicago, only a little more than half of the black hourly workers felt that they got along well with their foreman. But many of these were young and disadvantaged and, for this reason, at Chicago we find the greatest racial differences of all.

Promotion is probably the most difficult area in each of the plants studied. Even though some blacks have been promoted in the last few years, blacks are still very much underrepresented in craft, salaried and, supervisory ranks. While the perceptions of the black work forces were becoming more optimistic, between a third and a half were still not sure that blacks had a fair opportunity to obtain promotions.

We find a special problem with a minority of young black men in places like Chicago. These young Negroes are often uncertain, distrustful, impatient, and alienated. They demand to know the importance of what they are doing, although their demands are not always verbal. They may dislike their work, their boss, and their fellow workers; so they skip work, come in late, or quit. Personal relationships, even at work, seem to be more important to them than they are for the old-timers. If these young Negroes have good relationships with their foremen as well as their work group, they tend to remain on the job.

There are stereotypes about the way black people perform on the job. What did we find? The foreman is probably the best equipped individual to judge the performance of a worker. Even when there exists a more objective norm, such as production quotas and rejects, the foreman has access to this information. In our field studies the foremen generally judged that in quantity and quality of production, blacks do at least as good a job as the average worker, in spite of the fact that at Lynchburg, Memphis, and Chicago the blacks were generally younger and had less industrial experience. Not one foreman found blacks more difficult to deal with personally than whites—surely a significant finding. Two problems did emerge, especially in the northern locations: absenteeism and tardiness. But these were youth more than race problems. On the whole the blacks we observed were doing well.

Now that more blacks are getting into factory and office jobs, how do whites and blacks get along at work?

If we put into one factor several attitudes toward blacks, all four of our studies show that whites are quite open toward their black co-workers and supervisors. This fact is encouraging. We might have expected to find more racial antagonisms and prejudices since two of the plants were in the South where factories have traditionally been segregated, one plant draws from militantly white Cicero, Illinois, and at Buffalo the employees still have strong ethnic loyalties. Instead generally peaceful race relations exist in these plants. Blacks are understandably and significantly more favorable in acceptance of blacks than are their white co-workers. This is true in every plant.

One of the greatest triumphs and disappointments is the pattern of interpersonal relations on the job. Blacks and whites meet, talk, and get along very well on the job. They accept the right of management to place them side by side, and while working in this way they do not resist the opportunity to get acquainted and even to make new friends. In every plant, the fact that blacks and whites work side by side has helped to clarify biases and preconceptions each race often has toward the other.

At the same time, we noticed how the races tend to separate along racial lines when they are on their own time in the cafeteria and on breaks, and certainly after they leave work. This is not unlike the caste system in India, where Indian workers are "modern" while in the plant and return to their traditional ways when they are at home. " 'When I put on my shirt and go to the factory I take off my caste. When I come home and take off my shirt, I put on my caste.' This dramatizes the paradoxes in which modern Indians live."[1] The white worker is much the same way. He is modern while on the job, but often traditional when at home or in the cafeteria, which is also like home to him.

Not only in the South, but also in the North, factories such as those we have studied are notable agencies for social change, more influential often than the schools, churches, and neighborhoods of their cities, providing meeting places for the two races and opportunities for coming to know and trust one another. It is an unusual opportunity that American industry furnishes.

What kind of management action is needed to hire and advance black people more rapidly, especially craftsmen, foremen, middle managers, and professionals? Is preferential treatment necessary? Will this cause critical white reactions?

Our statistical predictions for the advancement of Negroes into crafts and into white collar jobs are gloomy unless strong and vigorous affirmative action plans emerge during the 1970s. These plans should call for a strong commitment on the part of top management, plus, at least for the larger corporation, a systems approach to minority manpower. Planning within the company will be coordinated, involving not only minority planning but manpower planning, economic and social forecasting. Since the company is also

[1] These comments are by M. N. Srinivas in Myron Weiner (ed.), *Modernization: The Dynamics of Growth* (New York: Basic Books, 1966), p. 64.

part of the larger social and economic systems, it will need to relate also to its environment.

Systems planning calls for six ways of implementing policy: clearly delegating responsibility for equal employment opportunity planning; communicating policy within and without the firm; identifying racial problem areas; establishing goals and timetables for minority programs; developing specific innovative programs to meet local plant targets; and using a system for measurement and sanctions.

The most important of these methods is the measurement of equal employment opportunity performance for all managers in the company including the foremen. In that way constructive behavior in racial relations and racial advancement is an integral part of the entire measurement-reward system. Without measurement being seriously attempted, no organization will turn itself around; but with it, the company can make the changes called for.

Because of the great shortage of skilled craftsmen and white collar professionals among blacks, management must work with the high schools and vocationals schools as well as encourage the entrance of Negroes into the business schools and engineering schools—the main source for its middle management and professional personnel. Companies are doing this in an increasingly imaginative way; but it is only the beginning.

In-plant training, especially apprentice programs, will be called for, and we find that many managers have not adequately recognized the talent already existing in their own work force. Sometimes college men are still sweeping floors and bright young men are stuck on dead-end jobs. With a crash training program, upgrading such employees can be done, as we have observed in our field studies.

Will a vigorous systems approach to more rapid assimilation of blacks in industry cause negative white reactions? In each of our four field studies, the hourly black work force has grown significantly during the last five years. In addition, blacks have entered into supervisory positions, even in southern plants, and into craft jobs and technical and professional jobs. Growth in these areas has been very modest; nevertheless, breakthroughs have occurred. In spite of this progress, we found only a small proportion of white workers complaining about, or even perceiving preferential hiring and promoting for their black fellow workers. The large-scale, brooding white backlash feared by some was significantly absent. It is encouraging that black employees can enter a plant rapidly and begin to move up its occupational ladders without antagonizing more than a few whites.

How does management hire, train, motivate, and retain young blacks who are disadvantaged?

An executive from a certain aircraft factory on Long Island stated, "It's hopeless! We bus blacks out from Bedford-Stuyvesant to our plant and nearly all of them quit within a short time. Until black people themselves want to become equal, there's nothing you can do for the disadvantaged!" Our findings, on the contrary, show that blacks who may be disadvantaged can be motivated and retained with time, effort, money, and innovation.

The disadvantaged performed their jobs adequately in both quantity and quality of work. It is true that widespread problems of absenteeism and retention did occur. But we found that even these obstinate problems could often be significantly reduced with sufficient orientation and foreman support. Absences and drop-outs have long been a problem with new young workers, disadvantaged or not.

Because of the costs and because of unequal competition between plants with black employees in their neighborhoods and those with none, government financial incentives will often be needed. Management can learn to live and work with the disadvantaged and with the New Work Force. It is happening.

How can the all-important first-line supervisor become racially sensitive and concerned?

Our findings are that the role of the foreman is crucial if racial integration and advancement are to succeed. The foreman has many obligations—product output, quality, flow of supplies, human relations, employee evaluations, and so forth. Now he is expected to become more sensitive and more outgoing with respect to new racial minorities, sometimes the disadvantaged, coming into his work force. The foreman's ability to deal satisfactorily with blacks should also be factored into his rewards and sanctions.

Second, extra efforts need to be made to give foremen an awareness of the differences in culture that may sometimes exist between the white foreman and the black community. There are many types and forms of foreman-sensitivity programs; they can work and they are important not only for old-line foremen but also for new black foremen who deal with whites and the Spanish-speaking.

From the black community: Does white big business really intend to hire and upgrade blacks in a hurry?

There are many questions from different sections of the black community regarding the sincerity of American management interest in the problems and opportunities of black Americans. Whitney Young, one civil rights leader who understood the problems of business and its opportunities, put it this way:

> A company's sincerity can be measured by the numbers of black supervisors and executives it hires. Simply opening up jobs is not enough.

Unless black people are given a share of corporate power and influence and are placed in positions *above* as well as *below* white people, "equal opportunity" will have a hollow sound and bitter taste. Businesses that cry about the lack of trained Negroes for supervisory jobs probably haven't looked at the talent in their own work force.[2]

This book should give some reassurance to American black communities that Negroes are moving into positions of first-line and middle management, and some into professional and higher management. Yet our forecasts of the time it will take for adequate black representation in management may be anything but reassuring. The approaches needed to make our forecasts wrong are only now emerging from their planning stages.

What have been the most important causes of change toward improving equal employment opportunities?

Looking over the history of black employment, chiefly in the electrical industry for the last 100 years, we conclude that until the mid-1960s the two major causes of improvement for the black community were (1) the need for labor especially during wars and (2) pressures of legislation, particularly the Civil Rights Act of 1964. We do not see the leadership of management or the concept of corporate social responsibility taking a decisive role in the past. However, toward the end of the 1960s and the beginning of the 1970s we see a new posture and a new thinking on the part of management, and to that central issue we now address ourselves.

CORPORATE RESPONSIBILITY TOWARD BLACKS—PAST AND FUTURE

The American public's expectations of the corporation are changing. The corporation is legally chartered to make a product: anything from breakfast cereal or missiles to lamp bulbs. Traditionally its social concerns were with the local YMCA and similar charities. This book asks how much further management should go in its social concerns, how directly and aggressively it should confront the major social problems of our times. What is the so-called ecology of the corporation?

Before we formulate our answers, we would like to recall the management era of the company town and its folk music: "I owe my soul to the company store." America does not welcome the paternalism of the Japanese factory or the company store era. On the other hand, Americans are no longer willing to accept unconcerned, irresponsible, absentee-owner corporations letting their environment shift for itself.

[2] Whitney M. Young, Jr., *Beyond Racism* (New York: McGraw-Hill, 1969), p. 209.

Critics like Friedman on the right and Harrington on the left agree when they say management should stick to its business of profits alone, and that corporate social responsibility is a delusion. Others such as Morse of Honeywell, Henry Ford II, and Clarence Walton write that corporate responsibility may be the only salvation of business in a world that challenges corporate legitimacy.

Our purpose in this book is not to theorize at length about corporate social responsibility. It is rather to get a better understanding of its meaning by observing its practical application in one area, namely, equal employment opportunity. In what ways, if any, have the companies and plants we observed in our studies acted in accord with the concept of corporate social responsibility as they dealt with issues of racial employment?

Admittedly the idea of corporate social responsibility is hard to pin down because the motivation of individual managers (or of anyone) is never a simple matter. One thing is clear: to proclaim the profit motive as the unique explanation of management's behavior is grossly simplistic. The motives of the managers we observed in this book and the motives they implanted in their companies by their behavior appeared to us to be multiple and complex. We found a mixture of altruism and self-interest—not a bad thing.

One manager criticized our discussing the motives of managers in dealing with the goals for minority hiring now being imposed by the Office of Federal Contract Compliance: "Why waste time discussing the question of *motives*? You *have* to fulfil the goals and the targets. That's all there is to it. That's all that matters." But we maintain that one's motives about goals will influence one's attitudes and the entire corporate system of implementation. An attitude of opposition can easily defeat implementation, whereas looking to the wisdom behind these goals, quite independently of government requirements, may make for much more effective applications. Motives are important.

The psychological theory of the functional autonomy of motivation is applicable here.[3] This theory opposes orthodox Freudian or behavioristic views of motivation that tie one's present motives irrevocably back to his far childhood or to some more recent past. Functional autonomy theory suggests that while such chains of influence are often present, motives can often change and become relatively independent of the past.

This theory was often verified: Managers became interested in equal employment opportunity because of community or government pressures, but then began to believe in it. Their motives changed and became autonomous. They became more socially responsible than they were at the beginning. One manager, for example, began work in minority employment because he was assigned to do so by his plant manager. Later he became a corporate officer in equal employment opportunity because his field work convinced him of its

---

[3] See Gordon W. Allport, *Personality* (New York: Holt, 1937), pp. 191–207, and *Personality and Social Encounter* (Boston: Beacon Press, 1960), p. 140.

importance. His motivation changed from merely fulfilling a management job to a sincere social concern.

Our findings: First, we summarize the corporate level equal employment activities of the four largest electrical companies in the United States: General Electric, Westinghouse, Radio Corporation of America, and Western Electric. The policies of these firms gradually evolved from an active commitment to nondiscrimination seen in their 1961 Plans for Progress to more vigorous affirmative action toward increasing the numbers of blacks they employed. The proportion of Negroes in the four companies increased significantly during the sixties. Two companies got an early start, while the racial growth curves in the other two rose most after 1965. Gradually, corporate departments were established to oversee minority employment. Spurred by the Civil Rights Act and by the riots of 1967 and 1968, managers began to think through the long-range issues and to look for more innovative programs. Toward the end of the 1960s these firms joined the new National Alliance for Businessmen efforts and undertook programs for the disadvantaged. Their involvement with community activities increased and much of it was aimed at the problems of the inner cities and of minority people, especially blacks.

Second, looking at the four plants described in this book, we saw National Acme management in Chicago dealing constructively with its rapidly changing work force and the complex problems of Chicago. Managers of GE-Lynchburg were working actively as individuals and as representatives of their company in their Middle South community to change the housing, educational, and newspaper situations for the good of blacks as well as whites. While their activity was somewhat recent, it is progressing. In Buffalo, with the Westinghouse plant at some distance from the Negro community, there was a modest growth in affirmative action activity and in Negro hiring. Finally, at Memphis we saw a plant facing the special problem of desegregating itself with success.

At these plants certain executives spent many hours on community affairs. A few we personally knew to have dedicated themselves quite beyond the call of duty to hours of work with black people away from the plant. At least in the late 1960s, and with differing degrees of aggressiveness, the managers of these plants were generally acting with a valid sense of corporate social responsibility regarding black employment.

As the plants and companies continued their new racial activities, they discovered that such action did not necessarily upset their customers or shareholders, injure the quality of their products, or cut into their profits. They began trying more innovative and constructive ways of dealing with minority employment. Putting together our observations and conversations, we conclude that these managers are beginning to act, regarding minority employment, with a spirit of corporate social responsibility as we defined it at the beginning of this book.

These managers are acting in equal employment not only as individuals but as corporate agents. They are undertaking some socially motivated actions not required by law or external pressures. They are going beyond traditional philanthropy to work with more complex interrelationships between their firms and society. In varying degrees they are sometimes exceeding the requirements of federal agencies and the Civil Rights Act. In several cases they set targets for Negro hiring higher than the targets they would publicize to a federal examiner. We find them concerned with black and white people outside the firm as well as within. They have continued to manage profitable companies producing quality products.

Lastly, we ask what is the ethical or moral component in their thinking? Here the answer is more elusive. Some managers seemed definitely to be motivated morally about racial employment; others appeared to be merely concerned with keeping the government off their backs. We have the impression of about as much ethical concern among these men as we would find in the American community generally.

Some limitations as to what management can do. Neither the four corporations nor the four plants we observed can do everything that is needed to meet the problem of racially fair employment. What are some of the boundaries to their involvement in social responsibility toward blacks?

Issues of competition and profits constantly confront management as it looks at its social responsibility toward blacks. The old distinction arises between the short run and the long run. Management of these companies is seeing what Henry Ford claims: "Whatever seriously threatens the stability and progress of the country and its cities also threatens the growth of the economy and your company." The rationale of corporate social responsibility is by no means divorced from practical business wisdom. These companies and plants are making moderate longer run investments at shorter run costs in order to improve their black involvement. There is a limit to how far they can go, and this leads us to the next point.

While the federal government is anxious to involve the private sector in black employment since business is cost-conscious and has management know-how, obviously the private sector cannot do it alone. These companies and plants are beginning to cooperate, and will need to cooperate further, with other power structures in the cities in which they operate.

The National Urban League idea of a "domestic Marshall Plan" seems useful in coming to grips with the immense racial-urban problem of America, although it is not clear how such a plan is politically and economically viable. The racial problem is only a part of the urban economic problem, a problem that can be handled only by a combined federal-state-profit-sector-black community-white community approach on a massive scale. The corporation has social responsibility toward blacks but is limited in its ability to change the situation. It must not promise too much; although it can still do more.

The position of this book on corporate responsibility. Well-conceived corporate social responsibility is both workable and desirable. We say it must be well conceived because we do not advocate business becoming involved with every possible type of problem. We do not propose corporate pressures toward such dubious issues as company-owned housing, but we do advocate concern about open housing for employees. We do not necessarily advocate company pressure for off-plant marijuana laws, but we do advocate company support for adequate health care and education in the ghetto. It remains the difficult task of management to decide what to be responsible for and what not to be responsible for, how to be a leader rather than a follower in dealing with what wise people see as American social problems. Private business property has a social as well as an individual character. It is in their own interest that managers recognize this fact.

The manager who refuses to accept social responsibility in private enterprise decision-making or who, like Friedman, castigates such thinking as "unadulterated socialism" may be quite sincere but he is really an enemy of the American system. In effect, he offers socialism as the only alternative to the profit-compulsive, free competition against which so many are revolting.

But we have observed a middle ground between socialism and a market economy ruled by competition (often marred by advertising pressures or only partial competition). It is the middle road of corporate social responsibility. Only in this admittedly grey area, we assert, lies the legitimacy and the survival of American business management.

A FINAL WORD

What did we learn? The need for vigorous affirmative action by management is quite clear, and time is short. More rapid growth of black involvement in American industry is possible and practicable. The "how to do it" is not so elusive as has been thought. More elusive are the "how to want it" and the "how to pay for it." There are many benefits, or fallout values, in learning how to bring black employees into the work force and helping them to advance. These benefits are equally important for dealing with whites, especially the New Work Force. This new knowledge may also help raise the level of workers in the have-not, developing nations to help preserve world peace and to lessen poverty.

What will motivate management during the 1970s? Will stress on law cause a wave of legalism in civil rights laws that Douglass Brown finds in the field of labor relations?[4] We saw the need for law, but its overemphasis might actually defeat the harmonious and progressive efforts that are needed. Will change come about from revolution? This seems doubtful, but we cannot

---

[4] "Legalism and Industrial Relations in the United States," *Proceedings* of the Twenty-Third Annual Meeting, Industrial Relations Research Association, December 1970.

rule out the threat of guerrilla warfare in our cities. Will change come through increased managerial responsibility so that American management will lead and influence the other segments of our society? Our findings point to a cautious hope for such new management thinking.

Returning to the idea of the functional autonomy of motivation, the companies we studied are manifesting a growing concern for their social responsibility to blacks with more innovative leadership. It remains to be seen whether management creativity and leadership will really catch on and fire all business and the nation, or whether it will relax into tokenism once the popular appeal of civil rights subsides. Instead of operating defensively, corporate management may seize the initiative in racial employment. If by a systems approach, team work, and scientific and social know-how, we can rescue astronauts in a severely damaged spacecraft from an aborted moon flight, we can accomplish what may be a less dramatic but more important feat of getting a Negro to a job, and a good job.

Polarization between the races in America is not some kind of Marxian dialectical necessity. Our findings show that when blacks enter the industrial world they can enrich that world for whites as well as blacks, and that issues for the manager can become transformed into shared accomplishments and opportunities.

APPENDIX A

Research methods: did they tell us what they really think?

The field work for this book took about three and one-half years and included visits to corporate and union headquarters, union conventions and meetings, government and civil rights agencies. We had hundreds of conversations about the issues we have treated. In addition, we spent long hours at the Cambridge Center working up history, analyzing EEO statistics, turnover, and other items.

In particular, the four extensive field studies described in Chapters 4 through 7 occupied the authors for over six months in 1968 and 1969. Living in the workers' home neighborhoods, as we did, proved to be an invaluable source of both information and relaxed social relationships. In Lynchburg, Virginia, we lived a few houses away from the local Community Action Agency. In Memphis, Chicago, and Buffalo, we lived in the black neighborhoods. Memphis' black Catholic parish was our home during the early months of 1969 (the Fairbanks–International first black employee came from this parish). In the spring we moved to the Lawndale west side of Chicago at Presentation Parish—a center for community activities centering on black home ownership and the Contract Buyers League. In Buffalo we lived in the poorest of the black neighborhoods where the parish was a focus for the social and civic activities of the surrounding neighborhoods. Black poverty program workers and city councilmen were frequent visitors. In addition, we did shorter studies at Westinghouse, East Pittsburgh, and Raytheon, Bedford, Massachusetts.

Sunday afternoons often found the authors at union hall meetings of the various locals in Buffalo, Memphis, and Chicago.

We learned the troubles and few triumphs of the black community at the dinner table, walking the streets, and talking to teen-agers, their parents, and neighborhood leaders. We listened to the attitudes of the workingman, not only in plant interviews but also in the most informal situations. We have many friends and agreeable memories from those months, providing us with a framework that no reading or less direct contact could supply. Most importantly, this community living helped our credibility with the black people we interviewed at the plants. To these black and white working people we owe a debt for making this book possible.

HOW WE SAMPLED

At each plant we selected random samples of sixty hourly workers. In order to insure an adequate representation of blacks, we stratified all samples so that one-half were black and one-half white. If the sample of sixty had not been stratified at Lynchburg, for example, randomly only nine blacks would have fallen into it and, at Buffalo, only three. In the two southern plants, where the work force was largely women, the subsamples were also stratified so as to include ten hourly male workers of each race in each plant. All attitude percentages which included stratified groups, such as men and women, were weighted to account for the different representations.

Size of the work force and numbers of blacks and whites varied greatly among the plants. In some cases our sample of thirty whites was a small percentage of the total number of whites in the plant, while the sample of blacks might be a larger percentage. But the adequacy of a truly random sample depends much more on its absolute size than on its relative size or size in relation to the number in the population. The samples we drew were indeed random, since we used random numbers and applied them to employee payroll numbers.

Because there were a large number of Spanish-speaking workers in the Acme–Chicago work force, we interviewed ten of them, along with twenty-five blacks and twenty-five whites. The eight to ten foremen interviewed at each plant were also selected randomly, as were the union stewards.

At each plant the authors interviewed a dozen or more extra hourly or salaried employees for special reasons: our interest in NAB pledges, absenteeism, issues of white collar employment, for example, or simply because these people were recommended as articulate leaders. These men and women were not included in the random sample of hourly workers and their opinions are not reflected in those percentages.

STARTING THE INTERVIEWS

The principal research tool for the field studies in this book was the focused, nondirective interview. In addition to many hundreds of informal conversations, the authors interviewed more than 450 blacks and whites at the six plants. The interviews at the plants were conducted in such neutral territory as a general meeting or utility room off the cafeteria, near the plant floor, and away from the front office. All employees and union members were told of the research project by means of union hand bills, plant newspapers, and bulletin board announcements. Workers randomly selected were asked by a personal letter to participate. The interviews were voluntary and only nine whites and two blacks of the entire 450 chose not to be interviewed. The project was announced as a human relations, rather than a racial, project, making relationships between persons primary. Before beginning the study, the authors addressed not only plant managers, but also the foremen (in two plants) and the union officers in the three locals involved, asking their cooperation in presenting the project to the people in the plant. The authors did all the interviewing, dividing it about equally.

Before the interview began, we obtained from the company personnel offices such biographical background information on each person as age, education, work history, dependents, place of birth, skill level, type of job, and pay raises. We went over this so as to have in advance a good idea of the person's background.

After obtaining the interviewee's permission, we recorded the interviews. The microphone did not seem to bother the workers once the interview began; only three people did not want their comments recorded.

Generally the interviews began in a relaxed manner and the interviewer assured the worker that he was picked at random, "like out of a hat." The purpose of the study was explained once again, stating that we had the support of both union and company, that we were not working for either one, and that what was said would not get back to the foreman or union steward. We assured the people that while we hoped to use their ideas and suggestions, their names would all be disguised. We stressed with each person that his ideas were important to us, and that only if he spoke straightforwardly would the whole project be worthwhile. The interviews lasted nearly an hour, some less, some longer. After the interview, the interviewer dictated any relevant observations or insights such as the worker's physical appearance, and characteristics, and whether he seemed to be nervous or at ease.

DID THEY TELL US WHAT THEY REALLY THINK?

How can we be sure that the employees, unionists, managers, and community people did not tell us what they thought we wanted to hear? Will a black worker talk freely with a white interviewer? Will a white worker talk freely with a white interviewer about a sensitive black relationship problem?

Will a woman talk with a man? Will a southerner talk with a northern interviewer? Inevitably, the role and appearance of the interviewer affect the results. The question is, will it bias the results? As Kahn and Cannell put it:

> It is impossible to conceive of an interview as anything else but a process of interaction, and interaction means by definition that each individual is influencing the other in a variety of ways. To say, therefore, that we want an interview without interviewer influence is a contradiction in terms.[1]

Several studies show that black respondents do not always give the same responses equally to black and white interviewers. Thomas Pettigrew states:

> When questioned by a Negro rather than by a white interrogator, Negroes mentioned higher educational aspirations for their children, more often agreed that changes must be made "in the way our country is run," and more strongly approved of the student sit-in protest demonstrations and school desegregation.... Not only did Negro respondents again evidence less militancy to white interviewers, but they also admitted to fewer feelings of racial victimization.[2]

Differences that Pettigrew and others show in responses to black and white interviewers do not in themselves establish the fact that black interviewers were obtaining a valid measurement of black attitudes. A recent report concludes: "Negro respondents gave higher quality responses to white interviewers than to Negro interviewers in a personally sensitive area."[3] Black workers might well exaggerate their racial attitudes in the opposite direction to a black interviewer.

The evidence is mixed and inconclusive. There is a danger for any interviewer in looking at a person primarily as black or white. This very attitude can itself lead to bias. The black man can easily sense that he is being talked to as black and he may respond accordingly, thus exaggerating his racial attitudes. The essential point for the interviewer is to meet people as *individual persons*.

The authors agree with Kahn and Cannell that the personal relationship established is far more important than the color of one's skin:

> Experience shows that the atmosphere which the interviewer sets for the interview process, his reactions to the expressed attitudes of the respondent, and his technical skill are in most cases far more important than his background characteristics. These characteristics have importance primarily as they affect first impressions, while the basic skills of

---

[1] Robert L. Kahn and Charles F. Cannell, *The Dynamics of Interviewing* (New York: John Wiley & Sons, 1957), p. 157.

[2] Thomas F. Pettigrew, *A Profile of the Negro American* (Princeton: D. Van Nostrand, 1964), p. 50. See also Herbert H. Hyman *et al.*, *Interviewing for Social Research* (Chicago: University of Chicago Press, 1954), for a review of the research on interview bias.

[3] Leonard Weller and Elmer Luchterhand, "Interviewer-Respondent Interaction in Negro and White Family Life Research," *Human Organization*, 27, Spring 1968, p. 53.

Appendix A

the interviewer have deeper and more enduring effects upon the interviewer-respondent relationship and therefore on the product of the interview.[4]

First impressions are less important in the longer, free-flowing interview. The authors' experience was that after a few minutes of easy conversation, rapport was established and black workers mostly tended to be open and straightforward with their white interviewers.

An important factor in the personal relationships was our role as Catholic priests as well as social scientists. Had we been investigating attitudes toward religion, our role might have hindered openness. But since we were discussing race relations and industrial relations, our role seemed to help. It was a kind of guarantee to the workers, union, and management people that we were not members of either management or union, that we were outsiders and not merely university people, although we were also that. From time to time in our interviews there was evidence that the respondents felt free to express themselves openly, trusting that what they said would be kept in confidence. One man was asked how he happened to come to get his job. He said: "Well, through the police. This is what happens when talking to a man of the cloth. I have to be truthful." We were announced as priests and pictured as such in the company newspapers, although we often interviewed simply in shirt and tie, or open collar.

In talking to us as clergymen, did the workers tend to play down attitudes of conflict or criticism? In practically every interview some criticism came to the surface. Somewhat less profanity seemed to be the only restraint. The authors attempted to be nonjudgmental in their reactions to what they heard. We knew there was no quicker way to "turn a person off" and hinder communication than to indicate to him in any way that his attitudes were unacceptable.

The interview is a fallible instrument and contains possible sources of bias, but it is a personal approach, and when bias is recognized and compensated for, the interview can lead to a much more open, human, and honest response than other types of research methods. Of course, everything goes back to the interviewers' sincere belief in the dignity and importance of each worker. This is more important than any aspect of the role: white, male, priest, or layman.

Ultimately, the best test of the validity of our methods is the interviews themselves. Often during the interview, a worker would say: "I'm glad you picked me to talk to you"; or "This was a good chance for me to get a load off my mind"; "You gave me a good chance to say a lot of things I've been thinking for a long time"; "If you had more questions, I would like to answer them"; and a foreman: ". . . and I'm not saying it because this is the thing to

[4] Kahn and Cannell, *op. cit.*, pp. 198, 199. See also these authors' briefer and earlier "Collection of Data by Interviewing," in Leon Festinger and Daniel Katz (eds.), *Research Methods in the Behavioral Sciences* (New York: Dryden Press, 1953), especially pp. 354–361.

say, because I really basically believe this." Typical were comments like these of Hafford Rast, a fifty-two-year-old Acme–Chicago press operator:

RAST: What I'm gonna tell you is gonna be the way I feel; and that's the truth and I got reasons to believe it and I don't care.

INTERVIEWER: We want you to tell us exactly the way you see it.

RAST: Yeah, yeah, that's what we got to do. If we don't, we ain't gonna get anywhere.

CODING THE INTERVIEW

During the summer of 1968 at the Raytheon–Waltham plant, the authors pretested their use of the topics covered in the Coding Form (see Exhibit 4), thus enabling them to alter and improve their interviewing and coding method. Three qualified coders, working independently, later analyzed the taped interviews back in Cambridge, Massachusetts. Personal employment data provided the basis for coding seventeen biographical items. Thirty-six attitudes were scored from the recordings.

We coded attitudes toward the job, training, supervision, promotion opportunities, the union, and black and white fellow workers. Possible discrimination and/or preferential treatment were coded in relation to the employment process, promotion, and supervision. The special issues of outreach recruiting of the poor, black foremen, and race relations were also covered. For simplicity, the five-point scale was reduced to three in our tables.

Following another coding form, the coders also rated supervisors on their attitudes toward their own job, their chances for further promotion, recruiting blacks, anticipated reaction of their work group to a black foreman, preferential treatment, and relations between black and white workers. We coded the foreman's judgment about the relative performance of his black and white employees on quantity and quality of their work, attendance, promptness, accepting responsibility, discipline at work, ability to learn their jobs, and the relative performance of the previously hard-core unemployed.

These ratings were made not from a single response but from all parts of the interview where the respondent touched on a given topic. There was a high degree of agreement or reliability among the three coders. Our final score on each item was the consensus or average of the three coders.

COMPUTERIZING THE DATA

Each employee's background data and attitude scores were punched on data cards, given variable numbers and descriptive classifications for computer processing. We used the Data-Text System,[5] which is a computer language for social science research originally developed for the 7094 IBM computer. The vocabulary of Data-Text is modeled along the lines of Fortran, especially in regard to arithmetic statements and input controls. Several modifications were made to make the language more congruous with special problems of social science research.

Data-Text provided us with basic statistics, frequency distributions, cross tabulations of contingency tables, and correlations on background and attitude variables for each location. We used T-tests to determine statistical significance of variation by race, age, sex, and plant location, and F-tests for a one-way analysis of variance.

Factor analysis showed two major clusters of attitudes. The factors were extracted by the principal components method and the factor loadings were rotated according to the Varimax criterion. We identified two factors and in addition chose two indices. The "Tolerance of Blacks in the Work Setting" factor combines workers' attitudes on preferential treatment, the black foreman, work performance of blacks, black-white relations, and personal feelings about working with blacks. The index clearly measures attitudes toward and perceptions of the black workers. It does not measure black attitudes toward whites. Our second factor, the "Company, Boss, Work Satisfaction Index," incorporates coded items on workers' attitudes toward the job, training, foreman, chances for promotion, and the company. It also includes perceptions on discrimination or nondiscrimination in employment, promotion, and supervision. The Pro-Union Index combines attitudes toward having a union and toward current union leadership. The "Hire-More-Poor Index" incorporates attitudes toward whether the poor want to work and on whether the company should hire more poor people and engage in outreach recruiting.

USE OF QUOTATIONS

In addition to tables and statistics on employee attitudes, we have used hundreds of quotations from workers, union leaders, and managers to give a fuller picture of attitudes than numbers alone can convey. These quotations are not atypical or sensational statements but are chosen to deepen understanding of a majority or even a *minority* position. (We have indicated clearly when a person did not speak for the majority.) We quoted some men and women simply as individuals, because their experiences or ideas throw light on important problems.

[5] See Arthur S. Couch, "Data-Text System, Preliminary Manual," Harvard Social Relations Department, July 1969.

SUPPLEMENTAL IN-PLANT ISSUE

Westinghouse Buffalo Divisions News

Vol. 1, No. 1   JUNE 3, 1969

OUR PLANT INCLUDED IN HUMAN RELATIONS STUDY CURRENTLY BEING MADE IN ELECTRICAL INDUSTRY

Father Purcell   *Father Cavanagh*

Two interesting and interested men, Dr. Theodore V. Purcell and Dr. Gerald F. Cavanagh, both of the Cambridge (Mass.) Center for Social Studies, will have office space at our plant for the next few weeks as they conduct a Westinghouse portion of their two-year, nation-wide study of human relations in the electrical industry.

To obtain meaningful information for their industry study, Fathers Purcell and Cavanagh (they are Jesuits) will conduct interviews with both management and non-management employes selected at random from our employment files. To chat with these gentlemen will be an interesting and enjoyable experience for those of us who might be selected, and we will be giving significant help to an important study. (Of course, if your name is selected, your participation is still an entirely voluntary matter for you to decide.)

Fathers Purcell and Cavanagh will begin their interviews here this week and will continue until this phase of their study is completed -- a period of, perhaps, three weeks in all. They may not be wearing clerical garb, but you will know them by their warmth and sincerity to be good men, sharing the concern we all have for our fellow men and the society in which we work and live.

It goes without saying that we will all want to show them every courtesy and the warm hospitality that typifies the welcome that Westinghouse-Buffalo employes accord all visitors.

UNION MEMBER

Of, by & for the Westinghouse Workers
Cheektowaga Plant
Local 1581   IUE-AFL-CIO   Telephone: 632-7846

May 29, 1969   4499 Genesee St., Buffalo, NY (25)

WIERZBIC - UNITED VICTORIOUS

With the largest turnout ever to participate in a Local Union Electi~
~bers~ ~ ~ted into office the Un~i~ ~d Committee Candidates. Incumb~~
~ into Offic~ ~ 9th T~

Fra~ ~~ly & sincerely,

TED WIERZBIC.

N O T I C E : Beginning next week --
The Cambridge Center for Social Studies, an independent social science research center, is conducting a nation-wide study of human relations in the electrical industry. This two-year study is supported by the Ford Foundation.

Rev. Theodore V. Purcell and Rev. Gerald F. Cavanagh of the Cambridge Center staff have secured the cooperation of the major companies in the electrical industry.

Father Purcell's activity in the labor relations field is quite well known. He has been a guest at several of our IUE Conference Board meetings and was in attendance at our IUE Convention last fall. Several of your Officers have had the opportunity to meet and talk with him and his associate during the past few months. We have been convinced that he has a genuine interest in the opinions of those to whom he talks. We would like to assure our membership that the selection of volunteers in this survey will be done by Father Purcell and Father Cavanagh. We would also like to assure you that anything you say will be kept in confidence. If you have the opportunity and decide to participate we urge you to state your opinions very frankly, regardless of the subject, since this is the only way such a survey can show the true feelings of the people.

NOT~   Next EXECUTIV~   ~TNG -- ~TDAY, J~~ ~h

CAMBRIDGE CENTER FOR SOCIAL STUDIES
42 Kirkland Street   Cambridge, Massachusetts 02138   (617) 868-1210

Dr. Theodore V. Purcell
Dr. Gerald F. Cavanagh

June   , 1969

Attention: _____
                (Supervisor)

Dear

We are making a national study of human relations in the electrical industry--Westinghouse, General Electric, and others--sponsored by the Ford Foundation. Buffalo Westinghouse and the International Union of Electrical, Radio, and Machine Workers, Local 1581, have agreed to cooperate with us.

We would like to get your ideas and suggestions on working conditions and human relations.

We picked your name at random--like out of a hat. I would like to meet you and converse with you for about an hour. Our conversation will be in strict confidence, of course.

Would you please come to_____
where I have a desk and will be waiting at _____.

Thank you.

FORD-CCSS RESEARCH
CODING FORM: PERSONAL DATA

CCSS No._____
Coder_____

5. Location of the study:
   - (1) Lynchburg, Va.
   - (2) Memphis, Tenn.
   - (3) Chicago, Ill.
   - (4) Pittsburgh, Pa.
   - (5)
   - (6)
   - (7)
   - (8)
   - (9)

   5._____

6. Job status: (1) Hourly paid (sample) (2) Foreman (3) Technical (4) Hourly paid (sample)   6._____

7. Address: (1) City   (2) Suburbs   (3) Outlying town or countryside   7._____

8. Sex: (1) Male   (2) Female   8._____

9. Marital status:
   - (1) Single
   - (2) Married
   - (3) Separated
   - (4) Divorced
   - (5) Widowed
   - (6) Remarried

   9._____

10. Year of birth:
    - (1) 1909 or before
    - (2) 1910 - 1914
    - (3) 1915 - 1919
    - (4) 1920 - 1924
    - (5) 1925 - 1929
    - (6) 1930 - 1934
    - (7) 1935 - 1939
    - (8) 1940 - 1944
    - (9) 1945 or after

    10._____

11. Place of birth:
    - (1) Middle South (Ky., Va., Mo., Md.)
    - (2) Deep South
    - (3) West (Miss. River and West)
    - (4) Northeast (Penn. and East)
    - (5) North Central (Ohio to Miss. River)
    - (6) Outside U.S.

    11._____

12. Citizenship: (1) U.S. citizen   (2) Non-citizen   12._____

13. Dependents: 1 2 3 4 5 6 7 8 or more 9 (none)   13._____

14. Highest educational level completed:
    - (1) College grad
    - (2) Some college
    - (3) High school grad
    - (4) 3 or 4 yrs. H.S.
    - (5) 1 or 2 yrs. H.S.'
    - (6) 8th grade
    - (7) 6th - 7th grade
    - (8) 4th - 5th grade
    - (9) 3rd grade or less

    14._____

15. Shift: 1 2 3   15._____

16. Skill level: (EEO-1 categories)
    - (1) Official/manager
    - (2) Professional
    - (3) Technician
    - (4) Sales
    - (5) Office/clerical
    - (6) Craftsman (skilled)
    - (7) Operative (semiskilled)
    - (8) Service worker
    - (9) Laborer (unskilled)

    16._____

17. Continuous service date (began work at plant):
    - (1) 1929 or before
    - (2) 1930 - 1939
    - (3) 1940 - 1949
    - (4) 1950 - 1959
    - (5) 1960 - 1964
    - (6) 1965 - 1966
    - (7) 1967
    - (8) 1968
    - (9) 1969

    17._____

18. Race:
    - (1) Negro
    - (2) Oriental
    - (3) American Indian
    - (4) Spanish American
    - (5) White

    18._____

19. Performance appraisal rating: 1 2 3 4 5 9 (none)   19._____

20. Job obtained through:
    - (1) Ordinary channels
    - (2) Outreach recruiting
    - (3) Had been hard-core (NAB)
    - (4) Both 2 and 3

    20._____

21. Foreman of interviewee is: (1) Black   (2) White   (3) Other   21._____

22. Union steward of interviewee is: (1) Black   (2) White   (3) Other   (9) None   22._____

FORD-CCSS RESEARCH
CODING FORM: INTERVIEWS **

	Very Fav.	Fav.	Neut.	Un-Fav.	V.Un-Fav.	No Resp.

RECRUITING

24. I <u>like</u> my job.   1   2   3   4   5   6   24._____

25. Which one of the following was most influential for <u>your getting a job</u> in this plant?   25._____
    1. Employee grapevine   6. Visit to plant employment office
    2. Newspaper ads   7. High school visits by company
    3. Neighborhood recruiting by company   8. Job fairs
    4. Government Employment Service 9. Other (indicate)
    5. Community agency

26. The <u>selection methods</u> in this plant (testing, interviewing,   1   2   3   4   5   6   26._____
    criteria, and so forth) <u>are fair</u>.

27. The employment office does <u>not discriminate</u> against blacks.   1   2   3   4   5   6   27._____

28. <u>No preferential treatment</u> is given blacks by the employment   1   2   3   4   5   6   28._____
    office.

29. Most people from the slums really <u>want to work</u>.   1   2   3   4   5   6   29._____

30. It is good to recruit <u>more poor</u>.   1   2   3   4   5   6   30._____

31. The Company should make <u>special efforts</u> to recruit the poor   1   2   3   4   5   6   31._____
    (outreach).

32. All new employees should be required to <u>meet the same work</u>   1   2   3   4   5   6   32._____
    <u>standards</u> as other employees.

TRAINING

33. I received <u>adequate training</u> in how to do this job.   1   2   3   4   5   6   33._____

34. My <u>foreman or trainer helps me</u> in learning my job.   1   2   3   4   5   6   34._____

35. My fellow <u>employees help me</u> in learning my job.   1   2   3   4   5   6   35._____

36. I feel I am getting adequate <u>training for jobs above me</u>   1   2   3   4   5   6   36._____
    which I could be promoted to.

EDUCATIONAL AND SOCIAL TRAINING HARD-CORE

*37. <u>Educational</u> training (reading, arith., etc.) has helped me   1   2   3   4   5   6   37._____
     (others) <u>as a person</u>.

*38. Educational training has helped me (others) <u>to do my job</u>   1   2   3   4   5   6   38._____
     with the company.

*39. <u>Social</u> education (use of credit, bus, "grooming", etc.)   1   2   3   4   5   6   39._____
     has helped me (others) <u>as a person</u>.

*40. Social education has helped me (others) <u>to do my job</u> better   1   2   3   4   5   6   40._____
     with the company.

*41. The special <u>job skill training</u> I received has helped me   1   2   3   4   5   6   41._____
     <u>to do my job with the company</u>.

---

*Items with asterisk refer only to severely disadvantaged or hard-core trainees, or to those who know about them
and work with them. They were scored at Raytheon-Bedford only.   3/12/69

** Also note that items 25, 56, and 57 are not attitudes and that item
   72 is the coder's judgment based on the entire interview.

		very Fav.	Fav.	Neut.	un- Fav.	v.un- Fav.	No Resp.	

SUPPORT PROGRAMS

42.	Do you feel you can take a <u>personal problem to your foreman</u>? Yes (1) No (2)						6	42.____
43.	Have you received any <u>counselling</u> here in the plant? Yes (1) No (2)						6	43.____
44.	Counselling here <u>helps me</u> and others in our work.	1	2	3	4	5	6	44.____
*45.	A <u>buddy</u> or personal <u>advisor helps me as a person</u>.	1	2	3	4	5	6	45.____
*46.	A buddy or personal advisor helps me to <u>do my job better</u>.	1	2	3	4	5	6	46.____
*47.	Support programs are <u>necessary and helpful</u> to the previously unemployed.	1	2	3	4	5	6	47.____

PROMOTION

48.	I would <u>like a promotion</u>. Yes (1) No (2)						6	48.____
49.	I have a <u>fair chance to get promoted</u> to a better paying job.	1	2	3	4	5	6	49.____
50.	Blacks have an <u>equal chance of being promoted</u> to a better paying job in this plant.	1	2	3	4	5	6	50.____
51.	Blacks get <u>preferential treatment</u> for promotion.	1	2	3	4	5	6	51.____
52.	<u>Seniority is an obstacle</u> in the way of my promotion.	1	2	3	4	5	6	52.____
53.	Seniority as a basis for <u>layoffs</u> is just.	1	2	3	4	5	6	53.____
54.	I <u>like</u> having a <u>union</u> here.	1	2	3	4	5	6	54.____
55.	I am satisfied with the <u>union's leadership</u>.	1	2	3	4	5	6	55.____

INTERPERSONAL RELATIONS

56.	My <u>work group</u> has <u>both blacks</u> and whites. Yes (1) No (2)						6	56.____
57.	There are some formerly <u>hard-core</u> trainees in my work group. Yes (1) No (2) Do not know (3)						6	57.____
58.	I <u>get along</u> well with my <u>foreman</u>.	1	2	3	4	5	6	58.____
59.	A significant number of men in my work group would be <u>uncomfortable</u> with a <u>black foreman</u>.	1	2	3	4	5	6	59.____
60.	<u>I could work well</u> for a black foreman.	1	2	3	4	5	6	60.____
61.	A black foreman would <u>work out</u> here.	1	2	3	4	5	6	61.____
62.	My <u>boss does not racially discriminate</u>.	1	2	3	4	5	6	62.____
63.	My <u>boss</u> does <u>not</u> give blacks <u>preference</u>.	1	2	3	4	5	6	63.____
64.	I can <u>work well with blacks</u>.	1	2	3	4	5	6	64.____
65.	There may be a few exceptions, but in general Negroes are <u>pretty much alike</u>.	1	2	3	4	5	6	65.____
66.	Blacks <u>do their jobs as well</u> here on the average as other employees.	1	2	3	4	5	6	66.____
67.	Blacks, whites, etc. <u>get along</u> well here <u>on the job</u>.	1	2	3	4	5	6	67.____
68.	Blacks and whites get together at <u>lunch and breaks</u>.	1	2	3	4	5	6	68.____
69.	Blacks and whites here get along socially <u>outside the plant</u>.	1	2	3	4	5	6	69.____
70.	I feel that I am a <u>real part</u> of the firm--a member of a <u>team</u>.	1	2	3	4	5	6	70.____
71.	I would like my <u>boy or girl</u> to work for the <u>company</u>.	1	2	3	4	5	6	71.____
72.	This person is <u>prejudiced</u> against blacks. (coder's judgment)	1	2	3	4	5	6	72.____

CCSS FORD PROJECT HOURLY PAID SAMPLE

CONTINGENCY TABLE NO. 50   JUNE 5, 1970

CELL PERCENT BASED ON COLUMN SUM
ALL COUNTS ARE WEIGHTED

VAR 3 Q5Q18 LOCATION BL WH

VAR 51 Q50 BL PROM CHANCE FAIR	LYNCH BLACK	LYNCH WHITE	MEMPHS BLACK	MEMPHS WHITE	CHICGO BLACK	CHICGO WHITE	BUFFLO BLACK	BUFFLO WHITE	TOTAL	PERCENT
VERY FAVBLE		16.9	4.9		16.3	3.1	3.4			
		221	12		413	8	120	773	8.0
FAVOR-ABLE	45.1	78.2	36.6	79.9	66.0	74.0	51.2	76.4		
	147	1021	86	373	719	1868	131	2686	7031	72.4
NEUTRL	28.1	4.9	31.7	20.1	4.3	4.8	35.3	20.1		
	91	64	74	94	46	122	90	708	1290	13.3
UNFAV-ORABLE	20.1		26.7		17.0	4.8	10.4			
	65		63		185	122	26		462	4.8
VERY UNFAV	6.7				12.8					
	22				139				161	1.7
TOTAL	325	1306	235	467	1090	2524	255	3514	9716	
PERCENT	3.3	13.4	2.3	4.8	11.2	26.0	2.6	36.2		100.0

CHISQUARE STATISTIC = 3354.623** WITH 28 DEGREES OF FREEDOM → (SIGNIFICANT AT THE 0. LEVEL)
LAMBDA (ASYMMETRIC) = 0.
LAMBDA (SYMMETRIC) = 0.069
GAMMA (ORDINAL)   = 0.007
TAU B STATISTIC   = 0.005
TAU C STATISTIC   = 0.005
SOMMERS D STATISTIC = 0.003
PHI COEFFICIENT   = 0.588
C COEFFICIENT   = 0.507
CRAMER V STATISTIC = 0.294

NO. OF MISSING UNITS = 1046

ANALYSIS OF VARIANCE BY CITY AND RACE - CHICAGO

APRIL 17, 1970 PAGE 63

COMPARISON OF GROUP 5 VS GROUP 6

VARIABLE DESCRIPTION	VAR NO.		BLACK GROUP 5	WHITE GROUP 6	DIFFERENCE	S.E.	D.F.	T-TEST	SIGNIFICANCE
G26 SELECT METH FAIR	VAR. 2	MEAN SD N	1.960 0.455 25	2.000 0. 25	-0.040	0.091	48.0	-0.440	(P= 0.662)
G33 MY TRAINING ADEQUATE	VAR 9	MEAN SD N	2.320 0.945 25	2.280 0.980 25	0.040	0.272	48.0	0.147	(P= 1.000) APPROX
G34 FOREMAN HELPS ME LEARN	VAR 10	MEAN SD N	2.375 0.924 24	2.043 0.638 23	0.332	0.233	45.0	1.426	(P= 0.161)
G43 I HAVE HAD COUNSEL	VAR 14	MEAN SD N	1.875 0.338 24	1.667 0.483 21	0.208	0.123	43.0	1.693	(P= 0.098)
G46 I WANT A PROMOTION	VAR 15	MEAN SD N	1.083 0.282 24	1.375 0.495 24	-0.292	0.116	46.0	-2.509**	(P= 0.016)
G52 SNORITY OBSTCL PROM	VAR 19	MEAN SD N	2.792 1.318 24	4.043 0.367 23	-1.252	0.285	45.0	-4.393***	(P= 0.000)
G59 GRP UNCOMF BL FORMN	VAR 24	MEAN SD N	3.619 0.805 21	3.458 0.779 24	0.161	0.236	43.0	0.680	(P= 0.500)
G68 BL.WH MEET AT LUNCH	VAR 33	MEAN SD N	3.000 1.183 21	3.826 0.717 23	-0.826	0.292	42.0	-2.829**	(P= 0.007)
G69 BL.WH MEET OUTSIDE	VAR 34	MEAN SD N	3.941 1.029 17	3.952 0.740 21	-0.011	0.287	36.0	-0.039	(P= 1.000) APPROX
G72 PERSON PREJUDICED	VAR 37	MEAN SD N	4.400 0.500 25	3.560 1.003 25	0.840	0.224	48.0	3.747***	(P= 0.000)
RACIAL TOLERANCE	VAR 38	MEAN SD N	4.207 0.299 25	3.623 0.527 25	0.584	0.121	48.0	4.815***	(P= 0.000)
COMPANY, BOSS, WORK STAT	VAR 39	MEAN SD N	3.333 0.731 25	3.758 0.381 25	-0.424	0.165	48.0	-2.574*	(P= 0.013)
PRO-UNION INDEX	VAR 40	MEAN SD N	3.460 0.900 25	3.312 0.976 24	0.147	0.268	47.0	0.550	(P= 0.585)
HIRE MORE POOR INDEX	VAR 41	MEAN SD N	4.007 0.519 25	3.160 0.870 24	0.847	0.204	47.0	4.157***	(P= 0.000)

FACTOR ANALYZE SELECTED FORD PROJECT VARIABLES

ROTATION NO. 2 ROTATED FACTOR LOADINGS ORTHOGONAL VARIMAX ROTATION BY VARIABLE

VARIABLE DESCRIPTION	VAR	NO.	1	2	3	COMMUNALITY
Q24 I LIKE MY JOB	VAR	1	.110	.684	.070	.485
Q26 SELECT METH FAIR	VAR	2	.019	.321	.238	.160
Q27 BL NOT DISC EM OFC	VAR	3	.100	.404	.151	.196
Q28 BL NOT PREF EM CFC	VAR	4	.458	.088	-.161	.243
Q29 PJR WANT TO WORK	VAR	5	.462	.061	-.086	.224
Q30 SHD RECRUT MORE POOR	VAR	6	.553	.029	-.145	.328
Q31 CMP SPEC RECRUT GOOD	VAR	7	.571	.159	-.004	.351
Q32 ALL SAME STANDARDS	VAR	8	.279	.230	.154	.154
Q33 MY TRAINING ADEQUATE	VAR	9	.250	.484	-.346	.416
Q34 FORMAN HELPS ME LERN	VAR	10	.255	.433	-.368	.388
Q35 FELLOWS HELP ME LERN	VAR	11	.005	.510	-.097	.270
Q36 AM TRAINED FOR PROMO	VAR	12	.002	.485	-.075	.241
Q42 ASK FORMN PERS PROB	VAR	13	-.038	.607	-.073	.375
Q43 I HAVE HAD COUNSEL	VAR	14	-.004	.228	.167	.080
Q48 I WANT A PROMOTION	VAR	15	.187	.171	.047	.067
Q49 MY PROM CHANCE FAIR	VAR	16	.052	.539	.126	.309
Q50 BL PROM CHANCE FAIR	VAR	17	.343	.528	.278	.473
Q51 EL GET PROM PREFRNCE	VAR	18	.587	.045	.331	.457
Q52 SNORITY OBSTCL PROM	VAR	19	.247	.352	-.195	.222
Q53 SNORITY LAYOFFS FAIR	VAR	20	-.108	.366	-.012	.146
Q54 I LIKE UNION	VAR	21	-.114	.108	.636	.429
Q55 UNION LEADERS GOOD	VAR	22	.066	.173	.595	.389
Q58 I GET ALONG FORMN	VAR	23	.037	.720	-.063	.523
Q59 GRP UNCOMF BL FORMN	VAR	24	.326	.241	.444	.362
Q60 I ACCEPT BL FORMN	VAR	25	.635	.035	.196	.443
Q61 BL FOREMAN WORK OUT	VAR	26	.486	.121	.309	.347
Q62 BOSS NOT DISCRIM BL	VAR	27	.058	.495	-.254	.314
Q63 BOSS NOT PREFER BL	VAR	28	.455	.061	-.214	.256
Q64 I WORK WELL WITH BL	VAR	29	.691	.106	-.009	.489
Q65 NEGROES ALIKE	VAR	30	.775	.033	-.100	.611
Q66 BL DO JOBS AS WELL	VAR	31	.700	.052	-.019	.493
Q67 BL, WH GET ALONG JOB	VAR	32	.470	.215	.251	.330
Q68 BL,WH MEET AT LUNCH	VAR	33	.295	.164	.400	.273
Q69 BL,WH MEET OUTSIDE	VAR	34	.258	.115	.289	.163
Q70 I AM PART OF TEAM	VAR	35	.230	.694	.052	.538
Q71 MY CHILD WORK HERE	VAR	36	-.180	.534	-.108	.329
Q72 PERSON PREJUDICED	VAR	37	-.695	-.019	-.244	.543
SUMS OF SQUARES			5.341	4.772	2.305	12.418

APPENDIX B

Comparative statistical tables

In this section we have assembled tables on several major attitude items for the reader who wants to compare the different plants. The tables must be interpreted in the light of local circumstances, types of work, and employee differences in age, sex, and length of service presented in each case study. With this caution, the tables are useful for quick comparison. An explanation of the indices can be found in Appendix A. For our interpretation of the data, see Chapters 4 through 7.

Table B-1. Job Performance of Hourly Blacks
Percentage of foremen who judged that blacks do at least as well as the average worker
Four plants

	Chicago N = 9	Lynchburg N = 9	Buffalo N = 8	Memphis N = 8	Total N = 34
Quantity of Work	89%	100%	88%	100%	94%
Quality of Work	78	100	100	87	91
Attendance	44	89	75	75	71
Promptness	44	89	88	75	76
Accepting Responsibility	67	89	100	62	82
Personality at Work	100	100	100	100	100
Discipline at Work	78	78	100	100	91
Ability to Learn Job	100	100	75	62	85
Promotability	100	78	62	62	76

Most employees at each plant are relatively satisfied (Table B-2), but there is a significant variation between the four plants, with the highest scores at Lynchburg. There is also a significant variation within two plants, with blacks less favorable at Lynchburg and Chicago. Older whites seem *less*

322   Appendix B

Table B-2. *Company, Boss, Work Satisfaction Index*
Four plants by race and age

	CHICAGO			LYNCHBURG			BUFFALO			MEMPHIS		
	Young	Old	Combined	Young	Old	Combined	Young	Old	Combined	Young	Old	Combined
Black	3.0	3.9	3.3	3.6	3.6	3.6	3.3	3.6	3.5	3.4	3.4	3.4
White	3.9	3.7	3.8	4.0	3.8	3.8	3.7	3.5	3.5	3.7	3.4	3.4

(Five-point scale: 5 very favorable, 1 very unfavorable.)
(Young: 29 years and under; Old: 30 and above.)

Table B-3. *Tolerance of Blacks in the Work Setting Index*
Four plants by race and age

	CHICAGO			LYNCHBURG			BUFFALO			MEMPHIS		
	Young	Old	Combined	Young	Old	Combined	Young	Old	Combined	Young	Old	Combined
Black	4.2	4.2	4.2	4.3	4.4	4.4	4.0	4.0	4.0	4.0	4.0	4.0
White	4.0	3.5	3.6	4.1	3.9	4.0	3.5	3.7	3.7	3.7	3.5	3.5

(Five-point scale: 5 very favorable; 1 very unfavorable.)

Table B-4. *Pro-Union Index*
Four plants by race and age

	CHICAGO			LYNCHBURG			BUFFALO			MEMPHIS		
	Young	Old	Combined	Young	Old	Combined	Young	Old	Combined	Young	Old	Combined
Black	3.3	3.8	3.5	1.9	2.6	2.3	3.7	3.4	3.5	2.8	3.3	2.9
White	4.0	3.2	3.3	1.8	1.8	1.8	3.5	3.4	3.4	3.4	3.2	3.2

(Five-point scale: 5 very favorable; 1 very unfavorable.)

Appendix B

positive than younger whites in their relations with the company while in the North older blacks are *more* favorable than younger blacks. However, this age difference is statistically significant only at Chicago and for blacks.

This index (Table B-3) is mainly relevant to white attitudes and shows whites quite open toward black co-workers and supervisors at all plants, with Lynchburg most favorable. Younger whites at every plant, except Buffalo, were more tolerant than older whites.

With the exception of Lynchburg, which is not unionized, both blacks and whites were positive toward the union, with blacks slightly more favorable (Table B-4). Employees in northern plants were slightly more favorable than in southern plants (which employ mostly women). Older whites were less favorable toward the union than younger whites, while older blacks were more pro-union than younger blacks. Again the one exception is Buffalo.

Table B-5 gives additional data relevant to Chapter 3 and Table 3-2. In the middle of the best economic decade in American history, black employment rose from 3.8 per cent to 6.4 per cent, but with most of the improvement at the blue collar level and for women.

Table B–5. Black Employment by Sex and Occupation, 1964, 1966, and 1967
Electrical Manufacturing Industry

Occupational Group	ALL EMPLOYEES 1964	1966	1967	MALE 1964	1966	1967	FEMALE 1964	1966	1967
Officials and managers	0.3	0.4	0.6	0.3	0.4	0.6	0.5	1.8	2.5
Professionals	0.6	0.7	0.8	0.6	0.7	0.8	1.5	2.0	1.9
Technicians	1.7	2.2	2.7	1.7	2.2	2.6	2.2	2.6	3.8
Sales workers	0.4	0.2	0.2	0.2	0.2	0.2	2.0	1.2	0.8
Office and clerical	1.8	2.0	2.4	1.8	2.3	3.0	1.7	1.8	2.1
Total white collar	1.1	1.3	1.6	0.9	1.2	1.4	1.7	1.8	2.2
Craftsmen	2.1	3.0	3.8	1.8	2.6	3.3	7.2	7.6	10.0
Operatives	6.1	8.4	9.9	5.9	8.5	9.7	6.3	8.3	10.1
Laborers	6.1	9.9	11.9	7.1	11.4	13.9	4.8	8.6	10.3
Service workers	16.2	17.5	18.5	15.9	17.8	18.7	18.1	15.7	17.0
Total blue collar	5.6	7.8	9.3	5.1	7.3	8.5	6.2	8.4	10.2
Total	3.8	5.4	6.4	3.2	4.6	5.3	5.0	6.8	8.3

Source: 1964: Data in authors' possession.
1966: U.S. Equal Employment Opportunity Commission, *Job Patterns for Minorities and Women in Private Industry,* 1966, Report No. 1 (Washington: The Commission, 1968), Part II.
1967: *Ibid.*, 1967. Report No. 2 (1970) Vol. 1.

APPENDIX C

Structure and manpower of the electrical industry

The electrical manufacturing industry is most diversified. Its products range from radios, televisions, and communication equipment to electronic components, industrial and transportation control devices, and household appliances such as refrigerators, ranges, and washing machines. Wiring devices, lights of all sizes, tubes, switchgears, transformers, motors, batteries, huge turbines, and tiny diodes and transistors are all included.

For the tables in this book we define the electrical industry according to the U.S. Office of Statistical Standards, Standard Industrial Classification (SIC) No. 36: "establishments engaged in manufacturing machinery, apparatus, and supplies for the generation, storage, transmission, transformation, and utilization of electrical energy."[1] Establishments are individual plants and offices classified by product regardless of the primary business of the company.

We present our company data as based on all the plants in a given company, even though some plants produce goods that do not fall within the SIC No. 36 category. The firms are those *primarily* engaged in electrical manufacturing. General Electric and Westinghouse, for example, are designated "electrical manufacturers" although they both manufacture many nonelectrical products such as jet engines, steam turbines, and chemicals. The

[1] *Standard Industrial Classification Manual* (Washington, D.C.: U.S. Government Printing Office, 1967), p. 168, Executive Office of the President/Bureau of the Budget, prepared by the Office of Statistical Standards. We shall use the terms "electrical machinery," "electrical manufacturing," and "electrical equipment and supplies" to describe the same industry.

Appendix C

tables exclude such corporate giants as General Motors, Ford, and Union Carbide, even though they are important producers of some electrical products, because their primary interests are elsewhere.

INDUSTRIAL STRUCTURE

The electrical industry is one of the largest American industries. Table C-1 shows that in 1967 it handled shipments valued at over $40 billion and employed more than 1.8 million people, over 9 percent of the total employment in manufacturing.

Table C–1. Number of Employees, Value Added, and Value of Shipments, 1967
Electrical Manufacturing and All Manufacturers

	Total Employees (number)	Value Added by Manufacture ($1,000)	Value of Shipments ($1,000)
All manufacturing	19,398,000	259,301,000	554,564,000
Electrical machinery	1,884,000	24,855,000	43,606,000
Percent Electrical of Total	9.7	9.6	7.9

Source: U.S. Bureau of the Census, *Annual Survey of Manufactures*, Preliminary Report for 1967.

The leading position of the electrical industry in relation to other large industries is apparent in Table C-2. Electrical is fourth of the seven leading American industrial groups in adding value to its products. It is *second* in employment. Moreover, as we shall indicate later, the growth rate of electrical manufacture is such that the industry is likely to move upward in the future. The only "industry" that exceeds electrical machinery in employment is "transportation equipment," a statistical amalgam of automobiles, aerospace, shipbuilding, and other diverse industries that have little in common.

Table C–2. Number of Employees and Value Added, 1967
Electrical Manufacturing and Selected Industries

SIC Code	Industry Group	Total Employees (Number)	Rank	Value Added ($1,000)	Rank
37	Transportation Equipment	1,890,000	1	28,901,000	1
36	Electrical Machinery	1,884,000	2	24,855,000	4
35	Machinery Except Electrical	1,872,000	3	27,697,000	2
20	Food	1,654,000	4	26,352,000	3
34	Fabricated Metals	1,307,000	5	17,054,000	7
33	Primary Metals	1,283,000	6	20,148,000	6
28	Chemicals	854,000	7	23,440,000	5

Source: U.S. Bureau of Census, *Annual Survey of Manufactures*, Preliminary Report, 1967.

The size of the electrical manufacturing industry is further exemplified by an examination of the data in Table C-3. The four largest companies employed 873,619 persons in 1969—5.9 percent of the 14,813,809 employed by the 500 largest manufacturing companies; the fifteen largest employed 9.4 percent of the total employment of the 500.[2]

LARGE FIRM DOMINANCE

Like many basic American industries, the electrical industry is dominated by a small number of corporate giants. Although there are approximately 10,000 American companies in the electrical industry, the eight largest firms produce more than 90 percent of total sales in about a third of the electrical product groupings. In only seven groups do they produce less than 50 percent. The eight largest, for example, produce 91 percent of the household refrigerators and 98 percent of the batteries.[3]

Employment is similarly concentrated. With total employment in the industry close to 2 million, 90 percent of the companies hire fewer than 100 employees. About 167 companies employ more than 1,000 people.[4] The Big Four with more than 800,000 employees (see Table C-3), although not all working in the electrical industry, have a large minority of total electrical employment.

The concentration of an industry in a few key firms gives to the top managements of those companies opportunities for leadership far greater than those of the small or even the middle-sized firms. Clearly, their policies directly affect greater numbers of people and are most widely noted by other businessmen.

Large company size also allows managers greater flexibility in planning. Table C-3 shows the managers of the Big Four controlling approximately $14 billion in assets. The managers of such resources can afford to make larger investments of time and money for long-term benefits and strategic decisions involving growth, market share, and the security of the enterprise. These managers have long-range perspectives that they can apply to manpower planning and to the education and upgrading of the labor force, including Negroes. They have more resources to commit to the effort.

A large industry can often exercise a leadership role Eckstein and Wilson[5] identify electrical machinery as one of the key groups in collective bargaining which, they say, influences wage rates in other industries. Similarly, the electrical industry's policies and practices on Negro employment may influence patterns developing elsewhere in the economy, although other industries, of course, have different economic opportunities and manpower requirements.

[2] *Fortune*, May 1970, pp. 184–200.
[3] *Concentration Ratios in Manufacturing* (Washington: U.S. Government Printing Office, 1967).
[4] Data in authors' possession.
[5] Otto Eckstein and Thomas A. Wilson, "The Determination of Money Wages in American Industry," *Quarterly Journal of Economics*, Vol. LXXVI, August 1962, pp. 384–385, 394.

Table C-3. The Fifteen Largest Electrical Manufacturing Companies, 1969

Company and 1969 Rank Among Industrial Corporations	Headquarters	Sales	Assets	Net Income	Invested Capital	Number of Employees	Net Income as a Percent of Sales	Net Income as a Percent of Invested Capital
		Thousands of Dollars						
General Electric (4)	New York	8,447,965	6,007,490	278,015	2,539,977	400,000	3.3	10.9
Western Electric (11)	New York	4,883,221	3,171,867	227,025	2,006,248	203,608	4.6	11.3
Westinghouse Electric (17)	Pittsburgh	3,509,153	2,477,611	149,888	1,389,330	142,011	4.3	10.8
RCA (21)	New York	3,187,903	2,634,379	151,283	1,023,754	128,000	4.7	14.8
Singer (45)	New York	1,902,144	1,438,615	77,721	680,914	133,000	4.1	11.4
Honeywell (75)	Minneapolis	1,425,993	1,222,011	62,481	494,115	81,520	4.4	12.6
Raytheon (86)	Lexington, Mass.	1,285,134	538,836	35,232	259,825	53,300	2.7	13.6
Whirlpool (100)	Benton Harbor, Mich.	1,153,530	573,929	45,943	250,654	30,301	4.0	18.3
Motorola (132)	Franklin Park, Ill.	873,224	576,509	33,793	326,134	45,000	3.9	10.4
Texas Instruments (135)	Dallas	831,822	526,758	33,511	281,548	58,974	4.0	11.9
Zenith Radio (166)	Chicago	676,577	336,525	39,621	224,814	22,500	5.9	17.6
Emerson Electric (177)	St. Louis	628,427	397,380	49,935	280,526	25,800	7.9	17.8
McGraw-Edison (183)	Elgin, Ill.	609,102	360,706	32,971	280,398	25,000	5.4	11.8
North American Philips (199)	New York	548,960	418,785	27,424	218,452	18,000	5.0	12.6
Magnavox (204)	New York	539,843	284,824	39,107	173,347	20,100	7.2	22.6

Source: *Fortune*, Vol. LXXXI, May 1970, pp. 184–191.

GROWTH RATE

Size gives a static dimension to an industry but growth rate is a fundamental dynamic measure. Rowan, in his study, *The Negro in the Steel Industry*, points up the impact of rate of growth on employment of blacks. Employment in the basic steel industry is over half a million, but basic steel has not been a growth industry for the last ten years. Rowan asks: "How does an industry that is declining in terms of employment, and beset by financial, production, and marketing problems adjust to the contemporary problems of employing and upgrading the Negro sector of the labor force?"[6] Rowan finds that despite management's desire to improve minority employment patterns, the state of the steel industry has made improvement in employment and upgrading most difficult. Industry growth in sales and employment is almost always a prerequisite for solid accomplishment in placing and upgrading Negroes.[7]

The growth rate of electrical manufacturing is notable and enhances equal employment opportunities. Backman, writing of electrical manufacturing in the early 1960s, reports somewhat exuberantly of the industry's prior three decades:

> Since 1923 the growth [of the electrical manufacturing industry] has continued at an almost unbelievable rate. In thirty-five years [1958], value added by manufacture of electrical machinery has risen to $9.2 billion, more than eleven times as large as the 1923 total of $800 million —a tremendous increase even though in part this rise reflected the price inflation of the period. Total employment in 1958 was more than three times as large as in 1923. As compared with an output valued at $1.25 billion in 1923, total sales were $29.9 billion in 1958. The number of establishments increased from 1,782 in 1923 to 7,066 in 1958. Electric power consumption increased from 42.3 billion kilowatt hours in 1923 to 683.2 billion kilowatt hours in 1960, a sixteen-fold increase—and this is in physical terms and hence does not reflect price inflation.

> Regardless of the measurement used, the "extraordinary development" of the industry has continued despite the wide cyclical swings noted. The electrical machinery industry grew so rapidly after 1923 that by the late 1950's its relative share had doubled as compared with both all manufacturing and the entire economy. The electrical machinery industry has been one of the great growth industries in the United States. The beneficial effects of this growth have been reflected in more job

---

[6] Herbert R. Northrup, Richard L. Rowan, *et al.*, "Negro Employment in Basic Industry," *Studies of Negro Employment*, Vol. I (Philadelphia: Industrial Research Unit, Wharton School of Finance and Commerce, University of Pennsylvania, 1970), p. 234.

[7] The urban transit and shipbuilding industries have been exceptions to this rule. See Lester Rubin, "The Negro in the Shipbuilding Industry," *The Racial Policies of American Industry* (Philadelphia: Industrial Research Unit, Wharton School of Finance and Commerce, University of Pennsylvania, 1970), Report No. 17; and Philip W. Jeffress, "The Negro in the Urban Transit Industry," *The Racial Policies of American Industry, op. cit.*, Report No. 18.

opportunities, increasing productivity in our economy, a lightening of the worker's task and of the drudgery of the housewife, and better living for all of us as consumers.[8]

In the years between 1961 and 1965, the electrical machinery industry continued to achieve increases in output well above the average, along with nonelectrical machinery, instruments, primary metals, fabricated metals, lumber and wood products, transportation equipment, rubber and plastics, and chemicals.[9] Industry sales rose to $40.8 billion in 1966. *Fortune's* 500 in 1969 shows a 9 percent increase in sales for appliances and electronics and an 18.2 percent increase in profits.[10]

This growth is quite likely to continue. Present electrical energy capacity may well be doubled by 1980.[11] An increase in production of electrical energy will generate demand for capital goods such as electrical generators and transmission and distribution equipment. Production of consumer goods, such as household appliances, is more subject to cyclical fluctuation, but growth in population and increases in per-capita income, plus rising consumer aspirations, are likely to maintain or to raise the demand for consumer goods.

Furthermore, the technology connected with electrical power has been one of the most rapidly advancing sectors of the engineering field. The industry has been intimately concerned with four of the basic technological innovations of the century: electricity as a source of productive power, radio-television communications, electronic computers and servomechanisms, and nuclear power generation. The industrial products and consumer goods applications forthcoming from these innovations have not yet been exhausted if, indeed, the major potential has even been tapped. The evolution of new uses and new products connected with these innovations will make for growth in the electrical manufacturing industry both in sales and employment, and therefore opportunities for increased Negro employment.

There are three cautions, however: the close association of the electrical manufacturing industry with government and, in particular, with defense production; the rising tide of imports; and possible conflict over locations for electric power generating stations. In some sectors of the industry almost half the total shipments are for military orders or for space or aerospace usage. Several of the largest electrical machinery companies are large defense contractors, and for some of these firms the value of defense contracts alone amounts to 20 percent of their total sales. For Raytheon, defense amounted to

---

[8] Jules Backman, *The Economics of the Electrical Machinery Industry* (New York: New York University Press, 1962), p. 57.

[9] "The Production Expansion in Perspective," *Survey of Current Business*, U.S. Department of Commerce, Vol. 46, January 1966, p. 14.

[10] *Fortune*, May 1970, pp. 200–201.

[11] *Historical Statistics of the Electrical Utility Industry* (New York: Edison Electrical Institute, 1962), Sec. 1, p. 1. See also *Edison Electric Institute Statistical Yearbook of the Electrical Utility Industry* (New York: Edison Electric Institute, 1969).

39 percent in 1969.[12] Since 1969 our defense commitments have substantially declined. This has already significantly reduced production in certain areas of electrical manufacturing.

The import problem is already severe. Few radios are now manufactured in this country, and Japan's rising electronic technology threatens American jobs in appliances, wiring devices, television, and electronic circuitry, among other branches of the industry.

Finally, if we have unresolved or prolonged conflict between electric utilities and conservationists over locations of generating plants, or if we have delayed rulings by public agencies, electric power shortages could slow down the growth of the industry.

MANPOWER

As we have seen in Chapter 2, employment in the electrical machinery industry has grown significantly (see Figure C-1) since 1930. During World War II, employment in the industry more than doubled. In the postwar period, although it declined slightly, employment was buoyed up almost to wartime levels by pent-up consumer demand for appliances and industrial demand for utility apparatus equipment, motors, and control mechanisms. The 1950s saw an uneven advance in jobs, but a substantial one nevertheless, amounting to nearly one-half million jobs. In the 1960s a slightly larger total increase brought jobs in the industry to nearly 2 million. Although employment has declined from one year to another and suffers when general demand slackens, the trend is definitely upward.

As a matter of fact, Figure C-2 shows that the electrical manufacturing industry has accounted for a constantly growing share both of total manufacturing and of durable goods employment. In the period 1947–1969 employment in all manufacturing increased from 15,545,000 to 20,121,000, a gain of 29.4 percent, and employment in durable goods manufacturing increased from 8,385,000 to 11,880,000, an increase of 41.7 percent. Electrical manufacturing, however, grew at a faster rate than either durable goods and total manufacturing, as seen in Figure C-2. Electrical employment in the same period rose from 1,035,000 to 2,038,000, an increase of 96.9 percent. If its past growth rates are projected forward, the industry may expect an increase of approximately 45,000 new jobs per year during the decade of the 1970s.[13]

---

[12] Juan Cameron, "The Case for Cutting Defense Spending," *Fortune*, August 1969, p. 74.

[13] This extrapolation is based on the post-World War II trend in the industry, from 1947 to 1969. Such an average increase should not be anticipated every year. But our estimate is modest. In the decade of the 1960s, annual changes of employment in the electrical industry ranged from a drop of 10,000 (1963–1964) to a rise of 250,000 (1965–1966), and the average annual increase in this decade was 64,200. Of course, sliding defense requirements and rising imports could dampen this forecast.

Appendix C

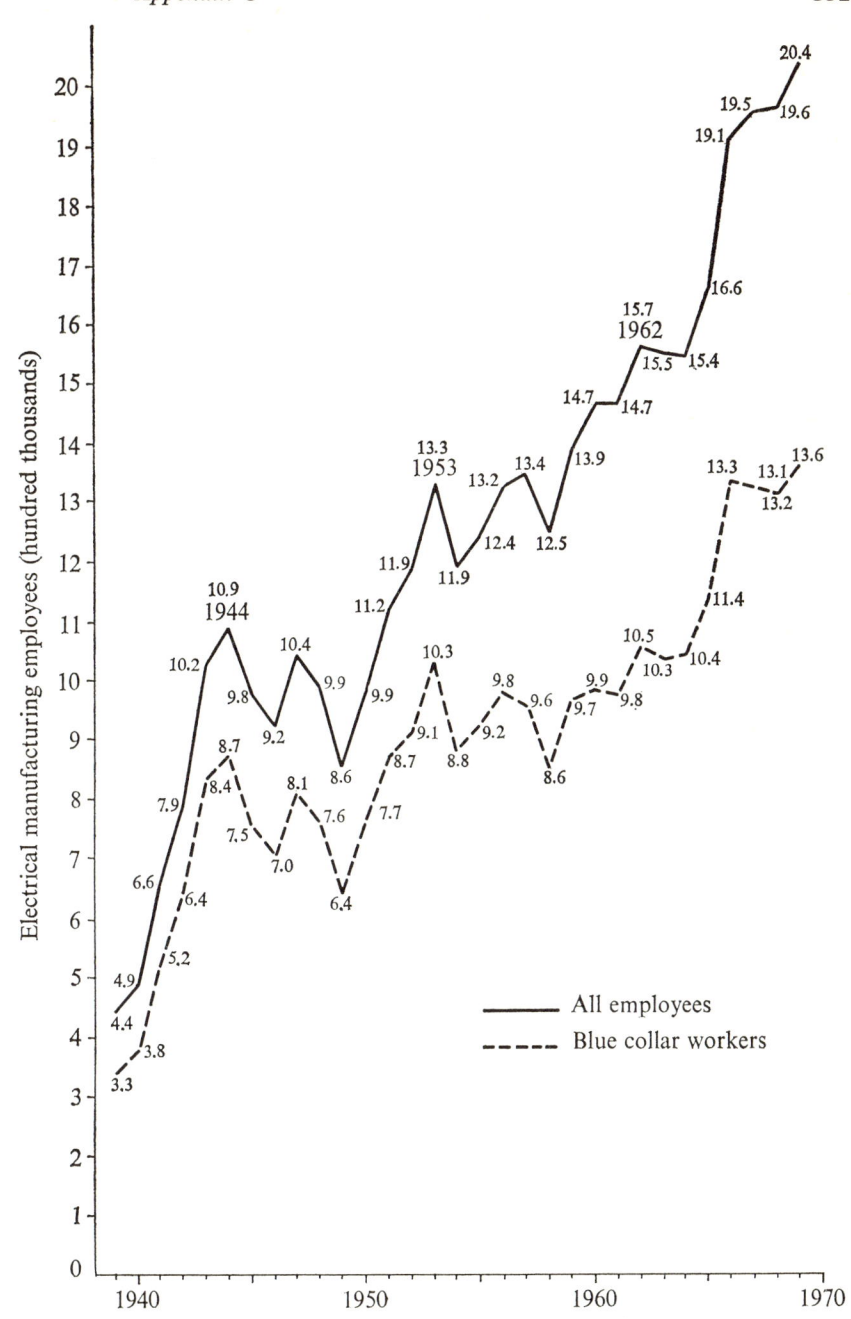

FIGURE C-1. **Growth of Total and Blue Collar Manpower Electrical Manufacturing Industry 1939–1969**

Source: Data for 1939–1968 from *Employment and Earnings Statistics for the United States, 1909–1968*, Bureau of Labor Statistics and the United States Department of Labor, August 1968. Data for 1969 from *Employment and Earnings Statistics for the United States* (Washington: Government Printing Office, March 1969), Tables B2- and B-3.

FIGURE C-2. **Electrical Manufacturing's Share of Total Manufacturing and Durable Goods Employment 1947–1969**

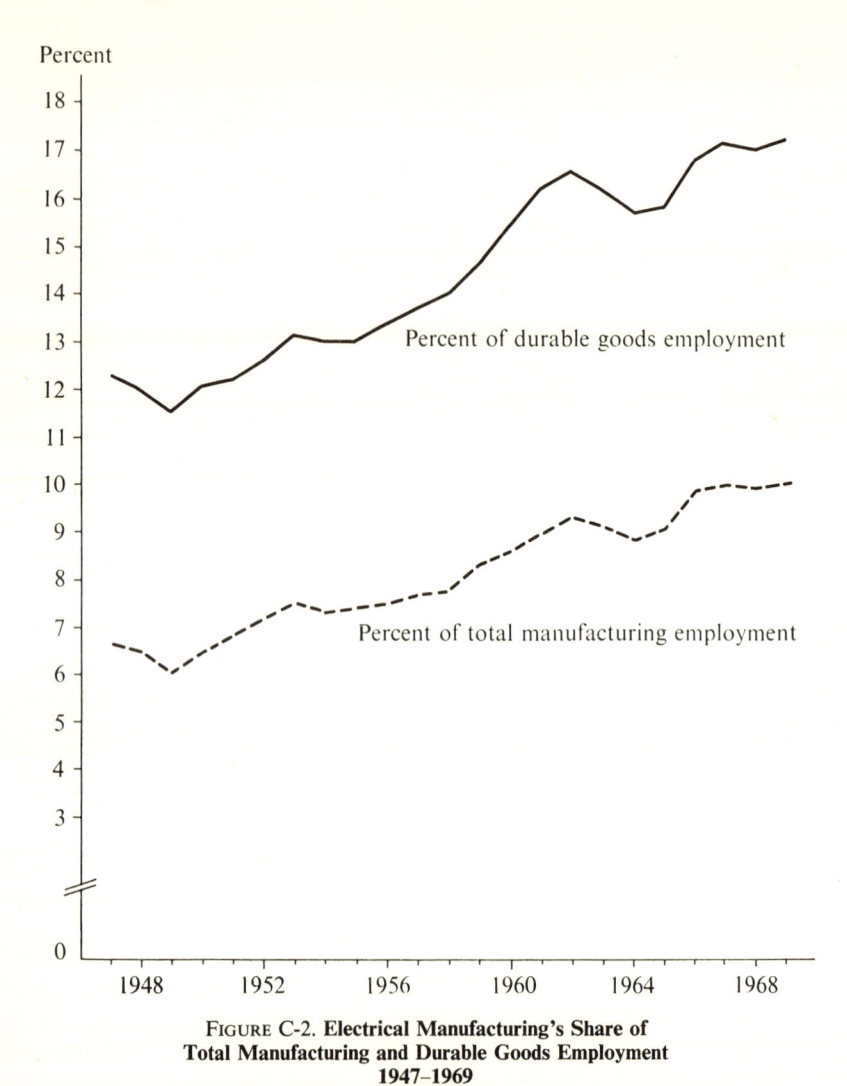

Source: U.S. Bureau of Labor Statistics, *Employment and Earnings Statistics for the United States, 1909–1968*, pp. 48, 55–56, 302; and *Employment and Earnings*, March 1969 and 1970, Table B-2 (Washington: Government Printing Office).

LABOR TURNOVER

Table C-4 shows the rate of monthly accessions and separations per 100 employees in the industry as compared with all manufacturing for selected recent years. Turnover is lower in the electrical industry than in all manufacturing, indicating that electrical manufacturing jobs are generally considered desirable. There are, however, sufficient separations to provide a substantial

Table C-4. *Average Monthly Turnover, 1958–1969 Electrical Manufacturing and All Manufacturers per 100 Employees*

	ELECTRICAL					ALL MANUFACTURING				
Year	Accessions	New Hires	Separations	Quits	Layoffs	Year	Accessions	New Hires	Separations	Quits	Layoffs
1958	3.3	1.5	3.5	1.0	2.1	1958	3.6	1.7	4.1	1.1	2.6
1959	4.0	2.6	3.2	1.4	1.2	1959	4.2	2.6	4.1	1.5	2.0
1960	3.2	2.0	3.5	1.2	1.6	1960	3.8	2.2	4.3	1.3	2.4
1961	3.6	2.1	3.3	1.2	1.4	1961	4.1	2.2	4.0	1.2	2.2
1962	3.6	2.4	3.3	1.4	1.1	1962	4.1	2.5	4.1	1.4	2.0
1963	3.1	1.9	3.4	1.3	1.4	1963	3.9	2.4	3.9	1.4	1.8
1964	3.3	2.1	3.2	1.2	1.2	1964	4.0	2.6	3.9	1.5	1.7
1965	3.9	2.9	3.1	1.6	0.8	1965	4.3	3.1	4.1	1.9	1.4
1966	4.7	3.8	3.8	2.3	0.5	1966	5.0	3.8	4.6	2.6	1.2
1967	3.6	2.5	4.0	2.0	1.1	1967	4.4	3.3	4.6	2.3	1.4
1968	3.7	2.7	3.8	2.0	0.8	1968	4.6	3.5	4.6	2.5	1.2
1969	4.0	3.1	4.0	2.3	0.7	1969	4.7	3.7	4.9	2.7	1.2

Source: U.S. Bureau of Labor Statistics, *Employment and Earnings Statistics for the United States, 1909–1968* (Washington: U.S. Government Printing Office, 1968) pp. 304–305; and *Employment and Earnings*, April 1969 and March 1970, Table D-2.

number of openings per year. If we estimate, for example, a separation rate of 3.5 per 100 employees and a layoff rate of 1.2 (which have been the averages for the industry since 1958), we can estimate that 2.3 new employees per 100 employed are required to maintain labor requirements in the industry. Based on 1969 employment, this would mean that normal turnover creates around 50,000 job openings in the industry monthly.

OCCUPATIONAL DISTRIBUTION

Despite its scientific advances and the consequent corps of professional and technical personnel employed in the industry, the electrical manufacturing industry continues to need a large percentage of production workers. Thus, in 1939, 74.4 percent of the employees in the industry were classified as production workers; in 1969 this percentage had declined to 66.6. But the number of production workers had risen from about 320,000 to about 1,300,000.

Growth in the electrical industry has thus had a substantial and rounded impact on employment. Unlike other growth industries with high technology, such as petroleum and chemicals, electrical manufacturing remains labor intensive—that is, the ratio of labor to capital is relatively high. The *Fortune* survey for 1969 reports $15,028 of assets committed for each employee in appliances and electronics, putting the electrical industry only eighteenth of the twenty-two industries listed and far outstripped by petroleum refining, for example, with $98,403 for each employee, by chemicals with $31,417 for each employee, or even by farm and industrial machinery with $19,555.[14]

The reason for this is that in many sectors of electrical manufacturing hand assembly is still a common method of manufacture. In the capital goods area, such as turbine generators and transmission equipment, production is frequently engineered and manufactured for individual specifications. But the product of electronic circuitry with sophisticated designs and rigid tolerances requires hand labor and human skills. Even in household appliances and radio or television assembly where automation and printed circuitry have replaced much hand labor, inspection, hand assembly, and parts manufacturing are still necessary and provide many jobs.

Nevertheless, the high proportion of white collar positions remains a challenge. The technical requirements of these jobs and their impact on Negro employment were discussed in Chapter 3.

FEMALE EMPLOYMENT

We have noted that jobs in the industry may be easier to secure for Negro females than males. Forty percent of the total labor force is female, concentrated in two occupational groups—clerical and operatives. The former is, of

---

[14] *Fortune*, May 1970, p. 203.

Appendix C

course, typical of all industry. The latter is the result of the large number of light assembly and small apparatus wiring jobs that exist in the industry.

Electronic advances and the miniaturization of equipment since World War II have created demands for thousands of female assemblers. Expansion in this sector of the labor force has been substantial in recent years and promises to continue. Typically, such jobs require little training and are now readily open to black women.

EARNINGS AND WORKING CONDITIONS

Working conditions in the industry are varied, but are becoming increasingly more pleasant. Most older plants of the major producers have some of the drawbacks of age, but are well kept up and modernized. Newer ones of all companies, however, tend to be in agreeable surroundings, well laid out, and often air-conditioned because electronic components and instruments now require strict temperature and dust control in the manufacturing process. Table C-5 shows wages moderately good but below some other major manufacturing industries.

Table C-5. Electrical Machinery and Other Industries Average Hourly and Average Weekly Earnings, 1969

	Average Hourly Earnings	Average Weekly Earnings
	(in dollars)	
All manufacturing	$3.19	$129.51
Durable goods	3.38	139.59
Nondurable goods	2.91	115.53
Fabricated metal products	3.33	138.53
Electrical equipment and supplies	3.09	124.84
Motor vehicles and equipment	4.10	170.97
Aircraft and parts	3.87	161.77

Source: Bureau of Labor Statistics, *Employment and Earnings* March 1970, Table C-2.

UNIONIZATION

Unlike the steel, automotive, and rubber industries, the electrical industry is not organized by a single powerful and cohesive union. The International Union of Electrical, Radio, and Machine Workers (IUE) has the largest membership—315,000 or about 30 percent of the blue collar employment. The United Electrical and Radio Workers (UE) follows with 165,000 members. The International Brotherhood of Electrical Workers (IBEW), the International Association of Machinists and Aerospace Workers (IAM), and the United Automobile, Aerospace and Agricultural Implement Workers

(UAW) also represent substantial numbers, while smaller groups are represented by several other unions.

The reasons for this multiplicity of union affiliation are found in history. The IBEW, the oldest union in the field, was primarily a building and metal trades craft organization, and when it did extend membership to noncraft factory workers, it offered them only "Class B" membership—one vote per local, instead of one per individual in national union affairs. The claims of other craft unions in the American Federation of Labor also precluded successful organization before 1933, despite the willingness of President Gerard T. Swope and Chairman Owen D. Young, of the General Electric Company:

> In 1926, Swope actually arranged a meeting with William Green, President of the American Federation of Labor, at which Young was also present. Swope proposed that Green establish an industrial union for electrical manufacturing employees. Swope noted in this conversation that the General Electric employee representation plan could be a nucleus for such an organization, but emphasized General Electric's poor World War I experience with, and its firm opposition to dealing with a conglomeration of craft unions, with their internal jealousies and jurisdictional problems. Green was, of course, helpless to act because of craft union control of AFL policies, and never even communicated with Swope after the meeting.[15]

After the inauguration of Franklin D. Roosevelt as President in 1933, unions sprang up in the electrical industry, as in other industries, and rather easily won management recognition. The major electrical union was the UE, affiliated with the newly formed Committee of Industrial Organization (CIO), organized by the late John L. Lewis. Following the passage of the National Labor Relations (Wagner) Act, the UE won bargaining rights in most plants of the large producers, except for those of Western Electric.

The UE, however, was successfully infiltrated and controlled by adherents of the Communist Party line,[16] and was expelled from the CIO in 1949. The CIO simultaneously chartered the rival IUE, which became the dominant union in the industry. The IUE, however, neither totally eliminated UE, nor garnered all its once-organized plants. The IBEW won several, and is now very strong in Westinghouse and the dominant union in RCA and in Western Electric. The Communications Workers of America, with a strong base in the Bell System, also represents employees in Western Electric and, as noted, many other unions, such as the International Association of Machinists (IAM) and the United Auto Workers (UAW), are now active in

---

[15] Herbert R. Northrup, *Boulwarism* (Ann Arbor: Bureau of Industrial Relations, Graduate School of Business Administration, The University of Michigan, 1964), p. 13. See also David Loth, *Swope of GE* (New York: Simon and Shuster, 1950), pp. 168–172; and Frances Perkins, *The Roosevelt I Knew* (New York: The Viking Press, 1946), p. 309.

[16] For details, see Northrup, *Boulwarism, op. cit.*, pp. 13–19, 39–45; and Walter Galenson, *The CIO Challenge to the AFL. A History of the American Labor Movement, 1935–1941* (Cambridge: Harvard University Press, 1960), pp. 239–265.

Appendix C   337

**Table C-6. Employment by Region,[a] 1967
Electrical Manufacturing Industry**

	Number of Employees in Region	Percent of All Employees in Region[b]	Percent of White Collar Employees in Region
Northeast	613,799	32	38
New England	61,768	8	37
Middle Atlantic	452,031	24	39
Midwest (North Central)	669,947	35	28
South	312,306	16	35
Mountain	33,442	2	42
West Coast (Pacific)	299,521	15	57
Total	1,929,015	100	37

Source: U.S. Equal Employment Opportunity Commission, *Job Patterns for Minorities and Women in Private Industry, 1967*, Report No. 2 (Washington: The Commission, 1970), Vol. 1.

[a] Geographical definitions are as follows:

New England:	Connecticut, Maine, Massachusetts, New Hampshire, Rhode Island, Vermont.
Middle Atlantic:	New Jersey, New York, Pennsylvania.
Midwest (North Central):	Illinois, Indiana, Iowa, Kansas, Michigan, Minnesota, Missouri, Nebraska, Ohio, South Dakota, Wisconsin.
South:	Alabama, Arkansas, Florida, Georgia, Kentucky, Louisiana, Maryland, Mississippi, North Carolina, Oklahoma, South Carolina, Tennessee, Texas, Virginia, West Virginia.
Mountain:	Arizona, Colorado, Nevada, New Mexico, Utah.
West Coast (Pacific):	California, Oregon, Washington.

[b] The sum of the regional totals was used for national employment figure. Not included are data from companies not reporting to the EEOC or from states with less than 2,000 employees and/or 5 establishments.

the industry. Perhaps more significant is the fact that nonunion plants are relatively common in the electrical industry, and General Electric, which once welcomed unions into its plants, since 1946 has followed the vigorous collective bargaining policies initiated by its now retired vice president of employee relations, Lemuel R. Boulware.

REGIONAL DISTRIBUTION

The electrical industry is located throughout the United States with heaviest concentration in the Northeast and Midwest. Table C-6 shows that 32 percent of electrical employment is in the Northeast, primarily in New York, Pennsylvania, New Jersey, and Massachusetts. The Midwest accounts for 35 percent of electrical manufacturing employment with Illinois, Ohio, and Indiana employing by far the greatest numbers. Midwest employment ranges from 225.9 thousand in Illinois to 4.3 thousand in Kansas. The South has 16 percent of electrical employees, the Rocky Mountain region only 2 percent. Despite the small percentage of 16, the electrical industry is the fourth largest employer in the South, after textiles, chemicals, and food products. The West accounts for 15 percent of electrical employment with 287.9 thousand of the 299.5 thousand employed in California.

Subject index

ability and preferential treatment, 276
absenteeism and attendance
  cost of, 61
  foremen compare black with white workers on, 62, 117, 155, 193-194, 295, 321
  of disadvantaged workers, 243, 244, 248-250, 257, 262-263, 298
  of the New Work Force, 60-85
    assembly work and, 72, 74
    discipline and, 84
    foreman style and, 80-81, 249-250
    promotion and, 77
    restlessness and, 67
    work satisfaction and, 66
absentees
  characteristics of, at National Acme, 60-61, 72
  counseling for, 71-72, 245
Acme, *see* National Acme Electric
administrative positions, blacks in, 121, 124, 151
aerospace industry, blacks in, 40, 41
affirmative action on equal employment
  corporate officers, importance of commitment of, 34, 110, 179, 223, 224, 229, 263
  corporate policy on, 32-35, 224-225, 301-302
  federal influence on, *see* federal government
  goals, 225, 230
  implementing, 225-232, 296-297
  in the South, 35-36, 104-105, 110, 172, 179-180
  industry growth rate and, 328
  Office of Federal Contract Compliance requirements, 32-33, 228, 230, 279-280
  plant level, 58, 104-105, 110, 141, 152, 154, 172, 179-180, 301-302
  preferential treatment and, 275
  see also specific areas such as selection criteria; promoting and upgrading; testing
Afro-American Committee, 87-91

age
  attitudes toward foreman and, 79, 82
  attitudes toward promotion and, 75-77
  attitudes toward union and, 322
  of disadvantaged workers, 235
  of hourly workers, 56, 104, 146, 186
  racial tolerance and, 160-161, 197, 207, 212, 322
  work satisfaction and, 66, 72, 322
aircraft and parts industry, earnings in, 335
Albrook, Robert C., cited, 8*n*.
Alexander, W. C., cited, 58
Alice Through the Looking Glass (Lewis Carroll), 30
Alinsky, Saul, cited, 53
Allport, Gordon W., cited, 300*n*., quoted, 223-224
American racial attitudes during World War II, 21
apprentice program
  at National Acme, 78
  need for, 297
  see also training, job
arrest record
  as a selection criterion, 241
  percent disadvantaged workers with, 235
assembly, hand, 334
assembly line
  absenteeism on, 61
  attitudes of workers on, 63, 72-75, 82, 243, 245
  challenge to foreman of, 85-86
assets, income, sales, and employees of fifteen largest electrical companies, 326, 327
aspirations of the poor, 238, 239
attendance, *see* absenteeism and attendance
attendance incentives, 72
authority, New Work Force attitudes toward, 64, 65
automation, effect of on black opportunities, 22
automobile industry, blacks in, 14, 40, 41

339

Subject Index

Backman, Jules, cited 13*n*., quoted, 328-329
Berry, Nicholas, 134
Berwyn, Illinois, 50, 52, 53
Besag, Frank, quoted, 143, 144
bias in interviews, 307-310
Big Four electrical companies
   affirmative action commitment of, 34, 301-302
   assets, income, sales of, 327
   employment in, 325-327
   see also General Electric; Radio Corporation of America; Western Electric; *and* Westinghouse
birth rate, black, in Buffalo, New York, 143
birthplace
   effect on turnover of, 244
   of disadvantaged workers, 235
   of hourly workers, 56, 104, 146, 186
black experience compared to immigrant's, 2, 143
black families, 68, 239
black foremen, 36, 91-95, 122-124, 167-170, 211-213
   appointment of, in field study plants, 90, 124, 154, 213
   black reactions to, 92-95, 168-170
   perceptions of differ from white foremen, 62
   selecting, 95, 170
   southern white reactions to the prospect of, 122-124, 211-212
   view their role, 93-95, 167-168
   white reactions to, 91-92, 124, 167-170
black identity
   black prejudice against blacks, 168
   blacks can share values of Middle America, 172
   generation gap in, 51
   school desegregation and, 136
   see also social relations between black and white workers
Black Labor Federation of Chicago, 88
black leadership and migration north, 133
black men
   dissatisfaction with promotion at General Electric–Lynchburg, 119-122
   jobs for, 36
   number of in electrical manufacturing, 14, 38, 39
   percent of all men in electrical manufacturing, 323
   percent of all men in field study plants, 111, 112, 153, 189-191

   white women and, 23, 127, 130, 206, 208-209, 212
black militants
   at National Acme, 87-91
   attitudes of a, 162
   in Lynchburg, Virginia, 132
   in Memphis, Tennessee, 178
black neighborhoods, 50-51, 131-139, 143, 176-179
black pioneers
   first black electrician in a northern plant, 149-150
   first black man in a mid-South plant, 127
   first black mechanics in a Deep-South plant, 205-209
   first black production worker in a northern plant, 59
   first black technician in a Deep-South plant, 205-209
   first blacks in a Deep-South plant, 181-185, 219
   first salaried blacks, 96-97, 128, 151-152, 209, 267, 290
   selection of, 109, 157, 181, 182-183, 210, 219
black power, workers' attitudes toward, 86
black protest
   at National Acme, 87-91
   at Westinghouse Occupational Training School, 262
   in Lynchburg, Virginia, 139
   in Memphis, Tennessee, 175-176, 178
   national, 18, 31
black women
   number of in electrical manufacturing, 14, 38
   percent of all women in electrical manufacturing, 14, 38, 323
   percent of all women in field study plants, 111, 112, 153
black workers, number of
   in all manufacturing industries, 39
   in electrical manufacturing: *1930-1960*, 14; *1930*, 14; *1940*, 17; *1944*, 19; *1957-1959*, 26; *1960*, 22, 29; *1960-1969*, 30; *1964, 1966*, 323; *1967*, 39, 323; *1969*, 36-39; *1966* compared to *1969*, 42; company size, 39; model of, 41-42; projections of, 2, 43
   in field study plants, 54-55; 106, 110-112, 114; 151-154, 172; 187-189, 191, 219
   in Raytheon, 253
   in selected industries, 40, 41

influences on, *see* affirmative action; federal government; labor market; location, plant; *and* state fair employment practice commissions
blacks, index of white attitudes toward, 128, 160, 195, 311, 322, 323
Blauner, Robert, cited, 74
blue collar jobs, number of in electrical manufacturing industry, 22, 331, 334
blue collar workers, percent black
  in electrical manufacturing industry, 30, 36, 38, 40, 42, 43, 323
  in field study plants, 54-55; 111, 112, 114; 151-153, 187
  in selected industries, 40
Bohemians
  at National Acme, 49 ff.
  in Cicero, Illinois, 51
boredom on the assembly line, 73
Boulware, Lemuel R., former vice president, General Electric, 338
Broom, Leonard, cited, 2*n*.
Brown, Douglass, cited, 303
Buffalo, New York
  description of, 142-145
  field study of Westinghouse plant in, 141-173
Burnham, Donald, president, Westinghouse, 263

cablemaking, disadvantaged trained for, 253, 255
Cameron, Juan, cited 330*n*.
Cannell, Charles F., quoted, 308, 309
Caples, William, former V.P., Inland Steel, 28
Carey, James, former president, IUE, 23
Cavanagh, Gerald F., cited, 250*n*.
Cayton, Horace R., cited, 22*n*.
Chamberlain, Neil W., cited, 272*n*.
chemical industry
  blacks in, 40, 41
  size of, 325
Chicago, Illinois
  description of Cicero and Lawndale, 50-54
  field study of National Acme plant in, 49-100
Chicago Black Labor Federation, 87
Chicago Riot Commission, 1
Chinoy, Ely, cited, 74
churches in field study cities, 51, 52, 102
Cicero, Illinois, description of, 50-54
civil disorder, *see* riot

Civil Rights Act of *1964*, 31, 32, 110, 279
civil rights groups and fair employment
  early efforts, 15, 18, 29
  ineffective in Fairbanks desegregation, 179-180
  influence of, on hiring, 26
  see also National Association for the Advancement of Colored People; *and* Urban League
Clark, Kenneth B., quoted, 5
clerical work
  disadvantaged trained for, 253, 259*n*.
  discrimination in, 16
clerical workers
  demand for in Boston, Massachusetts, 255
  first at Westinghouse-Buffalo, 151-152
  percent black
    in electrical manufacturing, 38, 40, 42, 43, 323
    in field study plants, 111-112, 114, 151, 153, 187
    in selected industries, 40
coding the interviews, 310
  coding form, 315
communication
  between foreman and worker, 82-84, 114, 252, 265, 270
  of policy, 228-229
  race relations and, 4, 144, 234, 292
  recruiting blacks and, 29, 37, 106, 229, 276
Communications Workers of America, 336
Community Action Program (CAP), Lynchburg, Virginia, 105, 113, 114, 139
community
  agencies and organizations, 131, 143, 178; *see also* civil rights groups
  managers' activities in, 135-140, 148, 154, 176, 301
  relations
    company policies on, 9, 225
    in the South, 34-35, 101, 103-104, 135-140
    in urban plants, 100, 141, 145
    measurement of, 231-232
    reevaluation of, 5
    see also corporate social responsibility *and* environment, social and economic
company
  index of workers' attitudes toward, 66, 115, 192-193, 294-295, 311, 321-323

size and black employment, 39
store era, 299
compliance reports, equal employment opportunity, 31-32, 34
Concentrated Employment Program (CEP) in Buffalo, 242, 246, 283
Congress of Industrial Organizations (CIO) civil rights committee, 23
corporate power, legitimacy of, 8
corporate social responsibility
  authors' views, 303-304
  discussion and definition of, 5-10
  management motivation and, 300
  evaluation of field studies, 301-302
  limitations on, 302
  see also community relations; *and* environment, social and economic
corporations, identity crisis of, 5
Couch, Arthur S., cited, 311*n*.
counseling
  need for, 273
  programs
    for absentees, 71-72, 245
    for disadvantaged workers, 245, 248, 253-254
    general, 114
  rapport with foremen, 81-82, 167
crafts, training in, 78
craftsmen, percent black
  in electrical manufacturing industry, 38, 40, 42, 43, 323
  in field study plants, 54, 111, 112, 114, 149, 151, 153, 187, 190, 191
  in selected industries, 40
credibility gap in recruiting blacks, 29, 37, 106, 229, 276
credit
  counseling, 78
  ratings as a selection criteria, 108-109
  see also debt, wage garnishment
crime and delinquency in field study locations, 51, 102, 143

Daily Advance, Lynchburg, Virginia, newspaper, 134-135
Daley, Richard, mayor, Chicago, 100
Data-Text, used in analysis of field work, 311
Davis, John A., cited, 19*n*.
Day, Virgil B., General Electric, cited, 16*n,* quoted, 37
deaf mute employees, 247
debt, effect on work incentive, 241
defense contract cutbacks, 258, 329, 330
Demaree, Allen T., quoted, 9
demographic variables, *see* hourly workers, characteristics of

Depression, decline of black employment during, 17
desegregation
  management's role in, 209-210, 218-219
  of a Deep-South plant, 179-185, 205-210, 218-219
  of production jobs in the 1940s, 18-19
  of women's jobs in Mississippi, 34-35
  see also black pioneers
disadvantaged workers, 233-274
  attitudes of, 234, 236-242, 256-258, 261
  background of, 239
  characteristics of, 234, 235, 272
  discipline and, 265-266, 284
  job placement of, 247, 262, 272
  motivation of, 256-257, 259-260, 273
  programs for, 225-226, 242-263, 272-274, 297-298
    financing, 274
    white attitudes toward, 257-258
  recruiting, 246, 254
  relationships of, with foremen, 236, 243, 249-250, 252, 255, 261-262, 266, 267-271, 298
  work performance of, 248-249, 255, 257, 273
discipline in the plant
  blacks compared to whites, 62-64, 155, 186
  double standards of, 84, 266, 291, 292
  importance of, 84, 265-266
  problems, 268-269
  rarely a reason for dismissal at National Acme, 244
  should be done in private, 81
  special procedures for the disadvantaged, 284
discrimination in education, 24
discrimination in employment
  before World War II, 16, 17
  effect of, 280
  institutionalized, 177, 280
  subtle, 29, 33, 276
  workers perception of
    in hiring, 107-109, 111, 148, 154, 183, 188
    in promoting, 76, 77, 96-97, 116-117, 119, 122-123, 151, 188
    in supervision, 127
discrimination in southern state employment services, 24, 188
distrust, disadvantaged workers feel, 236-237, 258
Doeringer, Peter B., cited, 240*n*., 250*n*.
Domestic Marshall Plan, 275, 278, 302
double standards of discipline, 84, 266, 291, 292

see also preferential treatment, workers' perception of in supervision
drafting, disadvantaged trained for, 253, 255
drug addict, former, 260
Dupont publication quoted, 9

earnings, *see* income *and* pay
Eckstein, Otto, cited, 326
education
  blacks disadvantaged in, 24, 29, 37, 95-96
  company programs, 37, 39, 78, 253-54, 260
  corporate support for, 225, 226, 297, 303
  see also schools
educational level
  in field study cities, 50, 177
  of disadvantaged workers, 235
  of hourly workers, 56, 104, 105, 107-108, 146, 147, 177, 185-86
Eisenhower, President Dwight D., 26
elections, municipal
  black elected in Lynchburg, Virginia, 131
  white backlash anticipated in Buffalo, New York, 144
elections, union, 87-88, 158-159
electric power consumption, 328, 330
Electrical Equipment Workers (fictitious name), 49, 87
electrical manufacturing industry, 3, 324-337
  definition of, 324-325
  dominance of large firms in, 326
  history and growth of, 13-29 *passim*, 328-330
  manpower in
    labor requirements, 14, 18, 22, 37, 44, 50, 329, 334
    number of employees, *1910-1930,* 13; *1940, 1943,* 18; *1947, 1949, 1951,* 19-20; *1950-1960,* 21-22; *1939-1969,* 331; *1960-1969,* 33; *1967,* 325; compared to all manufacturing and durable goods manufacturing, 330, 332; in 15 largest firms, 325, 327
    number of women, 14, 38, 323, 334-335
  occupational distribution, 334
  percent black of employees in, *see* black workers, percent of electrical manufacturing industry
  regional distribution of, 35, 337, 338
  turnover, 147, 332, 333
  wages and working conditions, 335
  products of, 324
  sales of, 325
  size of, 325
Electrical Workers of America (fictitious name), 180, 216-218
Emerson, Ralph Waldo, quoted, 223
employees
  characteristics of, *see* hourly workers, characteristics of
  neighborhoods of, *see* plant locales
  number of, *see* electrical manufacturing industry, number of employees; *or under specific company such as* Radio Corporation of America, number of employees
  percent black of, *see* black workers, number of
employment, *see specific aspects such as* affirmative action; hiring; testing
engineering requirements of electrical manufacturing industry, 37
English in Cicero, Illinois, 51
entry-level jobs, 36
environment, social and economic of the corporation
  a corporate concern, 7-8, 225
  important in planning affirmative action, 226-227
  the challenge at General Electric Lynchburg, 131; at National Acme–Chicago, 99-100
  see also community relations; corporate social responsibility; *and* plant locales
equal employment opportunity
  corporate departments of, 34, 227-228
  emblem, 228
  federal influence on, *see* federal government
  history of, 13-29, 299
  state influence on, *see* state fair employment practice commissions
  systems planning for, 225-227
  see also affirmative action
Equal Employment Opportunity Commission, 32
equalitarianism, not the rule in American society, 278-279
ethics and management decision-making, 10, 302
ethnic
  backlash, reasons for, 134, 144-145
  plants, racial change in, 54, 152-154
  population
    in Buffalo, New York, 142-145

Subject Index

in Cicero, Illinois, 51
voting in union, 158-159
Evers, Medgar, assassination of, 214
executive orders on fair employment, 18, 26, 31, 32
expectations, unrealistic, 69, 77

factor analysis of field data, 311, 320
fair employment, *see* affirmative action *and* equal employment
fair employment practice commissions (FEPC) (state), 21, 27
Fairbanks International (fictitious name), field study of Memphis plant, 174-220, 283, 284, 288, 290
   program for the disadvantaged in, 251-253, 272
fairness, high value placed on, 163, 172
fear of failure on the job, 237-238
federal government
   business cooperation with, 5, 8, 302
   in National Alliance of Businessmen, 233
   in Plans for Progress, 32, 176
   community action programs (CAP), 105, 113-114, 139
   influence on equal employment opportunity, 31-33
     Civil Rights Act of *1964,* 32, 279
     Equal Employment Opportunity Commission (EEOC), 32
     Executive Orders, 18, 21, 26, 31, 32
     Office of Federal Contract Compliance (OFCC), 32-33, 228, 229-330, 279-280
     Plans for Progress, 32, 176
   influence on hiring the disadvantaged, 274, 298
     Concentrated Employment Program (CEP), 242, 246, 283
     Manpower Administration Contracts (MA programs), 246, 253, 255, 259n., 274
     National Alliance of Businessmen, 233
   subsidies, 18, 278
feedback from foreman important to the disadvantaged, 252, 270
field work
   authors' residence during, 305
   locations, *see* plant locales
   methodology, 305-320
financing programs for the disadvantaged, 274
Folsom, Frank M., former president, Radio Corporation of America, cited, 16n., 19n., quoted, 28

food industry, size of, 325
Ford, Henry, II, cited 300, 302, quoted, 8
Foremen
   disadvantaged workers and, 236, 243, 247-249, 251, 252, 255, 261-262, 266, 268-271, 298
   evaluate work of blacks and whites, 61-65, 117, 154-155, 193-194, 295, 321
   evaluate work of the disadvantaged, 248-249, 255, 257, 273
   management's expectations of, 231, 297
   on the assembly line, 85-86
   the New Work Force and, 60-66, 78-86, 165-167
   training for, 210, 246, 273, 298
   white backlash and, 109-110, 128-130, 182, 184, 198, 208, 210, 218-219, 292
   workers' attitudes toward, 79, 82, 167, 193, 243, 249-250, 252, 295
   workers' perception of preferential treatment by, 85, 91, 127, 163, 290-292
   see also black foremen
"Forgotten American," 53
Friedman, Milton, 6, 300, 303

Galenson, Walter, cited, 336n.
Garfield Park, Illinois, 50
General Electric
   assets, sales, income of, 327
   black employment history of, 15-16, 19, 20, 21, 25, 27
   equal opportunity department in, 227, 229, 231-232
   equal opportunity policy of, 16, 32, 34, 223, 224-225, 301
   field study of Lynchburg plant, 101-140, 287-288, 284-285
   founded, 13
   number of employees in, 22, 327
   unions in, 336, 338
generation gap in black identity in Lawndale, Illinois, 51
Germans
   in Buffalo, New York, 142, 143
   in Cicero, Illinois, 51
ghetto employers, 240
Gifford, Richard P., Vice President, General Electric, 135, 136, 139
Glass, Carter, former U.S. Senator, 134
Glass, Carter, III, 135
Glenn, Norval D., cited, 2n.
Godwin, Milles, Jr., former governor of Virginia, 132

Subject Index

Goetze, A. B., former vice president, Western Electric, 20
Gooding, Judson, cited 73n.
government
   black representation in, 131, 143, 177, 178
   see also federal government and state fair employment practice commissions
Graham, Lloyd, cited, 142n., 145n.
Greeks in Cicero, Illinois, 51
gross national product, 1953-1965, 33
growth of black employment, see black workers, number of
growth of electrical manufacturing industry, 328-330
growth rate, industrial impact of on black employment, 328
Guest, Robert H., cited, 73n., 74, 85

Hamilton, Charles V., quoted, 278
Hannon, Richard, cited, 142-143
hard core, see disadvantaged
Harrington, Michael, cited, 7, 300
Harris, Abram L., 22n.
Health problems of the New Work Force, 58
Herzberg, Fredrick, cited, 74, 244n.
high school requirement, 57, 107-108, 188, 247
Hill, Herbert, cited, 25n.
hiring blacks
   at field study plants, 54-58, 106-114, 139, 147-157, 186-191
   workers' perceptions of discrimination in, 107-109, 111, 148, 154, 183, 188
   workers' perceptions of preferential treatment in, 111, 163, 191, 287-289
   corporate trends, 33-34, 301
   preferential treatment and, 281-283
   see also disadvantaged workers, programs for
hiring requirements, see selection criteria or labor requirements of the electrical manufacturing industry
Honeywell, 8, 300
Honore, Thomas, cited, 51n.
hourly workers
   characteristics of, in field study plants, 54-56, 104-105, 145-147, 185-186
   neighborhoods of, see plant locales
   number of, see blue collar jobs, number of
   number of black, see blue collar workers, percent black

housing conditions in field study cities, 50, 51, 102, 131, 137-138, 143, 176-177
housing, open
   as a corporate goal, 225, 303
   effect on recruiting black professionals, 137
   resistance to, 51-52
Howard University, 20, 95
human relations committee, union, 216
hypertension among New Work Force, 58

imported products, competition from, 330
income
   a disadvantage, 68-69, 241
   of black employees and affirmative action, 58
   median in field study areas, 50, 102, 143, 177
   see also pay
individuals and preferential treatment, 280-281, 283, 285
inferiority, sense of
   in assembly work, 72-73
institutionalized discrimination, 177, 280
integration, residential
   corporate position on, 225, 303
   resistance to in Berwyn and Cicero, Illinois, 51-52
International Association of Machinists and Aerospace Workers, 49, 335, 336
   racial stance of, 15-16, 17, 23
International Brotherhood of Electrical Workers, 49, 335, 336
   racial stance of, 17, 23
International Brotherhood of Teamsters, Chauffeurs, Warehousemen, and Helpers of America, 49
International Union of Electrical, Radio, and Machine Workers, 335, 336
   defeated at General Electric–Lynchburg, 115
   Local 1581, 157-159, 313
   racial stance of, 23, 35, 216
International Union of Operating Engineers, 49
interracial marriage and sex, fear of, 130, 203, 208, 209, 212
interview method, 307-310
interviewers, employment, 33, 57-58, 148
Invaders, 178
Irish
   in Cicero, Illinois, 51
   in Buffalo, New York, 142, 143
Italians in Buffalo, New York, 142

"Jackie Robinson syndrome," 109
Janger, Allen R., cited, 250n.
Jeffress, Philip W., cited, 328n.
Jennings, Paul, president, International Union of Electrical Workers, 35
Job Corps, employees from, 251, 271
job
  level of hourly workers, 56, 104, 146, 186
  placement of disadvantaged workers, 247, 262, 272
  redesign, 75
  security, 258
  training, see training, job
  variation, 73-74
  see also work and labor requirements of the electrical manufacturing industry
Johnson, Lawrence A., cited, 250n.

Kahn, Robert L., quoted, 308-309
Kellow, James Harry, cited, 175n.
Kennedy, President John F., 31, 32
keypunch, disadvantaged trained for, 253, 255
Killingsworth, Charles C., cited, 18n., quoted, 22
King, Martin Luther, 31, 178
  assassination of, 132, 178
  reaction to, 162
King, Wendell, 15
Korean War, effect on labor market, 21
Kornhauser, Arthur W., cited, 74
Ku Klux Klan, 31, 134n.

Labor, U.S. Department of, see Concentrated Employment Program; Manpower Administration contracts; and Office of Federal Contract Compliance
labor market
  effect on black employment
    in electrical manufacturing, 14, 17, 19, 21-22, 29, 33, 44, 299
    in field study plants, 49, 54, 105, 110, 147, 255
  secondary, 240
labor requirements of electrical manufacturing industry, 14, 18, 22, 37, 44, 50, 329, 334
laborers, percent black
  in electrical manufacturing, 38, 40, 42, 43, 323
  in field study plants, 112, 151, 153
  in selected industries, 40

law, equal employment opportunity
  effect of, 27, 28, 44, 299
  managers' attitudes toward, 21, 27-28
law and order, foreman sees lack of, 64-65
law on preferential treatment, 279-280
Lawndale, Illinois, description of, 50-51
Lawrence, R. G., cited, 16
layoffs
  absenteeism and, 71
  of the disadvantaged, 258, 286
  preferential treatment during, 285-287
  recall rate at General Electric–Lynchburg after, 105
legalism, danger of, 303
Leggett, Harold, quoted, 135
leisure, valued more than money, 67
Levitan, Sar A., cited, 272n.
Liebow, Eliot, cited, 233, 240
listening, importance of, 3-4
Lithuanians in Cicero, Illinois, 51
location, plant
  effect on employment of blacks, 14, 24-25, 29, 35-36, 39, 49, 226
  see also plant locales
Loth, David, cited, 16n., 336n.
Luchterhand, Elmer, cited, 308n.
lumber industry, blacks in, 36
Lynchburg, Virginia
  description of, 102-103, 131-139
  field study of General Electric plant in, 101-140, 284-285, 287-288
Lynchburg Community Action Program, 105, 113-114, 139
Lynchburg Voters League, 131
lynching, 175

management and equal employment opportunity, see affirmative action; corporate social responsibility; equal employment opportunity, history of; and specific aspects of such as community relations; desegregation; disadvantaged workers, programs for; hiring blacks
managers
  corporate, importance of commitment to affirmative action of, 25-26, 34, 110, 179, 223, 224, 229, 263
  community activities of, 136-139, 148, 154, 176, 301
  engineering background of, 37
  measurement of equal opportunity record of, 231
  motivation of, 300, 302
    business problems lead to interest in social causes, 226

influences on employment policy, 58, 104-105, 179-180
possible fear of white backlash, 96-97, 190
sincerity questioned, 265, 298-299
percent black
affirmative action needed, 275
in electrical manufacturing, 38, 40, 42, 43, 323
in field study plants, 54, 112, 151, 153
training in equal opportunity for, 20
see also foremen; black foremen; *and specific managers such* as A. B. Goetze, Louis Rader, David Sarnoff
Mangum, Garth L., cited, 272n.
Manpower Administration contracts to train the disadvantaged, 233
at National Acme, 246
at Raytheon, 253, 255
at Westinghouse, 259n.
need for, 274
number of, in Memphis, 253
manpower planning, minority, 225-227
recommendations of the National Advisory Commission on Civil Disorders on, 1-2
see also affirmative action
Maremont, Arnold, quoted, 7
Mark, Robert C., manager, General Electric, 135, 136-137
marriage
and absenteeism, 67-69
fear of interracial, 130
Marshall, F. Ray, cited, 22n., quoted, 177, 253, 274, 277-278
McDonnell Douglas, affirmative action settlement with the OFCC, 230
measurement and sanctions in implementing affirmative action policy, 231-232, 297, 298
compliance reports facilitate, 32
meatpacking industry, labor struggles in, 14
mechanics, black
at Fairbanks–Memphis, 190-191, 205-209
disadvantaged worker promoted to, 271
see also craftsmen
Memphis, Tennessee
description of, 175-179
field study of Fairbanks plant in, 174-220, 283, 284, 288, 290
men
influence of industry labor requirements on number of, 334-335

jobs for, integrated more slowly than women's, 39
number of in electrical manufacturing industry, 14, 38
number of in field study plants, 105, 146, 185
menial work, discontent with, 238
metals
fabricated
earnings in industry, 335
size of industry, 325
primary, size of industry, 325
Mexicans in Cicero, Illinois, 51
Middle America, 53-54, 141, 162-163, 172
some blacks share attitudes of, 172
Midwest
black population in, 36
electrical employment in, 337, 338
migration, *see* population migration
minority manpower policy
recommendations of the National Advisory Commission on Civil Disorders on, 1-2
see also affirmative action
Mitchell, George, cited, 22n.
moonlighting, 68
Morse, Gerry E., vice president, Honeywell, quoted 8, 300
motivation
of managers, *see* managers, motivation of
of the disadvantaged, 256-257, 259-260, 273
of the New Work Force, foremen's views on, 63, 64, 65, 77-78
see also work, attitudes toward
motor vehicle and equipment industry, earnings in, 335
Myrdal, Gunnar, cited, 32, 134, quoted, 17

Nader, Ralph, cited, 223
National Acme Electric (fictitious name)
field study of Chicago plant, 49-100, 285, 287
program for the disadvantaged in, 71, 99, 242-246, 272, 273
National Advisory Commission on Civil Disorders, 1, 2, 13, 144n.
One Year Later Report, by two members of, 2
National Alliance of Businessmen (NAB), 233
five programs for the disadvantaged, 242-263, 272-274
in Memphis, Tennessee, 253

National Association for the Advancement of Colored People (NAACP), 136, 175, 178, 291
National Urban League, *see* Urban League
Negro, *see* black
"Negro jobs," few in electrical manufacturing industry, 15
neighborhoods, changing, 53, 142, 176
New Work Force
 absenteeism, tardiness, and turnover of, 60-66
 background of, 49, 57-58, 66-69
 conclusions, 99-100, 297, 298
 reaction to an industrial plant, 66-86
 social relations of, 58-60, 97-99
New York State Employment Service, 246
News, The, Lynchburg, Virginia, paper, 134, 135
news coverage, racial bias in, 134-135
newspapers, black, 143
Nicholls, William H., cited, 25n.
"Nixon Committee" (President's Committee on Government Contracts), 26
Northeast
 blacks in, 36
 electrical manufacturing employment in, 337, 338
Northrup, Herbert R., cited, 2n., 14n., 16n., 22n., 25n., 36n., 328n., 336n.

occupational distribution of blacks
 affirmative action goal at National Acme, 58
 in electrical manufacturing, 29, 36-39, 40, 42, 43, 323
 in field study plants, 54, 112, 151, 153
 in selected industries, 40
 may affect perception of fairness, 117
 see also blue collar workers; clerical workers; craftsmen; professionals; operatives; technicians; *and* white collar workers
 see also labor requirements of electrical manufacturing industry
Office of Federal Contract Compliance (OFCC), 32-33, 228, 229-230, 279-280
 McDonnell Douglas and the, 230
One Year Later Report, 2
operative and production work
 desegregation of, 18
 discrimination in, 16
 number of jobs in electrical manufacturing increasing, 334

operatives, percent black
 in electrical manufacturing, 38, 40, 42, 43, 323
 in field study plants, 54, 112, 151, 153, 189
 in selected industries, 40
Opportunities Industrialization Center (OIC), 37, 246
orientation, employee
 need for, 69-70, 73, 77, 243, 264-265, 298
 programs for, 71, 245-246, 253-254, 260-261, 272-273
 value of, 65
Orwell, George, quoted, 275
overtime, attitudes toward, 63, 67, 166

paper industry, blacks in, 23, 36
paternalistic racism, 276
pay
 at field study plants, 56, 114, 145, 185, 260
 in electrical manufacturing and selected industries, 335
 misunderstandings about, 69, 237
pay differential, effect on turnover, 244
Perkins, Frances, cited, 336n.
Petit, Thomas A., quoted, 8
petroleum industry, blacks in, 40, 41
Pettigrew, Thomas, quoted, 308
philanthropy versus corporate social responsibility, 10
Piore, Michael, J., cited, 240n.
Pittsburgh, Westinghouse Occupational Training School in, 259-263
Plans for Progress, 32, 176
plant
 a foreign environment, 234-236, 255
 an integrator, 99, 126-127, 176, 195, 296
 contraction, effect on hiring blacks, 54, 154
 location, effect on employment of blacks, 14, 24-25, 29, 35-36, 39, 49, 226
plant locales, field study, 50-54, 102-103, 131-139, 142-145, 175-179
plantation atmosphere, 89
polarization, racial, 2, 304
Poles
 in Buffalo, New York, 142, 143
 in Cicero, Illinois, 51
policy, equal employment opportunity
 implementation of, 227-232, 296-297
 statements, 16, 224-225
policy statements, importance of, 223-224

politics, ethnic, 142, 158-159
population
  of field study areas, 50, 102, 143, 175
  percent black
    in field study areas, 50, 102, 141, 143, 176
    in Northeast and north central states, 14
    in United States, 2
  percent children in Lawndale, 51
population migration
  of blacks north, 19, 24, 36, 132-133
  through Memphis, 175
preferential treatment, 275-293
  distinguished from equalizing practice, 275-276, 281-287
  justification of, 280-281, 293
  law on, 279-280
  manager's view of, 165, 250
  nonracial examples of, 278-279
  summary, 293, 297
  views on, 277-278
  workers' perception of
    in hiring, 111, 163, 191, 287-289
    in promotion, 117, 163, 289-290
    in supervision, 85, 91, 127, 163, 290-292
    prejudice and, 291-292
prejudice and age, 160-161, 197, 207, 212, 322
President's Committee on Civil Rights, *1946,* 21
President's Committee on Fair Employment, *1941,* 18
President's Committee on Government Contracts, *1953,* 26
President's Committee on Government Contracts, *1961,* 31
President's Test Job Program, 253
Price, Gwilym, former president, Westinghouse, 24, 28
priests, effect on interview of authors' role as, 309
product quality, not hurt by New Work Force, 100
production jobs, *see* operative and production work
professionals
  growing need for in electrical manufacturing, 22, 37, 334
  percent black
    in electrical manufacturing, 38, 40, 42, 43, 323
    in field study plants, 54, 111, 112, 114, 151, 153
    in selected industries, 40
  recruiting black, 20, 95-97, 125, 137

profit
  maximization, 6, 7, 300
  motive, 300
profits
  importance of, 10
  long-run versus short-run, 7-8, 302
promoting and upgrading blacks
  at field study plants, 75-78, 116-125, 139-140, 149-150, 155-156, 188, 190, 191, 295
  frustration of young with, 74, 87, 155-156, 238
  of the disadvantaged, 262
  to salaried positions, 96-97, 151, 157, 209
  workers' perception of discrimination in, 76, 77, 96-97, 116-117, 119-123, 151, 188
  workers' perception of preferential treatment in, 117, 163, 289-290
  corporate trends, 34, 39, 224, 231
  effect of on motivation, 77, 121, 156
  preferential treatment and, 284-285
public relations or corporate social responsibility, 10
Purcell, Theodore V., cited, 14*n.*, 74, 234*n.*, 250*n.*

quotas, affirmative action
  importance of, 230, 277-278
  Office of Federal Contract Compliance on, 32, 280
  whites critical of, 163, 164
quotations from field interviews, use of, 311

racial conflict
  social justice and, 281
  see also riots
Rader, Louis, vice president, General Electric, 25, 105
Radio Corporation of America (RCA)
  affirmative action of, 32, 34, 301
  assets, sales, income of, 327
  black employment history of, 16, 18, 19, 20, 27, 28, 79, 225
  number of employees in, 327
  unions in, 336
Randolph, A. Philip, 18
rapport in interviews, 307-310
Raytheon
  assets, sales, income of, 327
  employment in, 327
    black, 253
  field study of Job Training Center for the disadvantaged, 253-258, 272-274

inspected by Massachusetts fair employment practice commission, 27
recession, effect on black employment, *see* labor market, effect on black employment
recreation, company sponsored, 128-130, 204-205, 281-282
recreation, union sponsored, 204-205
recruiting blacks
  affirmative action and, 33-34, 231
  after desegregation, 189-191
  at Howard University, 20
  credibility gap in, 29, 37, 106, 229, 276
  disadvantaged, 246, 254
  for mechanics jobs, 190-191
  and opening a southern plant, 106, 110
  for professional positions, 20, 95-96, 125
    effect of housing problems on, 137
  preferential treatment and, 281-282
  through a community agency, 113-114, 246, 254
recruiting the poor, white attitudes toward, 163
regional distribution of electrical manufacturing employees, 35, 337, 338
research methodology, 305-320
residence
  authors' during field work, 51, 305
  of workers interviewed, 56, 104, 146-147, 186
residential integration, resistance to, 52
  see also housing, open
responsibility, sense of
  and attendance, 74, 77
  foremen evaluate employees on, 62, 63, 155, 186
restlessness of youth, 67
retention of the disadvantaged
  characteristics of drop-outs, 244-245
  effect of birthplace on, 244-245
  effect of pay on, 244
  importance of, 273-274
  rates, 243, 246, 247, 251, 254, 263, 298
  reasons for leaving, 244, 254-255
  reasons for staying, 236, 256-257
Riot Report, Chicago, *1919,* quoted, 1
Riot Report (National Advisory Commission on Civil Disorders), 1, 2
riots, 31, 141, 178, 226
  anti-Negro, 144
Robinson, Haywood, black community leader, 137

Rocky Mountain states, percent of electrical employees in, 337, 338
Roosevelt, President Franklin D., 18
Ross, Arthur M., cited, 25*n*.
Ross, Richard, former director, Westinghouse Occupational Training School, 241, 259-260
Rowan, Richard L., cited, 8*n*., 14*n*., 16*n*., 36*n*., 328
rubber tire industry, blacks in, 14, 40, 41
Rubin, Lester, cited, 328*n*.
rumors and backlash, 292
Russians in Cicero, Illinois, 51

salaried employees, *see* white collar workers
sales of electrical manufacturing industry, 325, 328
salesmen
  engineering requirement for, 37
  percent black
    in electrical manufacturing, 38, 40, 42, 43, 323
    in field study plants, 112, 151, 153
    in selected industries, 40
sampling methods, 306
sanctions in implementing affirmative action policy, 231-232, 297, 298
sanitation workers' strike, Memphis, 178, 199, 215-216
Sarnoff, David, former president, Radio Corporation of America, 18
Scandinavians in Cicero, Illinois, 51
Schaeffer, Ruth G., cited, 250*n*.
school
  background of the disadvantaged, 239
  desegregation, 25, 31, 136
  system, business interest in, 226
  system in Lynchburg, Virginia, 136
  system in Memphis, Tennessee, 176, 179, 186
  see also education
Schrag, Peter, cited, 53*n*.
Scotch in Cicero, Illinois, 51
Seay, C. W., black city councilor, 131
secondary labor market, 240
segregation
  at Tennessee Division of Employment Security, 188
  in Lynchburg, Virginia, 102
  in Memphis, Tennessee, 175-176
  see also desegregation
segrationist behavior of Fairbanks-Memphis union, 213-214
selection criteria
  and the New Work Force, 57

at field study plants, 57, 107-109, 110, 112-114, 139, 147-148, 151, 152, 188, 190-191, 282
before *1960*, 24, 29, 147-148, 151
for black foremen, 93, 95, 170
for blacks when desegregating a plant or department, 109, 157, 181, 182-183, 210, 219
General Electric policy on, 224
in programs for the disadvantaged, 241-242, 246-247, 251-252, 253, 254, 259-261, 272, 283
modified at two northern plants, 57, 282
seniority
attitudes toward, 76, 118-119, 155-156
effect on job assignments, 72, 247
of hourly workers, 56-57, 104-105, 145-147, 185-186
provisions
at field study plants, 75, 116-117, 154, 247
in electrical manufacturing, 23
sensitivity training for foremen, 210, 231, 246, 298
service workers, percent black
in electrical manufacturing, 38, 40, 42, 43, 323
in field study plants, 112, 151, 153
in selected industries, 40
sex
interracial, 123, 130, 206, 208-209, 212
number of workers by, 14, 38, 105, 146, 185
rate of integration by, 39
see also black men *and* black women
Shelley, E. F., cited, 272*n*.
shift
race relations and, 200, 207, 212
turnover and, 245
worked by hourly employees sampled, 56, 104, 146, 185, 186
Shlensky, Bertram C., cited, 244*n*.
Silberman, Charles E., quoted, 277
size, company
black employment and, 39
in electrical manufacturing, 325-326
leadership and, 326
skilled jobs, *see specific positions such as* craftsmen, technicians
Slavs in Cicero, Illinois, 51
social activities during desegregation, 204-205
social auditing of corporations, needed, 9
social conscience, 179
social demands on the corporation, 5

social environment, *see* environment, social and economic, *and* corporate social responsibility
social relations at work, related to turnover, 97, 266-267
social relations between black and white workers, 58-60, 97-99, 125-130, 159-165, 194-205, 295-296
after desegregation, 194-205, 219
age and, 160-161, 197, 207, 212, 322
black fear of rejection, 201-202
blacks adjust to white prejudice, 17, 199-200, 127
blacks demand respect, 200, 238
blacks get used to whites, 125-126
blacks may be suspicious of white union stewards, 159
in an ethnic plant, 159-165, 172, 173
in an integrated southern plant, 125-130
in plant compared to city, 99, 126-127, 176, 195, 296
of salaried workers, 96-97, 128-130, 209, 267
social pressure to maintain racial barriers, 129-130, 199, 201-202, 203
summary of field study findings, 295-296
white attitudes toward blacks, an index, 128, 160, 195, 311, 322, 323
white fear of interracial marriage or sex, 130, 203, 208-209, 212
white isolated by blacks, 266-267
whites get used to blacks, 97-98, 125, 184-185, 194-198
whites resist integration, 109-110, 127-130, 160-163, 198
with the New Work Force, 58-60, 97-99
see also black pioneers *and* white backlash
for relationships with foremen, see foremen
social responsibility, *see* corporate social responsibility
social stability and social justice, 281
socialism or corporate social responsibility, 303
South
employment policies in, 24-25, 34-36
field studies in, 101-140, 174-220
percent electrical employment in, 35, 337-338
school crisis in, 25, 31
southern rural background, effect on work habits, 67, 244
Spanish population in Cicero, Illinois, 51

Spanish-speaking workers
  at National Acme–Chicago
    as a buffer group, 100
    hired, 54
    reaction to black foremen, 92
    reaction to black workers, 59
    turnover of, 61
  at Raytheon, 255
Spero, Sterling D., cited, 22n.
Srinivas, M. N., cited, 296n.
state employment services
  New York, 146
  southern, 24, 29
  Tennessee, 188-189
  Virginia, 110
state fair employment practice commissions, 21, 27
statistical analysis of field interviews, 310-311, 318-320
steel industry
  blacks in, 14, 23, 40-41
  contraction of hampers affirmative action, 328
stereotyped view of blacks, 52, 197
Stewart, Donald D., cited, 177n.
strike
  of the Afro-American Committee, 89-91
  of the Memphis sanitation workers, 178, 199, 215-216
  resisting integration, 15-16, 25
  see also walkouts
Striner, Herbert R., cited, 272n.
suburbs, whites flee to, 142, 176
Sullivan, Rev. Leon, founder, Opportunities Industrialization Center, 246
supervisors, see foremen
supportive relationships
  for black pioneers, 181-184
  in programs for the disadvantaged, 236, 261, 271
  need of the disadvantaged for, 263-265, 273
  with the foreman, 81-82
Swope, Gerard T., former president, General Electric, 16, 336
systems planning for equal opportunity, 225-227, 296-297

Taggart, Robert III, cited, 272n.
tardiness
  a youth problem, 61
  foremen evaluate employees on, 62, 117, 155, 193, 295
  reasons for, 66, 72, 80-81, 84
team work, importance of, 265

technical positions, number of in electrical manufacturing, 22, 37, 334
technicians, percent black
  in electrical manufacturing, 38, 40, 42, 43, 323
  in field study plants, 54, 111, 112, 114, 151, 153, 187, 209
  in selected industries, 40
technological innovation, effect of on electrical manufacturing labor force, 22, 329, 334
Tennessee Division of Employment Security at Memphis, 188-189
tent city, 175
testing, employment, 57, 112-113, 282
textile industry, blacks in, 36
Thomas, Julius, Urban League, 18, 20
Thompson, Stewart, cited, 223n.
tobacco industry, blacks in, 23, 36
tolerance of whites for blacks, an index, 128, 160, 195, 311, 322, 323
trainees, see disadvantaged workers
training, job
  by co-workers, 118, 207
  need for, 39, 96, 191, 224, 279-280, 297
  preferential treatment and, 164, 250-251, 283-284
  programs, 78, 124, 245-246, 253-256, 258
  workers' attitudes toward, 73, 205-208, 237-238, 256, 271
transportation industry, size of, 325
  see also aerospace industry; aircraft and parts industry; and automobile industry
transportation problems
  effect on black employment, 24, 29, 36, 254-255
  General Electric policy on, 225
Truman, President Harry S., 21
Turner, Arthur N. cited, 85
turnover
  cost of, 71
  low, slows hiring of blacks, 152
  of the disadvantaged, see retention of the disadvantaged
  of the New Work Force, 57, 60-61, 64
  reasons for, 66-84, 97, 99
  rates
    in electrical manufacturing, 147, 332, 333
    in field study plants, 57, 61, 105, 147

Uncle Tom, black foreman seen as, 169
underutilization of minority people, concept discussed, 229-230, 279-280

Subject Index

unemployment and underemployment
   effect of, 1, 239, 240
   in field study cities, 50, 102, 143, 177
   Kennedy policy on, 33
   national rates, 17, 21, 33, 44
   of disadvantaged workers before joining programs, 235
union
   elections, 87-88, 158-159
   human relations committee, 216
   leadership
      black, 88, 90-91, 158, 218
      desegregation and, 219
      workers' attitudes toward, 158, 214-215
   procedures, education in, 218
unions
   black caucus in, 213, 216-218
   civil rights stance of internationals, 22-23, 35
   defeated at General Electric–Lynchburg, 115
   desegregation not influenced by, 180
   ethnic influence in, 158-159
   field work supported by, 307, 313
   history and membership of, 335, 336
   resistance to integration of, 15-16, 17
   segregationist orientation of, 213-214
   support for integration of, 19
   workers' attitudes toward, 87, 115, 158, 214-215, 322, 323
United Automobile, Aerospace, and Agricultural Implement Workers, 335, 336
United Black Protest Committee, 262
United Electrical and Radio Workers
   civil rights stance of, 16, 23
   defeated at General Electric–Lynchburg, 115
   history and membership of, 335, 336
   supported integration at Pittsburgh plant, 19
United Security Association, 213, 216-218
United States Bureau of Employment Security report on discrimination in war industries, 16
United States government, see federal government
upgrading, see promotion and upgrading
Urban America, 2
Urban Coalition, 2
Urban League
   cited, Paul Jennings, IUE, 35
   corporate consultation with, 20, 29
   Domestic Marshall Plan of, 275, 278, 302
   founded, 15
   in Buffalo, New York, 148, 283
   in Memphis, Tennessee, 178-180
urban plants, field study of, 49-100, 141-173

value of shipments, selected industries, *1967*, 325
Van Adams, Arvil, quoted, 177, 253
Virginia Employment Commission, 110, 113
vocational education for blacks, inadequate in Memphis, Tennessee, 191
voting
   ethnic, 142, 158
   racial, 216

wage garnishment, 63, 78
wages, see pay *and* income
Walker, Charles R., cited, 73*n*., 74, 85
walkout, black, 89-91
walkouts
   attitude toward at Fairbanks–Memphis, 214-215
Walton, Clarence, cited, 300
Watts riot, 31
Webster, Rosalind, cited, 234*n*., 250*n*.
Weiner, Myron, cited, 296*n*.
welfare, resentment of, 170-172, 196
Weller, Leonard, cited, 308*n*.
West, percent of electrical manufacturing employment in, 337, 338
Western Electric
   affirmative action of, 32, 34, 229, 301
   assets, sales, income of, 327
   black employment history of, 16, 18, 20, 27, 32
   founded, 13
   ghetto plant of, 227, 274
   number of employees in, 327
   unions in, 336
Westinghouse
   affirmative action in, 32, 34, 224, 286, 301
   assets, sales, income of, 327
   black employment history in, 19, 20, 24-25, 27-28, 34-35
   field study
      of Buffalo plant, 141-173, 282, 284, 285, 288, 292
      of Buffalo program for the disadvantaged, 246-251, 272-274
      of East Pittsburgh program for the disadvantaged, 259-263, 273-274, 282
   number of employees in, 327
   unions in, 336

white attitudes toward blacks, an index of, 128, 160, 195, 311, 322, 323
  age and, 160-161, 197, 207, 212, 322
  see also social relations between black and white workers
white backlash
  absence of in Raytheon program for the disadvantaged, 257-258
  against disadvantaged trainees, 262
  against residential integration in Cicero, Illinois, 52-53
  during desegregation of a Deep-South plant, 181-182, 206-210, 218-219, 292
  during desegregation of production jobs in the North, 19, 25
  during desegregation of women's jobs in Mississippi, 34-35
  effectiveness of strong management stand against, 19, 25, 34-35, 109-110, 128, 173, 219, 292
  general absence of during desegregation of production jobs in the North, 18, 19
  general absence of in an ethnic plant, 172-173
  in *1917*, 15, 16
  in an integrated southern plant, 109-110, 128-130
  individual examples of, 160-163, 288-289
  management anticipation of, 96-97, 190
  uncommon in plants studied, 100, 172, 173, 293, 297
  see also black pioneers; black foremen, reaction to; *and* ethnic backlash
White Citizens Council, 31, 213
white collar jobs
  number of in electrical manufacturing industry, 22, 37, 334
  number of at Westinghouse–Buffalo, 145
white collar workers, black
  in electrical manufacturing, 20, 26-27, 30, 36, 38, 40, 42, 323
  in field study plants, 54, 111-112, 114, 150-157, 187, 209
  in the South, 36, 111-112, 114, 187, 209
  social relations of, 96-97, 128-230, 209, 267
  see also black foremen
white fear of interracial marriage or sex, 130, 203, 208-209, 212
white liberal, black militant's reaction to, 162

white minority at National Acme–Chicago, 54
White Power, 53
Wilson, Charles, former president, General Electric, 21
Wilson, Richard, quoted, 277
Wilson, Thomas A., cited, 326
women
  influence of industry labor requirements on number of, 334-335
  jobs for, integrated more quickly than men's jobs, 39
  number and occupational distribution of in electrical manufacturing industry, 14, 38
  number of, in field study plants, 105, 146, 185
Wood, Robert C., quoted, 53
work
  attitudes toward influenced by
    age, 66, 67, 72, 322
    assembly line, 63, 72-75
    debts, 241
    discontent with menial work, 238
    distrust, 236-237
    false expectations, 69
    fear of failure, 237-238
    marriage, 68-69
    past work experience, 240
    promotion aspirations, 77, 121, 155-156
    rural backgrand, 66-67
    status of hustlers, 271
  fulfillment, lack of in assembly work, 72-75
  habits, nonindustrial, 66-67
  motivation of the disadvantaged, 256-257, 259-260, 273
  performance of hourly workers
    foremen compare blacks and whites, 61-65, 117, 154-155, 193-194, 295, 321
    foremen evaluate disadvantaged workers, 248-249, 255, 257, 273
    white co-workers' opinions of blacks, 59, 99
    white co-workers' opinions of the disadvantaged, 257
  satisfaction with, an index of, 66, 115, 192-193, 294-295, 311, 321-323
  see also job
workers
  characteristics of, *see* hourly workers, characteristics of
  neighborhoods of, *see* plant locales

number of, *see* electrical manufacturing industry, number of employees; *or under specific company such as* Radio Corporation of America, number of employees
percent black of, *see* black workers, number of
working conditions
  at General Electric–Lynchburg, 114
  at Westinghouse–Buffalo, 145
  change in attitudes toward, 64-65
  in electrical manufacturing compared to other industries, 335
World War II, effect on labor market, 17, 18

Young, Owen D., former chairman, General Electric, 336

Young, Whitney, Urban League, 275, 276, 294, 298-299
young blacks
  absent-prone, 62-63
  attitudes of, compared to older blacks and whites, 66, 72, 75-76, 77, 79-82, 322
  special problems of, 295
youth
  absenteeism of, 61
  attitudes of, compared to older workers, 322
  frustration of, with promotion opportunities, 155-156
  perplexing to the foremen, 165-167
  restlessness, 67

Index of interviewees

Afesi, John, *black foreman,* 69, 77, 86
Anderson, Madeleine, 112, 115, 125-126
Andrews, Robert, 212
Arnolds, Dora, 126
Asbury, Iantha, 185, 201-202
Atkins, Todd, 68

Bailey, James, *black salaried employee,* 121
Baxter, Willie, 248-249
Becker, Bruce, 283
Beliard, Henry, *manager,* 255, 267
Bennett, Wynell, *black salaried employee,* 109, 121-122, 127, 137-138
Billingslee, Cliff, 119
Boler, Leonard, 59
Bosworth, Franklin, 264-265
Boyd, Henry, 132
Brewer, Irene, 129
Brigham, Nancy, 197
Brook, Amos, 267
Buford, Shipp, 113, 119
Burrell, Thomas, *foreman,* 164
Byrd, Jesse, 242, 269-270

Cairnes, Ambrose, *black foreman,* 68-69, 94, 98
Carter, Ronald, *community leader, Lynchburg,* 137
Chaffee, Randall, *foreman,* 127
Chamberlain, James, *black college student,* 133
Chisholm, James, *black college student,* 133
Chisholm, Todd, 119-120
Cipriano, John, *foreman,* 166, 268-269
Clay, John, *black foreman,* 84, 95, 97, 237, 265-266
Cleaver Mary Ann, 291
Clifford, Hank, 266-267
Clinton, Daryl, *black foreman,* 124, 129
Colbert, Essie, 204, 234, 236
Coleman, Mollie, 189, 200, 217
Collins, Jeremiah, 83, 90
Comeau, Verna, 85, 92
Corcoran, Garfield, 133

Cornell, Martha, 118-119
Crawford, Paula, 127
Croswell, Jane, 212
Crowley, Kevin, *foreman,* 204, 209
Cummings, Edward, *manager,* 101, 103-104, 105, 138
Czajkowski, John, 158

daCorta, Cesar, 59, 92
Dahle, John, 86, 91, 98-99
Dalton, Reginald, 192, 211
Daniels, Joseph, *union officer,* 87, 88
Davis, Lillian, 148
Dawson, Fred, *foreman,* 63-64
Dawson, Leroy, 236
Dennison, Walter, *manager,* 148
Dinkins, Harrel, 162, 168-169
Dixon, Freddy, 151, 166-167
Dolan, Edgar, 207, 270-271, 292
Drake, Gerald, 161-162, 288
Draper, DeWitt, 81, 89-90
Drumlin, Ken, *foreman,* 127
Duggins, Ted, *foreman,* 236
Duncan, Jake, 107

Eliot, Charles, *black foreman,* 59, 73, 81-82, 91, 241
Ellcock, Harry, *black foreman,* 62-63, 64, 82, 84, 86, 94-95
Ellington, Richard, 189-190, 202

Farland, Mildred, 150, 171
Farmer, Roland, 268-269
Favreau, Chester, 238
Fay, Virginia, 201
Filkins, Roscoe, 149, 264
Flaherty, Daniel, *foreman,* 188, 203-204, 206, 209-210
Fleck, William, 49, 73, 237, 243
Ford, Cyril, 80, 93, 265
Ford, Valerie, 130
Fox, Augustus, *Urban League,* 179-180
Fraley, Eric, 191, 202, 206, 207-208, 217-218
French, Dale, *foreman,* 288
Fuller, Katie, 181-183, 185, 196

Index of Interviewees

Gale, Annie, 200
Garrett, Linda Sue, 201
Gilbert, Diana, 106, 107
Gill, Frank, *black community leader, Lynchburg,* 108
Gladden, Viola, 88
Gomez, Baldamar, 76
Goode, Quentin, *black union steward,* 158-159, 168
Gordon, June, 112
Grand, Reverend Jimmy, *black community leader, Memphis,* 175, 188, 189
Grant, Samuel, *union officer,* 205, 214, 216
Green, Calvin, *black foreman,* 209, 213, 290
Green, Roger, 236, 237-238, 258
Griggs, Neil, *black instructor,* 236
Grogam, Daniel, *foreman,* 208, 271, 283, 292
Grossman, Jack, *foreman,* 63, 77-78
Grovitz, Louis, *general foreman,* 85
Grumbacker, Steven, 141, 161
Grushow, Mayer, 92-93

Hadden, Jorel, 87, 88, 89, 90
Hadley, Reverend Richard, *black community leader, Memphis,* 188-189
Haight, Shirley, 124, 126
Hall, Thomas, *manager,* 104-105, 108, 110, 114, 116, 117, 129, 130, 137
Hall, Winthrop, 290
Harris, Grady, 162
Havlin, Ben, 80
Haynes, Norma, 52-53, 79, 86
Hebemann, Lawrence, 164
Hemphill, Dolores, 184-185, 215
Henderson, Joyce, 197
Hennessey, Robert, *foreman,* 261-262
Herman, George, *black salaried employee,* 157
Hillman, Donna, 211
Hobbs, Avery, 150-151
Holden, Edwin, 164
Holley, Arlene, 198, 211, 215
Holmes, Fred, 163
Holmes, Paul, *black salaried employee,* 122, 129-130
Howard, Benjamin, 67, 70
Hughes, Phillip E., *manager,* 148, 151-152, 250-251
Humphrey, Glen, *foreman,* 165-166
Hunt, Theodore, *manager,* 246-247, 251
Hurley, Aaron, 76
Hutchins, Leroy, 238, 256-257

Iannelli, Mario, *foreman,* 82-83
Ivy, Bernard, 182-183, 217

James, Hosea, *black salaried employee,* 157
Jarvis, Ray, *black salaried,* 159, 171
Jemison, Idell, 192
Jennings, Alvin, *black foreman,* 93
Jezak, Walter, *foreman,* 65, 80
Jodka, Len, *foreman,* 149, 166
Johnson, Rosalie, 195-196

Kadey, Nelson, 97-98
Keith, Don, *manager,* 61, 245
Kelly, Eugene, 241-242
Kingwell, Jacob, 199-200
Kolinski, Ed, *foreman,* 62, 63, 64, 95
Kramer, Rosa Lee, 115

Larkin, Nora, 181, 290, 291
Larson, Bill, 160, 171
Lazlo, Michael, *foreman,* 255
Leodas, John, 163-164
Lewis, Art, *black union officer,* 73, 88, 90-91, 93
Livingston, Lois, 106, 113
Loder, Edward, *manager,* 109-110, 135
Lohr, Dean, 164, 291
Longfield, Tony, 199, 206-207
Luckey, Brenda, 202-203
Luzzio, Frank, 91

MacCauley, Francis, 205
MacGregor, Roger, 176, 179-180, 183, 198
Madden, Joe, 256
Magner, Alfred, *black union officer,* 182-183, 184, 190, 205, 211, 218
Marlow, Terry, *foreman,* 249
Masterson, Richard, 68
Matthews, George, *union officer,* 88
May, Thomas, *foreman,* 176, 194, 195, 291-292
McAvoy, Craig, *foreman,* 236
McClintock, Hazel, 118
McCoy, Rodney, 270
McCray, Anita, 174, 183
Meadows, Emily, 195, 200
Megget, Jerry, 156, 170
Mendez, Raphael, 60
Michner, Steve, 291
Miller, Charles, *manager,* 212
Millmore, Grace, 125
Mitchell, Fred, 73-74
Mitchell, Neal, 93
Mitchell, Tom, 260, 261
Mobley, Earline, 148, 156-157

Index of Interviewees

Montgomery, Willie, 240, 256
Morgan, Jeffrey, *foreman*, 255
Morgan, Ralph, *manager*, 61
Moses, Walter, *black salaried employee*, 120-121, 128
Mullen, Ora, 88, 93
Myers, Nancy, 203
Myers, Rosa Lee, 197

Nason, Clarence, *National Alliance of Businessmen, Buffalo*, 250
Newell, Linda, 130
Nichols, Reginald, *Concentrated Employment Program, Buffalo*, 246
Norton, Harvey, 73, 77, 79-80
Norton, Matt, *foreman*, 81

Ober, Tracey, *foreman*, 252
Olszak, Stanley, 59, 65, 97
Orkin, Stuart, *black foreman*, 167-170
Otis, Deirdre, 200

Pace, Delvin, 90
Packard, Dirk, 115
Parker, Jasper, 52
Patterson, Sal, 149-150
Patton, Ira, 156, 160, 170
Penton, Suzannah, 123-124
Pesch, James, *manager*, 97
Phillips, Bill, *manager*, 191
Pierce, Barbara, 289
Pierce, Lawton, 69-70, 86, 98, 239
Pope, Sidney, *black salaried employee*, 94, 96
Porter, Alfred, 73, 87
Poultney, Wilson, 118
Powers, Otis, 86
Pratt, Earl, 243
Pratt, Leo, 256
Prezioso, William, 289
Pritchett, Kathleen, 208-209, 212
Proctor, Claude, *foreman*, 123
Pruett, Ken, 238
Putnam, Roger, *foreman*, 169-170

Ramsey, Thomas, 67, 86, 98
Rast, Hafford, 310
Resnick, Bart, 248-249, 269-270
Ricker, James, 72-74, 76, 81
Roberts, Peter, 286-287
Rodgers, Dave, *manager*, 188, 189, 190, 252
Rogers, Gary, 81
Roland, Carmen, 76
Rosario, José, 88
Rouse, Andrew, *manager*, 61

Sampson, Ben, *black instructor*, 236
Sanborn, Elvin, 256
Sanford, Arthur, *manager*, 247-248
Scott, Ernest, *foreman*, 210, 211
Scruggs, Marian, 177-178
Seevers, Charles, 125
Shepherd, Paul, *manager*, 53, 75, 84, 95-96
Silverman, Edwin, *foreman*, 166, 270
Sifnas, James, 60
Simpson, Russell, 74, 237
Sims, Richard, 76
Singleton, Everlee, *black salaried employee*, 265
Slater, David, *counselor*, 127, 132
Small, Peggy, 289
Smith, Kenneth, 179
Smith, Marjorie, 60
Smith, Paul, 283
Stagg, Catherine, 180-181, 196-197
Stickney, Lewis, *black salaried employee*, 96-97
Strauss, Suzanne, 60

Tate, Paul, *foreman*, 192, 198
Tate, Sylvester, 93
Taylor, Ed, *counselor*, 71-72
Tenco, Pearl, 256
Thayer, Charles, *manager*, 180, 184
Tobias, Louis, *manager*, 64-65, 83
Tompkins, Elliot, 69, 237, 266
Troy, Wilbert, 155-156
Tuggle, Charles, 149
Tunstal, Eric, 264
Turesky, James, *union steward*, 144-145, 158, 288

Venson, Rosemary, 189

Walker, Ella, 107, 136
Walker, Estelle, 215
Warlick, Melvin, *black salaried employee*, 102-103, 120, 122-23, 129-130, 138
Watkins, Al, *black instructor*, 256
Watkins, Edgar, 113-114, 115
Webb, Monroe, 198-199
Whalum, Audrey, 108-109
Winfield, James, 169
Wing, Willis, *black community leader, Memphis*, 176
Withers, Brenda, 107, 111-112
Woiczak, Lavern, 93
Wolodsky, Morris, 160
Woodyard, Zita, 203

Yanchuk, George, *foreman*, 62